WITHDRAWN

WILLIAM FAULKNER'S CHARACTERS

GARLAND REFERENCE LIBRARY
OF THE HUMANITIES
(VOL. 270)

WILLIAM FAULKNER'S CHARACTERS
An Index to the Published and Unpublished Fiction

Thomas E. Dasher

GARLAND PUBLISHING, INC. • NEW YORK & LONDON
1981

© 1981 Thomas E. Dasher
All rights reserved

Library of Congress Cataloging in Publication Data
Dasher, Thomas E.
  William Faulkner's characters.

  (Garland reference library of the humanities ; v. 270)
  Includes index.
  1. Faulkner, William, 1897–1962—Characters—Indexes.
I. Title. II. Series.
PS3511.A86Z7816   813'.52   80-9033
ISBN 0-8240-9305-4   AACR2

Printed on acid-free, 250-year-life paper
Manufactured in the United States of America

To
Ella Ann

CONTENTS

Introduction	ix
Texts	xvii
Acknowledgments	xxi
Novels	1
Short Fiction	191
Unpublished Fiction	343
Title Index	357
Master Character Index	359

INTRODUCTION

Ideally, an index of characters in the fiction of any author should be done only once. However, nine indices, guides, and encyclopedias to the works of William Faulkner have heretofore been completed. Appearing at regular intervals from 1955 to 1969, they each purport to help readers identify and find Faulkner's characters quickly and easily. Unfortunately, none of these potentially valuable reference works succeeds in satisfying the need for a reliable, accurate, and complete character index in the Faulkner field.

Mona Margaret Melrose submitted the first guide to Faulkner's characters as an M.A. thesis at the University of Hawaii in 1955[1] and promised to continue and to enlarge her encyclopedia at a later date. Encouraged by William Van O'Connor, she attempted to identify each named character and a few of the unnamed characters, but none of the historical characters, in the novels from *Soldiers' Pay* to *Requiem for a Nun*. Her encyclopedia is not an index nor is it finally a very satisfactory guide.[2] She seems most concerned with her own critical estimates, Faulkner's inconsistencies, his descriptive patterns (the "gray" women and the idiots), and his use of generations. She handles only those short stories which, she claims, Faulkner grouped together to form novels such as *The Hamlet, The Unvanquished*, and *Knight's Gambit*, and she treats Negro characters by listing them under their owner or employer; *e.g.*, Joby is found as "Sartoris negro, Joby."

Robert Kirk and Marvin Klotz acknowledge the "helpful hints" they gained from Melrose in *Faulkner's People: A Complete Guide and Index to Characters in the Fiction of William Faulkner*,[3] published in 1963. Based mainly upon Kirk's 1959 dissertation,[4] the Kirk and Klotz volume, now out of print, was far more comprehensive. But unfortunately, it too falls far short of what an index should be. In his dissertation, Kirk precedes his index with brief discussions analyzing Faulkner's handling of nine different characters. He wisely deletes these essays from the published book, but as does Melrose, he and Klotz identify characters with critical interpretations. Furthermore, they claim that by focusing upon the characters printed in boldface type, the reader should be able to follow the action of the novels and short stories. They choose to interpret characters and their roles, too often misleading the reader, and index only named fictional characters and only where they appear by name. Significant unnamed characters and valuable pronoun references to named characters are ignored. Practices such as indexing "Horace's sister" only under "Horace" deceive the reader. They sometimes choose inferior texts, index only those stories which Faulkner never revised as parts of novels, and never indicate where Faulkner changed characters' names. They treat *Go Down, Moses* as a collection of stories while they treat *Knight's Gambit* as a novel. Finally, they fail to deal with the works and characters consistently; for example, they index the horses in *The Reivers* but never mention Lion in *Go Down, Moses*. With its separate listings of characters in individual works and its alphabetical listing of all characters in a Master Index, Kirk and Klotz's index should have satisfied the need for a character index in the Faulkner field. It does not.

Who's Who in Faulkner by Margaret Patricia Ford and Suzanne Kincaid[5] also appeared in 1963. With its many inaccuracies and its careless biographical sketch and bibliography, the Ford and Kincaid volume seems to have been rushed into print to capitalize on Faulkner's death. It is not an index and thus gives no page references; instead, it tries to give brief, interpretative sketches of the characters in Faulkner's novels. Of no use in any area of Faulkner studies, it has been superseded by later guides and longer critical interpretations.

One of these critical studies is Cleanth Brooks' *William Faulkner: The Yoknapatawpha Country*.[6] Brooks includes a character index which is quite helpful; he gives some page references to all the fictional, several unnamed, and a few historical characters in all the fiction with the exception of the *New Orleans Sketches* and those stories which Faulkner later revised as parts of novels. Yet he chooses to use *passim* and occasionally confuses relationships and names.[7] His index is primarily for quick reference, and because he lists characters only alphabetically in one Master List, the index is of limited use.

Harry Runyan's *A Faulkner Glossary* (1964),[8] Dorothy Tuck's *Crowell's Handbook of Faulkner* (1964),[9] and Walter Everett's *Faulkner's Art and Characters* (1969)[10] are not indices. Tuck's "Dictionary of Characters" is only a partial listing of characters with brief descriptive identifications, and she refers the reader to Kirk and Klotz for a complete listing. Runyan attempts to cover all areas—biography, bibliography, genealogy, family sketches, and character annotations—and fails to cover any of them satisfactorily. Everett comes up with perhaps the most original and bizarre approach to a list of Faulkner's characters. When the reader wants to identify Frankie, for example, he finds this listing: "Frankie: Cau.—Sartoris (1929)—Bkg.—young girl tennis player at Belle Mitchell's."[11] Everett has assigned each character such categories—major, minor, background; Caucasian, Negro, Indian; etc. His approach, however inventive, fails to delineate either Faulkner's art or his characters.

The most satisfactory previously available index to Faulkner's characters remains an early one, E.O. Hawkins' 1961 unpublished dissertation, "A Handbook of Yoknapatawpha."[12] Not only does Hawkins help to guide the reader through the novels themselves, but he also indexes historical and named fictional characters in the Yoknapatawpha novels from *Sartoris* through *The Mansion*. He tends to avoid both interpreting characters and inaccurate readings of relationships and roles; he usually is accurate and concise. Yet he also chooses to use *passim*, infers names from one work to another, and ignores unnamed characters. By putting all characters in only one alphabetical list, he, like Brooks, limits the index's usefulness. Furthermore, he deals only with those novels and short stories which relate in some way to Yoknapatawpha County and, unfortunately, he never expanded nor published his index.

Thus nineteen years after Faulkner's death, the Faulkner field has remained until now without one of its most basic research and reference tools; a satisfactory index to the characters in his fiction.[13] In a field where articles and books are proliferating tremendously, such an index has long been needed to help clarify character and novel relationships, to make readily accessible information about the growth and development of Faulkner's characterizations, and to identify historical, fictional, and unnamed characters and references throughout the Faulkner canon.

This index to characters and names in the published and unpublished fiction of William Faulkner is in two parts. The first, divided into novels, short stories, and unpublished fiction, lists the characters within each individual work. The second is an index of all named characters. Within each division of the first part of the index, works are listed alphabetically. The characters and names in each work are divided into fictional, unnamed, historical, Biblical, and literary/mythic. The Master Index of named characters is a conflation of all the fictional characters as well as historical/Biblical/literary/mythic characters and names which appear in all the fiction. All characters are identified as clearly and succinctly as possible without interpretation of their roles in the work.

Each fictional character is indexed on every page on which he appears whether he is referred to by name or pronoun. (If he is mentioned more than once on a page, this is not indicated.) The character is listed by the name by which he is referred to in the work itself with nicknames and titles included in parentheses. No names are inferred from one work to another. For example, characters and events similar to Rider's story in "Pantaloon in Black" are referred to in *Requiem*. These characters appear under the unnamed characters in *Requiem*. If more than one name is used in a work, the names are cross-referenced within the work; women who are referred to both by maiden and married names appear under the married name with the maiden name cross-referenced. When several generations with the same name appear in a work, Roman numerals differentiate among them. Unnamed family relations of named characters are listed with the named character; for example, in *The Unvanquished* Col. John Sartoris' first wife, never named, is listed under "Sartoris, Col. John" as "His wife," with page references. The index of all named characters lists only those characters who are named in the individual works. In the case of characters with the

Introduction xiii

same surname, those with the least identification are listed first.

Some unnamed characters, such as the Tall Convict in *The Wild Palms* and the Reporter in *Pylon*, should obviously be indexed. Other unnamed characters who figure prominently in a work or who help the reader locate significant scenes and named characters within the work are also listed. For example, the man who pulls the knife on Jewel Bundren as the Bundrens enter Jefferson in *As I Lay Dying* is indexed. Unnamed characters are listed only with the work in which they appear.

Faulkner often refers to historical figures in his fiction. Those who are referred to, such as Jack Dempsey, are not divided from the few historical characters who actually appear in the fiction, such as General Nathan Bedford Forrest in "My Grandmother Millard." All historical figures are listed by full given name, regardless of how Faulkner refers to them, followed by their birth and death dates, if known, and the pages on which they appear. Faulkner's spelling of these names is in parentheses if it varies from the standard spelling. Biblical, literary, and mythic names which are mentioned in the fiction are also indexed.

Many characters in Faulkner's novels appear on twenty-five or more pages in an individual novel. The page numbers on which such characters appear have been divided and their appearance identified to help the reader locate them at specific points throughout the novels. Although an attempt was made to pinpoint significant actions or descriptions, the identifications are selective. Also, the narrative stance which identifies the characters has not been indicated. For example, in *Absalom, Absalom!*, much of the action of the Sutpen family is Quentin and Shreve's speculation. The division simply identifies that the character is discussed at that point whether he actually does the action or not. Furthermore, the divisions indicate only where a particular event, action, or description begins, not necessarily the entire passage where the action appears. Finally, in the Short Fiction section, the page numbers of the characters in *Notes on a Horsethief, Mayday, The Wishing Tree*, and "Knight's Gambit," and in the Unpublished Fiction section, in "Elmer," have been divided like the novels.

NOTES

1. Mona Margaret Melrose, "An Encyclopedia of Characters in the Novels of William Faulkner," Unpublished Master's Thesis, University of Hawaii, 1955.

2. For example, Melrose placed the characters with an "M. A. D." system: M. for first mention of the character, A. for first appearance, and D. for first description; she gave only these three page references.

3. Robert Kirk and Marvin Klotz, *Faulkner's People: A Complete Guide and Index to Characters in the Fiction of William Faulkner* (Berkeley: University of California Press, 1963).

4. Robert Warner Kirk, "An Index and Encyclopedia of the Characters in the Fictional Works of William Faulkner," Unpublished Dissertation, University of Southern California, 1959.

5. Margaret Patricia Ford and Suzanne Kincaid, *Who's Who in Faulkner* (Baton Rouge: Louisiana State University Press, 1963).

6. Cleanth Brooks, *William Faulkner: The Yoknapatawpha Country* (New Haven: Yale University Press, 1963).

7. For example, Brooks identifies Lafe, Dewey Dell Bundren's lover in *As I Lay Dying*, as Rafe McCallum's twin brother.

8. Harry Runyan, *A Faulkner Glossary* (New York: The Citadel Press, 1964).

9. Dorothy Tuck, *Crowell's Handbook of Faulkner* (New York: T.Y. Crowell, 1964).

10. Walter K. Everett, *Faulkner's Art and Characters* (Woodbury, N.Y.: Barron's Educational Series, 1969).

11. Everett, p. 219.

12. E.O. Hawkins, "A Handbook of Yoknapatawpha," Unpublished Dissertation, University of Arkansas, 1961.

13. The volumes of *The Faulkner Concordances*, while useful for showing named characters in sentence context, will have very limited use as a character index. See *The Faulkner Concordances*, ed. Jack L. Capps (Faulkner Concordance Advisory Board: Produced on demand by University Microfilms International, Ann Arbor, Michigan, 1977–). The concordances to *As I Lay Dying, Go Down, Moses, Light in August,*

Introduction

Requiem for a Nun, and *The Sound and the Fury* have been published. Interim concordances to *The Hamlet* and the poetry are located in certain libraries throughout the country. The concordance to *A Fable* will soon be published.

TEXTS

In compiling the index, I have used the Faulkner texts recommended by James B. Meriwether in "The Books of William Faulkner: A Guide for Students and Scholars," *Mississippi Quarterly*, 30 (Summer 1977), 417–428. Because Faulkner often revised his short stories between published appearances, both the initial publication of each story and its subsequent appearances in collections have been indexed. I have particularly depended upon James B. Meriwether, "The Short Fiction of William Faulkner: A Bibliography," *Proof*, 1 (1971), 293–329. A headnote for each story indicates the appearances of the story chronologically. Page and column are indicated, if necessary, by 1.1, 1.2, 1.3. For early short fiction published in *The Mississippian*, New Orleans *Times-Picayune*, and *Double-Dealer*, the texts edited by Carvel Collins and Leland Cox have been used.

NOVELS:

Soldiers' Pay. New York: Boni & Liveright, 1926. 319 pp.

Mosquitoes. New York: Boni & Liveright, 1927. 349 pp.

Sartoris. New York: Harcourt, Brace & Company, 1929. 380 pp. *Flags in the Dust* (New York: Random House, 1973. 370 pp.), the original text of the novel, is the preferable text. I have included pagination for *Sartoris* along with *Flags*.

The Sound and the Fury. New York: Jonathan Cape & Harrison Smith, 1929. 401 pp.

As I Lay Dying. New York: Random House, 1964. 250 pp.

Sanctuary. New York: Jonathan Cape & Harrison Smith, 1931. 380 pp.
>Corrections in the 1932 Modern Library reissue do not affect the index. (The correction of a spelling error in later printings is noted in the index.) The 1981 Random House edition of the original *Sanctuary* has also been indexed and included.

Light in August. New York: Harrison Smith & Robert Haas, 1932. 480 pp.

Pylon. New York: Harrison Smith & Robert Haas, 1935. 315 pp.

Absalom, Absalom! New York: Random House, 1936. 384 pp.

The Unvanquished. New York: Random House, 1938. 293 pp.

The Wild Palms. New York: Random House, 1939. 339 pp.

The Hamlet. New York: Random House, 1940. 421 pp.
>The 1964 (New York: Random House, 366 pp.) edition contains one character change which is noted in the index.

Go Down, Moses. New York: Random House, 1942. 383 pp.

Intruder in the Dust. New York: Random House, 1948. 247 pp.

Requiem for a Nun. New York: Random House, 1951. 286 pp.

A Fable. New York: Random House, 1954. 437 pp.

The Town. New York: Random House, 1957. 371 pp.
>Character changes made in the 1961 Vintage and 1964 Random House texts are noted in the index.

The Mansion. New York: Random House, 1959. 436 pp.

The Reivers. New York: Random House, 1962. 305 pp.

SHORT STORIES:

These 13. New York: Jonathan Cape & Harrison Smith, 1931. 358 pp.

Idyll in the Desert. New York: Random House, 1931. 17 pp.

Miss Zilphia Gant. [Dallas:] Book Club of Texas, 1932. 29 pp.

Doctor Martino and Other Stories. New York: Harrison Smith & Robert Haas, 1934. 371 pp.

Knight's Gambit. New York: Random House, 1949. 246 pp.

Collected Stories. New York: Random House, 1950. 900 pp.

Notes on a Horsethief. Greenville, Miss.: Levee Press, 1951. 71 pp.

Big Woods. New York: Random House, 1955. 198 pp.
  This book has been treated as a unified work rather than as a collection of short stories because the prologues and epilogues, which Faulkner revised from previously published works, differ so greatly from their prior appearances. However, divisions in the text are indicated so that the reader can deal with the text in its parts as well as in its entirety. In the index, it appears in the Novels section.

Early Prose and Poetry, ed. Carvel Collins. Boston: Little, Brown, 1962. 134 pp.

The Wishing Tree. New York: Random House, 1967. 81 pp.

New Orleans Sketches, ed. Carvel Collins. New York: Random House, 1968. 139 pp.

Mayday. [South Bend, Indiana:] University of Notre Dame Press, 1977. (Limited edition; trade edition with different pagination published in 1980.)

Uncollected Stories of William Faulkner, ed. Joseph Blotner. New York: Random House, 1979. 716 pp.

Sinbad in New Orleans, ed. Leland Cox. Spartanburg, S.C.: The Reprint Company [scheduled for publication in 1981].

UNPUBLISHED FICTION:

The material in the Alderman Library at the University of Virginia and in the "Rowanoak" papers, a Xerox of which is available at the University of Virginia, has been indexed. In all cases, the latest, as far as could be determined, and most complete typescript or manuscript of each unpublished work was used.

ACKNOWLEDGMENTS

I would like to thank Jill Faulkner Summers for giving me permission to see the Xerox of the "Rowanoak" papers at the University of Virginia, Leland Cox for allowing me to see page proof of *Sinbad in New Orleans*, and the staff of the Alderman Library at the University of Virginia for their help. Professors Joel Myerson, Thomas Rice, and Herbert Johnson of the University of South Carolina offered helpful suggestions for improving the index in an earlier version.

The Southern Studies Program at the University of South Carolina, under the direction of James B. Meriwether, provided a research assistantship when I was a graduate student and the opportunity to use its important William Faulkner collection. Professors Bruce Harkness of Kent State University, Thomas L. McHaney of Georgia State University, and Stephen E. Meats of Pittsburgh State University, visiting scholars at the Southern Studies Program, willingly gave me advice and assistance. Edwin Arnold, Dianne Cox, Gail Morrison, Elisabeth Muhlenfeld, and Paul Ragan, former graduate students in the Program, helped in numerous ways with their friendship, support, and work on Faulkner.

Professor Noel Polk of the University of Southern Mississippi allowed me to see page proof of the original version of *Sanctuary*, offered valuable advice at several stages of this work, and provided vital assistance in getting this index published. His friendship has meant much to my family and me for many years. Professor James B. Meriwether of the University of South Carolina, as teacher, director, and advisor, was essential as I began and worked on this index and completed my graduate work. I especially benefited from his guidance and his bibliographical work on Faulkner.

Finally, I am indebted to the Faculty Research Committee at

Acknowledgments

Georgia Southern College for a Faculty Research Grant which helped me finish the index, to Professor Barbara W. Bitter, Head of the Special Studies Department at Georgia Southern College, for her continued support and encouragement, and, as always, to my wife, Ella Ann.

Novels

ABSALOM, ABSALOM!

[New York: Random House, 1936. 384 pp.]

Akers: Coon-hunter who stepped on one of Thomas Sutpen's
    Negroes covered with mud. 36, 44

Benbow, Judge: Jefferson judge. 46, 170, 211, 212

Benbow, Percy: Judge Benbow's son. 212

Bon, Charles: Son of Thomas Sutpen and Eulalia Bon. 18, 62,
    67, 70, 71; becomes Henry Sutpen's friend, 74-76, 78,
    79, 82, 87; Mr. Compson's speculations about events at
    Sutpen's Hundred, 89-126; letter to Judith Sutpen, 128-
    133, 135, 138, 141, 142, 145-150; buried, 151-153, 158,
    159, 162, 172, 179, 182; tombstone, 190, 192, 201, 203,
    207, 216, 262; speculation about Sutpen's response to
    Bon, 264-272, 274, 276, 277; Sutpen tells Henry that Bon
    is Henry's brother, 293-323, 325-351; Sutpen and Henry
    meet during war, 353-357; picture, 358-360, 364, 374, 377,
    378; Chronology, 380-383

Bon, Charles Etienne Saint-Valery (C.E. de St. Velery Bon in
    Genealogy): Son of Charles Bon and octoroon. 90, 91, 93,
    94, 100, 103, 104, 109, 114, 118, 119; tombstone, 191;
    with mother at Bon's grave, 193, 194; brought back to
    Sutpen's Hundred, 195, 196-204; returns with wife and
    farms, 205-210, 215, 307, 308, 336, 339, 358; Chronology,
    381, 384
  His wife: 205, 206, 208, 209, 215, 381, 384

Bon, Eulalia: See Sutpen, Eulalia Bon

Bond, Jim: Son of Charles Etienne Bon and Negro woman. 205-
    210, 214-216, 364, 370, 371, 374-376, 378, 381, 384

Clytemnestra (Clytie): Daughter of Thomas Sutpen and Negro
    slave. 30; named by Sutpen, 61, 62, 70, 87, 94, 101,
    109, 125, 126, 128, 132; Miss Rosa arrives after Bon's
    death, 135-140, 142, 150; helps to bury Bon, 152-164,
    168, 172, 180, 182, 183, 186, 187, 190, 191; tends to
    octoroon and son, 194-201, 204, 208-210; takes care of
    Jim Bond, 214-216, 259, 266, 271, 274, 276, 277, 281,
    285, 293; tries to stop Miss Rosa, 350, 351, 353, 358,
    364, 366; Quentin and Miss Rosa enter Sutpen house, 368-

371; house burns, 374-376, 378; Chronology, 380, 381, 383
  Her mother: 61, 383

Coldfield, Ellen: See Sutpen, Ellen Coldfield

Coldfield, Goodhue: Father of Ellen Coldfield Sutpen and Rosa
    Coldfield. 7, 15-17, 19-21, 23; visits daughter, 25-28;
    Sutpen's siege, 42-44, 46, 47; wedding of Ellen and Sutpen,
    48, 49-55, 57; Miss Rosa's childhood, 59-64, 66-68, 71,
    73, 77, 78; War, 80-82; dies, 83, 84; Sutpen's siege, 106,
    126, 145, 146, 148, 154, 162, 169, 170, 176-178, 211, 212;
    deal with Sutpen, 259, 260, 262, 347; Chronology, 380-383
  His father: 21
  His mother: 42, 50, 380
  His wife: 21, 42, 59, 82, 170, 347, 380

Coldfield, Rosa: Ellen Sutpen's sister; younger daughter of
    Goodhue Coldfield. Talks to Quentin Compson, 7-30, 33,
    36, 37, 40-43; Ellen and Sutpen married, 48, 51; her
    childhood, 59-71, 73-79; war, 80-89, 94, 102, 104, 126;
    goes to Sutpen's Hundred after Bon's death, 133-172; her
    death, 173, 174-178, 180, 182, 190, 196; Judith's death,
    210-212, 216, 266, 269, 277-280, 284, 296, 297, 302,
    304, 322, 325, 350, 358; trip with Quentin Compson, 362-
    377; Chronology, 380, 381, 383
  Her aunt: 16, 21, 23, 25, 26, 28, 42; Ellen and Sutpen married,
    48, 50-57; Miss Rosa's childhood, 59-63; climbs out
    window, 64, 66, 68-70, 73, 76, 77; War, 81-85, 134, 145,
    149, 176; Chronology, 380

Compson, General: Quentin Compson's grandfather. 12, 13; Sutpen
    arrives in Jefferson, 33-41, 45-47; Ellen Coldfield and
    Sutpen married, 48, 52-54, 56, 63, 70; opinion of Mr.
    Coldfield, 82, 83, 86, 191, 192; Bon's son arrives, 195,
    196, 198-200; Judith visits, 201-205, 208-210, 218, 219;
    Sutpen discusses his past, 220, 222-224, 226, 227; Sutpen
    turned away at door, 229, 230, 234, 237-257; Sutpen con-
    tinues story thirty years later, 258, 259; Sutpen's de-
    sign, 260-268; Henry Sutpen and Bon in his regiment, 270-
    276; overhears Wash Jones and Sutpen, 283, 284, 292, 344,
    370; Genealogy, 384

Compson, Mrs.: Wife of General Compson. 54-56, 71, 73, 76, 77,
    94, 126-129, 207, 281

Compson, Jason: Quentin Compson's father. 11-13, 31, 37, 41,
    43-47; Ellen and Sutpen married, 48, 49-58; Miss Rosa's
    childhood, 59-87; speculates about Henry, Judith, and Bon,

Absalom, Absalom!

89-129, 132, 133; Miss Rosa's death, 173, 174, 181; with
    Quentin at cemetery, 187-191; octoroon's visit, 192-211,
    213-215; Mr. Coldfield and Sutpen, 259-262; speculates
    about Bon and Sutpen, 265-270, 274; Sutpen's return after
    War, 277-283; Milly Jones and baby, 285-291, 296, 297,
    303, 320, 329, 335, 336; Bon and Henry join regiment,
    342-344, 358, 359, 374, 377

Compson, Quentin: Jason Compson's son, Harvard student. At
    Miss Rosa's, 7-14, 20-22, 31, 33, 35-38, 40, 41, 43, 45-
    49, 53, 54; talks with father, 59, 61, 63, 65, 70, 71,
    73, 76, 77, 82, 83, 86, 88; father shows Bon's letter,
    89, 94, 126-129, 132; Miss Rosa goes to Sutpen's Hundred
    after Bon's death, 134, 136, 143, 151, 154, 158, 159,
    166-169; at Harvard, 171, 172; Miss Rosa's death, 173,
    174-176, 178, 179, 181; Wash Jones and Sutpen, 182-186;
    with father at cemetery, 187-193; Bon's son, 195, 196,
    198-204, 207-209; Judith's death, 210, 211-219; Sutpen's
    past, 220-269; War, 270-297, 299, 303-305, 310, 311, 314,
    316; speculation about Henry, Judith, and Bon, 320-325,
    327-329, 333, 334; Henry meets Bon's mother, 335, 336;
    Henry and Bon in war, 342-350, 351; Henry shoots Bon, 358-
    361; trip to Sutpen's Hundred with Miss Rosa, 362, 363-
    378; Chronology, 381, 384
  His aunt and her kinswoman: 192

De Spain, Major: Sheriff who comes for Wash Jones after he
    kills Thomas Sutpen. 291, 292

Hamblett, Jim: Justice who tries Charles Etienne Bon. 203,
    209

Holston, Alexander: One of the founders of Jefferson. 31-33,
    36, 43-45, 63, 275

Ikkemotubbe: Chickasaw chief. 44, 54, 178

Jones, Melicent: Daughter of Wash Jones. 125, 171, 380, 383

Jones, Milly: Melicent Jones' daughter; granddaughter of Wash
    Jones. 125, 134, 171, 177; relationship with Sutpen,
    182, 185; Sutpen and Wash Jones, 281-291, 363, 364;
    Chronology, 380, 381, 383, 384
  Her daughter: 185, 285, 286, 292, 381, 384

Jones, Wash: Man who lives on Thomas Sutpen's land. 26, 72,
    81, 87, 125; fetches Miss Rosa, 133-136, 150, 151; helps
    to bury Bon, 152, 154, 156, 161, 166, 168, 171, 172, 177;

relationship with Sutpen, 181-187, 271, 276-278; relationship with Sutpen, 280-285; child born, 286, 287; kills Sutpen, 288-292, 358; Chronology, 380, 381, 383

Luster: Compson servant. 187, 213-215

McCannon, Shrevlin (Shreve): Harvard roommate of Quentin Compson. Miss Rosa's death, 173, 174, 176-181; Quentin and father in cemetery, 187, 207, 211, 215-218; Sutpen's past, 220, 223, 232, 246, 247, 255, 256, 258, 259; Sutpen's design, 260-262, 265-267, 270, 274, 275, 277, 280, 286, 289, 292; Henry confronted by Sutpen, 293; described, 294; continues speculation about Henry and Bon, 295-315; Bon's love, 316-334; Bon and Henry in New Orleans, 335-340; War, 341-351, 358-361; Quentin and Miss Rosa travel to Sutpen's Hundred, 362, 373, 374, 376-378; Genealogy, 384

McCaslin, Theophilus: Old Yoknapatawpha resident. 152, 275

Pettibone: Large landowner for whom Thomas Sutpen's father worked in Virginia. 227-229, 231, 235-238, 260

Sartoris, Col. John: Confederate officer. 80, 121, 124, 126, 152, 189

Sutpen, Ellen Coldfield: Thomas Sutpen's second wife; Goodhue Coldfield's elder daughter. 7, 9, 11, 13, 14; asks Miss Rosa to save Sutpen children, 15-30, 34, 35, 43, 46; marriage to Sutpen, 48-76, 78-82, 85-87, 93, 97, 99; first sees Bon, 101-106, 121, 125, 126; after Bon's death, 134-136, 138, 140-142; summer after Bon's first visit, 145-147, 149, 158, 162, 164, 165, 167, 169-171, 176, 178, 183, 185; her tombstone, 188, 190, 211, 253, 259, 268, 271, 279, 281, 282, 287, 294, 301; her reaction to Bon, 320-322, 326, 327, 329, 330, 347, 354, 363, 367; Chronology, 380-383

Sutpen, Eulalia Bon: Thomas Sutpen's first wife. 240; Sutpen's past, 247-249, 252-255, 262; repudiated, 264-266, 268, 269, 272, 274; son matures, 296-315, 319, 321, 327, 329, 331, 332; visited by Henry and Bon, 335-337, 339, 340, 343; Sutpen tells Henry about Bon's Negro blood, 354, 355, 377, 378; Chronology, 380, 382
  Her mother: 378
  Her father: 246-247, 249, 252-254, 262, 264, 266, 274, 335, 354, 355, 382

Sutpen, Henry: Son of Thomas and Ellen Sutpen. 9, 11, 13-15, 18, 21-23; trips to church, 24, 25-28; watches father fight Negro, 29, 30, 34, 40, 59, 62, 64, 65, 67, 69; father goes to New Orleans, 70, 71-75, 78, 79, 82, 86, 87; his love for Bon, 89-126, 132, 133; Miss Rosa travels to Sutpen's Hundred after Bon's death, 135, 136, 138-141, 145-147, 152-155, 157, 158; Sutpen returns from War, 159, 162, 167, 169, 172, 174, 176, 177, 179-181; Sutpen's relationship with Wash Jones, 182, 190, 201, 208, 216, 259, 261, 262, 265; brings Bon home for first time, 266, 267-271, 276, 277, 287, 292; father tells him that Bon is his brother, 293-295, 301, 309, 313-315; Bon's love, 316-322, 325-330, 332-334; visits Bon's mother, 335-337, 340; War, 341-354; learns of Bon's Negro blood, 355-357; shoots Bon, 358, 359, 360, 364, 370; visited by Quentin Compson, 373, 374, 378; Chronology, 380, 381, 383

Sutpen, Judith: Daughter of Thomas and Ellen Sutpen. 9, 11, 13-15, 18, 21-23; trips to church, 24-29; watches father fight Negro, 30, 40; Miss Rosa's past and relationship with Sutpens, 59, 61, 62, 64, 65, 67-71, 73-80, 82, 84, 86, 87; Henry's love for Bon, 89-105, 107-109, 119-128; Bon's letter, 129-132; Miss Rosa travels to Sutpen's Hundred after Bon's death, 135-142, 145-164, 167, 170, 172, 174, 177, 179-181; father's relationship with Wash Jones, 182-186, 187, 188, 190, 191; Bon's octoroon mistress visits, 192-195; Bon's son comes to live at Sutpen's Hundred, 197-201, 203-209; dies, 210, 211, 216, 259, 261, 262; Bon's first visit, 266-271, 276, 277, 281, 283, 285, 287; Sutpen tells Henry that Bon is his brother, 293-295, 301, 309, 310, 314; Bon's love, 316-322, 325-335, 337; Bon and Henry join regiment, 341-345; Bon and Henry in War, 347-350, 353, 354, 356, 357; picture on Bon's body, 358, 359, 370, 377; Chronology, 380, 381, 383

Sutpen, Thomas: Large landowner in Yoknapatawpha. 8, 9, 11-47; marriage to Ellen Coldfield, 48, 49-68; goes to New Orleans, 70-72, 74, 75; enters War, 78-85, 87, 90-97, 99, 100; Bon's first visit, 101, 102-107, 118, 120-122, 124-126, 128; Miss Rosa travels to Sutpen's Hundred after Bon's death, 134-136, 138, 140, 141, 145, 149, 154-172, 176-181; relationship with Wash Jones, 182-186, 188-190, 201-203, 208, 209, 211, 213; talks with General Compson about his past, 217-259; his design, 260, 261-265; awaits Bon's first visit, 266, 267-281; Wash Jones, 281-292; tells Henry that Bon is his brother,

293, 294-297, 301, 302, 304, 305, 309, 313, 314; Bon's
love, 317-322, 325-327, 329-335, 340; Bon and Henry join
regiment, 341, 342, 344, 347-350; talks to Henry in tent,
352-357, 362, 363, 377; Chronology, 380-384
His mother: 223, 241
His father: 223-225, 227-231, 234-237, 240, 241, 260
His family: 222-232, 235-238, 380, 382

Willow, Colonel: Confederate officer. 353, 355

UNNAMED

French architect whom Thomas Sutpen brings to Yoknapatawpha.
8, 16, 35-38, 41, 42, 161, 218-220, 238, 239, 244, 245, 256-258, 261

Twenty Sutpen Negroes. 8, 9, 16, 17, 35-38, 40, 43, 44, 61, 124, 178, 218-220, 239, 240, 243-247, 256, 257, 259, 262, 263

Mistress of Charles Bon. 90, 91, 93, 94, 100, 103, 104, 107, 109; discussed by Bon and Henry, 114-119, 121; visits Bon's grave, 192-197, 201, 207, 266, 301; Bon goes to college, 307, 308, 310, 312, 315, 336, 339, 340; her picture on Bon's body, 358, 359, 377

Eulalia Bon's lawyer. 300-315, 322, 331, 332, 336-340, 343

Juno, Missylena, Chlory: hypothetical names of female slaves. 110

Horse and mule trader with whom Rosa Coldfield's aunt eloped. 76, 81, 85, 176

Midwife who tends Milly Jones when her baby is born. 185, 285-288

Slave who turns Thomas Sutpen away from front door at Pettibone's. 228, 229, 231-235, 237, 260

HISTORICAL

Bayard, Pierre Terrail de (1473?-1524): French soldier-hero. 174, 360

Beardsley, Aubrey V. (1872-1898): English artist. 193

Absalom, Absalom!

Blackstone, William (1723-1780): English jurist. 102

Coke, Edward (1552-1634): English jurist. 102, 303

Davis, Jefferson (1808-1889): President of Confederacy. 177

Du Guesclin, Bertrand (1320?-1380): Constable of France. 345

Forrest, Nathan Bedford (1821-1877): Confederate general. 152

Jackson, Thomas J. "Stonewall" (1824-1863): Confederate general. 279

John V, Count of Armagnac (1420?-1473?): Henry Sutpen's "Duke of Lorraine." 342, 343, 346, 347

Johnston, Joseph E. (1807-1891): Confederate general. 276, 346, 355

Lee, Robert E. (1807-1870): Confederate general. 20, 68, 177, 276, 284, 290, 346, 348, 355

Lincoln, Abraham (1809-1865): President of United States, 1861-1865. 78, 184, 276, 340, 341

Littleton, Thomas (1407?-1481): English jurist. 303

Longstreet, James (1821-1904): Confederate general. 347

Pickett, George E. (1825-1875): Confederate general. 361

Richard I (1157-1199): King of England. 345

Scott, Sir Walter (1771-1832): Scottish novelist. 80

Shakespeare, William (1564-1616): English poet and playwright. 280

Sherman, William T. (1820-1891): Union general. 130, 184, 349, 350, 355, 361

Sullivan, John L. (1858-1918): American boxer. 46

Wilde, Oscar (1854-1900): Irish author. 193

BIBLICAL

Abraham: Old Testament patriarch in Genesis. 325, 326

Beelzebub: Satan's chief lieutenant. 178

Eve: Adam's wife in Genesis. 144

God: 11, 21, 28, 29, 44, 109, 115, 116, 130, 147, 166, 169, 198, 282, 297, 298, 303, 314, 321, 324, 346, 347, 349, 354, 363, 364

Ham: Second son of Noah in Genesis. 196

Jesus: 324

LITERARY/MYTHIC

Agamemnon: Leader of Greek forces at Troy. 177

Ben Hur: Central character in Lew Wallace's *Ben Hur*, 1880. 217

Bluebeard: Fairy-tale character who married and murdered one wife after another. 60

Cassandra: Daughter of Priam and Hecuba. 22, 60, 62, 177

Don Juan: Legendary hero of Spain; subject of many authors, especially Byron. 108

Fauntleroy, Little Lord: Hero of novel by Frances Hodgson Burnett, 1886. 194

Faustus: Central character in works by Goethe and Marlowe. 178, 182

Guinevere: King Arthur's queen. 174

Hamlet: Central character in Shakespeare's *Hamlet*, 1600-1601, 174

Lancelot: Knight of King Arthur's Round Table. 320

Lilith: First wife of Adam in Hebrew folklore. 196

Lothario: Character in Rowe's *The Fair Penitent*, 1703. 102

Moloch: Phoenician god to whom children were sacrificed by
    burning. 137

Niobe: Mother whose children were killed by Artemis and Apollo.
    13

Priapus: Roman god of male generative power. 122

Pyramus: Babylonian lover of Thisbe. 177

Roland: Hero of *Chanson de Roland*; defender of Christians
    against Saracens in Charlemagne legends. 345

Thisbe: Babylonian lover of Pyramus. 177

AS I LAY DYING

[New York: Random House, 1964. 250 pp.]

Albert: Clerk in Moseley's drugstore. 189, 193

Alford: Jefferson physician. 231

Armstid: Yoknapatawpha farmer; Bundrens' neighbor. 81-86, 172-184, 186, 218, 224, 229

Armstid, Lula: Wife of Armstid. 173, 174, 178, 179

Bundren, Addie: First wife of Anse Bundren. 4, 5, 8, 9, 14, 15, 17-24, 26-29, 31, 34-40, 42-48; dies, 49, 50-54, 57, 60, 62-67, 69, 70, 74, 76, 79, 81-83, 86, 89, 91, 92, 94, 95; family leaves for Jefferson, 98-100, 102, 107-111, 114, 122-130, 133, 137, 138, 140, 141; coffin falls into river, 143, 144; talk with Cora Tull, 158-160; her past, 161-168, 169-174, 176, 185, 187, 190, 202, 204-207, 212-215, 218; in Jefferson, 223-225, 230, 246
   Addie's father: 161, 162, 165, 167

Bundren, Anse: Husband of Addie Bundren. 8, 10, 11, 15-23, 25, 26, 28-32, 34-37, 39-44, 46-48; Addie dies, 49, 58, 59, 62-64, 68-70, 72-75, 80-82, 84, 86, 87, 90-92, 94-96; leaves for town, 98-102, 104-113, 115, 116; at river, 117-123, 125-131, 133, 137, 145-148, 150-157; Addie, 162-171, 173-179; trades with Snopes, 180-184, 186, 187; in Mottson, 193-196, 197-199, 203, 206; barn burns, 209, 211, 213, 214, 216-220; arrives in Jefferson, 221, 222-226; Addie buried, 227, 229, 230, 241, 245-249; introduces new Mrs. Bundren, 250
   His mother: 41

Bundren, Mrs. Anse: Second wife of Anse Bundren. 225, 226, 249, 250

Bundren, Cash: Oldest son of Anse and Addie Bundren. Building Addie's coffin, 4, 8, 9, 11, 14, 15, 18, 19, 22, 23, 25, 29-32, 35, 41-43, 47, 48; Addie dies, 49, 50, 55, 57-59, 62-64, 67-75, 77, 78, 82, 84, 85, 90, 91, 92, 94, 95; leaves for town, 98-103, 105-112, 115, 116; at river, 117-120, 122-128, 130, 131, 133-139; attempts to cross river, 140-143, 145-151, 155-157, 163-167, 172-174; broken leg set, 176, 177, 181, 182, 185-187, 193-

As I Lay Dying   13

   195, 197; cement poured on leg, 198, 200, 203, 205, 213,
   214, 216-219; arrives in Jefferson, 221-226; Addie buried,
   227, 228-230, 241, 243, 244, 247-249; meets new Mrs.
   Bundren, 250

Bundren, Darl: Second son of Anse and Addie Bundren. 3-5,
   8-13; with Jewel, 16-21, 23-27, 29, 32, 34-36, 38, 39,
   43, 46-48; Addie dies, 49-51, 57, 68, 71-76, 80, 86-89,
   90, 91-93, 95, 97; leaves for town, 98-103, 105-112, 115,
   116; at river, 117-131, 133-139; attempts to cross river,
   140-147, 149-157, 159, 164-167; at Armstid's, 172-174,
   177-181, 185-187; in Mottson, 193-195, 196-200, 202-
   205; barn burns, 208, 209-220; arrives in Jefferson,
   221, 222-226; Addie buried, 227, 228, 230, 240-242; on
   train to Jackson, 243, 244, 247, 250

Bundren, Dewey Dell: Daughter of Anse and Addie Bundren. 8,
   9, 15, 23; with Lafe, 25-27, 30, 31, 38, 39, 42-44, 46-
   48; Addie dies, 49-51, 55-62, 64, 73, 81, 87, 95, 97;
   leaves for Jefferson, 98, 100-102, 105-112, 114-116;
   at river, 117-124, 126, 127, 129-131, 133, 137, 139, 142,
   143, 146, 148, 149, 153-156, 168; at Armstid's, 172-174,
   177, 179, 180, 186, 187; in Mottson, 188-195, 196-198,
   200, 201, 203, 205-207; barn burns, 209, 211, 213-215,
   216-220; arrives in Jefferson, 221, 222, 224-226; Addie
   buried, 227; visits MacGowan, 231-242, 244-249; meets
   new Mrs. Bundren, 250

Bundren, Jewel: Son of Addie Bundren and Whitfield. 3, 4, 8,
   10-15; with Darl, 16-21, 23, 25, 27, 29, 30, 32, 34,
   36, 38, 39, 41, 43, 46, 48; Addie dies, 49, 51, 54, 57,
   73, 74, 76, 80, 86-96; leaves for Jefferson, 98, 99, 101,
   102, 105-112, 115, 116; at river, 117-120; works to buy
   horse, 121-131, 133-139; attempts to cross river, 140-
   142, 145-147, 150-157, 159, 160, 167, 168; at Armstid's,
   172-174, 176-182; trades horse, 183, 184, 186, 187,
   195, 198-200, 202, 203, 205; barn burns, 208-215, 216-
   220; arrives in Jefferson, 221, 222-226; Addie buried,
   227, 240, 241, 244, 247-249; meets new Mrs. Bundren,
   250

Bundren, Vardaman: Youngest son of Addie and Anse Bundren.
   8, 22, 29, 30, 32, 33, 37; gives rope to Peabody, 41-
   44, 46-48, 50; scares Peabody's horses, 52-55, 57, 58,
   60-68; bores holes in coffin, 69, 79, 81, 82, 87, 94-
   96; leaves for Jefferson, 98, 99, 101, 105-112, 115,
   116; at river, 117-120, 123, 126-133, 137, 139, 142-
   144, 146-148, 150, 151, 153, 168; at Armstid's, 174,

178, 179, 182; watches buzzards, 185-187; in Mottson, 193, 195, 198, 200-202, 204-207; barn burns, 209, 213-219; arrives in Jefferson, 221, 222, 224-226; Addie buried, 227, 237, 239-242, 244, 247-249; meets new Mrs. Bundren, 250

Gillespie, Mr.: Man whose barn Darl Bundren burns down. 206, 207, 209, 211, 214, 218, 222, 224, 227

Gillespie, Mack: Gillespie's son. 206, 207, 209-212

Grimm, Eustace: Man who works on Snope's place. 183

Grummet: Owner of hardware store in Mottson. 193, 194

Houston: One of men at Bundren's house after Addie's death. 83-86

Jody: Man who works in Jefferson drugstore with Skeet MacGowan. 231-232, 234-237

Lafe: Lover of Dewey Dell Bundren. 25, 26, 57-59, 191-193, 233-235

Lawington, Miss: Home demonstration agent. 6, 7

Littlejohn: One of men at Bundrens' house after Addie's death. 81-86, 176

MacCallum: Man on porch with Samson. 106, 107, 112, 113

MacCallum, Rafe: Twin of MacCallum. 106

MacGowan, Skeet: Jefferson drugstore clerk. 231-240

Moseley: Druggist in Mottson. 188-195

Peabody, Dr.: Yoknapatawpha physician. 18, 36, 39; attends Addie Bundren, 40-45, 50, 52, 53, 56-61, 65, 66, 75; Tull returns team, 80, 81, 83-85, 97, 176, 225, 226; attends Cash Bundren, 229, 230, 248, 249

Quick, "big" Lon: Man from whom Jewel Bundren bought his horse. 107, 127, 128, 154

Quick, "little" Lon: Son of big Lon Quick; at Bundrens' after Addie's death. 80-86, 106, 107, 154

As I Lay Dying

Samson: Owner of country store. 87, 105-113, 116

Samson, Rachel: Samson's wife. 108-112

Snopes: Flem's nephew with whom Anse Bundren trades. 175-177, 179, 180, 183, 187

Snopes, Flem: Man who apparently brought spotted horses to area. 106, 127, 183

Suratt: Sewing machine salesman. 181, 226, 248

Tull, Cora: Vernon Tull's wife. Thinks about cakes, 6-9, 11, 14, 17; comments on Darl, 20-24, 26, 30-33, 45; Addie dead, 65-70, 73-75, 81, 86, 87, 95, 124, 132, 145, 146; talk with Addie, 158-160, 165-168, 245

Tull, Eula: Daughter of Vernon and Cora Tull. 9, 14, 17, 21, 30, 32, 170, 171

Tull, Kate: Older daughter of Vernon and Cora Tull. 7-9, 14, 17, 21, 30, 32, 33

Tull, Vernon: Farmer; neighbor of Bundrens. 4; at Bundrens', 6-11, 16-19, 21, 22, 28-33, 40, 42, 49, 55, 64; Cora announces Addie's death, 65-70, 73-75; returns Peabody's team, 80-87, 94, 95, 98, 99, 101, 107, 116; tries to help Bundrens across river, 117-121, 124, 130-133, 135-139, 142-148, 150-156, 169, 170, 172, 173
  Tull's parents: 29

Varner, "Uncle Billy": One of men at Bundrens' after Addie's death; sets Cash Bundren's broken leg. 81-86, 176, 177, 229
  His wife: 83

Varner, Jody: "Uncle Billy" Varner's son. 83

Whitfield, Rev.: Addie Bundren's lover and Jewel Bundren's father. 82, 83, 86, 119, 136, 158, 159, 166, 167, 169-171

UNNAMED

Marshal in Mottson. 193-195

Drugstore owner in Jefferson. 232, 234, 236, 237

Rich town lady who does not buy Cora Tull's cakes. 7, 8, 33

Man who pulls knife on Jewel Bundren. 219-221

BIBLICAL

Lord: 7, 8, 15, 21-23, 29, 31, 32, 34-36, 41, 51, 56, 63, 67, 68,
      70, 81, 83-87, 100, 104, 105, 108, 113, 116, 119, 141,
      145, 146, 158-160, 166, 169-171, 180, 181, 182, 186,
      192, 204, 220, 223, 246

Satan: 169, 170

MYTHIC

Santa Claus: 94, 176, 206

BIG WOODS

[New York: Random House, 1955. 198 pp.]

Contains four stories, (I) "The Bear," pp. 11-97, (II) "The Old People," pp. 113-138, (III) "A Bear Hunt," pp. 145-164, (IV) "Race at Morning," pp. 175-198; also five greatly revised segments from stories and novels which Faulkner called "interrupted catalysts"—(V) *Requiem for a Nun*, [pp. 3-7], (VI) "Red Leaves," [pp. 99-109], (VII) "A Justice," [pp. 139-142], (VIII) "Mississippi," [pp. 165-171], (IX) "Delta Autumn," [pp. 199-212]. Since they are unnumbered in the text, page numbers for the segments appear here in brackets.

Baker, Joe (Jobaker): Chickasaw friend of Sam Fathers, I, II. 35, 66, 67, 122-124, 135

Basket, Herman: Chickasaw; Doom's friend, VII. [139-142]

Basket, John: Old Chickasaw moonshiner, III. 155, 156, 158, 159, 162

Basket, Three: Chickasaw, VI. [105-109]

Compson, General: Old hunter at de Spain's camp, I, II, III, IX. 14, 15, 22, 25, 26, 34-38, 42, 47-49, 54, 60, 61, 71, 74-77, 80, 81, 85, 89, 92, 114, 119, 126-128, 130, 136, 145, [204], [208]
  His son, I: 60

Compson, Quentin: Young narrator of III. 145-164

Crawford, Dr.: Physician who cares for Lion and Sam Fathers, I. 68, 70, 71, 73-75

De Spain, Major: Large landowner in Yoknapatawpha, I, II, III, VIII, IX. 11, 14, 15, 20-23, 25-27, 34, 35, 37-39, 42-46, 48, 49, 51-55, 58-64, 67-71, 73, 74, 76-78, 80-83, 85, 87-90, 92-94, 114, 119, 120, 123, 125-128, 130, 136, 137, 145-147, [167], [204, 206, 208, 209]

De Spain, young Major: Son of the large landowner; Jefferson banker, III. 145-147, 149-155, 157-164

De Spain, Mrs.: Young Major de Spain's wife, III. 145
  Their daughters, III: 145

Doom: See Ikkemotubbe

Edmondses: Yoknapatawpha family, I. 76

Edmonds, Carothers (Roth): McCaslin Edmonds' grandson, IV, IX.
    175-177, 179, 193, 195, 197, 198, [204, 205, 210, 211]

Edmonds, McCaslin: Ike McCaslin's cousin, I, II, III, IX. 12,
    14, 15, 21, 22, 25, 26, 31, 35, 39-44, 49, 51, 54-56, 58,
    59, 61, 71, 73-81, 85, 89, 92-94, 114, 117-120, 122-
    128, 130, 136-138, 145, 147, [204, 207, 211]
  His mother, I: 114

Ernest, Mister: Young narrator's guardian in IV. 175-198
  His wife, IV: 194

Ewell, Walter, I: Hunter with old Major de Spain, I, II, III,
    IX. 14, 20, 22, 25, 26, 31, 32, 37, 42, 44, 49, 61, 63,
    74, 80, 81, 84, 85, 89, 92, 114, 119, 126-132, 134-136,
    145, [204, 208]

Ewell, Walter, II: Son of Walter Ewell I; IV, IX. 176, 193,
    197, [204, 205]

Fathers, Sam: Ike McCaslin's tutor in the woods, I, II, VIII,
    IX. 11, 14-24, 26-46, 48, 49, 62-64, 66-71, 73, 75, 78-80,
    89, 92-94, 96, 113-136, 138, [170], [207, 209]
  His mother, I, II, VIII, IX: 27, 115, 116, 118, [170], [207]

Fraser, Mr.: Hunter with young Major de Spain's group, III.
    157-159, 161

Hogganbeck, Boon: Worker for old Major de Spain, I, II, III,
    IX. 11, 14, 18, 22, 25, 26, 35, 37-39, 41-62, 64-72,
    74-82, 84-90, 92-94, 96, 97, 114, 119, 120, 126-132,
    145, 147, [204, 208]
  His grandmother, I, II: 50, 120
  His father, I: 50
  His mother, I: 50

Hogganbeck, Lucius: Boon Hogganbeck's son, III. 145-147, 149-
    164

Hogganbeck, Mrs. Lucius: Lucius Hogganbeck's wife, III. 145,
    146
  Their three children, III: 146

Ikkemotubbe (Doom): Chickasaw chief, I, II, VII, VIII, IX. 11,
    27, 92, 114-116, 118, 120, [139-142], [170], [207]

Big Woods   19

Isham: Cook in IX. [209]

Issetibbeha: Chickasaw chief, VI, II. [99, 101, 102, 105, 106], 115, 116

Joseph: Young Negro in IX. [203, 206]

Legate, Willy: Hunter, IV, IX. 175, 176, 180, 181, 183, 193, 197, [203-205, 210, 211]
  His grandfather, IX: [204]

McCaslin, Amodeus (Uncle Buddy): Uncle Buck McCaslin's twin brother, II. 118, 119, 122

McCaslin, Carothers: Ike McCaslin's grandfather, II. 115, 116, 119, 122

McCaslin, Isaac: Son of Uncle Buck McCaslin; hunter, I, II, III, VIII, IV, IX. 11-97, 113-138, 145, 152, 153, 157-159, 161, [166], 177, 179, 181, 193-195, 197, 198, [199-212]

McCaslin, Theophilus (Uncle Buck): Ike McCaslin's father, I, II, IX. 57, 114, 118, 119, 122, [206]

Moketubbe: Issetibbeha's son, VI, II. [102, 103, 106], 116
  His son, II: 116

Provine: Two brothers who form gang with Lucius Hogganbeck, III. 146, 147, 164

Ratliff: Sewing machine salesman, III. 145, 147, 149-164

Sartorises: Yoknapatawpha family, I. 76

Sartoris, Bayard: Son of Col. John Sartoris, I. 60
  His son, I: 60

Sartoris, Col. John: Confederate officer, I. 57

Semmes, Mr.: Liquor dealer in Memphis, I. 49, 57

Simon: Negro who works for Mr. Ernest in IV. 177-181, 193

Snopeses: Yoknapatawpha family, VIII. [167]

Sutpen, Thomas: Yoknapatawpha landowner, I. 11

Tennie's Jim: Negro worker for old Major de Spain, I, II. 14,
     19, 20, 22, 23, 25, 37, 38, 45, 50, 51, 56, 61-64, 66-
     68, 71, 75, 77, 81, 89, 90, 114, 119, 125, 127, 128

Vitry, Chevalier Soeur-Blonde de: Doom's French companion, II,
     VII. 115, 116, [140]

Wylie, Ash, I: Negro cook for old Major de Spain's group of
     hunters, I, II, III. 18, 20, 22, 25, 27, 43, 47, 51-53,
     57, 60, 70, 72, 74, 81, 82, 84, 85, 87-91, 95, 126-128,
     145

Wylie, Ash, II: Negro; son of Ash Wylie I; III, IX. 145, 149,
     151, 153, 155-157, 159, 161-164, [205, 206]

Wylie, Daisy: Wife of Ash Wylie I; I. 81, 90

UNNAMED

Old hunter in VIII. 165-171

Narrator, a young boy, in IV. 175-198

Narrator's parents in IV. 192, 194

Roadhouse man who runs away with narrator's mother in IV.
     192, 194

Guinea Negro, Issetibbeha's slave, in VI. [99-109]

Headman in VI. [100, 101]

Conductor on train in I. 53, 59, 86, 87

Brakeman on train in I. 53, 59, 86

Two Indians who pursue Negro in VI. [99, 100, 102, 103, 105]

Negro who is husband of Sam Fathers' mother in II. 116

The People, the Chickasaws in II, VII. 116, 121, [139-142]

Big Woods   21

                                  HISTORICAL

Dempsey, William H. "Jack" (1895-   ): American boxer, I. 53

Fink, Mike (1770?-1822?): Keelboatman on Mississippi River, V.
    [6]

Forrest, Nathan Bedford (1821-1877): Confederate general, I.
    57

Hare, Joseph T. (?-1818): Bandit on Natchez Trace, V. [6, 7]

Harpe: Micajah (1768-1799) or/and Wiley (1770-1804), American
    bandits on Natchez Trace, V. [6]

Kilrain, Jake (1859-1937): American boxer, I. 53

Mason, Samuel (1750?-1804?): Bandit on Natchez Trace, V. [6,
    7]

Murrell, John A. (1804-1844): American Bandit on Natchez
    Trace, V. [6]

Sherman, William T. (1820-1891): Union general, III. 148

Sullivan, John L. (1858-1918): American boxer, I. 53

Tunney, James J. "Gene" (1898-1978): American boxer, I. 53

                                   BIBLICAL

God: IX. [205]

Ham: Second son of Noah in Genesis, II. 117

                                    MYTHIC

Priam: King of Troy, I. 13

A FABLE

[New York: Random House, 1954.   437 pp.]

Angélique: Old French woman who is blind and curses Marthe,
    Marya, and the Corporal's wife.   213-218
  Old man with her: 213, 214, 216-218

Beale, Colonel: British officer who calls the Corporal "Boggan."
    273-280, 282

Beauchamp, Philip Manigault: American Negro who helps to kill
    Gragnon.   370-376, 378-381

"Bidet": See unnamed characters, French group commander

Bledsoe, Sgt.: British sergeant whom the Runner knocks out.
    317-319

Blum, Major: French officer who saw the Corporal at Chalons.
    273, 274, 277, 279-282

Boggan: See Stefan

Bouc, Pierre: See Piotr

Bridesman: Flight commander of G.D. Levine's group.   89-91,
    95; reports mutiny, 97-100; flies one of planes which
    meet German general, 102-116, 324, 325

Brzewski: See Stefan

Buchwald: American soldier who helps to kill Gen. Charles
    Gragnon.   370-381

Burk: RAF aviator.   116, 117, 323

"Casse-tête": One of murderers executed with the Corporal.
    357-361, 384, 385

Collyer: British adjutant with aviators.   92-95, 99, 100,
    108, 109, 112, 114-117, 325

Conventicle: Flight sergeant with G.D. Levine's group.   91,
    92, 96, 325

A Fable   23

Corporal, the: See Stefan

Cowrie, RAF aviator. 97-99, 115

Demarchi: RAF aviator. 99, 117, 323

Demont, Marthe Demont's husband. 292-299, 387, 389, 392,
    395-401, 423, 426, 430

Demont, Marthe (Magda): Sister of Marya and the Corporal.
    Arrives in Chaulnesmont, 213-223; taken to Mayor's
    office, 272-275; meets old general, 282-301; receives
    Corporal's body, 387-400; body disappears, 401, 423,
    425; visited by two men, 426-433

De Montigny: French officer. 282

Gargne, Monsieur: French patron of the Runner's garret before
    World War I. 149
  His wife: 149

Gragnon, General Charles: Commander of French division which
    refuses to fight. 12; offered command of attack, 20-24;
    mutiny, 25, 26-32; meets group commander, 33, 34-55,
    123, 127; arrives in Chaulnesmont, 133-137; confronts
    old general, 228-235, 330, 331, 352, 362, 365, 366;
    killed, 376-380

Hanley: RAF aviator. 323

Harry: English groom; the Sentry. 56; described, 57-60, 65,
    74-80; hits Runner, 84, 85; Sutterfield looking for him,
    141-148; steals horse, 150-158, 160, 161; shoots horse,
    162-166, 168, 172, 179, 180, 188-190; taken into Masons,
    191, 192-202, 207, 312; Runner's plan, 314-321; death, 322

Henri: French army commander. 28, 30, 31, 33, 34, 124, 127

Horn: British soldier whom Runner knocks out. 316, 317, 319

Irey: Turnkey who holds Negro groom in custody. 168-171, 173-
    182, 186-188
  His wife: 168, 170
  His relatives: 174-176, 178

James, Lieutenant Colonel: British officer. 64-66, 71

Jean: One of the Corporal's men. Brought to Chaulnesmont,
    16, 17; Runner hears of thirteen men, 66-70, 74, 79;

described, 126-128, 205, 206, 223; in cell, 226, 227,
   233; faces generals, 274, 275; eats in cell, 333-342;
   old general talks with Corporal, 346-348, 352, 355, 366,
   369; Corporal's execution, 383, 384

Lallemont: French Corps Commander. 22-24, 26-31, 36, 37, 43,
   124, 127, 230

Landry: Sergeant of group sent to Verdun to retrieve body of
   soldier. 402-414, 417, 418, 420

Lapin: Man executed with the Corporal. 357-361, 384, 385

Levine, Gerald David: Young RAF aviator. 86-96; hears of
   mutiny, 97-102; flies to meet German general, 103-108;
   German shoots pilot, 109, 110-120, 318, 322-325; commits
   suicide, 326
 His father: 118
 His mother: 88, 89, 91, 100-102, 118, 119

Luluque: One of the Corporal's men, a Midian. Brought to
   Chaulnesmont, 16, 17; Runner hears of thirteen men, 66-
   70, 74, 79; described, 126-128, 205, 206, 223; in cell,
   226, 227, 233; faces generals, 274, 275; eats in cell,
   333-342; old general talks with Corporal, 346-348, 352,
   355, 366, 369; Corporal's execution, 383, 384

Martel, General: French officer; Grand commander from whose
   desk citation blows away which was to be awarded to the
   man who becomes the Generalissimo. 269

Marthe: See Demont, Marthe

Marya: Marthe Demont and the Corporal's sister. Arrives in
   Chaulnesmont, 213-223; taken to Mayor's office, 272-
   275; meets old general, 282-300; receives Corporal's
   body, 387, 389-400; body disappears, 401, 423, 425;
   visited by two men, 426-433
 Their mother: 286-291, 296
 Their father: 286-290, 300

Middleton, Captain: American officer who calls the Corporal
   "Brzewski." 273-282

Milhaud, Madame: Owner of French restaurant. 116

Monaghan: American aviator in RAF. 93, 99, 104, 108-110, 120,
   323

A Fable   25

Morache: One of the soldiers sent to retrieve soldier's body.
    402-425

Osgood: RAF aviator. 99

Paul: One of the Corporal's men; the Breton. Brought to
    Chaulnesmont, 16, 17; Runner hears of thirteen men, 66-
    70, 74, 79; described, 126-128, 205, 206, 223; in cell,
    226, 227, 233; faces generals, 274, 275; eats in cell,
    333-342; old general talks with Corporal, 346-348, 352,
    355, 366, 369; Corporal's execution, 383, 384

Picklock: One of men sent to retrieve soldier's body. 402-
    425

Piotr (Pierre Bouc; Zsettlani): One of Corporal's men who
    denies him, then recants. Brought to Chaulnesmont, 16,
    17; Runner hears of thirteen, 66-70, 74, 79; described,
    126-128, 205, 206, 223; in cell, 226, 227, 233; faces
    generals, 274, 275; eats in cell, 333-338; denies Cor-
    poral, 339-342; old general talks with Corporal, 346;
    struggles to return, 355, 356, 366, 369; Corporal's
    execution, 383, 384

Polchek: One of the Corporal's men who informs on him and later
    tries to pay the Corporal's sisters for soup. Brought
    to Chaulnesmont, 16, 17; Runner hears of thirteen, 66-
    70, 74, 79; described, 126-128, 205, 206, 223; in cell,
    226, 227, 233; faces generals, 274, 275; betrays Corporal,
    330; eats in cell, 333-342, 346, 347, 355; visits Cor-
    poral's sisters, 426-432

Sibleigh: RAF aviator. 91, 95

Smith, Lieutenant: British officer whom the Runner knocks out.
    317-319

Stefan (the Corporal): Young corporal who leads the regiment
    in its refusal to fight. Brought to Chaulnesmont, 16,
    17; Runner hears of thirteen, 66-70, 74, 79; described,
    126, 128, 134, 205, 206; sisters search for him, 214-
    218, 221, 223; in cell, 226, 227, 233; faces generals,
    274-283, 285, 287, 291-301; betrayal revealed, 330-340;
    discussion with old general, 341-354; joins two murderers,
    357-360; with priest, 361-367; execution, 384-386, 389,
    391; buried, 397-399; sisters visited by two men, 428-
    431

Sutterfield, Tobe: Negro groom and minister. 141, 143-146, 149, 150; tale of racehorse and groom, 151-161; Harry shoots horse, 162, 164-166, 168, 169, 171-178; talks with lawyer, 179-182, 186-196; Mr. Harry returns to England, 197-199; mission in France, 200-204, 207; Runner reports deception about German general, 310-313; with Sentry and Runner, 314-321

Theodule: Young soldier killed at Fort Valaumont. 404, 405, 415-417
 His mother: 404, 405, 415-417

Thorpe: RAF aviator. 99, 108, 109, 114

Wilson, Sergeant: Sergeant in American army. 375

Witt: RAF aviator. 91, 95

UNNAMED

Young woman who is engaged to Corporal. With crowd in Chaulnesmont, 7-10, 12, 18, 19, 121, 122; runs to meet Corporal's sisters, 212-223; taken to Mayor's office, 272-275; meets old general, 282-285, 300, 389; helps to take Corporal's body away, 390-401, 429; returned to brothel, 430
 Her grandmother: 300, 430

The Generalissimo; the old general. 12; arrives in Chaulnesmont, 13, 15-18, 23, 122, 124, 125, 133, 136; confronts Gragnon, 228-230, 232-234, 236-238, 242, 243; his background, 244-265; story of camel and soldier, 266-282; sees three women, 283-288, 291, 294-300; with three generals, 301-304, 306-309, 317-319; talks with Quartermaster General, 326-333; talks with Corporal, 341-356, 362-366, 369, 389; his funeral, 433-436
 His family: 246, 247, 249-251, 253, 254, 259, 261, 262, 300

Negro youth with Tobe Sutterfield. 143, 150; tale of racehorse and groom, 151-154, 157-159, 161; Harry shoots horse, 162, 164-166, 168, 178, 186-191, 194, 195; Harry returns to Europe, 197-201, 207, 310, 313; Sentry, Runner, Sutterfield together, 314
 His mother: 199

Battalion Runner. 56; background, 60-65; learns of thirteen men, 66-73; with Sentry, 74-85; joins battalion, 140-150; listens to story of racehorse and groom, 151, 153, 154, 158, 189, 191; talks with Sutterfield, 195-211; plan

A Fable   27

          to lead troops out of trenches, 310-320; bombardment,
          321-322; visits Corporal's sisters, 426-432; at General-
          issimo's funeral, 435-437

British general who meets with the Generalissimo. Arrives in
     Chaulnesmont, 13, 15-18, 136; confronts Gragnon, 228,
     230, 232, 234, 236, 239; woman and spoon, 271, 272,
     274, 280; with generals in study, 301-309, 318, 319

American general who meets with the Generalissimo. Arrives
     in Chaulnesmont, 13, 15-18, 136; confronts Gragnon, 228,
     230, 232, 234, 236, 239; woman and spoon, 274, 271, 272,
     274, 280; with generals in study, 301-304, 306-309, 318,
     319

Quartermaster General; old general's classmate. Past relation-
     ship with old general, 246, 247, 249, 253; background,
     254, 255, 257-271; talks with old general, 326-333, 437
  His family: 254

The Generalissimo's batman. 230, 244, 245, 433, 434

Lieutenant who alerts Headquarters of regiment's refusal to
     fight. 331

German general who meets with Allies. 107, 108; shoots pilot,
     109, 110, 112-114, 238, 283; with generals in study,
     301-309, 316, 318, 319, 325, 327, 377
  His pilot: 108, 109, 113, 238

Major of air corps in which G.D. Levine serves. 87, 90-95,
     97-100, 103-106, 108, 109

Sergeant-major in charge of Corporal's execution. 383-390,
     429

Young couple for whom Corporal gathers money. 282

British Army Signal Corps private who tells Runner about
     Sentry's activities. 67, 74, 80, 81

General Charles Gragnon's aide. 26, 38-41, 43, 48

Federal deputy marshal who pursues grooms and horse. 151,
     153, 157-165, 189, 195, 196
  His father: 159, 160

New Orleans lawyer. 151; arrives in Missouri town, 163-168, 171-179; Sutterfield's witnessing, 180-187, 198
  His father: 183

U.S. oil baron who owns racehorse. 152-156, 159, 160, 166, 168, 192, 193

Iowan; American private; one of three men sent to kill Gragnon. 370-379

Stranger who trades body with soldiers at Verdun. 420-425

Sergeant in charge of Corporal and his men in prison. 333, 334, 338-342, 355-357, 361, 367

Priest who visits Corporal. 361-370

Soldier sacrificed in Africa by French officer who became Generalissimo. 256, 257, 266-270

Generalissimo's aide. 230, 234-238, 272-275, 279, 282-284, 326

French group commander; called "Bidet," "Mama Bidet," "General Cabinet," "Marshall d'Aisance" in army. 23, 27, 28, 31-37, 50-55, 127, 230, 231
  His wife: 50

HISTORICAL

Alexander (356-323 B.C.): King of Macedonia. 181, 260

Anthony, Saint (c.250-350): First Christian monk. 259

Antipas, Herod (d. after 40 A.D.): Ruler of Judea. 241

Archimedes (287?-212 B.C.): Greek mathematician and inventor. 260

Ball, Albert (1896-1917): English aviator in RFC. 88, 89, 112, 120

Barcas: Surname of Hannibal's father, Mamilcar. 260

Barker, Major William G. (?-?): RAF aviator. 88, 89, 120

A Fable

Bishop, William Avery (1894-1956): Canadian aviator in RFC.
    88, 89, 91, 112, 120

Blackstone, William (1723-1780): English jurist. 171

Boelcke, Oswald (1891-1916): German aviator. 89, 120

Booth, General William (1829-1912): Founder of Salvation Army.
    181

Brown, John (1800-1859): American abolitionist. 186

Bryan, William Jennings (1860-1925): American lawyer and
    political figure. 181

Byron, Lord (1788-1824): English poet. 259

Caesar, Julius (100?-44 B.C.): Roman general and emperor. 7,
    171, 179, 181, 205, 260, 304

Calhoun, John C. (1782-1850): American statesman. 186

Capet: Family name of third dynasty of French kings from Hugh
    Capet (940?-996). 173

Charlemagne (742-814): King of the Franks. 133, 173

Cicero, Marcus Tullius (106-43 B.C.): Roman orator and states-
    man. 186

Clovis (466?-511): King of Salian Franks. 133

Coke, Edward (1552-1634): English jurist. 171

Cyrano de Bergerac (1619-1655): French poet and soldier; central
    character in Rostand's *Cyrano de Bergerac*, 1898. 45

Demosthenes (385?-322 B.C.): Athenian orator. 186

Desmoulins, Camille (1760-1794): French journalist and Revolu-
    tionary leader. 254

Dickens, Charles (1812-1870): English novelist. 173

Ericsson, John (1803-1889): Swedish engineer and inventor. 260

Fonck, René (1894-1953): French aviator. 89

[Ford, Henry (1863-1947)]: American automobile manufacturer. 187

Gaudier-Brzeska, Henri (1891-1915): French sculptor. 283

Gauguin, Paul (1848-1903): French artist. 53

Genghis Khan (1162-1227): Mongol leader. 181, 186

Guynemer, Georges Marie (1894-1917): French aviator. 89, 120

Haig, Douglas (1861-1928): British general. 96

Hannibal (247-183 B.C.): Carthaginian general. 7, 304

Heliogabulus (204-222): Roman emperor. 259, 260

Homer: Greek epic poet. 159

Hugo, Victor (1802-1885): French novelist. 173, 268

Immelmann, Max (1890-1916): German aviator. 89, 120

Krupp: Family name of German armaments manufacturers. 260

Kubla Khan (1216-1294): Mongol khan and founder of Mongol dynasty in China. 348

Littleton, Thomas (1589-1645): English jurist. 171

McCudden, Major James T.B. (?-?): RFC aviator. 88, 89, 91, 112, 119, 120

Mannock, Edward (1888-1918): RFC aviator. 88, 89, 91, 112

Marlborough, first Duke of (John Churchill, 1650-1722): English military commander. 181

Mazarin, Jules (1602-1661): French cardinal and statesman. 181

Michelangelo (1475-1564): Italian sculptor. 260

Mithridates (c.132-63 B.C.): King of Parthia. 259, 260

Murat, Joachim (1767?-1815): French cavalry commander. 186

Murrell, John A. (1804?-1844): American bandit. 168

A Fable

Napoleon (1769-1821): French emperor. 4, 7, 48, 96, 171, 181, 256, 260, 304

Newton, Isaac (1642-1727): English natural philosopher and mathematician. 260

Nungesser, Charles (1892-1927): French aviator. 89, 120

Orleans: Name of Cadet branch of Valois and Bourbon houses of France. 173

Peter I (1672-1725): Czar of Russia. 181, 260

Phidias (5th century B.C.): Greek sculptor. 260

Philip II (382-336 B.C.): King of Macedonia. 260

Pitt, William (1759-1806): English statesman. 186

Prester John: Name of alleged Christian priest/king in Middle Ages. 181

Rhys-Davies, A.P.E. (?-?): RFC aviator. 88, 120

Richthofen, Baron Manfred von (1892-1918): German aviator. 89, 120

Robespierre (1758-1794): French revolutionary. 254

Simeon, Saint (390?-459): Syrian ascetic. 259

Sunday, Bill (1862-1935): American evangelist. 181

Talleyrand-Perigord, Charles Maurice de (1754-1838): French statesman. 181

Tiberius Caesar (42 B.C.-37 A.D.): Roman emperor. 241, 348

Voss, Leutnant Werner (?-1917): German aviator. 89

Warwick: Name of English earldom, created c.1088. 181

Webster, Daniel (1782-1852): American statesman. 186

Wilson, Woodrow (1856-1924): President of United States, 1913-1921. 375

BIBLICAL

Abraham: Old Testament patriarch in Genesis. 159

Adam: First man in Genesis. 83, 153

David: King of Israel. 162

Eve: Adam's wife in Genesis. 161, 248

God: 156, 158, 159, 173, 180, 198, 199, 202, 203, 206, 218, 232, 260, 262, 264, 286, 293, 308, 328, 333, 362, 365, 406, 425

Goliath: Philistine giant killed by David in I Samuel. 162

He (Christ): 69, 74, 81, 83, 181, 204, 264, 337, 363-365, 370

Isaac: Old Testament patriarch; Abraham's son. 159

Mary: Mother of Jesus. 161

Moses: Old Testament patriarch. 186

Paul: Apostle of Christ. 186, 364, 365

Peter: Disciple of Christ. 364

Rachel: Jacob's second wife. 248

Samuel's father: Elkanah; father of the first great prophet. 159

Satan: 180, 407

LITERARY/MYTHIC

Ahab: Character in Melville's *Moby Dick*, 1851. 161

Androcles: Roman slave saved by his kindness to lion. 161

Andromeda: Ethiopian princess rescued by Perseus. 248

Bacchus: Greek and Roman god of wine and revelry. 203

Balzac's African deserter: Character in "A Passion in the Desert," 1832. 161

A Fable

Helen: Wife of Menelaus in Homer's *Iliad*. 153

Henry V: Central figure in Shakespeare's *Henry V*, 1599. 45

Juliet: Character in Shakespeare's *Romeo and Juliet*, 1594-1595. 153

Lilith: Adam's first wife in Hebrew folklore. 248, 249

Lochinvar: Hero of ballad in Scott's *Marmion*, 1808. 153

Niobe: Mother whose children were killed by Apollo and Artemis. 248

Paris: Prince of Troy in Homer's *Iliad*. 153

Pyramus: Babylonian lover of Thisbe. 153

Romeo: Character in Shakespeare's *Romeo and Juliet*, 1594-1595. 153

Tartuffe: Central character in Moliere's *Tartuffe*, 1669. 45

Thisbe: Pyramus' lover. 153

Venus: Goddess of love and beauty. 203

FLAGS IN THE DUST

[New York: Random House, 1973. 370 pp.]

Abe: Negro servant of Doctor Lucius Peabody. 279, 367

Alford, Doctor: Young doctor in Jefferson. 79; attends Bayard Sartoris II, 84; described, 85-89, 91, 92, 111; visits Narcissa Benbow, 137, 139, 205, 219, 226; travels to Memphis, 227-229, 247
  His aunt and uncle: 85

Allan: Officer with J.E.B. Stuart. 18, 19

Beard, Virgil: Young boy to whom Byron Snopes dictates letters to Narcissa Benbow. 96-101, 215-218, 250, 251

Beard, Will C.: Virgil Beard's father who owns a boarding house in Jefferson and runs a grist mill. 95-97, 100, 150, 216

Beard, Mrs. W.C.: Wife of Will Beard who runs the boarding house. 96, 97, 216, 217

Benbow, Belle Mitchell: Wife of Harry Mitchell whom she divorces to marry Horace Benbow. Described, 25-27, 157-159, 161; Horace Benbow visits, 166-171, 173-181; party for little Belle, 182-188, 190, 192-194; Horace plans to marry Belle, 242-245, 247, 276, 277; in Reno, 287, 288; her sister visits Jefferson, 291, 293-297, 299; married to Horace, 340-347, 355, 361

Benbow, Francis: Ancestor of Horace and Narcissa Benbow. 152

Benbow, Horace: Young lawyer in Jefferson, brother of Narcissa, second husband of Belle Mitchell. 27-29, 45, 46, 60, 62, 65-67, 138; returns from War, 145-158; relationship with sister, 159-165; visits Belle, 166-190, 192-194, 206, 241; plans to marry Belle, 242-245, 247; visits Narcissa after her marriage, 276-278, 280, 281, 283-289; Joan Heppleton visits, 290-299; married to Belle, 339-342; picks up shrimp, 343-347, 350, 351, 355, 368

Benbow, Julia: Mother of Horace and Narcissa Benbow; wife of Will Benbow. 29, 156, 159, 160, 165

Benbow, Narcissa: See Sartoris, Narcissa Benbow

Benbow, Will: Father of Horace and Narcissa Benbow; husband of Julia Benbow. 152, 156, 159-161, 163, 165, 291

Bird, Uncle: One of Negroes who comes for money from Simon Strother. 261-265

Brandt, Doctor: Specialist in Memphis who examines Bayard Sartoris II. 227-229

Buck: Marshal in Jefferson. 141-143, 254, 257

"Butler, Joe": Fictitious character to whom Byron Snopes has Virgil Beard address letter. 99.

Comyn: Irish aviator in RAF. 354

Du Pre, Virginia: Sister of Col. John Sartoris; aunt of Bayard Sartoris II. 3; family background, 11-14, 19, 20, 22; at Belle Mitchell's, 25-36, 38; greets Bayard III, 39-52, 55, 57; discusses letters with Narcissa, 58-63, 67, 68; rides in car, 69, 70, 72, 74-79; takes Bayard II to Jefferson doctors, 83-94, 102, 103, 111, 121, 125, 129, 136, 139, 142, 150, 151, 160; visited by Narcissa, 190-193, 195, 196, 202, 203, 205-207, 210, 219, 220, 225, 226; takes Bayard II to Memphis specialist, 227-231, 235, 236, 242, 244-247; Negroes come for money, 261, 262, 264-267, 270, 275-281; tells Narcissa not to ride with Bayard, 282, 283; alone with Narcissa, 347-351, 356, 358-370
  Her husband: 350

Elnora: Sartorises' cook; sister of Caspey Strother and mother of Isom. 11, 20, 21, 33, 34, 36, 37; listens to Caspey in kitchen, 52-55, 72, 73, 102, 204, 205, 219, 225-227, 233, 235, 361-363, 369

Eunice: Benbows' cook. 283, 284, 298

Eustace: Lawyer who introduces Gratton to Bayard Sartoris III. 115, 116

Falls, Will: Bayard Sartoris II's friend who served under Col. John Sartoris in Civil War. John Sartoris I's escape, 3-6; relationship with Bayard II, 70-72, 74, 81, 89, 91, 92; treats Bayard II's face, 208-210; John Sartoris I and Zeb Fothergill, 211-216, 219, 220, 223-226, 229,

277, 278, 368
His grandmother: 210

Fothergill, Zeb: Man who races Col. John Sartoris into the
Yankee camp. 212-214

Frankie: Young girl who visits Belle Mitchell and plays tennis
with Horace Benbow. 168-177, 179

Gratton, Mr.: Stranger in Jefferson whom Bayard Sartoris III
tries to fight. 115, 116

Harris, Meloney: Negro servant of Belle Mitchell's. 24, 25,
167, 168, 361

Henry, Uncle: Negro who lives near Sartorises where Bayard
Sartoris III hunts. 270

Heppleton, Joan: Belle Mitchell's sister. 290-299
Her husbands: 295
Her mother: 296
Her father: 296

Houston: Negro waiter at Rogers' restaurant. 110-112, 114

Hub: Young man who drinks with Bayard Sartoris III. 121-131,
134, 140-142

Isom: Sartorises' servant; son of Elnora. 11, 21, 31, 43,
44; wears Caspey's uniform, 45, 48-50; listens to Caspey
in kitchen, 52-57, 69, 70, 72, 73, 75, 77, 78, 102, 104,
191, 207, 225, 226, 232, 234, 235, 266, 267; hunts with
Bayard III and Narcissa, 271-276, 278, 281, 351, 361,
362; takes Miss Jenny to cemetery, 363, 364, 366

Joby: Sartoris slave; Simon Strother's grandfather. 13, 14,
34

Joe: Bookkeeper in local department store who plays tennis at
Mitchells'. 168, 171-173, 176, 177

John Henry: Young Negro who rescues Bayard Sartoris III from
the wrecked car. 196-202, 205

Jones, "Doctor": Janitor in Sartoris bank. 96, 97, 208

Littlejohn, Mrs.: Boarding house owner. 257

Louvinia: Sartoris slave; wife of Joby. 3, 4

MacCallum, Henry: Second son of Virginius MacCallum. 109, 111, 112; Bayard III's visit, 305-308, 310-312, 318, 321-325, 328, 329

MacCallum, Jackson: Eldest son of Virginius MacCallum. 109; Bayard III's visit, 308, 310-312, 317-327, 329

MacCallum, Lee: Fifth son of Virginius MacCallum. 109; Bayard III's visit, 306-312, 317, 321, 322, 325, 327, 329

MacCallum, Raphael Semmes (Rafe): Son of Virginius MacCallum; twin of Stuart MacCallum. 109-118; Bayard III rides stallion, 119-121; Bayard III's visit, 304, 306-312, 314, 317-322, 325-327, 329

MacCallum, Stuart: Son of Virginius MacCallum; twin of Rafe MacCallum. 109; Bayard III's visit, 308-312, 317, 323-325, 327, 329

MacCallum, Virginius: Father of six MacCallum boys. 204; Bayard III's visit, 305-312, 314, 319-321, 323-329
  His wives: 305, 325
  His father: 305

MacCallum, Virginius, II (Buddy): Youngest son of Virginius MacCallum. 109, 112; Bayard III's visit, 304, 305, 308-315, 317-319, 321-329

Mandy: MacCallums' cook. 306, 308-310, 318, 319, 324, 328

Marders, Mrs. Sarah: Friend of Belle Mitchell. 168-171, 174-179, 183-185, 189, 193

Mitch: Freight agent at the railway station. 129-134, 140-142

Mitchell, Belle: See Benbow, Belle Mitchell

Mitchell, Belle, II: Daughter of Belle and Harry Mitchell. 166, 169, 175-177, 181-188, 287, 288, 340, 341, 345, 346

Mitchell, Harry: Husband of Belle. 26, 157, 161; Horace Benbow visits, 168-171, 174-180; party for little Belle, 182-188, 193, 242, 243; Belle in Reno, 287, 288, 294, 297, 341, 345-347; in Chicago, 353, 355

Monaghan: World War I aviator; friend of Bayard Sartoris III.
351-355

Moore, Brother: One of Negroes who comes for money from Simon
Strother. 261-265

Myrtle: Receptionist in Dr. Alford's office. 84-86

Peabody, Lucius Quintus: Physician in Jefferson; John Sartoris'
regimental surgeon in Civil War. Described, 87-93; attends
Bayard III, 121, 124, 125, 129, 130, 136, 205, 209, 219,
229; Thanksgiving dinner, 277-281, 358-361; at cemetery,
366-368
His wife: 367

Peabody, Lucius Quintus, II: Son of Dr. Peabody; New York
surgeon. 91, 366-368

Ploeckner: German flier who shoots down John Sartoris III in
World War I; pupil of Richthofen. 40, 114, 239

Rachel: The Mitchells' cook. 24, 25, 176, 177, 179, 181, 182,
299

Redlaw: Man who kills Col. John Sartoris. 6, 366

Reno: One of three Negroes who accompanies Bayard Sartoris
III on his drinking spree. 129-134, 140-142

Res: Cashier in the Sartoris bank. 76, 77, 94-97, 215, 216,
249-252

Richard: Negro at the MacCallums'. 309-311

Rogers, Deacon: Cafe proprietor in Jefferson. 110-112, 114,
115, 129

Sartoris, Bayard, I: Brother of John Sartoris I killed in Civil
War. 12-20, 41, 220, 350

Sartoris, Bayard, II: Son of John Sartoris I, grandfather of
Bayard Sartoris III. With Will Falls, 3-14, 20-22, 24-
26, 29-37; greets Bayard III, 38-41, 43, 44, 48, 51, 52,
58, 59, 61, 62, 67, 69-78; in attic, 79-83; taken to
Jefferson doctors, 84-95, 103, 104, 108, 111, 150, 151,
154, 191, 195, 196, 198, 202, 204, 205; with Will Falls,
208-210, 212, 213, 215, 216, 219-226; taken to Memphis,
227-229, 249, 250, 252; group of Negroes visit, 261-266,

Flags in the Dust 39

    270; Thanksgiving dinner, 277-283; dies, 300, 301, 306,
    307, 328, 329, 331, 348, 349, 358, 359; Aunt Jenny at
    cemetery, 364-366
  His wife: 51
  His grandfather: 3
  His aunt: 3-5

Sartoris, Bayard, III: Grandson of Bayard Sartoris II; brother
    of John Sartoris III. In Jefferson, 8-10, 20, 23, 29,
    30, 32, 33; arrives home, 38-42, 45, 46; Aunt Jenny's
    visit before Caroline's death, 47-49, 51; youth recalled,
    60-68; returns with car, 69-72, 74-80, 83, 89, 91, 96,
    102; takes Simon for a ride, 103-108; with Rafe MacCallum,
    109-117; rides stallion, 118-120; with Suratt, 121-137;
    Narcissa Benbow serenaded, 138-144, 149-151, 160, 171,
    191, 193-195; automobile accident, 196-207, 219, 220,
    226, 227; Narcissa visits, 229-241, 244-246; drives
    Narcissa's car, 247-249, 261, 266-269; takes Narcissa
    hunting, 270-283, 287, 297; in car with grandfather, 299-
    300; goes to MacCallums', 301-325, 327-330; spends night
    with Negro family, 331-338, 347-350; in Chicago, 351-
    355; flies plane, 356, 357; Narcissa's child born, 358-
    360, 364, 368

Sartoris, Benbow: Son of Narcissa and Bayard Sartoris III.
    266, 267, 282, 348-351, 358-362, 367-370

Sartoris, Caroline White: First wife of Bayard Sartoris III
    who died in childbirth. 20, 41, 46-48, 64, 67, 68, 83,
    150
  Her baby: 20, 47, 83

Sartoris, John, I: Father of Bayard Sartoris II; Confederate
    colonel. Escapes from Yankees, 3-6, 10, 11, 13, 19, 20,
    35, 37, 50, 71, 80; his words remembered, 82, 87, 102,
    107; rides into Yankee camp, 211-214, 219; kills two
    carpetbaggers, 224, 225, 300, 358; his grave, 364-366
  His mother: 11
  His wife: 359
  His two daughters: 3, 4, 13, 14, 19

Sartoris, John, II: Son of Bayard Sartoris II, father of Bayard
    Sartoris III and John Sartoris III. 51, 63, 79, 83, 365

Sartoris, John, III: Grandson of Bayard Sartoris II, brother
    of Bayard Sartoris III. 9, 20, 27; his death, 38-42,
    46, 48, 51; youth discussed, 61-68, 78, 109; discussed
    by Bayard III and Rafe MacCallum, 113-115, 149, 171,

203, 204; Bayard III and Narcissa, 238, 239, 275, 307; his concern for Mandy, 309, 313, 315, 319, 323, 324; childhood, 348-351, 364

Sartoris, Lucy Cranston: Wife of John Sartoris II, mother of Bayard Sartoris III and John Sartoris III. 51, 63, 204, 348, 365

Sartoris, Narcissa Benbow: Sister of Horace Benbow; second wife of Bayard Sartoris III. 26-29; visits Aunt Jenny, 44-52, 57; shows letter to Aunt Jenny, 58, 59; discusses Sartorises, 60-68, 93, 94, 99, 100, 120, 134-140; Horace returns, 145-158; relationship with Horace, 159-162, 166, 170, 185, 187-194, 196, 202; after Bayard III's automobile accident, 205-207, 220, 227; reads to Bayard III, 229, 230-246; with Bayard III in her car, 247-249, 255, 261; pregnant, 266-269; goes hunting with husband, 270-283; misses letters, 284-290, 297, 299, 340, 341, 343-345; Bayard III's travels, 347-351, 355; child born, 358, 361, 362, 366; alone with Aunt Jenny and Benbow, 368-370

Sibleigh: World War I flier whom Bayard Sartoris III gets to act as decoy for a German flier who shot down his brother. 39

Smith, Mrs.: Switchboard operator for Dr. Brandt, the Memphis specialist. 227, 228

Snopes, Byron: Bookkeeper in Sartoris bank. 6-8, 58, 71, 72, 76, 77; waits on Narcissa Benbow in bank, 93-101, 139, 140, 154; with Virgil Beard, 216-219, 241, 243, 244, 248-250; frightens V. Beard, 251-254; enters Benbow house, 255, 256; steals money and leaves, 257-260

Snopes, Clarence: Son of I.O. Snopes. 218

Snopes, Flem: Vice-president of the Sartoris bank. 154
His wife and child: 154

Snopes, I.O.: Byron Snopes' cousin who runs restaurant. 97, 217, 218, 251

Snopes, Mrs. I.O.: I.O. Snopes' wife. 218

Snopes, Montgomery Ward: Snopes who goes to France with Horace Benbow in Y.M.C.A. 66, 154, 155

Sol: Railroad station porter. 146-148

Straud, Dr.: Physician referred to by young Dr. Peabody II. 368

Strother, Caspey: Servant of the Sartorises; son of Simon Strother and brother of Elnora. 45, 50; discusses War in kitchen, 52-58, 60, 69; confronted by Bayard II, 72-74, 191, 195, 225, 226; goes hunting, 270-276, 361

Strother, Euphrony: Simon Strother's wife; mother of Caspey Strother and Elnora. 277

Strother, Simon: Sartoris servant. 6-10; goes to Mitchells, 21-26, 28-30, 32-38, 40, 43, 44, 51; listens to Caspey, 52-56, 69, 73-75, 77, 78, 101, 102; rides in car, 103-107, 191, 202-205, 207, 219-223, 225-227, 229-236, 252; Negroes come for money, 261-266, 277-281, 348, 358-360; killed, 361, 363

Sue: Woman at Hub's cabin. 127

Suratt, V.K.: Sewing machine agent. 121-129, 203
  His father: 126
  His grandfather: 125

Tobe: Negro hostler who handles the stallion which Bayard Sartoris III rides. 117-120

Turpin: Man whom Byron Snopes visits before he flees. 258, 259

Turpin, Minnie Sue: Girl whom Byron Snopes visits before he flees. 258-260

Varner: Owner of Varner's store. 257

"Wagner, Hal": Fictitious name which Bryon Snopes has Virgil Beard sign to his letters. 100, 101

Watts: Hardware store owner. 99, 101

Winterbottom, Mrs.: Boarding house owner where two carpetbaggers stay whom Col. Sartoris kills. 224, 225

Wyatt, Captain: Officer with J.E.B. Stuart. 15, 16

Wyatt, Sally: Spinster who lives with Narcissa Benbow. 58; discusses Sartoris twins, 60-64, 66, 135-138, 148, 151, 152, 154-157, 159, 161, 162, 165, 167

Wyatt, Sophia: Aunt Sally Wyatt's older sister. 155, 161, 162
  Her younger sister: 155, 161, 162

UNNAMED

Two carpetbaggers whom John Sartoris I kills. 6, 224, 225

Hill man who built the house in which the Mitchells live. 22, 23

Horse trader who owns stallion which Bayard Sartoris III rides. 117-119

Negro beggar, wearing a uniform, to whom Bayard Sartoris III gives money. 108, 109

Old Negro with John Henry who rescues Bayard Sartoris III from car wreck. 196-202, 205

Negro who gets car for Byron Snopes. 251, 257

Negro family with whom Bayard Sartoris III stays on Christmas. 331-338

Scottish engineer who helps John Sartoris I build his railroad. 13, 19, 20

Country man, wife, children whom Narcissa Benbow Sartoris adopts. 66, 67

Woman whom Hub meets at his cabin. 127, 128

Telegraph operator who sends Miss Jenny Du Pre's telegram. 359, 360

Young woman with Bayard Sartoris III in Chicago. 351-355

Stocky man talking to Bayard Sartoris III in Chicago. 351-357

Negro minister who leads group to get money from Simon Strother. 261-265

Flags in the Dust 43

Yankee staff major captured by J.E.B. Stuart. 15-19

Australian major and two ladies with Bayard Sartoris III in
    Leicester lounge. 114

Ex-student who plays tennis at Mitchells. 168, 171-173, 176,
    177

Body servant of General Stuart. 14

Colonel elected to replace Col. John Sartoris. 220

HISTORICAL

Ahenobarbus: Name of plebeian Roman family which ended with
    Emperor Nero. 167

Arlen, Michael (1895-1956): English novelist. 158

Beauregard, P.G. (1818-1893): Confederate general. 149

Booth, General William (1829-1912): Founder of Salvation Army.
    182

Byron, Lord (1788-1824): English poet. 339

Caesar, Julius (100?-44 B.C.): Roman general and emperor. 170,
    281

Cincinnatus, Lucius Quinctius (519?-439? B.C.): Roman general
    and statesman. 267, 310

Corot, Jean B. (1796-1875): French artist. 84

Debs, Eugene V. (1855-1926): American Socialist leader. 112

Demosthenes (c.383-322 B.C.): Greek patriot and orator. 33

Dreiser, Theodore (1871-1945): American novelist. 158

Dumas, Alexandre (1802-1870): French novelist. 30, 76

Forrest, Nathan Bedford (1821-1877): Confederate general. 155,
    212

Grant, Ulysses S. (1822-1885): Union general; President of United
    States, 1869-1877. 211, 214

Halleck, Henry W. (1815-1872): Union general. 15

Homer: Greek epic poet. 267

Jackson, Thomas J. "Stonewall" (1824-1863): Confederate general. 149, 305, 314

Johnston, Joseph E. (1807-1891): Confederate general. 149, 155, 212

Lee, Robert E. (1807-1870): Confederate general. 15, 18, 19, 327

Milton, John (1608-1674): English poet. 154

[Pickens, Francis W. (1805-1869)]: Governor of South Carolina, 1860-1862. 12

Pope, John (1822-1892): Union general. 13-15, 17, 19, 20

Richard I (1157-1199): King of England, 1189-1199. 12

Richthofen, Baron Manfred von (1892-1918): German aviator. 40

Sabatini, Rafael (1875-1950): English novelist. 158

Shakespeare, William (1564-1616): English poet and playwright. 157, 158

Sherman, William T. (1820-1891): Union general. 212

Stuart, J.E.B. (1833-1864): Confederate general. 12-20, 52, 350

Van Dorn, Earl (1820-1863): Confederate general. 211, 212, 214

Vardaman, James K. (1861-1930): Mississippi governor and senator. 57, 112

Victoria (1819-1901): Queen of England, 1837-1901. 151

Wilson, Woodrow (1856-1924): President of the United States, 1913-1921. 112

BIBLICAL

Abraham: Old Testament patriarch in Genesis. 154

Delilah: Philistine mistress of Samson in Judges. 195

Lord: 37, 57, 74, 92, 106, 134, 166, 281, 342, 346, 360, 369

Uriah's wife [Bathsheba]: 182

LITERARY/MYTHIC

Atalanta: Grecian huntress who would marry only the man who could outrun her in a foot race. 167

Santa Claus: 298, 334

Semiramis: Mythical queen of Assyria, founder of Babylon and conqueror of Persia and Egypt. 96

Titania: Queen of the fairies in Shakespeare's *A Midsummer Night's Dream*, 1595. 175, 181

SARTORIS

[New York: Harcourt, Brace and Co., 1929. 380 pp.]

Abe: 293, 378

Alford, Doctor: 89; treats Bayard II, 94, 95; described, 96-101, 104; visits Narcissa Benbow, 153, 155, 156; visits Narcissa, 180, 215, 216, 220, 221, 229, 237; travels to Memphis, 238-241, 262

Allan: 17

Beard, Virgil: 106-112, 227, 229, 264, 265

Beard, Will C.: 106, 107, 110, 111, 168, 228

Beard, Mrs. W.C.: 106-108

Benbow, Belle Mitchell: Described, 29, 30, 176, 178, 180; Horace Benbow visits, 182-195; Little Belle's recital, 196, 197, 199, 201, 202; Horace reveals marriage plans, 256, 257, 259, 262, 290; married to Horace, 353, 361, 363, 370

Benbow, Francis: 169, 170

Benbow, Horace: 31-33, 53, 54, 70, 72, 73, 153, 154; returns home, 161-165, 167-178; relationship with Narcissa, 179-181; visits Mitchells', 182-199, 201-203, 217, 254, 255; plans to marry Belle, 256-259, 262; Thanksgiving dinner, 290-292, 294, 296, 299-303; married to Belle, 351-353, 358, 361, 363, 378

Benbow, Julia: 33, 174, 179, 180

Benbow, Narcissa: see Sartoris, Narcissa Benbow

Benbow, Will: 170, 174, 179, 180

Bird, Uncle: 270-276

Brandt, Doctor: 238-240

Buck: 157-160, 265, 269

"Butler, Joe": 109

Sartoris

Comyn: 362

Du Pre, Virginia: 7; family background, 8-11, 17-19, 20, 24, 25; at Belle Mitchell's, 28-34, 36-42, 44; greets Bayard III, 45-61, 64, 66-73, 75-77; rides in car, 78, 79, 81, 83-85, 87-89; takes Bayard II to doctors, 93-105, 113, 114, 123, 135, 140, 144, 152, 155, 159, 167, 168, 199; visited by Narcissa, 200-202, 204, 205, 212, 213, 216-218, 222, 229-231, 236, 237; takes Bayard II to Memphis, 238-243, 247, 248, 256, 259-262; Negroes come for money, 270-277, 281, 288; Thanksgiving dinner, 290-297; tells Narcissa not to ride with Bayard III, 298, 299, 349; alone with Narcissa, 353-359, 364; Narcissa's child born, 366-380
  Her husband: 357

Elnora: 7, 8, 19, 24, 38, 39, 41, 42; listens to Caspey in kitchen, 61-64, 81, 82, 112, 113, 215, 229, 236-238, 246, 248, 371-373, 380

Eunice: 153, 299, 300

Eustace: 128, 129

Falls, Will: 1, 2; John Sartoris I's escape from Yankees, 20-23; relationship with Bayard II, 79-81, 83, 91, 100, 101, 103, 104; treats Bayard II, 218-221; John Sartoris I and Zeb Fothergill, 222-229; John Sartoris I and carpetbaggers, 234-237, 241, 291, 378
  His grandmother: 221

Fothergill, Zeb: 224-226

Frankie: 182-190, 192

Gratton, Mr.: 128, 129

Harris, Meloney: 27, 28, 183, 370

Henry, Uncle: 282, 283, 285

Houston: 122-124, 126

Hub: 135-150, 156-159

Isom: 8, 19, 23, 35, 50, 51; wears Caspey's uniform, 52, 53, 56-59; listens to Caspey in kitchen, 61-66, 77, 78, 81, 82, 84, 87, 88, 112, 113, 115, 199, 200, 218, 236-238, 244, 247, 277; goes hunting, 281-289, 296, 358, 371; takes Miss Jenny to cemetery, 372-374, 376

Joby: 11, 39

Joe: 186, 187, 190, 192

John Henry: 205-212, 215

Jones, "Doctor": 219

Louvinia: 20, 21

MacCallum, Henry: 121, 123, 124; Bayard III visits, 309-318, 325, 329-338

MacCallum, Jackson: 121; Bayard III visits, 313-318, 325-336, 339

MacCallum, Lee: 121; Bayard III visits, 311, 312, 314-318, 325, 329-331, 333-336, 339

MacCallum, Raphael Semmes (Rafe): 121-131; Bayard III rides stallion, 132-135; Bayard III visits, 309-318, 320, 325-331, 333-336, 339

MacCallum, Stuart: 121; Bayard III visits, 313-318, 325, 329, 331-336, 339

MacCallum, Virginius, I: 124, 214; Bayard III visits, 309-318, 320, 321, 326-329, 331-339, 346
  His wives: 310, 334
  His father: 310

MacCallum, Virginius, II (Buddy): 121, 124; Bayard III visits, 308, 309, 313-322, 324-326, 329-338

Mandy: 310, 313-316, 325, 326, 332, 337

Marders, Mrs. Sarah: 182-190, 192, 197, 202

Mitch: 145-150, 156-159

Mitchell, Belle, I: See Benbow, Belle Mitchell

Mitchell, Belle, II: 184, 188-190, 195-197, 353

Mitchell, Harry: 26, 29, 30, 176, 180; Horace Benbow visits, 183, 185-195; Little Belle's recital, 196, 197, 202, 256, 257, 353; in Chicago, 361, 363, 364

Sartoris

Monaghan: 359-363

Moore, Brother: 270-276

Myrtle: 94, 95, 97
  Her mother: 95

Peabody, Lucius Quintus, I: Described, 97-105, 123; attends Bayard III, 135, 138, 140, 144, 152, 215, 220, 229, 241; Thanksgiving dinner, 290-296, 367-370; at cemetery, 376-378
  His wife: 377

Peabody, Lucius Quintus, II: 376-378

Ploeckner: 46, 127, 214, 252

Rachel: 25-28, 187, 189, 191, 193, 195, 196

Redlaw: 23, 375, 376
  His family: 375

Reno: 145-150, 154, 156-158

Res: 3, 86, 227, 228, 264, 265

Richard: 314-317

Rogers, Deacon: 122-129, 144, 145, 158

Sartoris, Bayard, I: 9-18, 47, 230, 357

Sartoris, Bayard, II: 1-3; Simon reveals that Bayard III is home, 4-11, 18-20, 22-25, 29, 30, 33-42; greets Bayard III, 43-47, 50, 51, 56, 59, 61, 68, 69, 71-73, 77-88; goes to attic, 89-92; taken to Jefferson doctors, 93-101, 103-106, 113, 119, 123, 167, 168, 172, 199, 200, 204, 205, 208, 214-216; Will Falls visits, 218-224, 227-237; taken to Memphis, 238-241, 264; visited by group of Negroes, 270-276, 281; Thanksgiving dinner, 291-294, 296-298; dies, 303-305, 310-312, 332, 338, 341, 354, 355, 357, 367, 370; Aunt Jenny at cemetery, 374, 375
  His aunt: 22
  His wife: 59
  His grandfather: 20

Sartoris, Bayard, III: In Jefferson, 4, 5, 7, 19, 33, 34, 37;
    arrives home, 43-49, 53; Aunt Jenny's visit before Caroline's death, 54-57, 59, 60; youth discussed, 70-76;
    returns with car, 77, 78, 80, 83-90, 101, 103, 113, 114;
    takes Simon for ride, 115-120; with Rafe MacCallum, 121-131; rides stallion, 132-134; with Suratt, 135-152, 154,
    155; Narcissa serenaded, 156-160, 167, 168, 186, 199,
    200, 202-204; automobile accident, 205-218, 229-231,
    238; Narcissa visits, 241-254, 258-261; drives Narcissa's
    car, 262, 263, 267, 268, 270, 277-280; takes Narcissa
    hunting, 281-289; Thanksgiving dinner, 290-298; drives
    grandfather in car, 303, 304; at MacCallums', 305-327,
    329-331, 333, 336-340; spends night with Negro family,
    341-350, 353-357; in Chicago, 359-363; flies plane, 364,
    365; Narcissa's child born, 366-369, 373, 376

Sartoris, Benbow: 277, 298, 354, 356, 358, 366-369, 371, 378-380

Sartoris, Caroline White: 19, 47, 48, 54-56, 74, 76, 93, 167
  Her child: 19, 55, 93

Sartoris, John, I: 1, 2, 5, 6, 8, 10, 11, 18; escapes from
    Yankees, 20-23, 40, 43, 59, 92, 98, 112-114; with Zeb
    Fothergill, 223-226, 230; kills two carpetbaggers, 235,
    236, 295, 304, 357, 367, 373; his grave, 375
  His two daughters: 10, 11, 18, 20, 22
  His mother: 8
  His wife: 367

Sartoris, John, II: 59, 74, 90, 374

Sartoris, John, III: 5, 31; his death, 43-48, 54, 56, 59, 60;
    youth discussed, 71-74, 76, 89, 93, 121; Bayard III and
    Rafe MacCallum, 125, 127, 167, 186, 214, 215; Bayard III
    and Narcissa, 251, 252, 288, 289, 298, 311; his concern
    for Mandy, 314, 319, 321, 322, 326, 332, 333, 349; childhood discussed, 354-358, 374

Sartoris, Lucy Cranston: 59, 74, 214, 354, 355, 374

Sartoris, Narcissa Benbow: 29-33; visits Aunt Jenny, 50-61,
    66, 67; shows letter to Aunt Jenny, 68, 69; discusses
    Sartorises, 70-77, 105, 106, 109, 110, 134, 136, 150-153; serenaded by Negroes, 154-157; Horace returns, 161-165, 167-172, 174-178; relationship with Horace, 179-182, 184, 197-203, 205, 212; after Bayard III's automobile accident, 216-218, 231, 238; reads to Bayard III,

Sartoris

241-255; Horace's marriage plans, 256-261; Bayard III drives her car, 262, 263, 267, 268, 270; pregnant, 276-280; goes hunting, 281-299; misses letters, 300-303, 352; Bayard III's travels, 353-359, 363; Benbow born, 366, 370-372, 376; alone with Aunt Jenny and Benbow, 378-380

Sibleigh: 44

Smith, Mrs.: 239

Snopes, Byron: 2, 3, 68, 69, 80, 81, 86, 87; waits on Narcissa Benbow in bank, 105, 106; with Virgil Beard, 107-111, 155, 156, 172; with Virgil Beard, 228, 229, 254, 257, 258, 264; frightens V. Beard, 265; enters Benbow house, 266-268; steals money, 269

Snopes, Flem: 172, 173
  His wife: 173
    Her baby: 173

Snopes, Montgomery Ward: 172-174

Sol: 162, 163, 165

Straud, Doctor: 378

Strother, Caspey: 52, 53, 59; discusses War in kitchen, 61-67, 70; confronted by Bayard II, 81-83, 199, 203, 236-238; goes hunting, 281-289, 371

Strother, Euphrony: 290

Strother, Simon: 2-6; at Mitchells', 24-28, 30, 32-34, 36-40, 42, 44, 46, 50-52, 60; listens to Caspey in kitchen, 61-66, 77, 78, 82-84, 86-88, 112-114; rides in car, 115-119, 199, 212-216, 218, 229, 231-234, 236-238, 241-249; Negroes come for money, 270-276, 290-294, 296, 349, 354, 355, 357, 366-369; killed, 370, 372, 373

Sue: 142

Suratt, V.K.: 135-144, 213
  His brother: 141
  His grandfather: 140
  His parents: 141

Tobe: 130-132, 134

"Wagner, Hal": 110, 111

Watts: 109, 111

Winterbottom, Mrs.: 235, 236

Wyatt, Sally: 68; discusses Sartoris twins, 70-72, 74, 75,
    151-154, 165, 168, 170, 172-176, 179-182
  Her mother: 151
  Her younger sister: 174, 181

Wyatt, Sophia: 174, 181, 182

Wylie, Captain: 12-14

UNNAMED

Two carpetbaggers. 22, 23, 235, 236

Hill man. 24-26

Horse trader. 130-133

Negro beggar. 120, 121

Old Negro. 205-212, 215

Negro family with whom Bayard III stays. 341-350

Scottish engineer. 10, 11, 18

Woman whom Hub meets at his cabin. 142, 143

Young woman. 359-363

Shabby man. 359-365

Negro minister. 232-234, 270-276

Yankees. 6, 20-22

Yankee staff major. 12-16, 18

Ex-student. 186, 187, 190, 192

Sartoris

Anzac major and two ladies. 127

General Stuart's body servant. 11

Colonel elected to replace Colonel John Sartoris. 230

HISTORICAL

Arlen, Michael: 177

Beauregard, P.G.: 166

Byron, Lord: 351

Caesar, Julius: 184, 296

Cincinnatus: 315

Corot, Jean B.: 94

Debs, Eugene V.: 124

Demosthenes: 38

Dreiser, Theodore: 177

Dumas, Alexandre: 34, 85

Forrest, Nathan Bedford: 174, 224

Grant, Ulysses S.: 223, 226

Halleck, Henry W.: 13

Homer: 278

Jackson, Thomas J.: 166, 310, 321

Johnston, Joseph E.: 166, 174, 224

Lee, Robert E.: 13, 16, 17, 336

Milton, John: 172

[Pickens, Francis W.]: 10

Pope, John: 10, 12, 13, 16, 17, 19

Richard I: 9

Richthofen, Baron Manfred von: 46

Sabatini, Rafael: 177

Shakespeare, William: 176, 177

Sherman, William T.: 224

Stuart, J.E.B.: 9-19, 61, 357

Van Dorn, Earl: 223, 226

Vardaman, James K.: 67, 124

Victoria: 169

Wilson, Woodrow: 124

BIBLICAL

Abraham: 172

Delilah: 204

God: 43, 66, 83, 104, 117, 150, 296, 369, 379

LITERARY/MYTHIC

Santa Claus: 345

Titania: 188, 195

GO DOWN, MOSES

[New York: Random House, 1942. 383 pp.]

Acey: Negro who works in sawmill with Rider. 136

Alec, Unc: Husband of Rider's aunt. 144, 145, 148, 150

Ash, Uncle: Negro cook. 175-178; at camp hunting Old Ben, 198-202, 204-206, 220, 224, 228-230, 233, 236; after Old Ben's death, 245, 247, 249, 316, 317, 319-326, 329

Baker, Joe (Jobaker): Chickasaw hermit. 172, 174, 184, 214, 242

Beauchamp, Amodeus McCaslin: Son of Tomey's Turl and Tennie Beauchamp who died in infancy. 271, 272

Beauchamp, Callina McCaslin: Daughter of Tomey's Turl and Tennie Beauchamp who died in infancy. 272

Beauchamp, Fonsiba: Daughter of Tomey's Turl and Tennie Beauchamp. 105, 107-109, 273-281, 283, 293
  Her husband: 274-276, 278-280, 283, 293
  His father: 275, 279

Beauchamp, Henry: Son of Lucas and Molly Beauchamp. 45, 50, 51, 58, 100, 110-114

Beauchamp, Hubert: Uncle of Ike McCaslin. 5, 6, 8; Uncle Buck and Cass at Warwick, 9-24; plays cards with Uncle Buddy, 25-29, 105, 271; his legacy to Ike, 300-309, 359
  His father: 305, 309

Beauchamp, James Thucydus (Tennie's Jim): Son of Tomey's Turl and Tennie Beauchamp. Background, 104-109, 164, 169; at hunting camp, 175-178; hunts Old Ben, 194, 199, 201, 202, 204, 205, 215, 216, 222, 227, 228, 232, 233, 237-240; Old Ben killed, 241-243, 246, 249, 251, 252; Ike McCaslin's search, 271-273, 276, 277, 293, 316, 323, 324, 361, 362

Beauchamp, Lucas Quintus Carothers McCaslin: Son of Tomey's Turl and Tennie Beauchamp. Plots against George Wilkins, 33-51; confronts Zack Edmonds, 52, 53-77; search for gold, 78-83, 85-98, 100-103; background, 104, 105, 107-

131, 138; Ike McCaslin's search, 273, 274, 281, 282, 293, 360, 373, 377

Beauchamp, Molly (Mollie): Wife of Lucas. 34, 41-43; enters Zack Edmonds' house, 45-52, 58-63, 65, 70, 73, 75, 76, 81, 98; wants divorce, 99-104; marriage to Lucas, 110, 111, 113, 115, 117, 119-122, 124-131, 360; seeks help from Gavin Stevens, 370-383

Beauchamp, Nat: See Wilkins, Nathalie Beauchamp

Beauchamp, Samuel Worsham: Grandson of Lucas and Molly Beauchamp. 369-378, 380, 382, 383
  His mother, daughter of Lucas and Molly Beauchamp: 372, 376
  His father: 372, 375

Beauchamp, Sophonsiba: See McCaslin, Sophonsiba Beauchamp

Beauchamp, Tennie: Wife of Tomey's Turl Beauchamp. At Warwick, 5, 15, 17, 18, 23, 24, 26, 28; won by Uncle Buddy, 29, 44, 55; her children, 105, 263; Ike McCaslin's search, 271, 272, 275, 276, 281, 300-305, 307, 310, 359
  Her unnamed child: 272
  Her great-grandfather: 304, 305, 310

Beauchamp, Tomey's Turl: Husband of Tennie. Runs away, 4-20, 23-25; deals cards, 27-29, 44, 47, 57; his children, 105, 106, 108; Ike McCaslin's search, 269-273, 281, 292, 294, 300, 302, 359

Birdsong: White night watchman at sawmill. 152-157
  His family: 155-158

Brownlee, Percival: Slave bought by Buck McCaslin from N.B. Forrest. 263-265, 292, 293

Compson, General: Confederate brigadier general and hunter. 164, 169, 175-179, 185; hunts Old Ben, 194, 201, 202, 204, 205, 212, 215-218, 220, 225, 226, 230, 237; after Old Ben is killed, 246, 248-251, 300, 309, 315, 316, 319, 320, 324, 327, 344, 352, 362
  His son: 236

Crawford, Doctor: Physician who attends Sam Fathers, Boon Hogganbeck, and Lion. 243, 245-249

Daisy: Wife of Uncle Ash. 316, 325

Go Down, Moses   57

Dan: Roth Edmonds' stableman. 83-86, 88, 96, 119, 120, 123-
     125

De Spain, Major: Hunting camp host and landowner. 164, 169,
     170, 173, 175-179, 185; hunts Old Ben, 191, 194, 199,
     201, 202, 204-206, 212-218, 220-223, 226-232, 234-240;
     Old Ben's death, 242-249, 251, 252, 255, 309, 315-325,
     327, 328, 344, 350, 352, 354

Doom: See Ikkemotubbe

Edmonds, Alice: Wife of McCaslin Edmonds. 276

Edmonds, Carothers (Roth): Son of Zack Edmonds. Lucas Beau-
     champ and George Wilkins, 33-36, 40, 42-46, 49-51, 58-
     62, 64-68, 70-73, 76, 77; Lucas and gold-finding machine,
     78-89, 96-100; Molly asks for divorce, 101-103; past
     with Lucas, 104-106, 109-131, 137, 138; hunts with Uncle
     Ike, 335-349, 352, 353, 355-361; kills doe, 364, 370,
     371, 373, 375, 377, 380

Edmonds, Carothers McCaslin (Cass): Great-grandson of Carothers
     McCaslin, cousin of Ike McCaslin. 3; pursues Tomsy's
     Turl, 4-24; poker game, 25-30, 35, 36, 43-46, 49, 52,
     56, 59, 60, 73, 97, 100, 104, 106, 107, 110, 116-120,
     126; at hunting camp, 164, 165, 167-179; discusses deer,
     185-187; hunts Old Ben, 192, 194, 201, 202, 204, 205,
     210, 214-222, 226-228, 231, 232, 234, 236, 237; after
     Old Ben's death, 246-253; discussion with Ike, 254-261,
     267-269, 271-276, 282, 283, 285-289, 291-302, 304-308,
     310-312, 315, 316, 319, 320, 323, 327, 328, 344, 350,
     351, 359, 360
  His grandmother, daughter of Carothers McCaslin: 3, 7, 10,
     52, 56, 114, 164, 256, 309, 311
  His father: 7, 10, 44
  His mother: 7, 44, 47

Edmonds, Zachary (Zack): Son of McCaslin Edmonds, father of
     Carothers McCaslin Edmonds. 35, 39, 43, 44; confronta-
     tion with Lucas Beauchamp, 45-60, 73, 80, 100, 101, 104-
     106, 109, 110; discusses heritage with his son, 114-117,
     120-122
  His wife: 45, 46, 50, 52, 58, 110, 121

Eunice: McCaslin slave, mother of Tomasina. 263, 267-271

Ewell, Walter: One of the hunters at de Spain's camp. At
     hunting camp, 164, 169, 175-181, 183-185; hunts Old Ben,

194, 199, 201, 204, 205, 210, 215-218, 220-222, 226, 237-239, 248, 249, 251, 315, 316, 319, 320, 323, 324, 327, 352

Fathers, Sam: Son of Doom and a slave. Ike kills first deer, 163, 164; background, 165, 166-183; shows Ike the buck, 184, 185, 187; hunts Old Ben, 191, 194-226, 238-240; collapses, 242-249; his burial, 252-254, 263, 295-297, 299, 300, 315, 323, 326-329, 350, 354
  His mother: 166, 168, 206, 263, 295, 326, 350

Gowan, Judge: Federal judge in Jefferson. 71-74

Henry: Deputy marshal in Jefferson. 72, 74

Hogganbeck, Boon: Member of hunting camp; grandson of Chickasaw woman. At hunting camp, 164, 169, 170, 175-181, 185; hunts Old Ben, 191, 194, 198, 201, 202, 204, 205, 213, 215, 216, 219-222, 224, 225; sent to Memphis, 226-240; kills Old Ben, 241, 242-253, 300, 315-317, 319, 320, 322-326, 328, 330; at Gum Tree, 331, 352
  His mother: 227
  His father: 227
  His grandmother: 170, 227

Hulett: Clerk in Jefferson court. 128, 129

Ikkemotubbe (Doom): Chickasaw chief. 164-166, 168, 170, 171, 191, 206, 255-259, 263, 295, 300, 326, 350

Isham: Negro cook for hunters. 348, 349, 354, 357, 361

Issetibbeha: Doom's uncle. 165, 166, 259
  His sister, Doom's mother: 165

Jonas: McCaslin slave. 7

Ketcham: Jefferson jailor. 157-159

Legate, Will: Hunter in Uncle Ike McCaslin's group. 335-347, 353, 354, 356, 364, 365
  His grandfather: 344

McAndrews: Foreman of logging gang. 143, 145, 146, 156

McCaslin, Amodeus (Buddy): Twin of Buck McCaslin; son of Carothers McCaslin. 4-8, 10-12, 21; plays poker with H. Beauchamp, 25-28; rescues Uncle Buck, 29, 30, 36,

Go Down, Moses   59

    39, 40, 45, 105, 106, 114, 115, 163, 168, 169, 171;
    discussion between Ike McCaslin and Cass Edmonds, 256,
    260-274, 281-283, 292, 299-302, 304, 309, 359

McCaslin, Carothers: Father of Buck and Buddy McCaslin. 6,
    36; Lucas Beauchamp's heritage, 44-46, 51-54, 56-58, 71;
    his descendents by slave, 104-106, 108, 114, 116, 118,
    126, 163, 165, 166, 169, 171; discussion about Ike
    McCaslin's heritage, 254, 256-259, 261-263, 265-267;
    birth of Tomey's Turl, 269-273, 281-283, 292-294, 299-
    301, 309, 310, 337, 359
  His grandfather: 299

McCaslin, Isaac: Son of Buck McCaslin and Sophonsiba Beauchamp.
    3, 4, 36, 39, 44, 52, 56, 57, 106-109, 114-116, 118;
    shoots first deer, 163-187; hunts Old Ben, 191-240; Old
    Ben's death, 241, 242-253; discusses heritage with Cass,
    254-264, 266-310; marriage, 311-314; last trip to Major
    de Spain's camp, 315-331; hunts with young men, 335-
    365
  His wife: 3, 4, 106-108, 281, 311-315, 351, 352
    Her father: 3, 106, 281, 311, 312
    Her sister and her sister's children: 4, 352 (identified
    as wife's niece on p. 352)

McCaslin, Sophonsiba Beauchamp: Wife of Buck McCaslin and
    mother of Ike McCaslin. 5, 6; Cass and Uncle Buck at
    Warwick, 9-16, 20; discovers Uncle Buck in bed, 21-24;
    poker game, 25-28, 109, 273; marriage to Buck McCaslin,
    301-307, 309
  Her mother: 303

McCaslin, Theophilus (Buck): Twin of Buddy McCaslin; son of
    Carothers McCaslin; father of Ike McCaslin. 3-8; at
    Warwick, 9-20; in wrong bed, 21, 22-28; rescued by
    brother, 29, 30, 36, 39, 40, 45, 105-107, 114, 115, 163,
    164, 168, 169, 171; in Civil War, 233; discussion between
    Ike McCaslin and Cass Edmonds, 256, 260-274, 281-283,
    288, 292, 293, 299-302, 304, 307, 308, 311, 339, 350,
    359

Mannie: Rider's wife. 135-141, 145, 151, 155

Maydew: Sheriff who arrests Rider for Birdsong's murder. 154-
    158

Moketubbe: Son of Issetibbeha. 166
  His son: 166

Oscar: Roth Edmonds' stableman. 83-86, 88, 96, 119, 120, 123-125

Phoebe (Fibby): McCaslin slave, wife of Roscius. 263, 266, 270

Rideout, Doctor: Physician who cares for Molly Beauchamp. 125

Rider (Spoot): Negro, husband of Mannie. 135-139; sees Mannie's ghost, 140-144; lifts log, 145, 146-152; slashes Birdsong, 153; deputy's story, 154-159
  His parents: 136
  His aunt, wife of Unc Alec: 144, 145, 148, 150

Roscius (Roskus): McCaslin slave, husband of Fibby. 263, 266, 270

Rouncewell: Jefferson merchant. 373

Sartoris, Bayard: Jefferson banker. 236
  His son: 236

Sartoris, Col. John: Confederate officer; father of Bayard. 234

Semmes, Mr.: Liquor dealer in Memphis. 227, 234

Sickymo: Ex-slave, U.S. marshal. 291, 292
  His sister: 292

Stevens, Gavin: Jefferson lawyer. 370-383

Sutpen, Thomas: Yoknapatawpha landowner. 191, 255

Tennie: See Beauchamp, Tennie

Tennie's Jim: See Beauchamp, James Thucydus (Tennie's Jim)

Thisbe, Aunt: Negro on Edmonds' plantation. 50

Thucydides: McCaslin slave, husband of Eunice. 263, 266, 267, 269, 270

Tom: Deputy. 63-66

Tomasina (Tomey): Mother of Tomey's Turl Beauchamp and daughter of Eunice. 57, 105, 269, 270, 271, 294

Tomey's Turl: See Beauchamp, Tomey's Turl

Vitry, Chevalier Soeur-Blonde de: Doom's French companion. 165, 166

Wilkins, George: Young Negro husband of Nat Beauchamp. Lucas Beauchamp's plot, 33-35, 39-45, 59, 60, 62-71; marriage certificate, 72, 74-77; Lucas Beauchamp and divining machine, 80-83, 85, 86, 88-96, 98, 101, 102, 117, 120, 122-127

Wilkins, Nathalie Beauchamp (Nat): Daughter of Lucas and Molly; wife of George. 34; foils father's plans, 41-43, 60, 62-71; marriage certificate, 72, 101, 117, 122-125, 127
  Her aunt: 70

Wilmoth, Mr.: Jefferson newspaper editor. 373-375, 377, 378, 381-383

Worsham, Miss Belle: Jefferson spinster. 374-383
  Her grandfather: 375

Worsham, Hamp: Molly Beauchamp's brother; servant of Belle Worsham. 117, 371, 374-376, 379-381
  His parents: 375
  His wife: 379, 381

Worsham, Samuel: Father of Belle Worsham. 375

Wyatt, Henry: Hunter. 344-348

UNNAMED

Mistress of Roth Edmonds; granddaughter of James Beauchamp. 356-363
  Her son: 357, 358, 360, 362, 363
  Her aunt: 360
  Her father: 360
  Her cousin: 357, 361

Sheriff's deputy who tells his wife about Rider. 154-159
  His wife. 154-156, 159

Salesman of gold hunting machine. 78-82, 86-98, 117

Hubert Beauchamp's Negro mistress. 302, 303

Slave who married Sam Fathers' mother. 166

U.S. Attorney. 73

Fireman at saw logging mill. 142, 143, 155

White bootlegger. 146, 147

Ike McCaslin's partner in carpentry. 310-312, 352

Bank president in Jefferson. 310

Ike McCaslin's landlady. 310, 311, 313

Sheriff. 43, 60, 62-68, 70, 76, 77, 84, 87-89

Conductor and brakeman on logging train. 230, 235, 320, 321

Commissioner in Jefferson. 63-66

Chancellor in Jefferson. 126-129

HISTORICAL

Ashby, Turner (1828-1862): Confederate cavalry general. 286, 287.
  His mother: 286

Brown, John (1800-1859): American abolitionist. 284, 285

Cleveland, Grover (1837-1908): President of the United States, 1885-1889, 1893-1897. 97

Dempsey, William H. "Jack" (1895-   ): American boxer. 230

Forrest, Nathan Bedford (1821-1877): Confederate general. 234, 263, 264, 272, 273, 280, 287

Hancock, Winfield S. (1824-1886): Union general. 286

Hitler, Adolf (1889-1945): German chancellor. 338

Hooker, Joseph (1814-1879): Union general. 286

Jackson, Thomas J. "Stonewall" (1824-1863): Confederate general. 286-288

Kilrain, Jake (1859-1937): American boxer. 230

Go Down, Moses 63

Lafayette, Marquis de (1757-1834): French statesman and officer. 305

Lee, Robert E. (1807-1870): Confederate general. 286

Lincoln, Abraham (1809-1865): President of United States, 1861-1865. 286

Longstreet, James (1821-1904): Confederate general. 286

Meade, George G. (1815-1872): Union general. 286

Morgan, John Hunt (1825-1864): Confederate general. 287, 288

Neville: Family name of English noble house. 307

Rand, Sally (1906-1979): American burlesque star. 339

Roosevelt, Franklin D. (1882-1945): President of United States, 1933-1945. 338

Stuart, J.E.B. (1833-1864): Confederate general. 286-288

Sullivan, John L. (1858-1918): American boxer. 230

Taft, William H. (1857-1930): President of United States, 1900-1913. 97

Tunney, James J. "Gene" (1898-1978): American boxer. 230

Washington, George (1732-1799): President of United States, 1789-1797. 338

Willkie, Wendell L. (1892-1944): Lawyer, Republican candidate for president in 1940. 338

BIBLICAL

Abraham: Old Testament patriarch in Genesis. 257, 283

God: 59, 102, 107, 121, 122, 145, 150, 257-259, 282-287, 289, 299, 300, 305, 339, 348, 349

Ham: Noah's second son in Genesis. 167, 260

Isaac: Old Testament patriarch; Abraham's son. 283

Jesus: 53, 291, 309, 310

Noah: Old Testament patriarch in Genesis. 289

LITERARY/MYTHIC

Aramis: One of heroes in Dumas' *Three Musketeers*, 1844. 166

Benjamin: Jacob's youngest son in Genesis. 371, 380, 381

Capulet: Family in Shakespeare's *Romeo and Juliet*, 1594-1595. 64

Montague: Family in Shakespeare's *Romeo and Juliet*, 1594-1595. 64

Priam: King of Troy. 194

THE HAMLET

[New York: Random House, 1940. 421 pp.]

Armstid: Family name of early settlers in Frenchman's Bend. 4.

Armstid, Henry: Farmer in Frenchman's Bend. 166, 167; at horse auction, 331-341; enters horse pen, 343-346; taken to Mrs. Littlejohn's, 348-352, 355; relationship with wife, 357-361, 367, 372-374, 376; at Old Frenchman's place, 383-401, 407-415; continues to dig, 417-421

Armstid, Mrs. Henry: Wife of Henry Armstid. At horse auction, 331-341, 345, 346, 348, 355; her relationship with husband, 357, 358; Flem Snopes and money, 359-363, 367; in court, 369-375, 384, 407, 419, 420
  Armstid children: 358, 359, 362, 373, 407, 419

Benbow, Judge: Judge in Jefferson. 5

Bolivar, Uncle Dick: Old man who uses divining rod. 391-400, 404, 407

Bookwright, Odom: One of three men who buys the old Frenchman's place. 65, 68, 70; Ratliff's illness, 78-82, 88, 90, 92-94, 97, 166, 167, 170; Houston and Mink Snopes, 184-187, 224, 301, 302, 304, 305, 315, 341, 352, 355, 366, 367, 372, 376; at Old Frenchman's place, 383-400, 403, 407-414, 417
  His father: 413
  His wife: 78 (However, on p. 407 Bookwright is described as a bachelor.)

Cain: Merchant in Jefferson from whom Ab Snopes buys milk separator. 44, 45, 53

De Spain, Major: Man for whom Ab Snopes once worked. 15-21

De Spain, Mrs.: Wife of Major de Spain. 17, 18

Doshey: Family name of early settlers in Frenchman's Bend. 4, 413

Freeman: One of the men at Frenchman's Bend who buys a spotted horse. 309, 313, 315-317, 325, 341-344, 352, 365, 400-403, 415-417

Freeman, Mrs.: Wife of Freeman. 365

George: Deputy sheriff. 292-295

Grimm, Eustace: Relative of Flem Snopes. 400-403, 405-409, 413
 His first wife who was a Calhoun County Doshey: 413
 His second wife who was a Fite: 400, 413
 His mother who was Ab Snopes' youngest sister: 413

Grumby, Major: Man who killed Mrs. Rosa Millard. 33

Haley: Family name of early settlers in Frenchman's Bend. 4

Hampton: Sheriff who arrests Mink Snopes. 262, 266, 267, 277, 281, 284, 285, 288, 289, 292-295

Harris: Farmer in Grenier County whose barn Ab Snopes burned. 11, 15

Hipps, Buck: Texan who sells the spotted horses. Arrives in Frenchman's Bend, 309-315, 317-322; horse auction, 324-336; gives back money to Mrs. Armstid, 337-341, 343-345, 352, 353, 357; Mrs. Armstid and money, 359-361, 365, 371-374, 377-379

Hoake: Father of Alison Hoake McCarron. 152-154

Holland, Anse: One of Ab Snopes' former landlords. 30, 34-36, 51, 53

Houston, Jack: Man murdered by Mink Snopes. 71-74, 79, 103, 104; sued by Mink Snopes, 180, 181, 184; Ike Snopes and cow, 191, 192, 200-202, 204, 213-217, 220, 221; "sells" cow to Ike, 223-225, 229, 231; background, 235-249; killed, 250, 258, 259, 267, 268, 275, 276, 277, 283, 285, 291-293, 296, 304, 305
 His father: 235, 236, 241, 243, 245
 His mother: 236, 237, 242

Houston, Lucy Pate: Jack Houston's wife who is killed by stallion. 213, 214, 235-240, 245-248

Jim: One of Hampton's deputies. 292-295

Jim: Negro who works for Pat Stamper. 34, 40-48, 50

Kemp, Beasley: Man who traded a horse to Ab Snopes. 35-43, 50, 51

The Hamlet   67

Labove: Father of football player/Frenchman's Bend school
    teacher. 116-123

Labove: Football star at University who becomes school teacher
    at Frenchman's Bend. 79, 114, 115; plays football, 116-
    123; opens school, 124-127; obsession with Eula Varner,
    128-144, 156, 406
  His great-grandmother: 116, 118

Leonard: Family name of early settlers in Frenchman's Bend.
    4

Littlejohn: Family name of early settlers in Frenchman's
    Bend. 4

Littlejohn, Mrs.: Woman who runs boarding house in Frenchman's
    Bend. 11, 32, 60, 87, 93-96; takes money from Ratliff
    for Ike Snopes, 100, 101, 113, 186-188, 193, 194, 208,
    216, 217; Houston, Ratliff, and Ike, 223-227, 229, 231,
    278, 304, 305, 312, 313; observes horse auction, 319-
    322, 324, 327-330, 332, 334, 335, 340, 342, 345; strikes
    horse, 346; Armstid brought to boarding house, 348-350,
    352, 353, 355, 356, 358-361, 367

McCallum: Family name of early settlers in Frenchman's Bend.
    4

McCallum: Whiskey maker. 56

McCallum, Anse: Man who tamed two Texas ponies earlier. 316,
    318

McCallum, "Old Man Hundred-and-One": Old man referred to by
    Ratliff. 185

McCarron: Husband of Alison Hoake. 153, 154

McCarron, Alison Hoake: Mother of Hoake McCarron. 152-155,
    157

McCarron, Hoake: Father of Eula Varner's child. 152, 154-
    160, 164, 416

McCaslin, Uncle Buck: Old man who helped Bayard Sartoris during
    Civil War. 19, 33

McCaslin, Ike: Man who allowed Ab Snopes to stay in his cotton
    house one winter. 11, 403

Millard, Rosa: Mother-in-law of Col. John Sartoris. 33, 37

Mitchell, Hugh: Farmer near Whiteleaf. 38, 40, 42

Murray: Family name of early settlers in Frenchman's Bend. 4

Odum, Cliff: Farmer near Whiteleaf. 51, 52

Peabody, Doctor: Yoknapatawpha physician. 45

Quick, Uncle Ben: Man who has goats. 88, 89, 92, 94, 95, 97

Quick, Lon: Sawmill operator. 65, 80, 184, 303, 304, 309-317, 341, 342, 352, 355, 377, 400, 401
 His boy: 401

Ratliff, V.K.: Sewing machine salesman. 7; Ab Snopes' past, 14-21; Ab Snopes and Pat Stamper, 28-65, 68, 70, 71; goat deal, 76-104; Flem, Eula, and Will Varner, 168-171, 179-187; Ike Snopes and cow, 224-234, 246; helps Mink Snopes' wife, 297-306; horse auction, 315-318, 342, 346, 348-362, 364-368, 370; at Old Frenchman's place, 383-414, 417, 420
 His sister: 70, 297, 298, 301
 His father: 30, 34, 50
 His nephew: 298, 301

Riddey: Family name of early settlers in Frenchman's Bend. 4

Rideout: Aaron's brother. 417

Rideout, Aaron: Ratliff's partner in a Jefferson restaurant; in 1964 edition replaced by Grover Cleveland Winbush. 417

Sam: Negro who works for the Varners. 30, 159, 163-165, 415, 416

Sartoris, Bayard: Son of Col. John Sartoris. 33

Sartoris, Col. John: Confederate officer. 19, 33, 37

Short, Herman: Man who traded a mule and buggy for a horse with Pat Stamper. 38-40

Snopes: Name of family tribe moving into Frenchman's Bend. 101, 184, 185, 230, 234, 299, 304, 305, 316, 319, 366, 367, 370, 403

The Hamlet 69

Snopes, Ab: Father of Flem Snopes. Arrives in Frenchman's
    Bend, 8-14; De Spain's barn, 15-25, 27, 29-32; trades
    with Pat Stamper, 33-57, 70, 299, 413

Snopes, Mrs. Ab: Second wife of Ab. 9-11, 15-17, 19, 23
  Her sister: 9-11, 15-17, 19, 23
  Her two daughters: 9-11, 15-19, 22, 24, 54
  Her younger son: 15, 30

Snopes, Eckrum (Eck): Cousin of Flem Snopes who becomes
    blacksmith. As blacksmith, 71-75, 79; Ike Snopes and
    cow, 227, 228, 231-234, 261, 275, 299, 303, 305, 306;
    horse auction, 312-315, 317-325, 328, 330-333; pursues
    horses, 343-346, 348, 352-357, 365-367; sued by Tull,
    370, 373, 375-379, 415, 416
  His first wife: 75, 306
  His second wife: 75, 315, 354
  Three children by second wife: 233, 234, 306

Snopes, Eula Varner: Daughter of Will Varner; wife of Flem
    Snopes. 6, 12; description, 107-115; Labove episode,
    128-140, 143; courtship, 145-151, 155; Hoake McCarron
    and marriage to Flem, 157-169, 171, 179, 181, 182; re-
    turns from Texas, 302-304, 349-351, 402, 404; leaves for
    Jefferson, 415-417
  Her daughter: 302, 415, 416

Snopes, Flem: Son of Ab Snopes; husband of Eula Varner. 9-11,
    15-20, 22; talk with Jody Varner, 25-28, 30-32, 55, 56;
    clerk in Varner's store, 58-62, 64-70, 75, 76; four
    Snopeses brought in, 79-88, 92; goat deal, 94-99, 101,
    102, 104, 107, 151, 162; marries Eula Varner, 165-169;
    meets Prince, 171-175, 179, 182, 185, 228, 232, 252, 298,
    301, 302, 304, 305; horse auction, 309, 311, 315, 317-
    319, 322, 324, 325, 334, 337-341, 349, 352, 354-356;
    Mrs. Armstid, 358-363, 366, 367, 370-375, 379, 382, 384,
    388-392; sells Old Frenchman's place, 402-407; leaves
    for Jefferson, 414-417, 420, 421

Snopes, I.O.: Cousin of Flem Snopes who succeeds Labove as
    schoolteacher in Frenchman's Bend. Leases blacksmith
    shop, 71-74, 79, 80, 183, 184; helps to buy cow, 227-
    234, 275, 299, 303, 304, 306, 364, 368
  His wife and child: 303, 304, 365

Snopes, Isaac (Ike): Flem Snopes' idiot cousin. 86, 87, 93,
    98-100; with cow, 188-213, 215-217, 222-224, 227, 229,
    231, 232, 305, 306

Snopes, Launcelot (Lump): Flem Snopes' cousin who succeeds him as clerk in Varner's store. 165, 183, 185-188; charges to watch Ike with cow, 225-227, 229, 232, 257, 261; confronts Mink Snopes, 266-269, 274-285, 287-289, 299, 342, 348; "defends" Flem Snopes, 354-364, 370, 371, 373-375, 401-403, 415, 416
  His mother: 225, 226

Snopes, Mink: Flem Snopes' cousin who kills Jack Houston. Ratliff brings sewing machine, 83-87, 103, 104; sues Houston, 180, 181, 183, 184, 227, 228, 232; kills Houston, 249-301, 304, 305, 366; sentenced, 380-382
  His grandmother: 86
  His father: 251, 270

Snopes, Mrs. Mink: Mink Snopes' wife. 83-85, 252-255, 266-269; at logging camp, 271-276; stays at house of Ratliff's sister, 297-299, 301, 302, 305
  Her father: 213, 271
  Her children: 83-85, 252, 254, 255, 267, 274, 297-299, 301, 302

Snopes, St. Elmo: Son of I.O. 357, 363-365

Snopes, Mrs. Vynie: Ab Snopes' first wife. 34-37, 39, 44, 47, 50-53
  Her father: 34

Snopes, Wallstreet Panic (Wall): Eck Snopes' son by his first wife. 75; Ike Snopes and cow, 185-187, 226, 261, 262, 265, 303, 305, 306; horse auction, 314, 315, 318-326, 334, 339, 341; pursues horse, 343-346, 348, 353, 354, 356, 357, 361-363, 365, 366, 370
  His grandparents: 306

Stamper, Pat: Horsetrader. 33-36, 38-49, 53, 55

Trumbull: Blacksmith who loses his job to the Snopeses. 67, 71-73, 75, 76, 101
  His wife: 75

Tull, Vernon: Farmer in Frenchman's Bend. 10-12, 70, 78-82, 166, 167, 170, 303, 304; accident with horse, 347, 348, 357; court case against Eck Snopes, 367, 369, 370, 373, 375-379, 415-417

Tull, Mrs. Vernon: Vernon's wife. 347, 348, 357, 367, 369, 370, 373, 375-379
  Four daughters of the Tulls: 347, 348, 369, 370, 373

Varner, Eula: See Snopes, Eula Varner

Varner, Jody: Son of Will; brother of Eula. Meets Ab and Flem Snopes, 6-31, 48, 53; Flem becomes clerk, 59-61, 64-70, 76, 88, 89, 92, 94, 95; usurped by Flem, 101, 102; relationship with Eula, 109-114, 128-130, 136, 138-141, 143, 144, 147-149, 152, 156; Eula's pregnancy, 159-164, 167, 168, 183, 269, 276, 310-312, 362-365, 413

Varner, Mrs. Maggie: Wife of Will Varner. 6, 8, 11, 12, 89; relationship with Eula, 107-112; Eula's courtship, 147-151; Eula's pregnancy, 161-165, 168, 304, 351, 402-404; Eula and Flem leave for Jefferson, 415, 416

Varner, Will: Father of Eula and Jody. 3-8, 11-13; discusses Snopes with Ratliff, 28-32, 54, 55, 58, 60, 61; pays for tobacco, 62, 64-66, 68-70, 73, 75, 76, 80, 82, 89, 95, 100-102, 104, 107-112; hires Labove, 115, 116, 118-121, 123-126, 130, 132, 134, 139, 146-149, 151, 152, 155-157; sets McCarron's arm, 158-164; marries Eula to Flem, 165-169, 179-185, 204, 230-232, 245-248, 257, 261, 269, 276, 285, 292, 293, 302, 304, 315, 324, 340, 341; attends Henry Armstid, 349-353, 368, 375, 384, 386, 391, 401-407, 413, 415-417, 419
  His fourteen children besides Eula and Jody: 6
  His mother: 351
  His grandfather: 163

Whitfield, Brother: Minister. 231-233

Whittington: Family name of early settlers in Frenchman's Bend. 4

Winterbottom: Frenchman's Bend resident who runs boarding house. 402

UNNAMED

Negro man who works for Houston. 204, 213, 217, 220, 223, 247, 248, 267

Prostitute with whom Houston lived. 242-245

The Professor who preceded Labove as school teacher. 115, 116, 124, 128

Original Frenchman. 3, 4

Young lawyer who defends Mink Snopes. 380, 381

Justice of Peace who hears spotted horses cases. 369-380

Farmer whose feed is stolen by Ike Snopes. 218-223

Labove's football coach. 122, 124

Negro companion of Bayard Sartoris during Civil War. 33

HISTORICAL

Blackstone, William (1723-1780): English jurist. 124

Caesar, Julius (100?-44 B.C.): Roman general and emperor. 184, 230

Coke, Edward (1552-1634): English jurist. 124

Grant, Ulysses S. (1822-1885): Union general; President of United States, 1869-77. 4

Horace (65-8 B.C.): Roman poet and satirist. 124, 128

Thucydides (471?-400? B.C.): Greek historian. 124, 128

Voltaire (1694-1778): French writer and philosopher. 125

BIBLICAL

Isaac: Old Testament patriarch; son of Abraham. 90

Jezebel: Ahab's wife in Old Testament books I and II Kings. 312

Job: Central figure in Old Testament book of Job. 312

Lord: 35, 36, 43, 90, 91, 93, 244, 249

Magdalen: Woman healed by Jesus in Luke 8:2. 243

Moses: Old Testament patriarch. 368

The Prince of Hell: 171-175
  His father: 173, 174

The Hamlet

LITERARY/MYTHIC

Brunhilde: Heroine in Wagner operas *Die Walkure*, *Siegfried*, and *Götterdammerung*. 350

Crane, Ichabod: Character in Irving's "The Legend of Sleepy Hollow," 1819. 138

Helen: Wife of Menelaus. 207, 213, 350

Juno: Jupiter's wife; queen of heaven. 208

Lilith: Adam's first wife in Hebrew folklore. 297

Venus: Goddess of love and beauty. 130, 135

Vulcan: Roman god of fire and metalworking. 135

INTRUDER IN THE DUST

[New York: Random House, 1948. 247 pp.]

Aleck Sander: Son of Paralee; Negro friend of Chick Mallison. Hunts with Chick Mallison, 4-13, 16, 17, 26, 27, 35, 36, 45, 71, 75, 78, 81, 83-85; Chick asks him to go to grave, 86, 89; goes to dig up body, 90-103; returns after body is dug up, 105, 106; goes to see sheriff, 108-114, 116-119, 121, 126, 128; details of digging up grave, 129-132, 141, 143-145, 147, 149, 150, 158, 159, 169, 170, 172, 174, 175, 185, 193, 196, 197, 209, 214, 215, 223, 230, 231, 237, 242-244

Armstead: Family name of farmers who settled in the valley. 149

Beauchamp, Lucas: Negro accused of killing Vinson Gowrie. 3; discovers Chick in creek, 6-20, 22-26; accused of killing Vinson Gowrie, 27-29, 31-34, 36-44; tells Chick to get Stevens, 45, 48, 49, 53, 54, 56; Chick and Stevens visit in jail, 57-66; tells Chick to look at body, 68-70, 72, 73, 78-89; Chick, Miss Habersham, and Aleck Sander, 90, 94, 101, 109, 113, 117; Miss Habersham sits at jail, 118, 119, 126, 128, 130, 133, 137, 138, 142, 144, 147, 151-153, 155, 161, 162, 178, 179, 181, 188, 189, 192, 193, 195-204, 208, 210-230, 232, 234, 236, 237; in Gavin Stevens' office, 240-247
  His father: 7
  His married daughter and husband: 23

Beauchamp, Molly: Wife of Lucas Beauchamp. 10, 11, 13-15, 22, 23, 25, 87, 119, 161, 242
  Her mother: 87
  Her first child: 87

Bookwright: Family name of farmers who settled in the valley. 149

Compson, General: One of the hunters at Major de Spain's. 93

Dandridge, Maggie: See Stevens, Maggie Dandridge

De Spain, Major: Cousin of Chick Mallison's grandfather who had hunting camp near Jefferson. 93

Intruder in the Dust

Downs, Mrs.: Old white woman who finds lost objects. 71

Edmonds, Carothers: Landowner on whose property Lucas Beau-
    champ lives. 3-10, 12, 13, 16-19, 22, 25, 28, 30, 36,
    44, 93, 151, 152
  His father: 8

Ephraim: Negro who is the father of Paralee. 63, 70, 71, 112,
    130

Fathers, Sam: Member of de Spain's hunting camp. 93
  His father: 93

Fraser: Family name of farmers who settled in the valley. 132,
    148, 149

Fraser, Squire Adam: Proprietor of store in Beat Four. 20,
    27, 30, 34, 39, 41, 219, 228, 229

Fraser, Doyle: Son of Adam Fraser. 20, 37

Gowrie: Family name of farmers who settled in the valley. 28,
    33-35, 38, 40, 45, 49, 53, 59, 61, 62, 65, 66, 69, 72,
    73, 74, 78, 81-84, 102, 117, 132, 139, 140, 148, 149,
    165, 200, 201, 218-220, 230, 232

Gowrie, Amanda W.: Wife of N.B. Forrest Gowrie. 101, 222, 237

Gowrie, Bilbo: Son of Nub Gowrie; twin of Vardaman Gowrie.
    159, 160, 162-167, 170, 171, 174-177, 179, 180, 219,
    220, 230

Gowrie, Bryan: Third son of Nub Gowrie. 165, 219

Gowrie, Crawford: Second son of Nub Gowrie. 62-64; moves body,
    100, 129-131; background, 164, 165, 167-169, 172-175,
    192, 197, 199-202, 204, 208, 210, 218-221; partnership
    with Vinson, 222-232; suicide's grave, 237, 243

Gowrie, Forrest: Oldest son of Nub Gowrie. 164, 219

Gowrie, N.B. Forrest (Nub): Moonshiner who lives in Beat Four.
    79-81, 101, 139; helps to look for body, 159-164, 167,
    168, 170, 171, 173-176; finds Vinson's body, 177-179,
    192, 193, 197, 219, 220, 230

Gowrie, Vardaman: Son of Nub Gowrie; twin of Bilbo Gowrie.
    159, 160, 162-167, 170, 171, 174-177, 179, 180, 219,
    220, 230

Gowrie, Vinson: Youngest son of Nub Gowrie. 3, 27, 28, 33-35, 37, 38, 40, 62-64, 68-70, 72-74, 79, 80, 82, 86, 89, 90, 93, 94; grave opened, 104, 109, 115, 117, 153, 161, 162, 164; grave reopened, 165, 167, 168, 173, 175; body found, 177-179, 188, 192, 193, 200, 201, 214, 219-221; partnership with Crawford, 222-231, 237

Greenleaf: Family name of farmers who settled in the valley. 149

Grenier, Louis: One of the original settlers of Yoknapatawpha County. 75, 76

Grinnup, Lonnie: Descendant of Louis Grenier. 76

Habersham, Doctor: One of the original settlers of Yoknapatawpha County. 75, 87

Habersham, Miss Eunice: Spinster who is granddaughter of Dr. Habersham. Visits Gavin Stevens, 75-78, 80, 82, 87-90; goes with Chick and Aleck Sander, 92-95, 98-103; grave opened, 104-106; goes to sheriff, 107-114, 116, 117; sits at jail, 118, 119, 121, 126-128; account of leaving grave, 129-133, 138, 142, 144, 145, 150, 158, 159, 169; in traffic, 185-189, 193, 196-198, 205, 208, 209, 212, 214; discusses crime, 221-223, 228, 230-232, 234, 237, 241-244
  Her father: 76

Halladay, Jim: District Attorney from Harrisburg. 65, 81, 109-111

Hampton, Hope: Sheriff of Yoknapatawpha County. 3, 27, 28, 31, 32, 34, 38-41, 43-45, 52-54, 56, 62, 64, 67, 70, 73, 74, 79-81, 83, 89; visited by Gavin Stevens and others, 107-118, 131, 136, 139-145, 151; at Beat Four, 156-163; empty grave, 166-176; discovers Vinson Gowrie's grave, 177-182, 185, 190, 192, 197, 203; plan to capture Crawford Gowrie, 204, 207-213, 215, 217-225, 229, 231-234, 240, 242, 245

Hampton, Mrs. Hope: Wife of sheriff. 107, 108
  Her daughter: 108

Hogganbeck, Boon: Member of Major de Spain's hunting camp. 93
  His mother: 93
  His grandmother: 93

Intruder in the Dust 77

Holston: Tavern keeper; one of the original settlers of Yoknapatawpha County. 75, 76

Ingraham: See Ingrum

Ingrum: Family name of farmers who settled in the valley; originally named Ingraham. 28, 33, 34, 38, 53, 148, 149

Ingrum, Willy: Jefferson marshal. 135, 136, 140-142, 184, 212, 221, 232, 237

Joe: Tenant's son on Carothers Edmonds' plantation. 4-10, 12, 13, 16, 17, 26, 27, 36

Legate, Will: Man who guards Lucas Beauchamp in jail. 52-54, 62, 66-68, 79, 80, 83, 114, 115, 117, 121, 138, 142, 224

Lilly, Mr.: Country man who owns small store in Jefferson. 47-49.
  His wife: 48

Littlejohn: Family name of farmers who settled in the valley. 149

McCallum: Family name of farmers who settled in the valley. 33, 148, 164

McCallum, Buddy: Farmer near Jefferson. 179, 192, 229

McCaslin, Carothers: Grandfather of Lucas Beauchamp. 7, 9, 17, 19, 24, 69, 152, 226

McCaslin, Uncle Ike: Carothers Edmonds' great-uncle who is member of De Spain's hunting camp. 93

McGowan, Skeets: Man who works in Jefferson drugstore. 66

Mallison, Charles, I (Charley): Father of Chick Mallison. 22, 32-34, 55, 71, 72, 75, 81, 82, 84, 105, 116, 123-129, 132, 133, 185, 208

Mallison, Charles, II (Chick): Son of Charles I and Maggie Mallison; nephew of Gavin Stevens. 3; hunts, 4-14; offers money to Lucas, 15-18, 21-36, 38-44; Lucas tells him to get Gavin Stevens, 45-53; goes to jail with Stevens, 54-90; goes to grave, 91-106; goes to sheriff,

107-119, 121-139, 141-143; returns to grave with uncle and sheriff, 144-153, 156-164, 166-176; Vinson Gowrie's body found, 177-196; discussion with G. Stevens, 197-214, 217-224, 226, 228-232, 234-236; resolution of crime, 237-239; Lucas visits G. Stevens, 240-247

Mallison, Maggie Stevens: Mother of Chick Mallison; sister of Gavin Stevens. 4, 8, 15, 21-23, 30, 32-34, 40, 41, 45, 55; loses ring, 70-72, 75, 77, 82; confronts Chick, 105-107, 116, 121-126; sits at jail, 127, 128, 130, 133, 138, 142, 152, 182, 184-186, 189-192, 208, 242

Maycox, Judge: Circuit judge. 59, 65, 110, 111

Millingham: Family name of farmers who settled in the valley. 149

Montgomery, Jake: Man who is killed by Crawford Gowrie and placed in Vinson Gowrie's grave. 104, 115, 162, 168, 174, 175, 178, 183, 185, 188, 193, 208, 220, 221, 223, 224, 229-232, 237

Mosby, Uncle Hogeye: Old epileptic. 184

Paralee: Mother of Aleck Sander. 12, 38, 39, 63, 70, 71, 75, 85, 96, 108, 116, 123, 124, 126-128, 130, 147

Skipworth: Constable at Beat Four. 27, 28, 33, 34, 37, 38, 40, 41, 64, 228, 240
  His wife: 33

Stevens, Judge: Father of Gavin Stevens and Maggie Mallison. 6, 8, 12, 24, 29, 93, 152

Stevens, Gavin: County attorney. 3, 4, 10, 15, 21-25, 28-34, 36, 40-43, 45-50, 52, 53; visits Lucas in jail, 54-68, 70-72, 74, 75, 77-82, 86-89; hears Chick's story, 105, 106; goes to sheriff, 107-112, 114, 116-119, 121-123, 125-129, 131, 133, 135, 137, 139, 141-143; goes to grave with sheriff, 144-150, 153-159, 161, 162, 164, 166-175; Vinson Gowrie's body found, 177, 178, 180, 182-186, 189-192, 194-196; discussion with Chick, 197-212, 215-218, 220-234, 236; Americans' love for automobile, 238, 239; Lucas comes to office, 240-247

Stevens, Maggie Dandridge: Mother of Gavin Stevens and Maggie Mallison. 15, 75, 130

Tubbs, Mr.: Jefferson jailor. 51-54, 56, 57, 66, 67, 80, 117

Tubbs, Mrs.: Wife of jailor. 118

Urquhart: See Workitt

Varner: Owner of store in Frenchman's Bend. 234

Workitt: Family name of farmers who settled in the valley; originally Urquhart. 28, 33, 34, 38, 132, 148, 149, 200, 201

Workitt, Uncle Sudley: Relative from whom Vinson and Crawford Gowrie were buying lumber. 220, 222-227

UNNAMED

Jailor's daughter who scratched her name in the glass at the jail. 50, 51

Lieutenant who marries the jailor's daughter. 51

Jailor in Jefferson during Civil War. 50

Three white sawmill workers who confront Lucas Beauchamp at Fraser's store. 18-20

Two Negro servants of Miss Eunice Habersham. 76, 77, 119

Two street-gang blacks taken to dig up the grave. 139, 140, 156-163, 171, 173, 174, 176, 177

Architect who insists upon being put into jail after he drives into store window. 54, 55

Old lady who taught the children to play Five Hundred. 60

HISTORICAL

Armistead, Lewis A. (1817-1863): Confederate general; Faulkner spells his name Armstead. 195

[Barnes, Djuna (1892-)]: American poet and novelist. 195

Brown, John (1800-1859): American abolitionist. 216

Garnett, Richard B. (1819-1863): Confederate general. 195

Kemper, James L. (1823-1895): Confederate general. 195

Lee, Robert E. (1807-1870): Confederate general. 217

Longstreet, James (1821-1904): Confederate general. 194

Pickett, George E. (1825-1875): Confederate general. 194

Pocahontas (1595?-1617): American Indian princess. 10

Wilcox, Cadmus M. (1824-1890): Confederate general. 195

BIBLICAL

Lord: 28, 36, 39, 100, 188

Noah: Old Testament patriarch in Genesis. 149

LIGHT IN AUGUST

[New York: Harrison Smith and Robert Haas, 1932. 480 pp.]

Alice: Twelve-year-old girl who helps Joe Christmas in orphanage. 127-129, 156

Allen, Bobbie: Waitress with whom Joe Christmas has an affair. 160, 161, 164-187, 191-193, 198-205, 207, 208

Armstid: Farmer who helps Lena Grove on her trip to Jefferson. 5-15, 18-23

Armstid, Martha: Armstid's wife. 10, 12-20, 22

Atkins, Miss: Dietician at orphanage where Joe Christmas stays. 112-126, 131-134, 363-365

Beard, Mrs.: Owner of boarding house where Byron Bunch lives. 43, 76, 78-80, 283, 395-398

Bedenberry, Brother: Negro preacher whose church is disrupted by Joe Christmas. 305-308

Brown, Joe: See Burch, Lucas

Buford (Bufe): Deputy who works with sheriff on Burden murder case. 274-276, 281, 302-304, 309-311, 400, 402-405, 409, 423, 433, 434

Bunch, Byron: Worker at planing mill who falls in love with Lena Grove. 22; meets Joe Christmas, 27, 29-34, 36, 38, 39; his lifestyle, 41-51; hears about Hightower, 55-57, 59, 62-65; Lena, Brown, Christmas, 67-94; goes to Hightower for help, 282-291, 294-300, 302-304, 342-345; brings Hines to see Hightower, 348-351, 353-355, 361, 365-370; Lena's child born, 371, 372-384, 388-403; fights Brown, 413-418, 422, 465; with Lena, 468-480

Burch, Lucas (Joe Brown): Joe Christmas's partner and the father of Lena Grove's child. 4-6, 9, 10, 13-18, 21, 22, 25; works at mill and meets Christmas, 32-42, 45, 46; identity revealed, 48-51; Joanna Burden's murder, 71-94; with Christmas in cabin, 95-98, 101, 102, 105, 106; relationship with Christmas, 255-260, 274; comes for reward, 277-279; after Joanna Burden's murder, 284-290, 296, 297, 299, 302-304, 309-311, 331, 344, 369, 380,

389, 390, 394, 397-400; sees Lena and fights Bunch, 402-417, 422, 423, 474, 478

Burden, Beck: Daughter of Calvin I and Evangeline Burden. 229-233, 237, 238

Burden, Calvin, I: Grandfather of Joanna Burden; killed by John Sartoris. 42, 48, 228-238, 241, 420

Burden, Calvin, II: Grandson of Calvin Burden I; half-brother of Joanna Burden. 42, 48, 231-239, 241, 251, 420

Burden, Evangeline: Wife of Calvin Burden I. 228-230, 233, 235

Burden, Joanna: Granddaughter of Calvin Burden I; Joe Christmas's mistress. 32, 39; town's response to her past, 42, 44, 45, 48, 72, 73, 77, 81; her murder discussed, 84-91, 98, 99, 104, 110, 214, 215; meets Christmas, 217-227; tells Christmas her family's history, 234-236, 238-241; second phase, 242-252; third phase, 253-257; plans for Christmas' future, 260-267, 270-273, 275; envelope with her instructions, 278, 279, 327, 331, 336, 369, 385, 394, 397, 420

Burden, Juana: First wife of Nathaniel Burden. 231-238

Burden, Nathaniel: Son of Calvin Burden I; father of Joanna Burden. 228-241, 251
  His second wife; mother of Joanna: 235-239

Burden, Sarah: Daughter of Calvin Burden I. 229-233, 237, 238

Burden, Vangie: Daughter of Calvin Burden I. 229-233, 237, 238

Burrington, Nathaniel: Father of Calvin Burden I. 228

Burrington, Nathaniel, II: Nephew of Joanna Burden. 86, 278

Bush, Lem: Neighbor of the Hines who takes Milly Hines to the circus. 352, 354

Carruthers, Miss: Organist at Rev. Hightower's church. 346

Charley: Intern who has affair with Miss Atkins. 112, 113, 115, 118, 119, 362-364

Light in August   83

Christmas, Joe: Son of Milly Hines. 27-30; relationship with
    Brown, 31-35; quits job, 36-42, 48-50; Bunch tells
    Hightower about Brown, Christmas, and J. Burden's murder,
    73, 74, 80, 81, 83, 86-94; on night of murder, 95-110;
    at orphanage, 111-132; with McEacherns, 133-160; rela-
    tionship with Bobbie Allen, 161-212; in Mississippi,
    213-218; with Joanna Burden, 219-227, 234-236, 240, 241;
    second phase of relationship, 242-252; third phase, 253-
    270, 277, 279, 281, 284, 286-288, 291-293, 303; disrupts
    Negro church, 305-322; Doc Hines' attack, 325-334, 336-
    338; his grandparents revealed, 343-345, 348, 350, 351,
    358-365, 367; Bunch asks Hightower to lie about Christ-
    mas, 369, 376, 387, 388, 391, 392, 394, 397, 399, 400,
    412; his death revealed, 418-425, 427; pursued by Percy
    Grimm, 433-439; his death, 440, 465, 466, 470

Cinthy: Wife of Pomp; cook for Gail Hightower I. 444-446,
    449-452, 457-459

Confrey, Mame: Wife of Max. 163-172, 175, 179-183, 185, 187,
    198, 200, 203-210

Confrey, Max: Proprietor of restaurant where Bobbie Allen works.
    166-168, 171, 172, 175, 179-183, 185-187, 198, 199, 201-
    205, 207-210

Conner, Buck: Marshal of Jefferson. 92, 93, 286

Dollar: Merchant in Jefferson. 338

Gillman, Mr.: Owner of sawmill where Hines works. 359

Grimm, Percy: Captain in State National Guard who kills Joe
    Christmas. 400, 425-439, 465, 466
  His father: 425, 427

Grove, Lena: Young country girl who bears child of Lucas
    Burch. 1-8; picked up by Armstid, 9-26; meets Byron
    Bunch, 45-51; Lena, Brown, Christmas, 71, 72, 74-82,
    86, 94, 278; plans to stay in Brown's cabin, 283-290,
    296-300, 302-304, 344, 345, 369; baby born, 371, 372,
    375-380, 384-391, 394, 397-400, 403; Brown brought to
    her, 406-410, 416, 418, 422, 465; picked up by furniture
    dealer, 468-480
  Her baby: 371, 375, 377, 379-381, 384-390, 394, 397, 403, 407,
    421-423, 465, 469, 470, 472-474, 477-480
  Her parents: 1, 2

Grove, McKinley: Lena's brother. 2-4, 17, 23, 25
   His family: 3, 17

Halliday: Man in Mottstown who captures Joe Christmas. 331, 332, 336

Hightower, Gail, I: Grandfather of Gail Hightower II; killed in Civil War. 56, 57, 59, 60, 445-448, 450-452, 457-459, 462, 465

Hightower, Gail, II: Deposed minister in Jefferson. 43, 44; background, 52-70; Lena, Brown, Christmas, 71-74, 76, 77, 80-83, 85, 93, 94; Byron Bunch visits, 282-301; Bunch brings Hines, 342-351, 353, 354, 358, 361, 365-370; Lena's baby born, 371-375, 377, 379-392, 395-397, 401, 407, 416; Christmas runs to house, 419, 421-425, 438, 439; remembers past and family, 441-445, 448-450, 452-467
   His father: 52, 442-452, 457, 459, 463
   His wife: 54-65, 441, 453-457, 459, 460, 462-465
   His mother: 442-447, 449, 450

Hines, Eupheus (Doc): Grandfather of Joe Christmas. Janitor in orphanage, 117-132; living in Mottstown, 322-330, 332-335; taken to see Hightower, 338-341, 348-370; in cabin with Lena, 375, 381; goes to Jefferson, 386, 387, 400, 420, 421, 423

Hines, Mrs. Eupheus: Wife of Doc Hines. Living in Mottstown, 322-324, 327-330, 332-335, 337-341; taken to see Hightower, 348-361, 365-370; in cabin with Lena, 373, 375-378, 380, 381, 386-388, 400; taken to train by Gavin Stevens, 420-424

Hines, Milly: Mother of Joe Christmas. 330, 350, 352-358, 360, 367, 376, 423

Jupe: Negro whom Joe Christmas meets in Jefferson. 109, 110

Kennedy, Wat: Sheriff in Jefferson. 45, 80, 86, 88-92, 94; at Burden house, 271-279, 281, 286-288, 292; Lena living in cabin, 302-304, 307-313, 335-337, 390, 393; visited by Bunch, 398-400, 404, 405, 411-414, 423; Percy Grimm, 429-431, 433

McEachern, Simon: Man who adopts Joe Christmas. 132-136; Joe and catechism, 137-146, 149-155, 157-160; Joe's affair, 161-164, 166, 170, 171, 173, 175, 178, 179, 185, 187-191; hit by chair, 192-194, 204, 217, 365

McEachern, Mrs. Simon: Wife of Simon McEachern. 99, 100, 134, 138-142, 144, 145; unpredictability, 149, 152, 154-156; her kindness, 157, 158, 160, 161, 171, 175, 178, 179, 185, 188, 189; Joe returns from dance, 194-196, 217, 247, 365

McLendon, Captain: Man in barbershop who listens to Joe Brown talk about his activities with Joe Christmas. 81

Maxey, Mr.: Man with Captain McLendon in barbershop who listens to Joe Brown. 81

Metcalf: Jailor in Mottstown. 334, 335

Mooney: Foreman at planing mill where Christmas, Bunch, and Brown work. 28, 29, 32-35, 37-41, 391, 392

Peebles, E.E.: Negro lawyer for Joanna Burden. 220, 221, 261, 278

Pomp: One of Negro slaves of Gail Hightower I; husband of Cinthy. 444-446, 450-452

Russell: Sheriff's deputy in Mottstown. 334, 335

Salmon: Garage owner in Mottstown who has a car for rent. 338, 339

Sartoris, Col. John: Ex-Confederate officer who kills two Burdens in Jefferson. 42, 235, 239-241, 420

Simms: Superintendent of planing-mill where Joe Christmas works. 28, 29, 31, 32, 38

Stevens, Gavin: District attorney in Jefferson. 419-425, 433
  His grandfather: 420

Thompson, Pappy: Old Negro assaulted by Joe Christmas. 306, 307

Thompson, Roz: Grandson of Pappy Thompson. 306, 307

Varner, Jody: Son of Will Varner who tells Lena Grove about Byron Bunch. 21-23

Varner, Will: Owner of store in Frenchman's Bend. 11, 19, 24

Vines, Deacon: Negro at church meeting disrupted by Joe Christmas. 307

Waller, Hamp: Country man who finds Joanna Burden's body. 83–85, 90, 271, 274, 278
  His wife: 83, 84, 90

Winterbottom: Farmer who discusses cultivator with Armstid. 5–8

UNNAMED

Doctor who arrives too late to deliver Lena Grove's baby. 374–380

Old Negro woman whose help Joe Brown tries to enlist in getting a message to town after he flees from Lena Grove and the baby. 410–413

Negro who takes message to town and tells Bunch where Brown is. 412–415

Furniture dealer and repairer who picks up Lena Grove and Byron Bunch. 468–480
  His wife: 468, 470, 472, 474, 476, 478, 479

Boy and girl in car who stop for Joe Christmas. 267–270, 281

Matron of the orphanage. 120–126, 129, 132–136, 362, 363

Stranger at restaurant when Bobbie Allen and the Confreys flee; helps to beat up Joe Christmas. 200–210

"Mexican" in carnival who is Joe Christmas's father. 353–357

Negro who works in yard at orphanage whom Joe Christmas follows around the yard. 363

American Legion commander in Jefferson. 427–429

College professor, friend of Gavin Stevens, who listens to Stevens tell about Joe Christmas. 420–422, 424

Negro girl whom Joe Christmas kicks and hits in his youth. 146, 147, 166, 173, 184

Four boys who struggle with Joe Christmas after he kicks and hits the Negro girl. 146–148, 173, 174

Light in August 87

Two men who take Hines home after he attacks Joe Christmas.
   327-329, 332

Sheriff in Mottstown. 334-337

HISTORICAL

Astor, John Jacob, II (1822-1890): American fur trader and
   financier. 180

Beardsley, Aubrey V. (1872-1898): English artist. 245

Casanova, Giovanni Jacopo (1725-1798): Italian adventurer.
   4

Grant, Ulysses S. (1822-1885): Union general, President of the
   United States, 1869-1877. 56, 451

Lincoln, Abraham (1809-1865): President of the United States,
   1861-1865. 238

Petronius: Roman satirist in 1st century A.D. 245

Tennyson, Alfred (1809-1892): English poet. 301, 383

Van Dorn, Earl (1820-1863): Confederate general. 451

BIBLICAL

Jezebel: Ahab's wife in Old Testament Books of I and II Kings.
   123, 292, 363, 364

Lord: 18, 22, 56, 57, 59, 60, 66, 98, 119-121, 123, 124, 134,
   135, 140, 143, 153, 155, 170, 171, 240, 250, 265, 285,
   287, 290, 298-300, 306, 307, 310, 319, 325, 344-346,
   351-354, 356-358, 360-365, 369, 372, 391, 399, 441, 442,
   446, 449, 452, 459, 460, 462-464, 471

Michael: 190

Moses: Old Testament patriarch. 238

Satan: 63, 191, 305

LITERARY

Faustus: Character in works of Marlowe and Goethe. 194

Juliet: Character in Shakespeare's *Romeo and Juliet*, 1594–1595. 180

Katzenjammer kids: Comic strip characters created by Rudolph Dirks on 12 December 1897. 335

Romeo: Character in Shakespeare's *Romeo and Juliet*, 1594–1595. 180–182, 199, 207

THE MANSION

[New York: Random House, 1959. 436 pp.]

Albert: Ex-marine; member of Goodyhay's congregation. 274-279

Allanovna, Myra: Owner of New York tie store. 167-170, 172, 176, 177, 231, 320

Allison, Miss: Old Major de Spain's niece. 422, 429

Allison, Mrs.: Old Major de Spain's only sister. 422, 428, 429

Armstid, Henry: Farmer in Frenchman's Bend. 127, 138, 142
His wife: 138

Backus, Mr.: Father of Melisandre Harriss Stevens. 195, 196, 357

Baddrington, Harold (Plex): Pilot of plane in which Chick Mallison is shot down. 294, 295

Barron, Jake: Convict at Parchman. 96-98

Benbow, Narcissa: See Sartoris, Narcissa Benbow

Biglin, Luther: Jefferson jailer. 206, 408-411, 428
His mother: 408

Biglin, Mrs. Luther: Wife of jailer; niece of husband of Sheriff Bishop's wife's sister. 408-410, 428

Binfords: Boys who squired Eula. 117, 119-125

Binford, Lucius: Common-law husband of Reba Rivers. 72, 78, 79

Bishop, Ephriam (Eef): Sheriff who alternates terms with Hub Hampton II as Jefferson sheriff. 370, 372, 373, 377, 379, 381, 389, 393-395, 408-410, 428, 429, 432

Bookwrights: Boys who squired Eula Varner. 117, 118, 119, 120-125

Bookwright, Calvin: Bootlegger. 170, 171, 231, 372

Bookwright, Herman: Rival for Eula Varner. 126

Bookwright, Homer: Farmer in Frenchman's Bend. 63

Bookwright, Odom: Farmer in Frenchman's Bend who is partner of Armstid and Ratliff. 127, 138, 142

Brummage, Judge: Judge who presides at Mink Snopes' trial. 3, 40-46, 48, 49, 92

Buffaloe: Jefferson electrician. 34

Burden, Joanna: Jefferson resident. 185

Christian, Uncle Willy: Drugstore owner in Jefferson. 55-57, 59, 69, 134, 135, 137, 187, 201

Compson, Benjy: Idiot brother of Jason Compson. 322, 328

Compson, Candace: Jason Compson's sister. 322

Compson, Jason: Man who sold rest of Compson place to Flem Snopes. 322-328, 330, 332, 334
  His mother: 322
  His forebear, Brigadier general in Civil War: 325
  His father: 323, 334

Compson, Quentin: Governor of Mississippi; forebear of Jason Compson. 325, 334

Compson, Quentin: Older brother of Jason Compson. 322, 323

Compson, Quentin: Daughter of Candace Compson. 322

Crack: Sergeant in McLendon's company. 183, 184

Dad: Man who steals Mink Snopes' money at Goodyhay's. 266-273

De Spain, Major: Father of Manfred de Spain. 127, 135, 153, 154, 215, 422
  His mother: 215

De Spain, Manfred: Jefferson mayor and bank president. 34, 56, 62, 86, 125; his background, 127-130, 135; affair with Eula V. Snopes, 137-145; Eula's suicide, 146, 148, 152, 153, 155, 156, 193, 202, 211, 212, 245, 328, 355, 358, 360, 401; Flem Snopes' house returned to De Spains, 421, 422

The Mansion 91

Devries, Colonel: Clarence Snopes' opponent for Congress. 307-318, 320
  His sister and her family: 315-317, 319, 320

Dilazuck: Livery stable owner. 181

Dukinfield, Judge: Jefferson judge. 130

Du Pre, Virginia: Bayard Sartoris III aunt. 189

Ewell, Walter: Yoknapatawpha hunter. 31

Gihon: Federal agent investigating Linda Snopes Kohl. 233-236, 242, 243

Goodyhay, Brother Joe C.: Ex-marine; preacher. 265-277, 279-282
  His wife: 267

Gowrie, Nub: Farmer in Beat Nine. 10, 14, 61

Grier, Res: Farmer in Frenchman's Bend. 316

Hait, Lonzo: Horse and mule trader. 181-188

Hampton, Hub, I: Jefferson sheriff. 52-56, 58-63, 102, 171, 367, 369, 370

Hampton, Hub, II: Son of Hub Hampton I who succeeds his father as sheriff. 103, 171, 369, 370

Harriss: First husband of Melisandre Backus. 195, 196, 358

Harriss, Melisandre Backus: See Stevens, Melisandre Backus Harriss

Henry: Negro with scrub bull; works for Jack Houston. 8-11, 13-17, 23, 25, 29, 35

Hogganbeck, Lucius: Resident of Jefferson; automobile jitney operator. 35

Holcomb, Beth: Member of Goodyhay's group. 264, 265, 268-270, 277

Holland, Mr.: Bank president in Jefferson. 34, 328, 329

Holston, Alexander: One of the original founders of Jefferson. 383

Houston, Jack: Farmer murdered by Mink Snopes. 3; relationship with Mink Snopes, 5-27, 29, 30, 35, 37, 38; shot, 39, 41, 42, 44, 64, 67, 82, 89, 90, 99-101, 378, 381
His wife: 7, 8, 10, 11

Jabbo, Cap'm: Guard at Parchman. 97, 98

Killegrew, Hunter: Deputy who takes Montgomery Ward Snopes to Parchman. 64

Kohl, Barton: Husband of Linda Snopes; sculptor. 93, 109, 110, 112, 113; background, 157-164; wedding reception, 170-174; killed, 178, 179, 192, 199; sculpture bequeathed to Ratliff, 200, 203, 210, 217-219, 229, 230, 232, 233, 235, 237, 238, 248, 355

Kohl, Linda Snopes: Wife of Barton; daughter of Eula Varner and Hoake McCarron. 65, 86, 93; her name on petition to free Mink Snopes, 102, 109; background, 111-115, 119, 124, 126-128, 133-145; Eula's suicide, 146-149, 151, 152, 154, 157-159, 161-164; wedding reception, 170-175, 177; Kohl killed, 178, 179, 192-194, 197-199; returns to Jefferson, 200-207, 209-223, 225-241, 243-245; in Pascagoula, 246-254, 256, 320; after War, 350-374, 376-379, 381, 389-391, 394, 395, 401, 410; Flem killed, 412-416, 419-425; leaves Jefferson, 426, 427, 429, 431, 433, 434

Kyrilytch, Vladimir: See Ratcliffe, V.K.

Ledbetter, Mrs.: Customer of Ratliff's. 142

Littlejohn: Owner of Airdale. 316

Long, Judge: Judge who sentenced Montgomery Ward Snopes to prison. 52, 63, 69, 369, 370, 373. [See Judge Brummage.]

Ludus: Minnie's husband. 80

McCallum, Rafe: Farmer who owns stallion which young Harriss used to try to kill Argentine. 255

McCarron, Mrs.: Hoake McCarron's mother. 125, 127

McCarron, Hoake: Linda Snopes Kohl's father. 4; affair with Eula Varner, 116-125; leaves Frenchman's Bend, 126-128, 135, 136, 139, 141, 148; in New York, 169, 170; at Linda's wedding reception, 171-175, 177

McCaslin, Ike: Old hunter who owns hardware store. 31, 32, 323, 370

McGowan, Skeets: Clerk in Christian's drugstore. 187, 188

McLendon, Captain: Cotton buyer. 183-187
   His family: 184

Mallison, Charles, I: Father of Chick Mallison. 129, 199, 206, 207, 254, 321, 383

Mallison, Charles, II (Chick): Son of Charles I and Maggie Stevens; nephew of Gavin Stevens. 109-113, 148, 149, 179-199; Linda Kohl returns to Jefferson, 200-232, 238, 244; Gavin Stevens marries, 254-256; Clarence Snopes' defeat, 294-297, 299-309, 311-316, 318-325; Meadowfill vs. Res Snopes, 327, 330-335, 337-339, 341-349; Linda's return after War, 350-361, 383

Mallison, Maggie: Mother of Chick Mallison; sister of Gavin Stevens. 112, 113, 129, 146, 187; discusses Sartorises, 189-191, 193, 196, 199, 205-207, 209, 210, 212; Linda comes to dinner, 215-218, 254, 255, 354, 383

Meadowfill: Father of Essie Meadowfill Smith. 327-348, 361

Meadowfill, Mrs.: Wife of Meadowfill. 328, 329, 331, 332, 339, 346, 348

Meadowfill, Essie: See Smith, Essie Meadowfill

Meeks, Doc: Jefferson Watkins Products salesman. 154

Minnie: Maid at Miss Reba Rivers' in Memphis. 72, 73, 75, 77, 79-82

Mohataha: Chickasaw matriarch. 334

Nightingale, Mr.: Tug Nightingale's father. 181-185, 187, 213

Nightingale, Tug: Painter recruited for War by McLendon. 181-188

Quick, Solon: Constable at Frenchman's Bend. 16-18, 20, 23, 24, 26, 29, 31, 37, 316

Quick, Theron: Suitor of Eula Varner. 117-122, 123, 124, 125, 126, 388

Ratcliffe, Nelly: Virginia farm girl who married the first
    Vladimir Kyrilytch. 162, 165, 166

Ratcliffe, V.K.: Name of Russian mercenary after he marries
    Nelly Ratcliffe. 162, 164-166, 177

Ratliff, V.K.: Sewing machine agent. 32; Montgomery Ward
    Snopes sent to Parchman, 52-64, 103, 109-114; Eula,
    Flem, Gavin, De Spain, 115-165; at tie shop, 166-170;
    wedding reception, 171-177; Barton Kohl killed, 178, 187,
    192-194, 196-198; Linda Kohl returns, 200, 203-206, 211,
    218-222, 227, 228, 230-232, 242, 254, 256; eliminates
    Clarence Snopes, 295, 296, 298, 302, 304-307, 309, 312,
    313, 315-322, 332, 333, 344, 349; after War, 351, 356,
    359-361; Linda asks Gavin Stevens about Mink Snopes,
    366, 368-374, 376-378, 381-393, 395; Flem Snopes dead,
    417-419, 421, 425-431; finds Mink Snopes, 432-434

Rivers, Reba: Memphis madam. 72, 73, 75-82, 85

Rouncewell: Owner of Commercial Hotel. 128

Rouncewell, Mrs.: Wife of owner of Hotel. 128
  Their son: 55, 56, 59

Sartoris, Bayard: President of Farmers and Merchants Bank.
    34, 128, 135, 142, 145, 152, 153, 156, 189, 298, 379,
    406

Sartoris, Bayard: Grandson of old Bayard Sartoris. 135, 183,
    186, 188-192, 209

Sartoris, Benbow: Son of Narcissa Benbow and young Bayard
    Sartoris. 206

Sartoris, Col. John: Father of old Bayard Sartoris; Civil
    War Colonel. 183, 191, 406

Sartoris, John: Twin of young Bayard Sartoris; grandson of old
    Bayard Sartoris. 183, 186, 189-191, 209

Sartoris, Narcissa Benbow: Wife of young Bayard Sartoris;
    mother of Benbow Sartoris. 189

Smith, Essie Meadowfill: Wife of McKinley Smith. 328-330,
    334-336, 338-340, 342-344, 346-348, 361

The Mansion

Smith, McKinley: Ex-Marine; husband of Essie Meadowfill. 338-341, 343-349, 361
   His father: 339

Snopes, Ab: Father of Flem Snopes. 87, 123, 152

Snopes, Admiral Dewey: Younger son of Eck Snopes. 83, 87, 153, 420

Snopes, Bilbo: Twin of Vardaman Snopes; son of I.O. Snopes. 87

Snopes, Byron: Clerk in Sartoris Bank. 83, 87, 152, 298
   His children: 152, 298

Snopes, Clarence Eggleston: Mississippi Senator. 61-63, 70, 71; in Memphis with Virgil and Fonzo, 73, 74, 82, 83, 87, 101, 102, 161; eliminated from race, 295-315, 317-320, 322
   His grandfather: 102

Snopes, Doris: Clarence Snopes' youngest brother. 298

Snopes, Eck: Father of Wallstreet Panic and Admiral Dewey Snopes. 83, 87, 102, 153
   His mother: 87

Snopes, Eula Varner: Wife of Flem Snopes; mother of Linda Snopes. 4, 17, 27, 32, 65, 70, 86; G. Stevens first sees her, 114, 115; affair with McCarron, 116-121, 123-125; married to Flem, 126-131, 133, 135-145; commits suicide, 146-148; headstone, 149-152, 155, 158, 163, 170, 172, 174, 192, 193, 197, 198, 202, 211, 212, 219, 229, 232, 233, 240, 241, 245, 325, 326, 355, 359, 360, 367, 373, 377, 420, 424, 430, 431, 434

Snopes, Flem: Husband of Eula Varner Snopes; president of bank. 3-6, 17, 26, 27, 32, 35, 37, 40-43; Mink vows to kill Flem, 51-64; talks with Montgomery Ward Snopes, 65-71, 74, 82-89, 92-94, 98, 102, 103, 115-117, 123; married to Eula Varner, 126-130, 135, 137-139, 141-145; Eula commits suicide, 146, 147-149, 152-159, 162, 164, 192, 193, 197, 198; Linda returns, 200-202, 206, 212, 213, 215, 216, 219-223, 226-229, 240-244, 246, 259; owns rest of Compson place, 322-330, 332, 333, 335, 348; after War, 351, 355, 356, 358, 359, 364, 365; Linda asks about Mink, 366-370, 372-382, 386, 387, 389-391, 393, 394, 396, 397, 401, 408-414; faces Mink Snopes, 415, 416, 419-423, 425, 428, 430, 431
   His grandfather: 102

Snopes, I.O.: Father of Clarence, Montgomery Ward, Vardaman, Bilbo, and Doris Snopes. 68, 83, 87, 152

Snopes, Linda: See Kohl, Linda Snopes

Snopes, Lump: Clerk who followed Flem Snopes in Varner's store. 27, 28

Snopes, Mink: Farmer near Frenchman's Bend who murders Jack Houston. 3, 4; relationship with Houston, 5-42; sent to Parchman, 43-51, 64-70, 82-84; tries to escape, 85-101; petition signed by Linda Kohl, 102-106, 152, 259-264; with Goodyhay, 265-279, 281; arrives in Memphis, 282-293, 366-373; Stevens visits Parchman, 374-382, 384-402; arrives near Jefferson, 403-409, 411-415; kills Flem, 416-419, 425, 426, 428-431; found by Stevens and Ratliff, 432-435
His two daughters: 10, 13, 24, 30, 38, 50, 90, 93, 101, 290, 369, 374, 394
His father: 99, 104, 105
His grandfather: 38, 102
His mother: 88, 99, 104
His uncle: 89
His father's second wife: 99, 104, 105

Snopes, Montgomery Ward: Son of I.O. Snopes. 52-64; talks with Flem Snopes, 65-70; in Memphis, 71-82; at Parchman, 83-89, 91, 92, 97, 152, 259, 367, 368

Snopes, Orestes (Res): Small farmer near Jefferson. 294, 295, 322, 328, 330, 331, 333-344, 346-349

Snopes, Vardaman: Twin of Bilbo Snopes. 87

Snopes, Virgil: Son of Wesley Snopes who goes to barber college in Memphis. 71-74, 83, 87

Snopes, Wallstreet Panic: Oldest son of Eck Snopes. 83, 87, 102, 153, 213, 214, 420

Snopes, Watkins Products: Jefferson carpenter. 153, 154, 156, 158, 328, 333, 411

Snopes, Wesley: Father of Virgil Snopes; revival song leader. 71, 83, 87

Snopes, Mrs. Yettie: Wife of Mink Snopes. 10, 13, 24, 30, 38, 50, 51, 90, 93, 101, 369, 374, 394

The Mansion   97

Spoade I: Classmate of Gavin Stevens at Harvard in 1909. 206

Spoade II: Friend of Chick Mallison who invites him to Charleston. 206

Stevens, Judge: Father of Gavin Stevens and Maggie Mallison. 130

Stevens, Gavin: Jefferson lawyer. 52-56, 58-60, 62, 63, 77, 109-115; first sees Eula V. Snopes, 116, 119, 125, 128-141, 143, 144; Eula commits suicide, 146-151, 157-170; Linda's wedding reception, 171-181, 187, 189, 190, 192-197; meets Linda after her becoming deaf, 198-213, 215-226, 229-246; in Pascagoula with Linda, 247-255; Clarence Snopes eliminated from race, 295-297, 299-307, 309-316, 318-326; Meadowfill vs. Res Snopes, 327, 330-334, 337, 338, 341-349; after War, 350-357, 359-365; Linda asks about Mink Snopes, 366-395, 409, 410, 417-431; finds Mink Snopes, 432-434

Stevens, Melisandre Backus Harriss: Wife of Gavin Stevens. 194-196, 198, 254-256, 352, 355-357, 359, 362-365, 382, 383, 427
  Her son: 196, 255, 256, 356
  Her daughter: 195, 196, 358

Stillwell, Shuford H.: Prisoner at Parchman who escapes. 96-101

Strutterbuck, Captain: Visitor to Miss Reba Rivers' brothel. 75-77, 80, 81

Strutterbuck, Q'Milla: Name signed to Strutterbuck's money order. 81

Thelma: One of Miss Reba Rivers' girls. 75-77, 80, 81

Triplett, Earl: Man who takes over Ike McCaslin's hardware store. 323

Tubbs, Euphus: Jefferson jailor. 60, 63, 65, 71

Tubbs, Mrs. Euphus: Jailor's wife. 63

Tulls: Boys who squired Eula. 117-125, 388

Tull, Vernon: Farmer at Frenchman's Bend. 31

Tull, Mrs. Vernon: Wife of Vernon Tull. 50

Turpins: Boys who squired Eula Varner. 119-125, 388

Turpin: Draft-evader hiding in Mink Snopes' cabin. 418

Varner, Eula: See Snopes, Eula Varner

Varner, Jody: Son of Will Varner; brother of Eula Varner Snopes. 4, 27, 28, 367, 420, 421

Varner, Will: Father of Jody Varner and Eula Varner Snopes. 4, 7, 10; involvement with Mink Snopes and Houston, 16-24, 26-32, 37-40, 62, 65, 66, 89, 93, 115, 117-120, 123; Eula pregnant, 124-127, 135, 138, 139; Flem Snopes' move to become president of bank, 142-148, 152, 155, 197, 202, 284; Clarence Snopes eliminated from race, 295-299, 301, 302, 306, 310, 311, 313-317, 319, 320, 355, 394, 403, 408, 413, 417, 420, 427
  His father: 17
  His second wife: 417
  His grandson: 417

Varner, Mrs. Will: Will Varner's first wife; mother of Jody Varner and Eula Varner Snopes. 144, 146

Wattman, Jakeleg: Bootlegger. 220, 221, 355, 356

Winbush, Fonzo: Nephew of Grover Cleveland Winbush. 71-73

Winbush, Grover Cleveland: Night watchman in Jefferson. 52-57, 59, 68, 69, 71, 73, 115, 117, 127, 128, 138

Winbush, Mrs. G.C.: Wife of Grover Cleveland. 69, 71

UNNAMED

Two men who robbed Christian's store. 55, 57, 59, 69

Parchman warden. 44, 49-51, 86, 88, 89, 95-103, 369, 373-376, 384-386

Flem Snopes's Negro cook and yardman. 154-156, 164, 203, 215, 226, 410-412, 423

Two Negro firemen at powerhouse who put brass in water tank. 164

Mail carrier whom Mink Snopes accuses of taking five dollars. 30-32, 34, 37, 38

The Mansion

Young lawyer who defended Mink Snopes. 41-45, 48, 91, 93, 94, 375

Two Finns who settle in Jefferson. 213-215, 222, 350

Proprietor of store where Mink Snopes buys food. 259-263

Negro family whom Mink Snopes helps to pick cotton. 399-404, 414

Gavin Stevens's Harvard classmate. 371, 387, 389, 390, 395, 429

Argentine who marries Melisandre Harriss' daughter. 255, 256

Russian poet who was killed in Spain. 217

HISTORICAL

Astor, John Jacob, II (1822-1890): American fur trader and financier. 154

Bach, Johann Sebastian (1685-1750): German composer. 132

Bacon, Francis (1561-1626): English philosopher and author. 218

Beethoven, Ludwig van (1770-1827): German composer. 132

Bilbo, Theodore G. (1877-1947): Mississippi governor and senator. 161, 301

Burgoyne, John (1722?-1792): English general. 165

Burr, Aaron (1756-1836): United States Vice President, 1801-1805. 154

Carver, George Washington (1864-1943): Negro educator. 224

Catullus, Gaius Valerius (84?-54 B.C.): Roman lyric poet. 357

Chaplin, Charles (1889-1977): Film comedian. 211

Churchill, Winston (1874-1965): English statesman and author. 233

Cincinnatus, Lucius Quinctius (519?-439? B.C.): Roman general and statesman. 296, 320, 387

Debs, Eugene V. (1855-1926): American Socialist leader. 214

Dickens, Charles (1812-1870): English novelist. 218

Donne, John (1572-1631): English poet. 200

Fielding, Henry (1707-1754): English author. 218

Fitzgerald, F. Scott (1896-1940): American novelist. 209

Forrest, Nathan Bedford (1821-1877): Confederate general. 17

Francesca da Rimini (d. 1285?): Mistress of Paolo, her husband's brother; murdered by her husband; in Dante's *Inferno*. 133

Franco, Francisco (1892-1976): Spanish dictator. 160, 164, 192, 193, 208

Gamelin, Maurice G. (1872-1958): French general. 208

Hamilton, Alexander (1757-1804): American statesman. 154

Harriman, Edward H. (1848-1909): American railroad magnate. 154

Hemingway, Ernest (1899-1961): American novelist. 209, 217

Herrick, Robert (1591-1674): English poet. 200

Hill, James J. (1838-1916): American railway promoter. 154

Hitler, Adolf (1889-1945): German dictator. 109, 160, 164, 178, 193, 208, 218, 228, 233

Hoover, Herbert C. (1874-1964): President of United States, 1929-1933. 242, 243

Hoover, J. Edgar (1895-1972): FBI Director. 242, 243

Hopkins, Harry (1890-1946): American cabinet member and politician. 214

Horace (65-8 B.C.): Roman poet and satirist. 195, 357

Johnson, Hugh S. (1882-1942): Director of the National Recovery Administration. 214

Jonson, Ben (1573?-1637): English playwright. 200

Kreisler, Fritz (1875-1962): Violinist. 182

Lee, Robert E. (1807-1870): Confederate general. 181, 182, 184

Lenin, Nikolai (1870-1924): Russian Bolshevik leader. 233

Lewis, John L. (1880-1969): American labor leader. 213

Long, Huey P. (1893-1935): Louisiana governor and senator. 161, 301, 305

Malraux, André (1901-1976): French writer. 217

Marlowe, Christopher (1564-1593): English dramatist. 218

Messalina (?-48 A.D.): Third wife of Roman Emperor Claudius. 262

Milton, John (1608-1674): English poet. 194, 218

Morgan, John P. (1837-1913): American banker and financier. 154

Mozart, Wolfgang A. (1756-1791): Austrian composer. 132

Murat, Joachim (1767?-1815): French cavalry commander. 408

Mussolini, Benito (1883-1945): Italian dictator. 160, 164, 193, 208, 218

Newton, Isaac (1642-1727): English natural philosopher and mathematician. 182

Pershing, John J. (1860-1948): American general. 75, 76

Ptolemy: Alexandrian astronomer second century A.D. 182

Pushkin, Aleksander S. (1799-1837): Russian poet. 217

Rickenbacker, Eddie (1890-1973): American fighter pilot. 75, 76

Roosevelt, Franklin D. (1882-1945): President of the United
    States, 1933-1945. 193, 213, 242, 272, 304, 320, 333

Shakespeare, William (1564-1616): English poet and playwright.
    218

Smollett, Tobias George (1721-1771): English novelist. 218

Spenser, Edmund (1552-1599): English poet. 194

Stalin, Josef (1879-1953): Russian dictator. 161, 228, 233

Suckling, Sir John (1609-1642): English poet. 200

Thackeray, William Makepeace (1811-1863): English novelist.
    179, 254, 356

Thomas, Norman M. (1884-1968): American Socialist leader.
    272

Truman, Harry S. (1884-1972): President of United States,
    1945-1953. 272

Wagner, Richard (1813-1883): German composer. 132

Washington, Booker T. (1856-1915): American Negro educator.
    224

Wilson, Woodrow (1856-1924): President of United States, 1913-
    1921. 160, 183

                              BIBLICAL

Delilah: Philistine mistress of Samson in Judges. 121

Eve: Adam's wife in Genesis. 290

Galilean: 212, 268, 269, 271, 272, 280-282

Jacob: Son of Isaac in Genesis. 164

Judith: Jewish heroine who killed Assyrian general Holofernes
    in the Old Testament Apocrypha. 133

Lord (Old Moster): 5, 99, 100, 105, 116, 128, 131, 161, 173,
    264, 267, 272, 312, 315, 321, 364, 389, 398, 401, 403, 407
    414, 416, 431, 434

The Mansion

Samson: Hebrew judge of great stength betrayed by Delilah in Judges. 121

Satan: 209, 326

LITERARY/MYTHIC

Crusoe, Robinson: Character in Defoe's novel *Robinson Crusoe*, 1719. 234

Helen: Wife of Menelaus. 130, 131, 133, 139-141, 143, 163, 290, 360, 436

Holmes, Sherlock: Character created by Arthur Conan Doyle. 69

Isolde: Tristan's beloved; heroine in Wagner opera. 133

Legree, Simon: Character in Stowe's *Uncle Tom's Cabin*, 1852. 69

Lilith: In Hebrew folklore, the first wife of Adam. 111, 133, 290

Paris: Prince of Troy. 133, 139, 360

Semiramis: Assyrian queen and legendary founder of Babylon. 133, 262

Venus: Goddess of love and beauty. 211

MOSQUITOES

[New York: Boni & Liveright, 1927. 349 pp.]

Ayers, Major: Britisher aboard the yacht. 55, 57; loses teeth, 61, 62; explains business scheme, 63-73; jumps overboard, 79-82, 84-88, 92, 97-99; after yacht runs aground, 114, 132, 155, 173, 178, 208, 210; Gordon missing, 217-220, 222-224, 245, 253, 258, 259, 261, 275, 277-279, 281-285, 288-293, 303; appointment with Mr. Reichman, 304
   His grandfather: 66

Broussard, George: Owner of restaurant and waiter. 33, 34, 37, 38, 40, 41, 44

Ed: Captain of the yacht. 57, 76-79, 89-91, 101, 109, 112, 122, 138, 191, 195, 198, 258-261, 291

Fairchild, Dawson: Novelist aboard the yacht. 27; described, 33-44, 49-54; boards yacht, 55, 57, 61-65; Al Jackson, 66-70; discusses Talliaferro, 71-73; jumps overboard, 79-81, 84-88, 92, 97-99; after yacht runs aground, 103, 104, 110, 112-114; background, 115-120, 122, 123, 126, 127, 130-132, 136, 138, 151, 155; Pat and David missing, 181-186; tries to free boat, 191-201; misses Gordon, 207-211, 217-222, 227-243; discusses poet/poetry, 245-257, 259-264; Gordon returns, 265-268, 274-285, 288-293, 302, 303; in New Orleans, 304, 305, 307-313, 317-321; discusses Mrs. Maurier, 322, 323, 325-329, 331; with Gordon and Kauffman, 335-345, 348, 349

Faulkner: Man who speaks to Jenny Steinbauer at Mandeville. 144-146, 203

Frost, Mark: Poet aboard the yacht. At lunch with Fairchild and others, 33-39, 41-44, 52; described, 54, 55; at lunch on yacht, 63-70, 79; doesn't swim, 80, 83-86, 88; continues to play bridge, 91-93, 95, 96, 102, 103, 132, 138, 151, 152, 155, 182, 183, 185, 186, 189; joins efforts to free yacht, 192-201, 208-210, 217-220, 227, 228, 230-234, 237, 239, 241, 243, 246, 255, 256, 258, 259, 262, 264, 275, 276; at Mrs. Maurier's house, 313, 314, 327; at Dorothy Jameson's house, 329-334

Ginotta, Mr.: Father of Joe and Pete Ginotta. 296, 297

Mosquitoes 105

Ginotta, Mrs.: Mother of Joe and Pete Ginotta. 296-301

Ginotta, Joe: Pete Ginotta's brother. 146, 286, 296-301

Ginotta, Pete: Younger son of the Ginottas; guest of Patricia Robyn on the yacht. Boards yacht, 55-61, 66, 70, 73-75, 80, 81, 83, 94, 95, 104; talks with D. Jameson, 105-109, 129, 130, 133, 134, 138, 141-148, 150, 151, 153, 155, 175-177, 192-195, 201, 237, 239-241, 244, 253, 254, 274, 276, 277, 283-288, 294; background, 295-302

Gordon: Sculptor aboard the yacht. 9-11; visited by Talliaferro, 12-14, 18-21; visited by Mrs. Maurier and niece, 22-30, 42-44; decides to go on yachting party, 47-51; boards yacht, 54, 55, 62, 69-72, 79, 80; helps Patricia out of water, 82, 92-97, 104, 132, 151; talks with Mrs. Maurier, 152-155, 183, 186, 187; joins efforts to free yacht, 194-201; disappears, 207, 211, 217, 218, 222, 225, 227, 237-239, 254, 255, 259, 263, 264; returns, 265-274, 283-285; in New Orleans, 313, 317, 318, 321; sculpture of Mrs. Maurier, 322, 323, 325, 327-329; with Fairchild and Kauffman, 335-339

Hooper, Mr.: Businessman who lunches with Fairchild. 33-40

Jackson, Al: Character in one of Fairchild's tales. 66, 67, 86-88, 276-279

Jackson, Claude: Al Jackson's brother. 87, 278-281

Jackson, "Old Man": Father of Al and Claude Jackson. 277-280

Jameson, Dorothy: Painter aboard the yacht. 27; boards yacht, 54-56, 60-63; plays bridge, 69, 70; swims with others, 79-81, 84, 88; continues to play bridge, 91-93, 95, 96; described, background, 101-104; talks with Pete, 105-108, 110, 111, 132-134, 141-143, 151, 153, 155, 169, 181, 182, 185, 186, 216, 217, 237, 259, 260, 275; dances, 284; asks Pete to dinner, 286, 287; with Mark Frost, 330-333
  Her family: 102, 330, 331
  Her lover: 102

Kauffman, Julius, I: Grandfather of Semitic man who helped Maurier make a fortune. 324, 327

Kauffman, Julius, II: The Semitic man, brother of Eva Wiseman, aboard the yacht. At lunch with Fairchild, 33-44; with Fairchild and Gordon, 49-55, 62-70; discusses Talliaferro,

71-73; jumps overboard, 79, 80, 84, 86, 97-99, 103, 110,
113, 114, 130-132, 154, 155, 181-186; joins efforts to
free yacht, 192-200; Gordon first missed, 207-211, 217-
222, 227-231, 233, 234, 236, 237, 239-243, 245-254, 261-
264, 266, 267, 274-276, 281, 282; dances, 283-285, 288-
290, 293; in New Orleans, 302, 303, 313; in Gordon's
studio, 317-329, 331; with Fairchild and Gordon, 335-
340

Maurier: Husband of Mrs. Maurier. 323-326

Maurier, Mrs. Patricia: Wealthy woman, owner of the *Nausikaa*.
12, 16-20; visits Gordon, 21-31, 43, 45, 50, 51; boards
yacht, 54-66, 68-72, 78; party goes swimming, 79, 83-88,
91-95, 97, 104, 109, 110, 122, 132-135, 147; talks with
Gordon, 151-156, 163, 169, 181, 183-185, 188; efforts
to free boat, 191-193, 198, 199, 201, 203; Patricia and
David return, 216, 217, 224, 225, 236-238, 254-261;
search for Gordon, 263, 264, 266, 268, 269, 275-277;
party dances, 284, 285, 287, 288, 290-292; in New Orleans,
303, 313, 314, 316; Gordon's sculpture, 322; background,
323-327, 329-331
 Her father: 324

Reichman, Mr.: Businessman whom Major Ayers visits. 304

Robyn, Henry (Hank): Father of Patricia and Theodore Robyn.
30, 114, 124, 125, 191, 256-258, 288

Robyn, Patricia: Sister of Theodore Robyn; niece of Mrs. Maurier.
16-22; in Gordon's studio, 23-31, 45, 46, 48; boards
yacht, 54-62, 69, 70, 74, 77-79; dives into water, 80-
82, 86, 88, 92-94, 97, 103-105, 108-111, 114, 115, 120;
first talks with David West, 121-126, 132-135; in cabin
with Jenny, 136-151, 153, 154; with David, 156-167; leaves
yacht, 168-172, 174-181, 187, 188, 190, 191, 201-207,
211, 212; meets man in swamp, 213, 214; returns to yacht,
215-220, 224, 227, 228, 237-241, 254-258, 267-274, 276,
281-283; dances with Gordon, 284, 285, 287, 288; at Mrs.
Maurier's, 313-317

Robyn, Theodore (Josh; Gus): Brother of Patricia Robyn. 16;
works on cylinder of wood, 45, 46, 57; boards yacht,
58, 60-62; discusses Major's scheme, 64, 65, 67, 70, 74-
78, 81; searches for wire, 88-91, 94, 104, 110; replaces
rod, 111, 112; discusses pipe with Fairchild, 113-116,
118, 120, 125, 127, 136, 143, 150, 157; discusses pipe
with Major, 173, 175-178, 212, 217, 224, 238-241; with
Jenny, 243, 244, 255-258; at Mrs. Maurier's, 313-317

Mosquitoes 107

Roy: Thelma's boy friend. 144-147

Steinbauer, Genevieve (Jenny): Guest of Patricia Robyn on the
    yacht. 54; aboard yacht, 55-61, 66, 69, 73-75; joins
    swimming party, 79-81, 83, 86, 87, 94, 95, 98, 103, 104,
    108, 109, 126; with Talliaferro on deck, 127-130, 132,
    133; in cabin with Patricia, 136-151, 153, 168; talks
    with Pete, 175-178, 188-190; joins efforts to free yacht,
    193-203; kissed by Eva Wiseman, 204, 207, 218; talks
    with Major Ayers, 222-227, 232, 237-241; with Josh Robyn,
    243, 244, 249, 251, 255, 271, 281-284; with Pete, 287-
    290; in New Orleans, 294; returns home, 295, 306, 307,
    309-312; with Talliaferro, 342-344, 348, 349
  Her father: 146, 295

Talliaferro, Ernest: Man who changed his name from Tarver;
    aboard yacht. At Gordon's, 9-15; meets Mrs. Maurier,
    16-30; background, 31, 32; eats lunch with Fairchild,
    33-44; aboard yacht, 54-57, 60-66, 69-72, 78, 79; joins
    swimming party, 80, 81, 83-89, 91-93, 95-99, 104, 111-
    113; with Jenny on deck, 126-132, 141, 143, 144; con-
    tinues to play bridge, 151, 152, 178, 184, 188-190;
    joins efforts to free yacht, 193-201; Gordon first missed,
    207, 208, 217, 218, 225, 232, 237-239, 249, 258-260;
    Gordon returns, 266, 269, 283-285, 288-290, 292; in New
    Orleans, 305-312; returns to Fairchild after evening with
    Jenny, 340-349
  His wife: 31, 33, 348
  His family: 32

Thelma Frances: Friend of Jenny Steinbauer. 144-147

Walter: Negro servant of Mrs. Maurier. 46, 58

Walter: One of the crew on the tugboat. 261, 262, 264-266

West, David: Steward on the *Nausikaa*. 54-57, 60, 61, 63, 65,
    66, 69; jumps overboard after Major, 79, 91, 93, 94,
    110, 112; first talks with P. Robyn, 121-126, 132, 135,
    136, 138; meets P. Robyn at night, 156-163, 165-167;
    leaves yacht with Patricia, 168-172, 174, 175, 177-181,
    187, 188, 190, 191, 201, 202, 204-207, 211, 212; meets
    man in swamp, 213, 214; returns to yacht, 215-219, 224,
    228, 235; leaves note for Fairchild, 236, 268

Wiseman, Eva: Sister of Julius Kauffman aboard the yacht.
    27, 44; aboard yacht, 54-57, 60-62, 64-67, 69, 70; joins
    swimming party, 79-81, 84-88; plays bridge, 91-97, 103,

104, 109, 110, 132, 136-138, 140, 151-156, 169, 178, 181-186; joins efforts to free yacht, 193-203; kisses Jenny, 204, 217, 220, 225; comforts Jenny in cabin, 226, 227, 237-239, 241, 242; discusses art, 245-251, 254, 255, 259, 260, 264, 268, 269, 274-276; dances, 283-285
Her husband: 103

UNNAMED

Deckhand on the *Nausikaa*. 79, 101, 112, 198

Helmsman on the *Nausikaa*. 57, 74, 79, 99, 101, 120, 198

Man in swamp who brings Patricia Robyn, David West, and later Gordon back to the *Nausikaa*. 213-215, 263, 264, 266-268

Malaria-ridden man in skiff. 263-266

HISTORICAL

Ashur-bani-pal (669-626 B.C.): Last great king of the Assyrians. 251

Balzac, Honoré de (1799-1850): French novelist. 243, 345

Berlioz, Hector (1803-1869): French composer. 185, 186

Butler, Benjamin Franklin (1818-1893): American general and politician. 324

Byron, Lord (1788-1824): English poet. 116

Caesar, Julius (100?-44 B.C.): Roman general and emperor. 131

Chopin, Frédéric (1810-1849): Polish composer. 182, 185

Cyrano de Bergerac (1619-1655): French poet and soldier; subject of Rostand's *Cyrano de Bergerac*, 1898. 269, 270

Dante (1265-1321): Italian poet. 339

Darwin, Charles (1809-1882): English naturalist. 116

Debussy, Claude (1862-1918): French composer. 185

Ellis, Havelock (1859-1939): English author and psychologist known for his research into psychology of sex. 251

Emerson, Ralph Waldo (1803-1882): American author. 242

Ford, Henry (1863-1947): American automobile manufacturer and inventor. 131

Freud, Sigmund (1856-1939): Austrian physician, founder of psychoanalysis. 248

Gershwin, George (1898-1937): American composer. 185

Greeley, Horace (1811-1872): American newspaper publisher. 32

Grieg, Edvard (1843-1907): Norwegian composer. 182

Held, Anna (1873?-1918): Comedienne. 240

Held, John (1889-1958): American illustrator, cartoonist, and writer. 230

Ibsen, Henrik (1828-1906): Norwegian playwright. 182

Jackson, Andrew (1767-1845): President of United States, 1829-1837. 14, 49, 66-68, 277

Lowell, James Russell (1819-1891): American poet. 242

Mackaill, Dorothy (1903-   ): Early American film actress. 204

Maecenas, Gaius (70?-8 B.C.): Roman statesman and patron of the arts. 18

Mussolini, Benito (1883-1945): Italian dictator. 131

Napoleon (1769-1821): Emperor of France. 312

Sassoon, Siegfried (1886-1967): English writer. 182

Shakespeare, William (1564-1616): English poet and playwright. 116, 248
  His mother: 248

Shelley, Percy Bysshe (1792-1822): English poet. 193, 195

Sibelius, Jean (1865-1957): Finnish composer. 182

Swedenborg, Emanuel (1688-1772): Swedish scientist, inventor
and mystical religious leader. 186

Swinburne, Algernon Charles (1837-1909): English poet. 116

Tanguay, Eva (1878-1947): American stage personality. 240

Turner, Joseph M.W. (1775-1851): English artist. 86

Verdi, Giuseppe (1813-1901): Italian opera composer. 185

BIBLICAL

Lord: 35-37, 40, 42, 48, 125, 130, 137, 185, 210, 242

LITERARY/MYTHIC

Beatrice: One of Dante's guides in the *Divine Comedy*; based
upon Beatrice Portinari (1266-1290). 339

Bluebeard: Fairy-tale character who killed one wife after
another. 9

Don Juan: Legendary hero of Spain; subject of many authors,
especially Byron. 31

Frankenstein: Scientist and his creation in Mary Shelley's
Frankenstein, 1818. 207

Israfel: Angel with sweetest voice of all God's creatures in
the Koran. 48, 187

Lear: Central character in Shakespeare's *King Lear*, 1605-1606.
320

Leda: Maiden ravished by Zeus in the form of a swan. 318

Lochinvar: Hero of ballad in Scott's *Marmion*, 1808. 326

Peer Gynt: Central figure in Ibsen's play *Peer Gynt* (1867) for
which Grieg composed incidental music. 182

[Roxane]: Cyrano's beloved. 269, 270

Tom O'Bedlam: Fool; idiot. 248, 319

Tristan: Knight who is sent to escort Isolde to her intended
    but who falls unwittingly in love with her; hero of
    Wagner opera, *Tristan and Isolde*. 339, 340

Venus: Goddess of love and beauty. 133

Western, Squire: Character in Fielding's *Tom Jones*, 1749. 72

Yseult of the White Hand: Tristan's wife in some versions of
    the medieval legend. 339

PYLON

[New York: Harrison Smith and Robert Haas, 1935. 315 pp.]

Atkinson: Matt Ord's partner. 168, 207, 214, 232

Bullitt, R.Q. (Bob): Flyer competing at airmeet. 24, 31-33, 52, 60, 160

Bullitt, Sharlie: Bob Bullitt's wife. 31

Burnham, Frank: Flyer who is killed in plane crash at meet. 27, 42, 52, 55, 57, 60, 64, 73, 142, 144, 150, 152, 153

Chance, Vic: Airplane builder. 31, 47

Cooper: Newspaperman on Reporter's paper. 142, 143, 178

Despleins, Jules: French stunt flyer. 27, 142, 229, 230, 231

Feinman, Col. H.I. ("Gen. Behindman"): Chairman of the Sewage Board of New Valois. 12, 14, 15, 17, 29, 32, 58, 64, 66, 73, 74, 141; meeting of pilots, 150-152, 170, 189, 214-216, 220; described, 222-226, 228, 232
 His secretary: 223-228

Grady: Reporter on duty at scene of Shumann's crash. 285-294, 297, 298

Grant, Joe: Flyer competing at airmeet. 31

Hagood: City editor of Reporter's paper. Discusses aviators with Reporter, 41-44, 46, 49-54, 59, 62; telephone conversation with Reporter, 66-69, 72, 74-76, 84-90; remembers Reporter's mother, 91-100, 112-115, 143, 158, 162; loans money to Reporter, 178, 179, 181, 187, 203-205, 230, 231, 238, 239, 241, 242, 266; loans money again to Reporter, 269-271, 274; reads Reporter's copy on Shumann, 314, 315
 His son: 315

Hank: Announcer at Feinman Airport. 26-33, 37-39, 48, 141, 144, 149-154, 160, 162, 163, 222, 231, 232

Holmes, Jack: Professional parachute jumper. 19-22, 29, 30, 32, 33; described, 34-39; relationship with Shumanns,

Pylon *113*

    43-51, 54-56, 62, 63, 66-74, 76; goes home with Reporter, 77-84, 97-101, 103-106, 110, 112, 113, 115-117, 119, 120; confrontation about Reporter's money, 121-132, 135, 138-142, 145; in Superintendent's office, 147-150, 154, 155; hits Reporter, 156, 157, 159-161; apologizes to Reporter, 164-167, 175-177, 179, 182; in Reporter's apartment, 187-191, 193, 204, 231, 244, 246; repays money to Reporter, 257-261, 264, 269, 272, 273, 280, 281; Reporter discusses Jack's relationship with Shumanns, 289-293, 296, 301; with Laverne and son in Ohio, 302-304, 308, 309, 311, 315

Hurtz: The Reporter's latest stepfather. 270

Jackson, Arthur (Art): Stunt flyer. 23, 39, 264, 282, 295, 296

Jiggs: Roger Shumann's mechanic. 7; buys boots, 8-19; teases boy, 20-24, 29, 30, 32-40, 45, 46, 49; with Reporter in New Orleans, 56-59, 62, 66-74; goes home with Reporter, 76-84, 89, 90; Hagood discusses Reporter, 96-104, 106; awakens in Reporter's apartment, 112-120; confrontation about Reporter's money, 121-133, 135, 138-142; at airfield, 145-149, 155-161; Shumann's first crash, 163, 164, 167, 175-178, 180-186; returns to Reporter's apartment, 187-193, 204; at airfield, 217-220; talks with Reporter after Shumann's death, 245-254, 257; at Reporter's apartment, 263-271; Reporter buys toy airplane, 272-283; says goodbye to Reporter at hotel, 294-297
  His wife and children: 16

Joe: Proprietor of bar. 205, 206, 299

Jug: Photographer with the Reporter's paper. 142, 143, 162, 230, 231, 236, 238-242, 247, 249

Laverne: See Shumann, Laverne

Leblanc: Policeman at airport. 156, 157, 182

Legendre, Dr.: Doctor in town whom Hagood recommends to the Reporter. 270

Leonora: Negro woman who cleans the Reporter's room. 132-139, 146, 160, 264, 265, 284, 300

Mac: Desk man at police station. 181, 182

Marchand: Assistant of Matt Ord. 212, 215, 216, 218, 219, 227, 243

Monk: One of Shumann's airplane's crew at the airport. 38, 39

Myers, Al: Flyer competing at airmeet. 31, 33, 53, 60, 64, 160

Ord, Matt: Airplane builder. 60, 97, 165; visited by Reporter and Shumann, 167-175, 188, 189, 192, 207; plane discussed, 213-215, 218-221; with Shumann in board room, 222-229; race, 232-234, 243, 244, 292

Ord, Mrs.: Matt's wife. 171

Ott, Jimmy: Flyer competing at airmeet. 31, 32, 60, 160

Pete: Restaurant proprietor from whom the Reporter wants to buy absinthe. 83, 84

Renaud: Ex-senator, now restaurateur. 75, 111, 209

Sales, Mac: Airplane inspector. 173, 220, 223-226, 230

Shumann, Dr. Carl: Father of Roger Shumann. 212-214, 227, 274-276, 296, 302-313, 315

Shumann, Mrs.: Wife of Carl Shumann; mother of Roger Shumann. 307, 308, 310-313, 315

Shumann, Jack: Laverne Shumann's son. 19; attacks Jiggs and Reporter, 20-23, 26-29, 33; Reporter discusses aviators, 43-46, 48, 49, 51, 54, 62-64, 67, 70-74; goes home with Reporter, 76-84, 98, 102, 106, 115-117, 123, 124, 126; at airfield, 127, 132, 135, 138-141, 176, 179; in Reporter's apartment, 191, 193, 204; at airfield, 221, 229-232; Shumann killed, 234, 235; on skiff in lake, 237, 244, 246, 251, 258, 260, 269; plan to give him money, 272-274, 280-282, 290, 293, 294, 296, 301; in Ohio, 302-313, 315

Shumann, Laverne: Wife of Roger Shumann; mother of Jack Shumann. 19-23; described, 24, 25, 27-29, 32-34; Reporter discusses aviators, 43-51, 54-57, 59, 62-74; goes home with Reporter, 76-82, 84, 98, 102, 103, 106, 110, 115-117; confrontation about Reporter's money, 121-126; at airfield, 127-132, 135, 138-142, 145, 147, 148, 155, 156, 160, 161; after Shumann's first crash, 164-166, 175-177, 179, 182; in Reporter's apartment, 187, 191-193; first parachute jump, 194-206, 209, 221,

Pylon 115

    222, 229-233; Shumann killed, 234, 235; on skiff, 237,
    238, 244-247, 249-252; at airfield, 255-258, 260-262,
    269, 272, 273; background discussed, 276-278, 280, 281,
    289-294, 296, 301; takes son to grandparents, 302-313,
    315
  Her family: 276-278

Shumann, Roger: Racing pilot; husband of Laverne Shumann.
    12, 14, 19-23, 28, 31-33, 35; Reporter discusses aviators,
    43-59, 62-74; goes home with Reporter, 76-82, 84, 98,
    102, 103, 106, 110, 112-117; confrontation about Reporter's money, 119-126; at airfield, 127-132, 135, 138-142, 145; in Superintendent's office, 147-151, 154-156, 159-161; first crash, 163-177, 179-186; in Reporter's apartment, 187-201, 204, 207; Ord's plane, 209, 211-233; killed, 234; final efforts to avoid crash, 237, 238, 240, 241, 246, 253, 255-257; tending to his body, 258-260, 272; Shumann's background, 274-276, 287, 289-294, 296, 299; Laverne takes son to grandparents, 302, 303, 305-309, 311-315

Smitty: Worker on the Reporter's paper. 204, 215

Uncle Issac: Man from whom Jiggs wants to borrow money. 272

UNNAMED

Reporter: Man assigned to cover the airmeet at New Valois by
    Hagood. Described, 20-23, 25-29, 33; tells Hagood about aviators, 41-76; takes aviators home with him, 77-85, 89, 90; mother described, 91-117, 119-126; Leonora comes to clean, 132-138; at airport, 139-148; struck by jumper, 156-162; Shumann's first crash, 163-166; talks to Matt Ord, 167-185, 189, 201-208; Ord's plane, 209-216; flies in plane, 217-224, 227-233; Shumann killed, 234, 235; at lake where Shumann crashed, 236-271; buys toy airplane, 272-274, 276, 278-284; at lake with reporters, 285-290, 293-295; sees Jiggs for last time, 296-303; copy about Shumann's death, 314, 315
  His mother: 91-97, 270

Young police officer who is obsessed with Laverne Shumann in
    small Kansas town. 196, 197, 199, 200

HISTORICAL

Antony (83?-30 B.C.): Roman general; character in Shakespeare's play *Antony and Cleopatra*, 1607. 204

Cleopatra (69-30 B.C.): Queen of Egypt; character in Shakespeare's play *Antony and Cleopatra*, 1607. 204

Dempsey, William H. "Jack" (1895-   ): American boxer. 21, 28, 45, 63, 64

Hardy, Oliver (1892-1957): American comedian. 57

Harlow, Jean (1911-1937): American film star. 44

Hemingway, Ernest (1899-1961): American novelist. 50

Lafitte, Jean (1780?-1826?): French pirate. 97

Laurel, Stan (1890-1965): American comedian. 57

Lewis, Sinclair (1885-1951): American novelist. 50

Lindbergh, Charles (1907-1976): American aviator and author. 220

Rembrandt (1606-1669): Dutch artist. 185

Tchekov, Anton (1860-1904): Russian dramatist and short story writer. 50

BIBLICAL

Lazarus: Man whom Jesus raised from the dead. 33

LITERARY/MYTHIC

Don Quixote: Central character in Cervantes' *Don Quixote*, 1605, 1615. 49

Jekyll and Hyde: Character with dual personality in Stevenson's novel, 1886. 290

Momus: God of mockery and pleasantry. 77

THE REIVERS

[New York: Random House, 1962. 305 pp.]

Alice: Miss Ballenbaugh's Negro cook. 76, 77, 79, 175

Avant, Jim: Hound man from Hickory Flat. 194

Ballenbaugh I: Man who took over Wyott's place. 69, 72-76

Ballenbaugh II: Son of Ballenbaugh I. 74-76

Ballenbaugh, Miss: Only child of Ballenbaugh II. 76-81, 93, 175, 212, 303

Ballott, Mr.: Priests' stable foreman. 7, 8, 10-14, 37, 56, 64, 65, 67, 299
  His first wife: 8

Beauchamp, Bobo: Van Tosch's groom. 22, 228-230, 285, 287-294, 298

Beauchamp, Lucas Quintus Carothers McCaslin: Bobo's cousin. 229

Beauchamp, Tennie: Bobo Beauchamp's great-grandmother. 229

Beauchamp, Tennie's Jim: Bobo Beauchamp's grandfather. 22

Binford, Mr.: Consort of Miss Reba. 99, 101, 106-114, 133, 142, 153, 154, 160, 164, 209, 278

Bookwright, Uncle Cal: Whiskey maker. 13

Briggins, Lycurgus: Uncle Parsham Hood's grandson. Ned, Boon, Lucius arrive at Parsham, 165-168, 171, 172, 174-176, 178, 180, 181, 185, 186, 189, 203, 221, 223, 224; goes to see Akron, 225-228, 230, 232-235, 245, 247, 248; returns from town, 249-251; Ned returns with horse, 252, 258; at races, 267, 269-271, 282, 283

Briggins, Mary: Lycurgus Briggins' mother. 171, 172, 189, 247, 248, 250, 251, 254

Buffaloe, Mr.: Jefferson mechanical wizard. 25-27, 29, 39, 49, 50, 57

Caldwell, Sam: Flagman on railroad. 130, 131; called by Miss
    Corrie, 133-141, 143-145; tries to get horse in boxcar,
    146-152, 162-164; train arrives in Parsham, 165, 167,
    171, 172, 198, 199, 204, 205, 217-220, 233; returns for
    race, 235-237, 241-244; posts bond for Boon, 250, 252,
    256, 258, 261, 274-276, 278, 279, 281, 282, 303

Callie, Aunt: Negro nurse of Priest children. 34, 36, 41,
    43, 45, 47-50, 52-60, 63, 64, 66, 300, 301

Charley: Railroad employee. 143-152

Christian: Jefferson drugstore owner. 15

Clapp, Mr. Walter: Van Tosch's horse trainer. 226-228, 231,
    232, 241, 253, 290

Compson, General: Hunter at Major de Spain's camp. 18, 19,
    21-23, 46, 82

De Spain, Major: Manfred de Spain's father; large landowner.
    18-22, 45, 72, 73, 78, 82

De Spain, Manfred: Jefferson banker and former mayor. 21,
    25

Doom: Chickasaw chief. 73

Ed: Judge at horse race. 266

Edmonds, Carothers: Cousin of Lucius Priest III. 61, 89

Edmonds, Louisa: Wife of Zachary Edmonds. 47, 54, 61, 62,
    66, 226

Edmonds, McCaslin: Father of Zachary Edmonds. 18, 19, 21-24,
    120, 121

Edmonds, Zachary: Son of McCaslin Edmonds. 18, 19, 24, 45,
    47, 49, 50, 53-56, 59; Priest children arrive, 61-67,
    89, 90, 120, 124, 169, 171, 182, 183, 226, 246

Ephum: Negro who works for Miss Ballenbaugh. 76, 77, 79, 175

Everbe Corinthia (Miss Corrie): See Hogganbeck, Everbe
    Corinthia (Miss Corrie)

Ewell, Walter: Hunter at Major de Spain's camp. 21, 23

The Reivers   119

Fathers, Sam: Woodman at Major de Spain's camp. 21, 22

Fittie, Aunt: Woman with whom Miss Corrie lived and worked after
    her mother died. 143, 154, 156, 157

Gabe: Priests' blacksmith. 6, 9, 10

Grenier, Louis: One of founders of Jefferson. 8

Grinnup, Dan (Dan Grenier): Priest employee at livery stable.
    8
  His father: 8

Hampton: Jefferson sheriff when Boon Hogganbeck tries to shoot
    Ludus. 10, 14, 15

Hampton, Little Hub: Grandson of sheriff; present sheriff of
    Jefferson. 14

Hightower, Hiram: Baptist minister who converted Ballenbaugh
    establishment. 75, 76

Hogganbeck, Boon: Mr. Ballott's assistant at livery stable.
    3; tries to shoot Ludus, 4-7, 9-17; background, 18-29,
    31-47; Priests leave for funeral, 48-66; leaves for
    Memphis, 67-72, 74; arrives at Ballenbaugh's, 76-81;
    Hell Creek crossing, 82-94; arrives in Memphis, 95, 96;
    at Miss Reba's, 97-107, 111, 112, 114; Ned arrives with
    horse, 115-120, 124-126, 128-141, 143-145; tries to get
    horse in boxcar, 146-153, 157-164; arrives in Parsham,
    165, 166, 172-178, 180, 181, 184-186, 189-200, 202-204,
    206, 207, 209-212; day of first race, 213-220, 222, 224,
    226, 227, 229-231, 233, 235, 236, 238, 239; arrested,
    241-245, 249-254; fights Butch, 255-260, 263, 275-277,
    279, 283, 287, 290, 298, 299, 303; married, 304, 305
  His grandmother: 19

Hogganbeck, Everbe Corinthia (Miss Corrie; Bee): Prostitute;
    Boon's wife. 95, 99, 100; described, 102, 106-108, 112,
    113, 115, 118, 124-127, 130; calls Sam, 131-140, 143-
    145; helps to get horse in boxcar, 149-153; background,
    154-165; arrives at Parsham, 171-181, 186; at doctor's,
    188-199, 201-212; day of first race, 213-218, 233, 250,
    252, 253; hit by Boon, 255-261, 263, 275, 276, 278-281,
    298, 299, 304; introduces son, 305
  Her mother: 156
  Her grandmother: 155

Hogganbeck, Lucius Priest: Son of Corrie and Boon Hogganbeck. 305

Hood, Uncle Parsham: Old Negro, grandfather of Lycurgus Briggins. 167, 168; discusses horse, 170-174, 176, 178, 181, 185, 190, 203, 205, 220, 222, 223; discusses race, 224, 225, 228-234, 239, 243, 244; Lucius II goes home with him, 245-252, 254-258, 262, 263, 267, 271, 279, 281, 282, 303

Issetibbeha: Chickasaw chief. 19, 73

Jackie: Prostitute. 201

Legate, Bob: Hunter at Major de Spain's camp. 21, 23

Lessep, Grandfather: Lucius II's maternal grandfather. 18, 41, 43, 44, 50, 133

Lessep, Grandmother: Lucius II's maternal grandmother. 44

Linscomb, Colonel: Owner of Acheron, the horse that races Lightning. 181, 191, 194, 219, 223, 225, 234, 241, 262, 268, 269, 275, 277, 278, 281, 284-286, 291, 293, 294, 296, 298

Little Chicago: Woman who once owned Rouncewell's boarding house. 24

Lovemaiden, Butch: Hardwick deputy. 172-178, 181, 184-186; takes Lucius II to doctor, 188-196, 203; confronts Miss Reba, 206-211, 215, 217, 229, 233; arrests Ned, 239-244, 249; fights Boon, 255-257, 259; Boon attacks him, 275-277, 298, 299

Ludus: Negro who works at Priests' livery stable. 5, 9-18, 42

Luster: Negro who works at Priests' livery stable. 6, 9, 10, 14, 15, 32

Lytle, Horace: Bird-dog specialist. 166, 194

McCaslin, Delphine: Ned McCaslin's wife. 30, 32-34, 36, 54, 55, 65, 299, 302

McCaslin, Isaac: Hunter at Major de Spain's camp. 14, 15, 17-23, 31, 45, 54, 55, 61-63, 65, 96

The Reivers

McCaslin, Lucius Quintus Carothers: Grandfather of Isaac and
    Ned McCaslin. 22, 31, 61, 69, 82, 89, 229, 285
  His wife: 70

McCaslin, Ned: Grandson of old Carothers McCaslin and Negro
    slave; Priests' coachman. Described, 30-37, 54-56, 58,
    59, 61, 64, 65; discovered in car, 69-72; arrives at
    Ballenbaugh's, 76-81; Hell Creek crossing, 82-94;
    arrives in Memphis, 95-98, 100; arrives with horse, 115-
    121, 123-145; tries to get horse in boxcar, 146-152,
    158, 162-164; arrives in Parsham, 165, 166; at Uncle
    Parsham's, 167-189, 191, 193, 197, 203-205, 211; day
    of first race, 213-226, 228-237; second race, 238;
    arrested, 239-244, 250-252; second day of races, 253-
    259, 261-265, 267-272; horse wins race, 273, 274, 278-
    286; story of Bobo and white man, 287-298; arrives home,
    299, 302-304
  His mother: 31
  His three wives, in addition to Delphine: 30

McCaslin, Theophilus: Ike McCaslin's father. 96

McDiarmid, Mr.: Judge at horse race. 235

McWillie: Negro who rides Acheron. 224-227, 231-233; first
    race, 236-238, 253; second race, 263-266; third race,
    271-273, 275, 278, 283, 284, 295-297
  His father, Col. Linscomb's chauffeur. 275, 278, 283, 284

Minnie: Miss Reba's Negro maid. 98, 99; teeth described,
    100-102, 107-109, 112-114; Ned arrives with horse, 115-
    118, 124, 126, 133-135, 139, 141, 142, 152-154, 158,
    164; arrives in Parsham, 199; gold tooth stolen, 200-
    202, 204-206, 216, 218, 220, 221, 229, 259, 261, 274,
    275; gold tooth restored, 278, 279, 283
  Her husband: 100

Moketubbe: Chickasaw chief. 73

Otis: Miss Corrie's nephew. 95, 99, 101, 102, 106-113, 125,
    126, 135, 137-140; described, 141-145, 151, 152; sleeps
    with Lucius, 153-156; fights with Lucius, 157-159, 163,
    165, 168; arrives in Parsham, 171, 172, 174-181, 186,
    190, 192-195, 198; Minnie's gold tooth stolen, 199-
    206, 209, 212, 216-218, 220, 221, 225, 234-236, 249, 250,
    261; tooth recovered, 282, 283

Parsham: Man who owned large farm and for whom town is named. 281

Patch, Dan: Man in horse business. 233

Peabody, Dr.: Jefferson physician. 15

Peyton, George: Bird-dog specialist. 194

Poleymus: Beat Four constable. 210, 211, 238-240, 242-244, 249, 254, 256-262, 276, 280, 281
 His wife and children: 257, 280, 281

Powell, John: Head employee at Priests' livery stable. 4, 6-12, 14, 15, 37, 38
 His father: 6, 7
 His wife: 7, 9

Priest, Alexander: One of Lucius Priest II's brothers. 4, 30, 34, 36, 41, 43, 45, 47, 50, 52-54, 56, 58-60, 63, 64, 100, 118, 246, 300

Priest, Alison Lessep: Lucius Priest II's mother. 30; rides in car, 34-36, 40, 41, 43-47; leaves for funeral, 48-51, 53-55, 63, 65, 66, 78, 100, 105, 107, 118, 139, 147, 155, 190, 191, 196, 212, 218, 251, 279; group returns to Jefferson, 299-301, 303, 304

Priest, Lessep: One of Lucius Priest II's brothers. 4, 30, 34, 36, 41, 43, 45, 47, 50, 52-54, 56, 58-60, 63, 64, 100, 118, 246, 300

Priest, Lucius, I (Boss; Grandfather): Father of Maury Priest I; Jefferson bank president. 18; buys automobile, 23-25, 28-34, 36-39; spits tobacco, 40, 41, 43-47; leaves for funeral, 48, 49, 51, 54-56, 60, 64-67, 71, 77, 81, 82, 86, 93, 96, 97, 100, 104, 105, 107, 116-118, 120, 126, 133, 143, 166, 167, 175, 186, 197, 213, 219, 222, 230, 242, 247, 250, 252, 254, 256; arrives at races, 274-278, 281, 283-286; story of Bobo and white man, 287-299; talks with grandson, 300-304
 His father: 285, 301
 His mother: 100, 285

Priest, Lucius, II (Loosh): Grandson of Lucius Priest I; grandfather of narrator. 3; story of Ludus and Boon, 4-17, 18-22; Boss buys automobile, 23-66; leaves for Memphis, 67-81; Hell Creek crossing, 82-91, 92-94;

arrives in Memphis, 95, 96-114; Ned arrives with horse, 115-145; tries to get horse in boxcar, 146-152; sleeps with Otis and has knife fight, 153-159, 160-164; in Parsham, 165-212; day of first race, 213-238; group arrested, 239-243; stays with Uncle Parsham, 244-252; day of second race, 253-270; third race, 271-273; Boss arrives, 274, 275-286; story of Bobo and white man, 287-298; returns home, 299-305

Priest, Lucius, III: Narrator; grandson of Lucius Priest II. 3-305. Lucius Priest II speaks directly to Lucius Priest III: 3, 31, 57, 61, 68, 121, 234
 His spinster aunts: 234

Priest, Maury, I: Lucius Priest II's father. 3; Boon and Ludus, 4-21, 27, 32; rides in car, 36-38, 41, 43-47; leaves for funeral, 48, 49, 51, 53-55, 63, 65, 69, 82, 96, 100, 105, 107, 117, 120, 123, 124, 139, 143, 196, 197, 212, 242, 246, 252, 286; group returns, 299-301, 303

Priest, Maury, II: One of Lucius Priest II's brothers. 4, 30, 34, 36, 41, 43, 45, 47, 50, 52-54, 56, 58-60, 63, 64, 100, 118, 246, 300

Priest, Sarah Edmonds: Lucius Priest II's grandmother. 28, 30, 32-34; rides in car, 35, 36; stops riding in car, 38-40, 44-47; leaves for funeral, 48, 54, 56, 65, 100, 105, 110, 147, 229; ancestry, 285, 302, 303
 Her mother: 229

Rainey, Paul: Hound specialist. 166, 194

Reba, Miss: Proprietor of bordello in Memphis. Described, 98-103, 106-116, 118-120, 124-139, 141, 152-154, 196; arrives at Parsham, 199-202, 204, 205; confronts Butch, 206-211, 215-218, 222, 233, 242, 250, 255, 256; arrested, 257, 259, 261; story of jail stay, 275-280; returns to Memphis, 281, 290

Rhodes, Miss: Teacher of Lucius Priest II. 303

Rouncewell, Mr.: Jefferson oil company agent. 47, 48, 50

Rouncewell, Mrs.: Boarding house owner in Jefferson. 24

Sande, Earl: Man in horse business. 233

Sartoris, Colonel Bayard: Jefferson bank president. 25, 27, 29, 30, 38, 50, 57, 74, 117

Sartoris, Colonel John: Confederate officer; Bayard Sartoris' father. 74, 194

Snopes, Flem: Banker murdered by kinsman. 24

Son Thomas: Priests' youngest Negro driver. 4, 15-17, 47, 56

Stevens, Judge: Jefferson judge. 15, 16

Sutpen, Thomas: Large Yoknapatawpha landowner. 20, 72, 78

Van Tosch, Mr.: Lightning's legal owner. 226, 229, 268, 269, 281, 284, 285, 287-290, 292-296, 298

Vera: One of prostitutes at Miss Reba's. 101

Virgil: Hotel clerk in Parsham. 199, 202, 208, 209, 211, 233

Watts, Birdie: Proprietor of Memphis brothel. 110, 131, 173

Winbush, Mack: Property owner near Jefferson. 13

Wordwin, Mr.: Bank cashier in Jefferson. 29, 31, 32, 68, 85, 86

Wyott I: Early settler who built store at river crossing. 72-74, 78

Wyott II: Family friend of Priests. 69, 72

UNNAMED

Man at Hell Creek with mules. 84-92, 105

Man who traded Lightning for the car. 117-120, 128, 129, 131, 166

White man with whom Bobo Beauchamp was once involved. 287-293

Negro girl whom Boon shot. 14, 15, 17

Stewart and marshal at race; a dog trainer. 235, 237, 253, 265, 296

The Reivers

Night telegraph operator at depot; judge at race. 235, 296

Physician in Parsham who looks at Lucius Priest II's hand.
    188-192, 206, 256

Flem Snopes' kinsman who killed him. 24

HISTORICAL

Caesar, Julius (100?-44 B.C.): Roman general and emperor.
    210, 259, 298

Cobb, Ty (1886-1961): American baseball player. 194

Ford, Henry (1864-1947): American automobile manufacturer.
    40

Forrest, Nathan Bedford (1821-1877): Confederate general. 75,
    96
  His brother: 96

Goldwater, Senator Barry (1909-   ): American senator. 169

Hampton, Wade (1818-1902): Confederate general. 285

Johnston, Joseph E. (1807-1891): Confederate general. 21

Porter, Fitz-John (1822-1901): Union brigadier. 285

Roosevelt, Eleanor (1884-1962): Wife of F.D. Roosevelt. 169

Ruth, George Herman "Babe" (1895-1948): American baseball
    player. 194

Sherman, William T. (1820-1891): Union general. 285

The Swan: William Shakespeare (1564-1616). 135

BIBLICAL

Lord: 62

Satan: 66, 68

LITERARY

Faustus: Central character in works by Marlowe and Goethe. 53, 60

Uncle Remus: Character created by Joel Chandler Harris. 177, 182, 261

REQUIEM FOR A NUN

[New York: Random House, 1951. 286 pp.]

Coldfield: Family name in Yoknapatawpha. 9

Compson: Family name in Yoknapatawpha. 9, 110

Compson, General: Confederate brigadier; son of Jason Compson. 237, 238

Compson, Jason: Man who traded Ikkemotubbe racehorse for land. Background, 13-15; bandits escape, 16, 17, 19, 20, 22-27; helps to name town, 32-34, 36-38, 41, 42, 45, 215-217, 219, 220, 237

Depre, Virginia: Sister of Colonel John Sartoris. 239

Drake, Temple: See Stevens, Temple Drake.

Farmer: Jefferson jailor during Civil War. 228, 229, 236, 257
His wife: 228, 229, 236

Farmer, Cecilia: Daughter of jailor who scratches her name in jail windowpane. 229, 232, 235-237, 253, 254, 256-262

Gombault, Uncle Pete: Old man in Jefferson. 242

Grenier, Louis: One of the founders of Jefferson. 7, 9, 33, 34, 41, 42, 44, 47, 214, 217, 219, 220

Habersham, Dr. Samuel: One of the founders of Jefferson. 7-9, 39, 47, 216, 217, 219, 220
His son: 7, 8, 217, 219
Son's Chickasaw wife; Issetibbeha's/Mohataha's granddaughter; Ikkemotubbe's daughter: 8, 217

Henry: State governor whom Temple Drake Stevens and Gavin Stevens visit. 90; in his office, 112-120, 122-140, 142, 144-152, 155, 156, 160, 162-164, 167; replaced by Gowan Stevens, 194-196, 201, 202; refuses to save Nancy, 206, 207, 209-211, 271, 273, 274

Holston, Alexander: One of the founders of Jefferson. Arrives
    in Yoknapatawpha County, 7-10; lock put on jail, 12-20,
    22-27, 30; town named, 32, 34, 36, 39, 41, 43, 44, 47,
    213; Mohataha in town, 216-220, 222, 251, 253

Ikkemotubbe: Issetibbeha's successor as Chickasaw chief. 13,
    18, 21, 30, 45, 215-217, 219, 220, 224, 229

Issetibbeha: Chickasaw chief; brother of Mohataha. 8, 9, 13,
    21

McCaslin: Family name in Yoknapatawpha. 9

Maggie: Gowan Stevens' aunt. 67, 96, 97, 204

Mannigoe, Nancy: Maid of the Gowan Stevenses; see Manigault
    and Maingault in Historical. Described, 50; sentenced,
    51, 54, 58, 60, 61, 63, 65, 69-71, 74, 78, 79, 82, 84-86,
    88, 90, 92, 93, 117-122, 124, 125, 132-134, 138, 142,
    152; relationship with Temple, 157-159, 168, 171, 172,
    175; events leading to infant's murder, 178-192, 194,
    196, 199-201, 207-211; visited by Temple, 264-285

Mohataha: Mother of Ikkemotubbe; sister of Issetibbeha. 21, 27,
    30, 34, 35, 215-217, 221, 222

Mulberry: Negro janitor in Jefferson. 242, 243

Peabody, Doctor: Dr. Habersham's successor. 15, 19, 20, 22,
    23, 25-29, 32, 34, 36, 38, 42, 45, 217

Pete: Red's brother with whom Temple Drake Stevens plans to
    run away. 160, 165, 167-171, 173-183, 186, 190

Pettigrew, Thomas Jefferson: Mail rider for whom Jefferson is
    named. 9, 10, 11, 17, 19-29, 32, 35, 36, 38, 215, 217,
    219, 224, 250
  His mother: 29

Ratcliffe: Owner of Jefferson trading post. 15, 20-28, 30,
    31, 34-38, 42, 43, 213, 216, 219, 220

Red: Nightclub bouncer in Memphis killed by Popeye Vitelli.
    144-146, 149, 151-153, 160, 167, 170, 178

Redmond: Man who killed Col. John Sartoris. 233, 238

Sartoris: Family name in Yoknapatawpha. 9, 10

Requiem for a Nun 129

Sartoris, Bayard: Son of Col. John Sartoris; Jefferson banker.
    242
  His grandson: 242

Sartoris, Colonel John: Confederate officer; father of Bayard
    Sartoris. 44, 45, 214, 230, 231, 237-239

Stevens: Family name in Yoknapatawpha. 9

Stevens: Unnamed infant daughter of Temple and Gowan. 50, 51,
    69-71, 74, 92, 118, 119, 132, 151, 158, 159; born, 164,
    168, 169, 173, 184-190; killed by Nancy, 191, 264, 265,
    268, 274, 277; in heaven, 279, 280

Stevens, Bucky: Son of Gowan and Temple Stevens. 50, 64, 66,
    67, 71; asleep, 76-79, 91, 92, 95, 97, 118, 119, 151,
    156-158; born, 162-165; on fishing trip, 172, 184, 185,
    187-190, 203, 204, 207-209

Stevens, Gavin: Gowan Stevens' uncle and Jefferson attorney.
    40; described, 49, 50; at Gowan Stevens', 53-75; four
    months later, 76-96; in Governor's office, 113, 115, 117-
    119, 121-123, 125-127, 129-140, 142, 144-147, 149, 151,
    152, 155, 156, 160-172, 194-196, 198, 199, 201-212, 214;
    visits Nancy in jail with Temple, 263-276, 278-286

Stevens, Gowan: Temple Drake Stevens' husband. 51; described,
    53-75, 77, 95, 97, 118, 121, 126, 127, 130-132, 135-
    139, 147, 150, 151, 154-158, 161, 165, 167, 169, 171,
    172, 176, 183-189; in Governor's office, 194-196, 201-
    209, 211, 286
  His mother: 136, 184

Stevens, Temple Drake: Wife of Gowan Stevens. 51, 52; described,
    at her home, 53-69, 71-74; four months later, 76-97;
    in Governor's office, 113-134; likes "evil," 135-140;
    in Memphis brothel, 141-148; Popeye dead, 149; her
    letters, 150-156; relationship with Nancy, 157-172; her
    dressing-room, 173-192; discovers dead child, 193;
    Gowan Stevens takes place of Governor, 194-205; Governor
    refuses to save Nancy, 206-212; visits Nancy in jail,
    263-277, 280-286
  Her father and brothers: 136, 139, 153, 186

Sutpen: Family name in Yoknapatawpha. 9

Sutpen, Thomas: Large landowner in Yoknapatawpha. 37, 40,
    41, 44, 45, 214, 225, 227, 228, 238, 244

Tubbs, Mr.: Jefferson jailor. 263-270, 282-286

Tubbs, Mrs.: Jailor's wife. 266, 267

Vitelli, Popeye: Memphis gangster. 74, 126, 127, 129-146, 148, 149, 153

Whitfield: Man whose cabin is church in early community which became Jefferson. 28

UNNAMED

Paris architect whom Sutpen brings to Yoknapatawpha. 37-40, 44, 46, 225, 227, 228, 238, 244

Lieutenant who returns to Jefferson for Cecilia Farmer. 232, 234-237, 256-260

Holston slave who is cook's husband, waiter-groom-hostler. 16, 17, 30, 34, 35

Stranger, outlander who visits Jefferson. 252-258, 260-262

Negro who kills white man; see *Go Down, Moses*. 198, 199

Deputy who helps to hold Negro. 198

White man killed by Negro whose wife had just died. 198

Man falsely accused of murder by Temple Drake Stevens. 127, 128, 136

Jailor who helped to subdue Negro. 198

Negro's wife who had just died. 198

Sheriff who arrested Negro. 198

Madam of Memphis bordello where Temple Drake Stevens stayed. 141, 142

Bank cashier accused by Nancy of not paying her. 121

Negro maid in Memphis bordello. 141, 143, 148

Requiem for a Nun

HISTORICAL

Alexander (356-323 B.C.): King of Macedonia. 226

Barksdale, William (1821-1863): Confederate general. 110

Bee, Barnard E. (1824-1861): Confederate general. 45

Bernhardt, Sarah (1845?-1923): French actress. 261

Burnside, Ambrose E. (1824-1881): Union general. 240

Caesar, Julius (100?-44 B.C.): Roman general and emperor. 200

Cincinnatus, Lucius Quinctius (519?-439? B.C.): Roman statesman and general. 49, 214

Claiborne, William C.C. (1775-1817): Territorial governor of Mississippi. 106, 110

Clay, Henry (1777-1852): American statesman. 108

Coke, Edward (1552-1634): English jurist. 199

David, Jacques Louis (1748-1825): French artist. 38

Davis, Jefferson (1808-1889): President of the Confederacy. 109, 110

DeFrance, Abraham (?-?): Superintendent of Washington, D.C., buildings. 106

Dickson, David (?-1836): Lieutenant Governor of Mississippi, 1823-1824. 110

Dillinger, John (1902-1934): American gangster. 7

Duse, Eleonora (1859-1924): Italian actress. 261

Eggleston, Beroth B. (?-1891): President of Mississippi's constitutional convention of 1868. 109

Fink, Mike (1770?-1822?): Mississippi River keelboatman. 104

Forrest, Nathan Bedford (1821-1877): Confederate general. 231, 233

Grant, Ulysses S. (1822-1885): Union general; President of United States, 1869-1877. 107, 240

Hare, Joseph T. (?-1818): Bandit on Natchez Trace. 103, 104, 223, 226

Harpe, Micajah (1768-1799): "Big Harpe," American bandit on Natchez Trace. 5, 16, 103, 104, 223, 226

Harpe, Wiley (1770-1804): "Little Harpe," American bandit on Natchez Trace. 5, 16, 103, 104, 223, 226, 229, 249

Hemingway, Ernest (1899-1961): American novelist. 154, 156, 159, 169

Henry, Judith (1776?-1861?): Widow around whose house Battle of First Manassas in Civil War was fought. 45

Hinds, Thomas (1775-1840): U.S. Cavalry commander and Mississippi congressman. 99, 105-107

Hooker, Joseph (1814-1879): Union general. 240

Humphreys, Benjamin G. (1808-1882): Mississippi governor, 1865-1868. 109, 110

Jackson, Andrew (1767-1845): President of United States, 1829-1837. 106-108

Jackson, Thomas J. "Stonewall" (1824-1863): Confederate general. 45, 240

James, Jesse W. (1847-1882): American bandit. 7

Jefferson, Thomas (1743-1826): President of United States, 1801-1809. 29, 106

Johnston, Albert S. (1803-1862): Confederate general. 240

Johnston, Joseph E. (1807-1891): Confederate general. 108, 233, 240, 259

Lamar, Lucius Q.C. (1825-1893): Mississippi statesman. 110

Lattimore, William (1774-1843): Physician and Mississippi public servant. 99, 105, 106

Lee, Robert E. (1807-1870): Confederate general. 234, 240

Requiem for a Nun

Le Fleur, Louis (?-?): Owner of trading-post store on Mississippi. 106

Leflore, Greenwood (1800-1865): Choctaw chief and planter. 106

Lind, Jenny (1820-1887): Swedish singer. 260, 261

Littleton, Thomas (1407?-1481): English jurist. 199

Longstreet, James (1821-1904): Confederate general. 240

Louis IX (1214-1270): King of France. 105

McClellan, George B. (1826-1885): Union general. 240

McLaurin, Anselm J. (1848-1909): Mississippi governor and senator. 110

Maingault: Norman family name. 118

Manigault: Charleston, South Carolina, family name. 118

Marion, Francis (1732?-1795): American Revolutionary War general. 218

Mason, Samuel (1750?-1804?): Bandit on Natchez Trace. 103, 104, 223, 226

Maximilian (1832-1867): Emperor of Mexico, Archduke of Austria. 261

Mistinguette (1875-1956): French actress. 261

Murrel, John A. (1804-?): American bandit. 5, 103, 226

Napoleon (1769-1821): Emperor of France. 4, 199

Patton, James (?-?): Lieutenant governor of Mississippi, 1820. 99, 105, 106

Pemberton, John C. (1818-1881): Confederate general. 108

Pope, John (1822-1892): Union general. 240

Prentiss, Seargent S. (1808-1850): Mississippi congressman. 110

Shakespeare, William (1564-1616): English playwright and poet. 150

Sherman, William T. (1820-1891): Union general. 107-109, 240

Twain, Mark (1835-1910): Pen name of Samuel Clemens, American author. 260

Victoria (1819-1901): Queen of England. 225

BIBLICAL

Gabriel: Archangel. 113

God: 113, 128, 157, 163, 164, 212, 257, 277, 278

Ham: Second son of Noah in Genesis. 42

MYTHIC

Damocles: Courier of ancient Syracuse. 169

Erinys: One of the Furies. 261

Lilith: Adam's first wife in Jewish folklore. 260

SANCTUARY

[New York: Jonathan Cape and Harrison Smith, 1931. 380 pp.]

Benbow, Belle Mitchell: Previously married to Harry Mitchell, now wife of Horace Benbow. 15, 16, 18, 26, 28, 54, 126-128, 139, 155, 313, 318, 319, 357-360
  Her father: 313

Benbow, Horace: Husband of Belle Mitchell, brother of Narcissa Benbow Sartoris. Meets Popeye, 1-6; at Old Frenchman's place, 7, 8, 11, 12; his situation at home, 13-24; at sister's house, 25-29, 54, 115, 116; at sister's, 126-133; with Lee Goodwin, 136, 137; Ruby at his house, 138-144; takes Ruby to hotel, 145-148, 150-160; learns of woman at Old Frenchman's place, 161; listens to Ruby, 192, 193, 197-200; takes train to Oxford, 201-207; meets Clarence Snopes, 208-214; Ruby at jail, 215-225, 240-243; meets C. Snopes again, 244-247; at Miss Reba's, 248-250, 252-255; talks with Temple Drake, 256-259, 261, 264-268, 313, 314, 316-322; trial begins, 323-332, 334-340; Temple on stand, 341-343, 346, 348-353; sees fire, 354, 355; returns home to Belle, 356-360
  His father: 133, 140, 221, 320
  His mother: 140, 221

Benbow, Narcissa: See Sartoris, Narcissa Benbow.

Beth: Girl who has ridden trains without paying. 204

Binford, Mr.: Consort of Miss Reba Rivers. 185, 189, 306, 307

Doc: One of the men with Gowan Stevens when he is looking for liquor. 34-38

Drake, Judge: Temple Drake's father. 59, 60, 62, 64-66, 71, 96, 187, 212, 224, 320, 342, 343, 346-348, 379, 380

Drake, Hubert (Buddy): Temple Drake's youngest brother. 62, 63, 66, 187, 347, 348
  His brothers: 62, 66, 187, 347, 348

Drake, Temple: Judge Drake's daughter. 28-30; at school, 31-34, 39; with Gowan Stevens, 41-43; wreck, 44, 46; at Old Frenchman's place, 47-50, 53, 55-92, 94-99; Gowan leaves, 100, 101-113, 118-120; Tommy shot, 121; raped,

122, 123; in car with Popeye, 161-169; at Miss Reba's, 170-198, 205-207, 212, 224, 246, 247, 251, 254, 255; visited by H. Benbow, 256-265, 268; at Miss Reba's, 269-279; at the Grotto, 280-290, 307, 308; Red, Temple, Popeye, 310-312, 321, 322, 339; at trial, 341-348, 352, 355, 361; in Paris, 378-380

Fonzo: Companion of Virgil Snopes who stays in Miss Reba Rivers' house. 214, 226-239, 303

Frank: A lover of Ruby Lamar. 67

Gene: Bootlegger at Red's funeral. 292-297, 304

George: Porter on train carrying Clarence Snopes and Horace Benbow. 213

Goodwin, Lee: Bootlegger. At Old Frenchman's place, 7-9; described, 11, 12, 16, 20, 22, 38, 43, 48, 52, 54, 57, 60, 65, 68, 71, 76, 78-80, 84-94, 110; confronted by Ruby, 113-121; Popeye and Temple gone, 124, 129, 130; in jail, 135; Horace Benbow visits, 136-139, 143, 144, 147, 150-153, 155-159, 193-196, 221, 222, 224, 255, 256, 265, 317; on trial, 323, 324, 326-338, 344, 345, 348, 350, 352; murdered, 355, 357

Graham, Eustace: District Attorney in Jefferson. 222-224, 314-318, 323-325, 329, 340-346, 348, 358

Harris, Mr.: Proprietor of livery stable. 315, 316

Isom: Negro servant of the Sartorises. 131, 145, 146, 148-150, 155, 158, 220

Jenny, Miss: Great aunt of Narcissa Benbow Sartoris' husband. 25-29, 127-129, 138-141, 150-155, 197-199, 219, 222, 223, 350

Joe: Proprietor of club where Red's funeral is held. 291-299

Jones, Herschell: Suitor of Narcissa Benbow Sartoris. 26

Lamar, Ruby: Woman who lives with Lee Goodwin. At Old Frenchman's place, 7-13, 15-20; Temple and Gowan arrive, 48, 56, 57; talks with Temple, 61-74, 76-78, 86, 88-91, 94-99; Gowan leaves, 100, 107, 108, 110; confronts Goodwin, 113-116; sees Temple and Popeye leave, 123-125, 130; Goodwin in jail, 137-147, 150-153, 156-160; tells about

Sanctuary 137

    Temple, 161, 162; talks to Horace Benbow, 192-199, 215-224, 240, 241, 245, 253, 256, 257, 265; Goodwin's trial, 323-338, 340, 348, 350
  Her baby: At Old Frenchman's place, 19, 20, 56, 60, 64-70, 73, 99, 107, 110, 113-116, 123, 124; Goodwin in jail, 137-140, 142-144, 146, 147, 150, 151, 157, 158, 160, 162, 192, 193, 197, 215, 219, 240, 253, 256, 265; Goodwin's trial, 323, 326-329, 331, 332, 348, 350
  Her father: 67
  Her brother: 67

Lorraine, Miss: Thin woman who visits Miss Reba Rivers. 300-312

Luke: Bootlegger near Oxford. 35, 36

Marge: Girl who has ridden train without paying. 204

Minnie: Negro maid at Miss Reba Rivers'. 170, 173-176, 184, 185, 234, 236, 237; Horace Benbow visits, 249-252, 254, 269; with Temple, 271-275, 300-303; Temple, Red, Popeye, 309-312, 321, 322
  Her husband: 251, 322

Mitchell, Belle: See Benbow, Belle Mitchell

Mitchell, "Little" Belle: Daughter of Harry and Belle Mitchell. 14-16, 28, 127, 199, 200, 211-213, 267, 268, 358-360

Mitchell, Harry: First husband of Belle Mitchell Benbow. 126, 128

Myrtle, Miss: Plump woman who visits Miss Reba Rivers. 300-311, 322

Pap: Old man who lives with Lee Goodwin and Ruby Lamar. 12, 49, 50, 52, 53, 59, 60, 64, 104, 105, 109, 115, 117, 122, 124, 130, 156, 157

Popeye: Bootlegger. Meets Horace Benbow, 1; described, 2, 3-6; at Old Frenchman's place, 7-14, 17, 21-23; Temple and Gowan in wreck, 44, 48, 50-58, 80, 84, 85, 87, 88, 91-93, 95, 96, 109, 110, 115-117, 120; kills Tommy, 121; rapes Temple, 122; leaves with Temple, 123, 129, 130, 137, 143, 147, 152, 156-158; on road to Memphis, 162-169; arrives at Miss Reba's, 170, 171, 174, 175, 190-192, 194, 196; at Miss Reba's, 251-253, 256-258, 261-265, 270, 272, 273, 277-279; at the Grotto, 280-286, 288, 290;

Temple, Red, Popeye, 307-313, 322, 326, 330, 334, 335;
    arrested, 361, 363-365, 367-378
  His mother: 307, 361-365, 368, 370
  His grandmother: 363-369
  His father: 361-363
  His stepfather: 363, 364

Quinn, Dr.: Physician who attends Temple Drake in Memphis.
    173, 176, 178, 179

Red: Young man brought by Popeye to Temple Drake in brothel.
    277-280; at the Grotto, 283-290; his funeral, 293-297,
    299, 301, 305, 307; Temple, Red, Popeye, 310-312, 361

Rivers, Miss Reba: Proprietor of brothel in Memphis. Popeye
    and Temple arrive, 170-180, 184, 185, 187-191; Fonzo and
    Virgil arrive, 229-232, 234, 236, 237; Horace Benbow
    visits, 248-257, 259, 261, 264, 265, 269, 272-276; after
    Red's funeral, 300-312, 321, 322

Sartoris, Benbow (Bory): Son of Narcissa Benbow Sartoris. 25,
    27-30, 127, 140, 153, 155, 198

Sartoris, Narcissa Benbow: Sister of Horace Benbow. With
    Gowan Stevens, 25, 26; described, 27-29; relationship
    with brother, 126-128, 130, 131; confronts Horace, 138-
    141, 145, 148; discussed by Aunt Jenny and Horace, 150-
    155, 158, 159, 197, 198, 215, 218-223, 242, 244, 314;
    visits Eustace Graham, 316-319, 349, 350, 358
  Her husband: 25, 140

Shack: Young man on train who cheats conductor on ticket. 203

Snopes, Clarence: State senator. On train, 207-214, 223, 224,
    238, 239; with Horace Benbow, 242-252, 313, 314, 317;
    "hit by car," 319, 320

Snopes, Virgil: One of two youths who stay in Miss Reba Rivers'
    house. 214, 226-239, 303

Stevens, Gowan: Young man who leaves Temple Drake with boot-
    leggers. Visits Narcissa Sartoris, 25-30, 33-40; picks
    up Temple, 41-43; wreck, 44, 46; at Old Frenchman's place,
    47, 48, 50-59, 61-63, 65, 66, 71, 75-80, 84-86, 88, 90,
    92, 94-96, 99; leaves Old Frenchman's place, 100-102,
    153; note to Narcissa, 154, 155, 163, 193-198, 223, 261

Sanctuary

Tommy: Man who works for Lee Goodwin. 7, 9-11, 20-24; discovers Gowan and Temple in wreck, 44, 46-48, 51-56, 75-88, 90-93, 95, 96, 115, 117-120; killed, 121, 125, 129, 134, 156, 157, 196, 323, 344, 345

Tull: Farmer who lives two miles from Old Frenchman's place. 100, 124, 125
  His family: 124, 125

Uncle Bud: Small boy visiting Miss Myrtle. 300-305, 308-310, 312

Van: Bootlegger with Lee Goodwin. 61, 73, 75-80, 82, 83, 85-88, 90, 91, 93, 101, 194-196

Walker, Ed: Jefferson jailor. 218, 326

Walker, Mrs.: The jailor's wife. 215, 217, 218

UNNAMED

Man in shirt sleeves exhorting the crowd against Goodwin. 351, 352

Sheriff. 124, 135, 150, 156, 157, 351

Negro murderer who cut wife's throat. 135, 136, 146, 148-150, 155, 159

Hotel proprietor who won't allow Ruby Lamar to stay in the hotel. 216, 217, 354

Old half-crazed white woman with whom Ruby Lamar stays in Jefferson. 240, 241, 325, 326

Judge at Goodwin's trial. 324, 339, 340, 342, 343, 346

Old man who meets trains in Kinston. 356, 357

Drummers who discuss Goodwin trial in hotel. 351-353

Man in crowd who catches fire when they burn Goodwin. 354, 355

Memphis Jew lawyer at trial. 320, 338, 348

Turnkey in jail where Popeye is held. 374-377

Minister who tries to pray for Popeye. 376-378

Judge at Popeye's trial. 371-374

District Attorney at Popeye's trial. 374

Popeye's lawyer in Alabama. 372-374

Original Frenchman. 7, 130

HISTORICAL

Berlioz, Louis Hector (1803-1869): French composer. 379

Blackstone, Mrs.: Reference to William Blackstone (1723-1780), English jurist. 140

Coolidge, Calvin (1872-1933): President of United States, 1923-1929. 367

Delsarte, François (1811-1871): French inventor of system of calisthenics. 323

Gilbert, John (1897-1936): American film star. 272

Grant, Ulysses S. (1822-1885): Union general; President of United States, 1869-1877. 7

Massenet, Jules Émile Frédéric (1842-1912): French composer. (Misspelled as Massanet in first printings.) 379

Scriabin, Alexander (1872-1915): Russian composer. (Spelled as Scriabine.) 379

Strauss, Johann (1825-1899): Austrian composer. 294

Tschaikovsky, Petr Ilich (1840-1893): Russian composer. 379

BIBLICAL

Adam: First man in Genesis. 181

Eve: Adam's wife in Genesis. 181

God: 208, 316, 337

LITERARY

Bovary: Central character in Flaubert's *Madame Bovary*, 1857. 6

SANCTUARY

[New York: Random House, 1981. 291 pp.]

Benbow, Belle Mitchell: 5, 6; relationship with Horace, 15-19, 27, 30, 32, 33, 35; Horace visits his sister, 37-40, 45, 46; Horace at Goodwin's house, 50, 56, 58, 60, 61, 64-67, 77, 78, 95, 199; Horace writes letter to Belle, 205, 219; Horace mails letter, 254, 258; Horace's letter to Narcissa, 281, 284

Benbow, Horace: 3; visits Goodwin in jail, 4-8; first sees Ruby's son, 9-13; discussion with Little Belle, 14; relationship with Belle, 15-18; leaves Belle, 19, 20; sees Popeye, 21, 22-30; at Jefferson house, 31; visits sister, 32-36, 40; looks at Sartoris portraits, 41-46; at Goodwin's house, 47-68; Goodwin in jail, 71-78; Ruby agrees to talk, 79, 95, 110, 111, 122, 141-148; rides train to Oxford, 149, 150-153; meets Clarence Snopes, 154-158; Ruby not at hotel, 159-161, 194-198; finds place for Ruby, 199, 200; C. Snopes' information, 201-205; at Miss Reba's, 206-215; returns to Jefferson, 218-220; mails letter to Belle, 254-259; trial opens, 260-271; sees Temple Drake in courtroom, 272-276, 279, 280; letter to Narcissa, 281-284
  His father: 6, 20, 62, 197
  His mother: 6, 20, 60, 62, 197, 272

Benbow, Narcissa: See Sartoris, Narcissa Benbow

Beth: 151

Binford, Mr.: 178, 179, 181, 210, 249

Doc: 81-85, 88

Drake, Judge: 99, 100, 102-104, 107, 113, 157, 180, 194, 195, 259, 276, 278, 279, 290, 291

Drake, Hubert (Buddy): 100, 102, 104, 180, 279
  His three brothers: 100, 104, 180, 279

Drake, Temple: 37, 39, 79; in Oxford, 80-82, 85; meets Gowan Stevens in Taylor, 87, 88; car wreck, 89, 90; at Goodwin's house, 91-99; talks with Ruby; 100-113; sleeps in barn, 114, 115-121, 125-139; raped, 140-142; Gowan leaves,

143-145, 147, 148, 152; Horace Benbow in Oxford, 153, 156-158; in car with Popeye, 162, 163-167; at Miss Reba's, 168-182; visited by Popeye, 183, 194-196, 204; Clarence Snopes' information, 205, 207-211; talks with Horace Benbow, 212-218, 220, 221; wrecks room, 222-227; at Grotto, 228-236; Temple, Popeye, and Red, 249-252, 254, 255, 260; at trial, 272, 274; her testimony, 275-279; in Paris, 290, 291

Ed: Jefferson jailor.   161, 196, 263, 264
  His wife: 160, 161

Elnora: Sartoris cook; mother of Sundy and Saddie.   44

Fonzo: 159, 184-193, 207, 246

Frank: 104

Gene: 238-241, 247

George: 158

Goodwin, Lee: in jail, 4-10, 12, 26, 28, 30, 32; Horace Benbow at Goodwin's house, 47-55, 57, 65, 66; in jail, 70-78, 85, 88; Gowan and Temple at Goodwin's house, 91, 93, 95, 97, 99-102, 105, 107, 108, 110-113, 118, 119; drunk, 121-123, 126-139; Temple raped, 140, 141, 144, 194, 196, 198, 209, 211; Temple talks to Horace, 213, 214, 218, 254-258; trial opens, 260-270, 272; Temple on witness stand, 274, 276, 277, 279; Horace's letter to Narcissa, 280, 283, 284

Graham, Eustace: 195, 199, 256-258, 260, 261, 265, 274-280

Harris, Mr.: 256, 257

Isom: 10-13, 38, 65, 76, 78, 142, 159, 160, 197, 199, 284

Jenny, Miss: 5-8; talks with Horace Benbow, 31-40; Sartoris portraits, 41-46, 58, 59, 63; talks with Horace, 71, 72; Gowan Stevens' note, 73, 74, 77, 78, 142, 146, 147, 196, 256; Narcissa's letter to Horace, 284
  Her husband: 44

Joe: 237-242, 247

Jones: Man who takes Horace Benbow home in Kinston.   281

Sanctuary 143

Jones, Herschell: 36

Lorraine, Miss: 244-252

Luke: 83

Marge: 151

Minnie: 168, 170-172, 178, 179, 189, 191, 192, 207-210, 221-225, 245, 247, 250-253
  Her husband: 208

Mitchell, Belle: See Benbow, Belle Mitchell

Mitchell, "Little" Belle: 5, 14, 15, 19, 32, 37, 46, 59, 67, 143, 145, 146, 157, 158, 205, 220, 282

Mitchell, Harry: 5, 16, 18, 19, 38, 46, 65, 67

Myrtle, Miss: 244-252

Pap: 46, 51-54, 75, 92-95, 99, 115, 116, 119, 122, 123, 140

Popeye: 4, 9, 12; sees Horace Benbow, 21-28, 30, 32, 39; Horace at Goodwin's house, 46-55, 60, 65, 66, 72, 74-76; sees car wreck, 89; Temple and Gowan at Goodwin's house, 91, 93-98, 101, 111, 113, 118, 122-124; curses Tommy, 125, 129, 132-134, 136, 137, 139; rapes Temple, 140, 144, 156; in car with Temple, 162-167; at Miss Reba's, 168-171; visits Temple, 183, 208-210; Temple talks with Horace, 212-218, 221-224, 226, 227; at Grotto, 228-234, 236; Temple, Popeye, and Red, 249-251, 255, 260, 263, 265, 269-271; in jail, 285-291
  His grandfather: 50
  His mother: 50, 249, 285

Quinn, Dr.: 170, 172-174, 183

Red: 227, 228, 230-235, 238-243, 245, 246, 248, 249, 251, 252

Rivers, Miss Reba: Popeye and Temple in Memphis, 168-175, 178-183, 186-192; Horace Benbow visits, 206-213, 215, 218, 221, 223-226; after Red's funeral, 244-253, 260

Ruby: Woman who lives with Lee Goodwin. Goodwin in jail, 4-12, 22, 23, 26, 30, 32, 39, 46; Horace Benbow at Goodwin's house, 47, 48, 51-58, 65, 66; in jail, 70-73, 75-79; Temple and Gowan at Goodwin's house, 91-93, 96, 97; talks with Temple, 100-110, 114, 117-123, 126, 127; Gowan

struck, 132-136; talks to Horace, 141, 143, 147, 156; leaves hotel, 159-162, 194-200, 203, 210, 211, 213, 217, 218, 254; trial opens, 260-272; Temple on witness stand, 274, 279, 280; Horace's letter, 283, 284
 Her child: Goodwin in jail, 4-12, 22, 23, 39; at Goodwin's house, 48, 52, 57; in jail, 70-72, 75-79; at Goodwin's house, 96, 99, 102, 104-106, 108, 110, 117, 119, 121-123; Ruby talks to Horace, 141, 161, 162, 196, 210, 211, 218, 254; trial opens, 260, 261, 263-267, 279, 280; Horace's letter, 283
 Her father: 104
 Her brother: 104

Sartoris, Bayard: Husband of Narcissa Benbow. 6, 16-18, 21, 35, 37, 41, 42, 44, 59, 63

Sartoris, Benbow (Bory): 6, 33-41, 44, 45, 59-61, 73, 74, 147, 199, 284

Sartoris, Johnny: Twin brother of Bayard Sartoris. 38, 41, 42, 45

Sartoris, Narcissa Benbow (Narcy): 5-8, 10, 11, 16-18, 20, 27, 29; visited by Horace, 31, 32; walks with Gowan Stevens, 33-41, 44-46; Horace stays, 58-65, 72; Gowan Stevens' note, 73, 74, 76, 77; Gowan's proposal, 147, 195-199, 201, 202, 254-256; visits Eustace Graham, 257-259, 281-283; her letter, 284

Saturday (Saddie): Sartoris Negro servant; daughter of Elnora; twin of Sundy. 33, 35, 36, 40, 42-45, 78

Shack: 150-152

Snopes, Clarence: 154-159, 192-195, 201-209, 255, 258, 259
 His father: 156

Snopes, Virgil: 159, 184-193, 207, 246

Stevens, Gowan: Visits Narcissa, 33-41, 44, 45; note to Narcissa, 73, 74, 81-88; wreck, 89, 90-98, 100-103, 107, 110-113, 125-128, 130, 131; struck by Van, 132-134, 136, 137; leaves Goodwin's house, 143, 144; proposal to Narcissa, 147, 148, 162; Horace talks to Temple, 213-215
 His mother: 73

Sunday (Sundy): Sartoris Negro servant; daughter of Elnora; twin of Saddie. 34, 44, 59, 284

Tommy: 26-30; Horace Benbow at Goodwin's house, 47, 49-55, 57, 65, 66; body on table, 69, 75; car wreck, 89-97, 113, 122, 123, 125-134, 136-139; killed, 140, 144, 213, 214, 254, 255, 260, 277

Uncle Bud: 244-248, 250-253

Van: 100, 101, 108, 110-112, 118, 125-134, 136, 137, 143, 144, 213, 214

UNNAMED

Sheriff. 75, 141

Negro murderer who cut wife's throat. 3, 4, 11, 12, 70, 76, 77

Hotel proprietor who won't allow Ruby to stay in the hotel. 159, 160

Old half-crazed woman with whom Ruby stays in Jefferson. 199, 200, 262

Judge at Lee Goodwin's trial. 10, 261, 272-276, 278

Memphis Jew lawyer at trial. 259, 272, 279, 280

Turnkey in jail where Popeye is held. 287, 288, 290

Minister who tries to pray for Popeye. 289, 290

Judge at Popeye's trial. 286, 287

District Attorney at Popeye's trial. 287

Popeye's lawyer in Alabama. 286, 287

Original owner of old house where Goodwin lives. 51

Man who wrote love letters to Narcissa Benbow. 74

Sartoris men in portraits beside Miss Jenny's bed. 41-44

HISTORICAL

Berlioz, Louis Hector (1803-1869): 291

Blackstone, Mrs.: 7

Gilbert, John (1897-1936): 223

Grant, Ulysses S. (1822-1885): 51, 65

Massenet, Jules Émile Frédéric (1842-1912): 291

Scriabin, Alexander (1872-1915): 291

Strauss, Johann (1825-1899): 239

Tschaikovsky, Petr Ilich (1840-1893): 291

BIBLICAL

Adam: 176

Christ: 52

Eve: 176

God: 43, 154, 257, 271

LITERARY

Bovary: 25, 60

SOLDIERS' PAY

[New York: Boni & Liveright, 1926. 319 pp.]

Alice: Name muttered by drunken soldiers on train. 9

Baird, Dr.: Eye specialist from Atlanta. 153-157, 168, 255, 285

Bleyth, Captain: RAF pilot remembered by Cadet Lowe. 9

Burney, Mr.: Dewey Burney's father. 180, 183

Burney, Mrs.: Dewey Burney's mother. 179-186, 257-259, 261-263

Burney, Dewey: Young soldier who kills Richard Powers. 180-186, 258, 261-263

Coleman, Mrs.: Friend of Mrs. Saunders. 233

Dough, James: Mrs. Wardle's nephew. 189-195, 201, 204, 205

Ed: Policeman who attempts to arrest Gilligan and Lowe. 21

Emmy: Girl who lives with the Mahons. 65, 66, 68-71, 73-75, 78, 79, 90-93, 109; not recognized by Donald Mahon, 110, 116, described, background, 120-123; relationship with Donald Mahon, 124-129, 133-135, 166, 167, 210, 250-253, 263; mothers Donald Mahon, 270-272; Margaret Powers asks her to marry Donald, 273, 274, 282-284, 286, 287, 289-291; Donald's death, 296; seduced by J. Jones, 297, 298; at pool, 300, 301, 313, 315, 317
  Her family: 120, 125, 126, 128

Farr, Cecily Saunders: Daughter of Minnie and Robert Saunders; fiancée of Donald Mahon; wife of George Farr. 40, 41, 43, 66; visits the Rector, 70-83; with George Farr, 84-93; sees Donald's face, 94-103, 106, 107, 111-115, 117-119; talks with her father, 129-133, 135; returns to Mahons, 136-142; her relationship with other women, 143-150, 152, 156, 160, 161, 165, 166, 168, 169, 182, 183; at dance with James Dough, 189-196, 198-200, 202-210, 212; with George Farr, 213-216; with J. Jones, 217-233, 237, 240-246, 249-251, 254-257, 259-262; visited by Margaret Powers, 263-268; calls George, 270-273, 275; won't marry Donald Mahon, 276, 277, 280; married to George Farr, 281, 290, 298, 304, 306, 307

Farr, George: Husband of Cecily Saunders. 77; picks up Cecily at Mahons, 84-89, 96, 132, 135, 138, 140, 142-146; affair with Cecily, 147-149, 152; at dance, 195, 196, 211, 212; note from Cecily, 213-218, 220, 225, 228, 230; lurks near Saunders' house, 233-238; attacks J. Jones, 239-244, 261-263; drunk, 268-270; married to Cecily Saunders, 281, 304, 306, 307

Gary, Doctor: Young physician who examines Donald Mahon and courts Cecily Saunders. 99, 166-168, 193, 198-200, 212, 285

Gilligan, Joe (Yaphank): Soldier who helps Donald Mahon and falls in love with Margaret Powers. On train, 7-30; meets Margaret Powers, 31-35; in hotel, 37-53, 55, 82, 93, 94; at Mahons, 100-110, 114, 115, 122, 123, 135, 136, 138, 149-154, 156-161; talks with Margaret Powers about her husband, 162-172, 182-184, 187; at dance, 196-203, 205-208, 210, 211, 246, 249-252, 254, 255, 257, 262, 263, 270, 271, 273, 278, 279, 282-292, 295; at train station with Margaret Powers, 301-312; fights J. Jones, 313-315; with Rector, 316-319
  His mother: 24

Green, Captain: Friend of Richard Powers and captain of his company; killed in World War I. 173-177, 179, 185

Henderson, Mrs.: Woman insulted on train by Gilligan and Lowe. 31, 32

Henry: Porter on train. 15, 16, 20, 22, 24-28, 30, 32-35. [Also called Claude, Othello, Charles, Ernest, and George by drunken soldiers on train.]

Jerks: Name which drunken soldier thinks he heard in play. 9

Jones, Januarius: Young man who pursues Cecily Saunders. Described, visits Rector, 56-84, 86, 89-94, 97, 133-138; at dance, 202-209; at Saunders', 216-232, 237; fights George Farr, 239-244; talks with Margaret Powers, 247-254, 257, 283, 284, 286-291, 295; seduces Emmy, 297, 298, 302, 304; fights Joe Gilligan, 313-316

Lowe, Julian: Young flying cadet who falls in love with Margaret Powers. On train, 7-30; meets Margaret Powers, 31-35; in hotel, 37, 38, 43, 45-53; promises to go home, 54, 55, 103, 104, 153, 186, 187, 246, 247, 277, 278, 280, 285, 315
  His mother: 50, 53, 54, 153, 247, 277

Soldiers' Pay   *149*

Madden, Rufus: Sergeant in Captain Green's company. 173-179,
    181, 185, 186, 191-194, 200-202, 205-207, 209-211, 262

Mahon, Reverend (Uncle Joe): Father of Donald Mahon. 40, 41,
    43; visited by J. Jones, 56-76, 78-80; visited by Mar-
    garet Powers, 81-87, 89-91, 93; Donald arrives home, 94,
    98, 104, 107-118, 121-123, 125, 129, 131, 136, 138, 149,
    151, 152, 154, 156, 157, 160, 166; told Donald is blind,
    167-169, 180-184, 217; visited by J. Jones, 252-258, 261,
    263, 266-268, 270, 272, 273, 275; Cecily won't marry
    Donald, 276, 277; Margaret Powers and Donald married,
    278, 280-282, 284-289, 291, 292; Donald dies, 294, 299-
    301, 303, 315; with Joe Gilligan, 316-319
  His wife: 68, 83

Mahon, Donald: Son of Rector Mahon; husband of Margaret Powers.
    On train, 25-35; in hotel, 37-49, 51-53, 55, 56; descrip-
    tion of his picture, 67, 68, 73, 76, 77, 81; photograph
    with Cecily, 82-85, 87, 89, 93; arrives home, 94-101,
    103-123; relationship with Emmy, 124-133, 135-141; his
    "homecoming," 149-156, 161, 165, 166; blind, 167-169;
    visited by Callie Nelson, 170-172, 181-184, 187; at dance
    in car, 197, 198, 200-207, 209, 210, 219, 221, 228, 244-
    246, 248, 250, 251, 253-266, 268, 270-274, 276, 277;
    marries M. Powers, 278-282, 285, 286, 289, 291-293; dies,
    294-297, 300, 301, 303, 315, 316

Mahon, Margaret Powers: Widow of Richard Powers; wife of Donald
    Mahon. On train, 31-34; in hotel, 35; remembers husband,
    36-45, 47-55, 75; visits Rector, 81-87, 89-91, 93; Donald
    Mahon arrives home, 94, 103-112, 114-119, 121-123; talks
    with Emmy, 124, 125, 127-129, 136, 137, 139-142, 150-
    152; specialist visits, 153-161; relationship with Richard
    Powers, 162-172, 181-184, 186, 187; at dance, 196-198,
    201-207, 209-211, 244-246; talks with J. Jones, 247-252,
    254, 255, 257, 258, 261, 262; visits Cecily, 263-267,
    270-275, 277; marries Donald Mahon, 278-292; Mahon's
    funeral, 295, 296, 299, 300; leaves on train, 301-309,
    311, 313, 315, 317
  Her mother: 162

Maurier, Harrison: Man from Atlanta who courts Cecily Saunders.
    99

Miller, Mrs.: Dressmaker for whom Emmy once worked. 128, 129,
    298

Mitchell, Mrs.: Town resident. 182

Nelson, Cal'line (Callie): Negro woman who worked for the
    Mahons. 170, 171, 259

Nelson, Loosh: Callie Nelson's grandson. 170, 171, 296

Powers, Margaret: See Mahon, Margaret Powers

Powers, Richard: Margaret Powers' husband; killed in World
    War I. 36, 39, 42, 44, 45, 52, 123, 162-164, 177-179,
    181-184, 186, 202, 210, 211, 262, 279

Rivers, Lee: Young man who has spent a year at Princeton.
    190-196, 203-204, 208, 209

Saunders, Cecily: See Farr, Cecily Saunders

Saunders, Minnie: Mother of Cecily and Robert Saunders II; wife
    of Robert Saunders I. 40; at home after Cecily sees
    scar, 95-100, 102, 103, 113, 116, 117, 119, 133; at home,
    138-140, 144, 146, 180, 181, 183; J. Jones at lunch, 218,
    219, 228-233, 255, 256; pleads with Cecily not to marry
    Donald, 259-261, 263, 264, 266, 267, 272, 273, 298

Saunders, Robert, I: Father of Cecily and Robert Saunders II;
    husband of Minnie Saunders. 40; at home after Cecily
    sees scar, 95-103; talks with Rector, 111-120; talks with
    Cecily, 129-133; at home, 138-142, 144, 146, 160, 218,
    219, 229, 230, 232, 233, 239, 242; visits Rector, 252-
    256, 259-261, 267, 268, 272, 273, 298; meets Mr. and Mrs.
    George Farr, 306, 307

Saunders, Robert, II: Son of Minnie and Robert Saunders I;
    brother of Cecily Saunders Farr. 95-97; meets Joe Gilli-
    gan, 100-103, 120, 130, 142, 148; brings friends to see
    D. Mahon, 149, 150, 152; spies on M. Powers and J. Gilli-
    gan, 159-161, 164-166, 168; talks with J. Jones, 218-
    220, 230, 231, 295; after sister's marriage and D. Mahon's
    death, 298, 299
  His grandfather: 220

Schluss: Ladies' "underthings" salesman on train with companion,
    Lowe, and Gilligan. 15-22

Tobe: Negro servant who works for the Saunderses. 97, 99, 100,
    102, 133, 138, 238

Wardle, Mrs.: Town resident. 181, 189, 192, 210

White, Hank: Gilligan's drunken companion on train. 9-20

Willard: Man who lives near the Mahons in a small house and grows fruit. 318

Worthington, Mrs.: Wealthy town resident. 152, 180-184, 187, 257, 282

UNNAMED

Pullman conductor on train carrying Lowe, Gilligan, Mahon, and Margaret Powers. 11-16, 18

Man at stream whom Gilligan meets after Margaret Powers Mahon has left. 309-312

Schluss's companion on train. 15-22

HISTORICAL

Aelia: Wife of Sylla, Roman nobleman. See *Mayday* in Short Fiction section. 134

Alexander (356-323 B.C.): King of Macedonia. 177

Austen, Jane (1775-1817): English novelist. 66

Beardsley, Aubrey (1872-1898): English artist. 31

Belasco, David (1853-1931): American theatrical producer and playwright. 188

Caesar, Julius (100?-44 B.C.): Roman general and emperor. 242, 294

Castle, Irene (1893-1969): Member of popular dancing team in American cabaret; later dramatic film actress. 200

Cellini, Benvenuto (1500-1571): Italian goldsmith and sculptor. 265

Gibbon, Edward (1737-1794): English historian. 169

Grant, Ulysses S. (1822-1885): Union general; President of the United States, 1869-1877. 177

Hoyle, Edmund (1672?-1769): First systematizer of the laws of whist and author of a book on games. 40

James, Henry (1843-1916): American novelist. 231

Kipling, Rudyard (1865-1936): English author. 200

Lindsay, Vachel (1879-1931): American writer. 116

Lufbery, Raoul (1885-1918): American aviator. 33

Milton, John (1608-1674): English poet. 200

Napoleon (1769-1821): Emperor of France. 107, 177, 288

Pershing, John J. (1860-1948): American general. 9, 13, 49, 135, 173

Pico della Mirandola (1463-1494): Italian humanist. 225

Rousseau, Jean Jacques (1712-1778): French philosopher. 285

Savonarola, Girolamo (1452-1498): Italian reformer and martyr. 288

Sherman, William T. (1820-1891): Union general. 12

Smith, Alfred E. (1873-1944): Governor of New York. 63

Swift, Jonathan (1667-1745): Irish author. 288

Swinburne, Algernon Charles (1837-1909): English poet and critic. 200

Washington, George (1732-1799): President of the United States, 1789-1797. 164

Watson, Tom (1856-1922): American journalist and political leader. 112

Wilcox, Ella (1850-1919): American poet and journalist. 200

Wilson, Woodrow (1856-1924): President of the United States, 1913-1921. 13, 149, 281

BIBLICAL

God: 45, 58, 64, 83, 85, 111, 112, 152, 169, 170, 183, 212, 268, 280, 288, 296, 297, 313, 317, 319

LITERARY/MYTHIC

Achilles: Leader of Greek army at Troy. 7, 46

Ancient Mariner: Character in Coleridge's *The Ancient Mariner*, 1798. 136

Atalanta: Mythological Grecian huntress who would marry only the man who could outrun her in a foot race. 78, 287, 292

Atthis: Girl in Sappho's poetry. 227

Cinderella: Fairy tale character created by Brothers Grimm. 123

Galahad: Knight of King Arthur's Round Table. 289

Jason: Leader of Argonauts. 31

Jove: King of the gods. 147, 200

Jurgen: Central character in James Branch Cabell's *Jurgen*, 1919. 67

Mercury: Messenger of the gods in Roman mythology. 7, 46, 135

Narcissus: Greek youth known for his beauty who fell in love with his own image. 92, 309

Niobe: Mother whose children were killed by Artemis and Apollo. 203

Othello: Character in Shakespeare's play, 1604. 24, 107, 108

Venus: Goddess of love and beauty. 65

THE SOUND AND THE FURY

[New York: Jonathan Cape and Harrison Smith, 1929. 401 pp.]

Ames, Dalton: Caddy Compson's lover. 98, 113, 126, 128, 130, 166, 183, 184, 187, 188, 192, 195-203, 217

Anse: Cambridge, Mass., marshal. 161, 162, 173, 174, 176-179, 181

Bascomb: Mrs. Compson's family name. 127, 225, 273, 279

Bascomb, Maury: Mrs. Compson's brother. 3, 4, 6, 7, 12, 14, 52, 53, 124, 128, 217, 218, 244, 245, 249, 250, 252, 254, 256, 277-280, 326

Beard: Owner of lot in Jefferson. 234

Bland, Mrs.: Gerald Bland's mother. 111-113, 125, 130-132, 175, 176, 181-184, 205, 207, 208, 213

Bland, Gerald: Harvard student. 111, 112, 125, 129-132, 137, 138, 149, 175, 176, 178, 181-185, 203-208
  His grandfather: 183-185

Burgess, Mr.: Compsons' neighbor. 328, 329

Burgess, Mrs.: Compsons' neighbor. 63
  Their daughter: 64, 329

Charlie: Beau of Caddy Compson. 56-58

Clay, Sis Beulah: Negro woman upon whose funeral Frony comments. 39

Compson: Family name. 116, 126-128, 221, 244, 245, 249, 329, 344

Compson, Benjamin (Benjy; Maury): Youngest Compson son. 7 April 1928, 1-12; letter to Mrs. Patterson, 13-18; his birthday, 19-46; Caddy climbs tree, 47-55; Caddy with Charlie, 56, 57; Miss Quentin with beau, 58-62; chases girls, 63-70; name changed, 71-83; pulls at Caddy's dress, 84-89; watches Miss Quentin climb down tree, 90-92; 2 June 1910, 100, 109, 111, 114; pasture sold to send Quentin to Harvard, 116, 124, 126, 127, 131, 138,

The Sound and the Fury   155

  139, 143, 153, 154, 160; paws at Caddy, 185-187, 189, 193,
  195, 196, 198, 210, 211, 215-217, 219, 220; 6 April 1928,
  224, 231, 232, 243-245, 254, 257, 258, 276, 278, 280,
  286, 290, 294, 302, 312, 313, 315, 318, 319, 326, 328,
  329; 8 April 1928, 335-346, 354-359; goes to church with
  Dilsey, 360-364; sermon, 366-368, 370-372, 374-376, 392-
  397; goes for ride, 398-401

Compson, Candace (Caddy): Only daughter of Caroline and Jason
  Compson. 7 April 1928, 3, 5-8; letter to Mrs. Patterson,
  13, 14; sits in branch, 19-23, 26-32, 39, 40, 42-46;
  climbs tree, 47-55; with Charlie, 56-58, 62, 63, 66, 68,
  69; Benjy's name changed, 71, 74-81; Benjy pulls at dress,
  84-90; in bed with Benjy, 91, 92; 2 June 1910, 95-98;
  wedding day, 100, 109, 113; Herbert Head, 114-119, 124,
  126-128, 130, 131; Quentin and Herbert talk, 132, 133-
  139, 142-144, 149, 151-154, 159, 160, 166, 167, 169-172;
  Quentin pleads with her, 183-198, 201-203, 210, 213, 215-
  218; Quentin discusses incest with father, 220, 221; 6
  April 1928, 230, 232; note to Jason, 236, 243-247; in
  cemetery, 250-257; pleads with Jason, 258-267, 272-275,
  278, 286, 290; 8 April 1928, 325-327, 329, 374, 394

Compson, Caroline Bascomb: Wife of Jason Compson. 7 April
  1928, 3, 4, 6, 7; goes to cemetery, 8-12, 14, 19, 20,
  29-32, 37, 40, 49, 50; Mr. Patterson and Maury, 52, 53,
  59, 62, 63, 66, 68, 70; Benjy's name changed, 71-81, 84,
  86-88; locks Miss Quentin in room, 90-92; 2 June 1910,
  95, 114-119; laments situation, 124-128, 133-136, 181,
  187, 193, 210, 211, 213-218, 221; 6 April 1928, 223-233;
  Caddy's baby sent home, 243-251, 253, 254, 256-259, 261-
  263, 266, 269; burns Caddy's check, 272-281; discussed
  by Earl, 283-286, 290, 291, 293-299, 301, 302, 307, 312,
  315-317, 319; talks with granddaughter, 320-328; 8 April
  1928, 332-334, 336-339, 342, 343, 346-349; struggle over
  key to Miss Quentin's room, 350-354, 356, 359, 373-375,
  379, 395, 396

Compson, Jason: Father of Quentin, Caddy, young Jason, Benjy.
  7 April 1928, 7, 12, 14, 27-32, 38, 39, 41, 43-47, 50;
  Mr. Patterson and Maury, 52-54, 63, 75-84, 86, 88, 92;
  2 June 1910, watch given to Quentin, 93-100, 105, 115-
  118; protects women, 119; Mrs. Compson's lamentation,
  124-129, 131, 133, 134, 138, 140, 143, 148, 152, 153;
  his drinking, 154, 159, 166, 184, 185, 187, 198, 214-
  218; conversation with Quentin about incest, 219-222;
  6 April 1928, 224-226; his funeral, 245-248, 250, 252,
  258, 260, 269, 274, 275, 281, 286, 290; 8 April 1928,
  relationship with Quentin and Caddy, 325-327, 339, 379

Compson, Jason: Second son of Caroline and Jason Compson.
7 April 1928, 7, 9, 12; plays at branch, 21-23, 26-28,
30-32, 39, 42, 43, 45, 46; Caddy climbs tree, 47, 49,
52, 54, 59, 63, 66, 69, 73, 76, 77; fights with Caddy,
79-83; argues with niece, 85-92; 2 June 1910, 95; Herbert
Head's promised job, 114, 116, 118, 124; Mrs. Compson
laments her situation, 126-128, 134, 210, 213, 215; with
Patterson boy, 217, 218; 6 April 1928, 223-228; threatens
Miss Quentin with belt, 229-234; at work, 235; note from
Caddy, 236-239; with Lorraine, 240, 241, 242; Caddy
sends infant home, 243, 244; father's funeral, 245-250;
Caddy's desire to see child, 251-261, 262-267; gives money
to Miss Quentin, 268-271; his mother burns Caddy's check,
272-276; letter from Uncle Maury, 277-282; Earl discusses
Mrs. Compson, 283-286, 287; sees Miss Quentin with beau,
288-295; sees car and pursues, 296-301; discovers flat
tires, 302-314; home for dinner, 315, 316; taunts Luster,
317-320; dinner with mother and Miss Quentin, 321-324;
father's relationship with Quentin and Caddie, 325-329;
8 April 1928, 334, 337-340, 343-349; struggles with
mother for key, 350-352; discovers money missing, 353-
357; pursues Miss Quentin and carnival man, 373-385;
attacked by man, 386-392, 399, 400

Compson, Quentin: Son of Jason and Caroline Compson. 7 April
1928, 7, 12; Caddy sits in branch, 19-27, 29-32, 47, 48;
Mr. Patterson and Uncle Maury, 52-55, 76; has been in
fight, 81-83, 88, 90-92; 2 June 1910, at Harvard, 93-
95; Shreve called his husband, 96, 97; breaks watch,
98, 99; Caddy on wedding day, 100, 101; in clock shop,
102-104; buys flat-irons, 105-110; Gerald Bland, 111-
118; protection of women, 119, 120-123; sees Shreve
after class, 124, 125; mother laments her situation,
126-131; talks with Herbert Head, 132-143; at bridge in
Cambridge, 143, 144; three boys fishing, 145-154; at
bakery with little Italian girl, 155-165; with Natalie,
166-169; sees boys swimming, 170-174; rescued by Mrs.
Bland's "party," 175-184; Dalton Ames and Caddy, 185-
202; fights Gerald Bland, 203, 204-212; returns to room,
213-218; talks with father about incest, 219-222; 6 April
1928, 224, 245, 246, 249, 251, 278, 281, 285, 290;
8 April 1928, father's relationship with Caddy and him,
325-327, 352, 373, 374
  His grandfather, Confederate officer: 84, 93, 101, 218, 219
  His great-grandfather, former governor: 93, 125

Compson, Quentin: Caddy's daughter. 10, 35-38, 56; with beau
in swing, 58-62, 67, 81, 82; Benjy hears her quarrel with

The Sound and the Fury 157

Jason, 85-90; 6 April 1928, 223-228; Jason threatens with belt, 229-236, 239, 242; Caddy sends her home, 243, 244, 246-249; Caddy in town, 252-269, 271, 272, 274-277, 281, 286; Jason sees with beau, 288-291, 295; pursued by Jason in car, 297-303, 307, 313, 315-317, 319; dinner with Jason and grandmother, 320-328; 8 April 1928, 338, 344, 346-349, 351; discovered missing, 352, 353, 355, 356; Luster and Benjy see her climb down tree, 357, 372-374; pursued by Jason, 377-380, 382-386, 388-390

Daingerfield, Miss: One of the girls at the Blands' picnic. 175, 180, 181, 184

Damuddy: Grandmother of Compson children. 22, 23, 27, 31, 40, 42, 43, 45, 77, 89, 92, 111, 188

Deacon: Negro handyman at Harvard. 101, 118-125

Dilsey: See Gibson, Dilsey

Earl: Store owner where young Jason Compson works. 234, 235, 237, 238, 242, 243, 261-263, 268, 269, 271, 280, 281; talks with Jason about Mrs. Compson, 283-286, 293, 299, 301, 305, 306, 309-311, 313

Frony: Dilsey's daughter. 34-41; Damuddy's funeral, 43-47, 54, 55, 68, 82, 223, 232, 318; goes to church, 361-364, 366, 371, 372

Gibson, Dilsey: Compsons' cook. 7 April 1928, 2, 3, 7, 9-12, 17, 19-22; after Damuddy's death, 28-39, 41, 43, 51-55, 58, 59, 63; Luster taunts Benjy, 66-70; Benjy's name changed, 71-76, 78, 80-84, 86, 87; puts children to bed, 89-92, 106, 109, 111, 140, 189, 210, 211; 6 April 1928, 223, 227, 228; stops Jason from beating Miss Quentin, 229-232, 243, 244; infant Quentin, 246-249, 254; Caddy in town, 256-258, 271, 275-277, 294, 302, 315-320; 8 April 1928, 330-351; Miss Quentin discovered gone, 352-360; goes to church, 361-364; sermon, 366-368, 370-376, 392-394; comforts Benjy, 395-398

Gibson, Roskus: Dilsey's husband. 9, 10, 19, 22, 23, 33-38, 40, 51, 86, 87, 106, 123, 312

Gibson, T.P.: Son of Dilsey. 9-12; kicked by Quentin, 23-26; funeral, 33-46; Caddy's wedding, 47, 48, 50, 55-57, 62, 63, 100, 185, 187, 197, 218, 223, 232, 244, 290, 372, 392, 395, 396, 398

Gibson, Versh: Son of Dilsey. 3-6, 8, 14; Caddy in branch, 19-35, 37, 39, 42, 44-47, 52, 53; Caddy in tree, 54-56, 70, 72, 75, 76; Benjy's name changed, 84-86, 90, 124, 139; with Quentin and Uncle Louis, 142, 143, 223, 232

Hatcher, Louis: Jefferson Negro. 114, 141, 142

Hatcher, Martha: Louis Hatcher's wife. 141

Head, Sidney Herbert: Caddy Compson's first husband. 114-117, 130, 132-139, 149, 152, 153, 245-247, 253, 274, 275, 290, 327

Henry: Student in Quentin Compson's class in Jefferson. 108

Holmes, Miss: Girl at Blands' picnic. 175, 180, 181

Hopkins: Man in telegraph office. 240

Job, Uncle: Negro who works for Earl. 235-237, 263, 287, 288, 307, 309, 311-313

Julio: Brother of little Italian girl in Massachusetts. 172-176, 178-180

Junkin, Professor: Teacher at Miss Quentin Compson's school. 224

Kenny: One of three boys fishing in Cambridge. 145-153, 169-171, 179, 183

Laura, Miss: Quentin Compson's Jefferson schoolteacher. 108

Little Sister Death: 94, 97

Lorraine: Young Jason Compson's Memphis mistress. 240, 241, 291, 307, 383

Luster: Frony's son. 1-3, 5, 8, 10, 13; looks for quarter, 15-19, 22, 23, 35, 36, 38-40, 42, 55, 56; Miss Quentin and beau, 58-62, 64, 65; teases Benjy, 66-74, 80-82, 85, 89; watches Miss Quentin climb down tree, 90, 91, 223, 231, 232, 272, 275, 276, 294, 313; taunted by Jason, 315-319; in cellar, 334-346, 354-356; saw Miss Quentin, 357-360; goes to church, 361-363, 371, 372, 375, 376, 392-395; drives Benjy in carriage, 396-401

Mac: Man in Jefferson drugstore. 314

The Sound and the Fury   159

MacKenzie, Shreve: Quentin Compson's Harvard roommate. 94,
    95; called Quentin's husband, 96, 99-101, 115, 122;
    meets Quentin after class, 124, 125, 131, 132; discovers
    Quentin arrested, 175-178; goes on picnic, 180-184; after
    Quentin's fight with Gerald Bland, 203-209, 212, 213,
    216, 222

Mike: Gymnasium owner near Cambridge. 206

Mink: Worker in Jefferson livery stable. 254, 255

Myrtle: Jefferson sheriff's daughter. 376, 377

Natalie: Playmate of Compson children. 166-169

Parker: Restaurant owner in Cambridge. 102

Patterson: Man whose wife is having affair with Uncle Maury
    Bascomb. 14, 15, 52

Patterson, Mrs.: Patterson's wife. 13-15

Patterson boy: Young Jason Compson's childhood companion.
    116, 217, 218

Peabody, Doc: Jefferson physician. 159

Rogers: Jefferson restaurant owner. 261, 268

Roskus: See Gibson, Roskus

Russell, Ab: Farmer near Jefferson. 299, 302, 303

Sartoris, Colonel John: Confederate officer. 218, 219

Shegog, Reverend: St. Louis Negro preacher. 361-371

Simmons: Jefferson man who has key to old opera house. 269

Snopes, I.O.: Cotton speculator. 271

Spoade: Harvard classmate of Quentin Compson. 96, 97, 113,
    118, 175-184, 205-208, 213

Thompson: Cafe owner in Cambridge. 97

T.P.: See Gibson, T.P.

Turpin, Buck: Town official who receives ten dollars for allow-
    ing the carnival to play in Jefferson. 287

Vernon: Myrtle's husband; sheriff's son-in-law. 376, 377

Versh: See Gibson, Versh

Walthall, Parson: Jefferson Methodist minister. 308

Wilkie: Blands' Negro servant. 184

Wright, Doc: Cotton speculator. 239, 240, 270, 271

UNNAMED

Little Italian girl who walks with Quentin Compson near Cambridge, Mass. 155-157; walks off with Quentin, 158-171; discovered by Julio, 172-175; sent home, 176, 178, 179, 181, 182

Carnival man with whom Miss Quentin Compson runs away. 56; with Miss Quentin in swing, 58-61, 82; Jason sees with Miss Quentin, 288-291; in car with Miss Quentin, 296-303, 359; Jason pursues, 377-380, 383-386, 388-390, 392

Salesman with whom young Jason Compson discusses farming. 237, 238

Telegraph operator. 239, 270, 282, 291, 293, 304, 305

Jefferson sheriff: Myrtle's father. 376-382

Carnival man who threatens to kill young Jason Compson. 385-390

Cambridge watchmaker. 102-105

Squire who hears case against Quentin Compson about kidnapping. 173, 176-180

Two boys fishing with Kenny. 145-153, 169-171, 179, 183

HISTORICAL

Byron, Lord (1788-1824): English poet. 115

Columbus, Christopher (1451-1506): Italian explorer. 101

De Soto, Hernando (1500?-1542): Spanish explorer. 108

Francis, Saint (1182-1226): Italian friar. 94, 97

Garibaldi, Giuseppe (1807-1882): Italian patriot. 101

Lincoln, Abraham (1809-1865): President of United States, 1861-1865. 120

Maingault: Norman family name. 113

Mortemar: Name of Anglo-Norman family of Welsh marches holding earldoms of March and Ulster; usually spelled Mortimer. 113

Ruth, George Herman "Babe" (1895-1948): American baseball player. 314

Washington, George (1732-1799): President of the United States, 1789-1797. 99

BIBLICAL

Jesus: 35, 94, 97-99, 139, 144, 212, 213, 221, 348, 368-370, 396

Lord: 9, 29, 30, 36, 112, 137, 138, 239, 244, 247, 249, 256-258, 261, 267, 272, 276, 281, 287, 290, 294, 298, 323, 337, 342, 362, 369, 370, 374, 396, 400, 401

Mary: 369

Moses: Old Testament patriarch. 216

LITERARY/MYTHIC

Euboeleus [Eubuleus]: Swineherd of Eleusis who saw one of his swine swallowed up by the earth. 184

Galahad: Knight of King Arthur's Round Table. 136

Leda: Maiden ravished by Zeus in the form of a swan. 207

Lochinvar: Hero of ballad in Sir Walter Scott's *Marmion*, 1808. 115

Santa Claus: 6, 107

Semiramis: Assyrian queen, legendary founder of Babylon. 125

THE TOWN

[New York: Random House, 1957. 371 pp.]

Adams, Mayor: Mayor of Jefferson before Manfred de Spain.
    11-13

Adams, "Miss Eve": Wife of the mayor. 11

Adams, Theron: Youngest son of the mayor. 12, 13

Aleck Sander: Negro friend of Chick Mallison. 45, 52-55, 63,
    111, 181, 244, 310, 311, 337-342, 362

Armstid, Henry: Former farmer in Frenchman's Bend. 7, 8, 34,
    228, 271, 292
  His wife: 292

Backus, Mr.: Father of Melisandre Backus. 50, 178

Backus, Melisandre: Woman whom Gavin Stevens once courted.
    50, 63, 178-180
  Her husband, New Orleans bootlegger: 178
  Her two children: 178

Beauchamp: Family name of early settlers in Yoknapatawpha
    County. 316

Beauchamp, Tomey's Turl: Night fireman of the Jefferson power
    plant. 15-30, 83-86, 142

Benbow: Family name of early settlers in Yoknapatawpha County.
    118, 280

Benbow, Narcissa: See Sartoris, Narcissa Benbow

Best, Henry: Jefferson alderman. 85-87

Binford, Dewitt: Man married to Snopes woman. 365-367, 369

Binford, Mrs. Dewitt: Wife of Dewitt. 365-367

Bird, Tom Tom: Negro day fireman at Jefferson power plant.
    15-30, 83-86, 109, 110, 142
  His wife: 16, 20, 21, 24, 25, 28

Birdsong, Preacher: Country man who boxes with Matt Levitt. 183

Bishop: Boy who dates Linda Snopes in high school. 212

Bookwright, Cal: Father-in-law of Zack Houston. 35, 78, 79

Buffaloe, Mr.: Jefferson electrician. 11-13, 16, 18, 30

Christian, Walter: Negro janitor in Christian's. 155, 159, 160
  His grandfather: 159

Christian, Uncle Willy: Drugstore owner in Jefferson. 60, 154-160, 162, 179, 180, 188, 194, 195, 202, 204, 205, 211, 212, 309, 341, 361, 362
  His grandfather: 159

Clefus: Courthouse janitor. 357

Compson: Family name of early settlers in Yoknapatawpha County. 118, 271, 316

Compson, General: Confederate officer. 69, 231

Compson, Mrs.: Wife of General Compson. 231

Compson, Jason: Jefferson man; grandson of General Compson. 151
  His mother: 151

Connors, Buck: Jefferson marshal. 23, 60, 61, 68, 69, 116, 124, 125, 157, 158, 161, 162, 195, 196, 319, 361-363

Connors, Buck, II: Son of marshal. 53-55

Crenshaw, Jack: Revenue agent in Jefferson. 172-174

De Spain: Family name of early settlers in Yoknapatawpha County. 271, 316

De Spain, Major: Father of Manfred. 10, 14, 43, 58, 117-119, 140, 362

De Spain, Manfred: Jefferson mayor, bank president, and Eula Varner Snopes' lover. 8; background, 10-15, 24, 29, 30, 36, 43, 44, 47, 49, 52; Christmas Cotillion, 56-75; fights Gavin Stevens, 76, 77, 83-87, 92-95, 97-101, 108, 111, 116, 117; Flem becomes V.P. of bank, 118-120, 133-

135, 137-140, 142, 147, 150, 151, 166, 186, 187, 194, 233, 265-267, 270, 272-275; replaces money stolen by Byron Snopes, 277-279, 281, 282, 286, 290, 293-295, 298, 300, 302-304; town's reaction to his affair, 307-309, 311-315, 318, 319, 328-332, 334; after Eula's suicide, 337-342; Eula's funeral, 344, 346-348, 360, 362

Doom: See Ikkemotubbe

Dukinfield, Judge: Jefferson judge. 87, 97

Du Pre, Mrs. Virginia: Bayard Sartoris' sister. 117, 118, 139, 140, 244, 310

Edmonds: Family name of early settlers in Yoknapatawpha County. 280, 316

Edmonds, McCaslin: Roth Edmonds' father. 58

Edmonds, Roth: Son of McCaslin Edmonds. 58

Elma, Miss: Sheriff Hampton's office deputy. 174

Frazier: Family name of early settlers in Yoknapatawpha County. 316

Gant, Miss Eunice: Clerk in Wildermark's store. 199, 200, 214

Garroway, Mr.: Jefferson merchant. 312-315
  His father: 313

Gatewood, Jabbo: Son of Uncle Noon; mechanic. 68, 69

Gatewood, Uncle Noon: Father of Jabbo; blacksmith. 65, 66, 68, 113

Gombault, Mr.: Federal marshal in Jefferson. 165, 166, 174

Gowrie: Family name of early settlers in Yoknapatawpha County. 316

Gowrie, Mr.: Moonshiner. 357

Grenier: Family name of early settlers in Yoknapatawpha County. 271, 316

Grenier, Louis: One of the founders of Jefferson. 323

The Town   165

Guster: Aleck Sander's mother; wife of Top I. 48, 52, 54, 63,
     64, 336-338, 340-342

Habersham: Family name of early settlers in Yoknapatawpha County.
     271, 280, 316

Habersham, Dr.: One of the founders of Jefferson. 323

Habersham, Miss Emily: Jefferson social worker. 370, 371

Habersham, Miss Eunice: Spinster who peddles vegetables. 71,
     118

Hait, Lonzo: Husband of Mannie Hait. 232-235, 241, 243, 248,
     249, 251, 255

Hait, Mannie: Wife of Lonzo Hait. 231; widowed, 232-240; house
     burns, 241-255; shoots mule, 256, 257

Hampton, Hub: Sheriff of Yoknapatawpha. 104, 130; catches
     Montgomery Ward Snopes, 158-166, 172-176, 192, 196, 197,
     257; Byron Snopes' children, 361-364, 367

Harker: Engineer at Jefferson power plant. 9, 15-19, 21-28,
     30, 109, 110

Harker, Otis: Night marshal in Jefferson. 25, 195, 196, 318,
     319, 321, 333, 361

Het: Old Negro woman who helps Mannie Hait. 231, 232, 234,
     237-245, 247, 248, 250-252, 254-256

Hogganbeck, Boon: Father of Lucius Hogganbeck. 58

Hogganbeck, Lucius: Son of Boon Hogganbeck. 58, 59, 71, 101

Hogganbeck, Miss Melissa: History teacher in Jefferson. 288

Holcomb, Ashley: Friend of Chick Mallison. 53-55

Holston: Family name of early settlers in Yoknapatawpha County.
     316

Holston, Alexander: One of the founders of Jefferson. 323

Houston, Letty Bookright: Wife of Zack Houston; daughter of
     Cal Bookwright; she is named Lucy Pate in 1961 Vintage
     printing and 1964 Random House printing. 78, 79

Houston, Zack: Farmer killed by Mink Snopes; he is called Jack on pp. 78 and 82 in later printings; Zack on p. 36. 36, 37, 78-80, 82

Hovis, Mr.: Sartoris bank cashier. 309

Ikkemotubbe (Doom): Son of Issetibbeha's sister. 307, 316
   His mother: 307, 316

Issetibbeha: Chickasaw chief. 307, 316

Job: Janitor of Judge Dukinfield. 97

Killebrew, Miss: Sartoris Bank teller. 309

Kneeland, Mr.: Tailor in Jefferson. 70

Ledbetter, Mrs.: Rockyford woman who buys sewing machine from Ratliff. 295, 296, 298, 299

Levitt, Matt: Suitor of Linda Snopes from Ohio. 183-189; hits Gavin Stevens, 190, 191, 194-198, 202, 204, 212, 285, 287, 325, 364

Littlejohn, Mrs.: Frenchman's Bend boarding house owner. 34, 35

Long, Judge: Federal judge in Jefferson. 165, 168, 169, 171, 172, 174

McCallum: Family name of early settlers in Yoknapatawpha County. 316

McCallum, Anse: Son of Buddy McCallum. 196, 197

McCallum, Buddy: Father of Anse McCallum. 196, 197

McCarron, Hoake: Father of Linda Snopes. 94, 95, 100, 101, 135, 136, 192, 204, 221, 263, 272, 273, 288

McCaslin: Family name of early settlers in Yoknapatawpha County. 271, 316

McCaslin, Ike: Hardware store owner in Jefferson; uncle of Roth Edmonds. 12, 58

McGowan, Skeets: Clerk in Christian's. 156, 160, 162, 180, 207, 361

The Town   167

McLendon, Jackson: Jefferson World War I veteran. 104, 116

Mallison, Charles, I: Father of Chick Mallison. 3, 16, 45-49,
    51-53; Christmas Cotillion, 55-57; De Spain's cut-out,
    58-61, 63, 65, 67-72, 76, 78, 83, 84, 179, 180; Matt
    Levitt and Linda Snopes, 184-187, 198, 200, 206; Manfred
    De Spain, Eula Snopes, and Will Varner, 302-304; after
    Eula V. Snopes' suicide, 336, 341, 343, 344, 357, 364

Mallison, Charles, II (Chick): Gavin Stevens' nephew; son of
    Margaret and Charles Mallison I. 3-14; Flem Snopes
    becomes power-plant supt., 15-29, 45-55; Christmas
    Cotillion, 56-74; G. Stevens fights Manfred De Spain,
    75-77, 103-106; Eck Snopes' death, 107-111; G. Stevens
    returns home, 112-119; "Atelier Monty," 120-132; Mont-
    gomery Ward Snopes caught, 154, 155-176, 178-182; Matt
    Levitt and Linda Snopes, 183-192, 194-197; Linda Snopes'
    graduation gift, 198-201, 205-208, 212, 215; Mannie Hait
    vs. I.O. Snopes, 231-256, 257-261, 301; M. De Spain,
    Eula V. Snopes, and Will Varner, 302-311, 320; after
    Eula's suicide, 336-346, 353, 354; Eula's tombstone,
    355-358; Byron Snopes' children, 359-371
  His grandmother: 45, 72

Mallison, Margaret: Sister of Gavin Stevens; mother of Chick.
    3, 16, 45-49; calls on Eula Snopes, 50-55; Christmas
    Cotillion, 56, 57; De Spain's cut-out, 58-64, 67-74;
    red rose for Gavin, 76-78, 87, 89, 102, 105, 106, 111,
    113, 116, 121, 133, 178-182; Matt Levitt and Linda Snopes,
    183-187, 194; Linda Snopes' graduation gift, 198-201, 205,
    214, 220; M. De Spain, Eula V. Snopes, and Will Varner,
    302-305, 309-311, 319, 334; after Eula's suicide, 336,
    337, 340-346
  Her mother: 89

Muir: Family name of early settlers in Yoknapatawpha County.
    316

Nunnery, Mrs.: Mother of Cedric. 108, 109, 143

Nunnery, Cedric: Small boy; Eck Snopes is killed looking for him.
    108-110, 143

Peabody: Family name of early settlers in Yoknapatawpha County.
    118

Peabody, Dr.: Jefferson physician. 117, 156, 161, 366

Priest, Maurice: Sally Hampton's husband; in 1964 printing changed to Parsons. 77, 78

Priest, Sally Hampton: Wife of Maurice Priest; in 1964 printing changed to Parsons. 70, 77, 78

Provine, Wilbur: Yoknapatawpha man sentenced to penitentiary by Judge Long. 168, 169, 171, 172
  His wife: 168, 169, 172

Quistenberry, Dink: Proprietor of Snopes Hotel. 360, 361
  His wife: 360

Ratliff: Vladimir Kyrilytch: Sewing machine salesman. 3-9; Flem Snopes becomes power-plant supt., 15, 29, 31-40, 43-46; Mink Snopes and Zack Houston, 78-82; G. Stevens' suit against De Spain's bonding company, 83-88, 94, 97-100; G. Stevens leaves for Germany, 101-106; Eck Snopes' death, 107, 111; Stevens returns home from War, 112-116; De Spain becomes bank president, 118-121, 123, 124, 126, 129, 134, 135; Flem Snopes at bank, 138-143, 149-153; Montgomery Ward Snopes caught, 154-158, 162, 166-171, 174-178, 189, 192, 195, 206, 219, 220, 223, 225; discusses Will Varner's will, 227-229; Mannie Hait vs. I.O. Snopes, 231-237, 241-243, 248, 256-258; Flem's ambition, 259-261, 264, 265, 271, 276, 278, 292; Flem's message to Will Varner, 295-300, 308, 318, 320; his ancestry, 322, 323, 331, 335; after Eula's suicide, 339, 342, 343, 346-354; Eula's tombstone, 355-358; Byron Snopes' children, 364-371
  His family: 322, 323

Renfrow: Oil tank owner. 33

Riddell: Family name of highway engineer whose son has polio. 301, 302, 310, 311, 337, 362

Roebuck, John Wesley: Friend of Chick Mallison. 53-55, 130

Rouncewell, Mrs.: Jefferson florist. 70, 71, 73, 77, 122, 199

Rouncewell, Whit: Boy who discovers robbery at Christian's. 160, 212

Samson: Hotel porter. 97
  His boy: 97

Sartoris: Family name of early settlers in Yoknapatawpha County.
    271, 280, 316

Sartoris, Col. Bayard: Son of Col. John Sartoris; president of
    bank. Horses scared by De Spain's car, 11, 13; Byron
    Snopes, 41-43, 104, 106; grandson returns from War, 116-
    119, 136, 137, 139, 140, 147, 151, 164, 169; Flem Snopes'
    attitude about bank presidents, 265-267, 274, 302, 312

Sartoris, Bayard: Grandson of Col. Bayard Sartoris. 104, 116-
    118, 120, 140, 274
  His twin brother killed in World War I: 104, 116, 140

Sartoris, Benbow: Son of young Bayard and Narcissa Benbow
    Sartoris. 244

Sartoris, Col. John: Father of Bayard Sartoris; Confederate
    officer. 4, 41, 42, 117, 140

Sartoris, Narcissa Benbow: Wife of young Bayard Sartoris; mother
    of Benbow Sartoris. 117, 118

Snopes: Family name in Yoknapatawpha County. 5, 8, 9, 31, 33,
    40, 42-46, 51, 79, 95, 102, 106, 107, 112, 114, 120, 126,
    127, 129, 136, 142, 149, 150, 182, 184, 217, 219, 226,
    228, 279, 282, 295, 347, 348, 365

Snopes: "Actual Snopes Schoolmaster"; father of Byron and
    Virgil Snopes. 40, 41

Snopes, Ab: Father of Flem Snopes. 4, 5, 41, 42, 55, 79, 129-
    131, 263
  His daughter: 129

Snopes, Admiral Dewey: Eck Snopes' younger son. 39, 40, 127,
    128, 144, 146

Snopes, Bilbo: Son of I.O. Snopes; twin of Vardaman Snopes.
    37, 39, 129-131

Snopes, Byron: Son of schoolmaster; brother of Virgil Snopes.
    Sent to business school, 41-43, 106, 107; steals money,
    117-119, 138, 140, 141, 262, 264-267, 274, 275, 277,
    278, 347; four children arrive, 359, 361, 364, 370
  His children: 359-371
  His squaw: 361

Snopes, Clarence: I.O. Snopes' oldest son; he is named Doris
    Snopes, Clarence's younger brother, in the 1961 Vintage
    printing on pp. 365, 368, and 369. 37, 39, 365, 368,
    369

Snopes, Eck: Flem Snopes' successor in restaurant; night watch-
    man of oil tank. 5, 8, 31-36, 39, 40, 79, 107-110, 127,
    128, 143, 144, 150, 168, 282
  His mother: 79

Snopes, Mrs. Eck: Wife of Eck Snopes. 32, 39, 40, 110, 127-
    129, 146

Snopes, Eula Varner: Daughter of Will Varner; wife of Flem
    Snopes. 3-10; first seen by M. De Spain, 14-16, 24,
    29, 31, 44, 46-49; visited by Maggie Mallison, 50, 52,
    53, 55; invited to Cotillion, 56, 57, 70; at Christmas
    Cotillion, 73-77; visits Gavin Stevens, 88-96, 99-101,
    119, 132-136; Flem becomes bank vice-president, 142,
    151, 179-181, 184, 189, 194, 205, 211, 214, 217, 218;
    visited by G. Stevens, 219-225; first asks Stevens to
    marry Linda, 226-228, 230, 259-261, 263; Flem's motives
    according to Stevens, 270-274, 276, 283, 286-294, 297,
    298, 300, 304, 307, 308; at beauty shop, 309-311; meets
    Stevens at his office, 313-315, 318-334; commits suicide,
    336-343; her funeral, 344, 346, 348, 349, 351, 354; her
    tombstone, 355; her "boredom," 358, 359

Snopes, Flem: Son of Ab Snopes; husband of Eula Varner Snopes.
    3-9; becomes power-plant supt., 15-20, 22-26, 28-34, 38,
    48, 50, 52, 53; invited to Cotillion, 56, 70, 73, 75,
    77; Mink Snopes, 78-84, 86, 92, 94-96, 99, 118, 120,
    124, 126, 129, 131, 134, 135; bank vice-president, 136-
    143, 146-152; helps to catch Montgomery Ward Snopes,
    166-172, 174-178, 188, 189, 201, 205, 214; refuses to
    allow Linda to leave town, 221-228; Hait vs. Snopes, 245-
    254, 257, 258; respectability, 259-261; his motives and
    actions according to Stevens, 262-295, 296-300, 308,
    309, 312-314, 318-322; his treatment of Linda, 323-330;
    his impotence, 331, 333, 338, 339, 342, 343, 346; bank
    president, 347-349, 351-354; Eula's tombstone, 355, 358-
    360, 364, 365, 367, 369, 370
  His grandfather: 222

Snopes, I.O.: Flem Snopes' cousin; bigamist. Background/
    described, 36-40, 79, 104, 129, 150, 196; vs. Mannie
    Hait, 232-240, 242-245, 247-258, 269, 347, 360, 365

The Town   171

Snopes, Mrs. I.O.: I.O. Snopes' first wife; mother of Monty
     Snopes. 37-40, 104, 129, 365

Snopes, Mrs. I.O.: I.O.'s second wife; mother of Clarence,
     Vardaman, and Bilbo; Mrs. Vernon Tull's sister's niece.
     37-39, 129, 365, 367, 369

Snopes, Linda: Daughter of Eula Varner Snopes and Hoake McCarron.
     3-6, 31, 50, 74, 94, 100; first seen by Gavin Stevens,
     131-135, 179-182; Matt Levitt, 183-196, 198-218; her
     inability to leave town discussed, 219, 221, 223-230,
     259-261, 263, 270, 271, 280; Stevens' speculations about
     Flem Snopes, 283-288, 290-292, 298, 300, 310; discussed
     by Eula and G. Stevens, 320-328, 330-333, 335; Eula's
     suicide, 336, 339-345; Stevens' lie about Flem, 346-
     348; plans for New York, 349-352, 354; Eula's tombstone,
     355, 358

Snopes, Mink: Cousin of Flem Snopes who kills Zack Houston.
     5, 78-82, 166

Snopes, Montgomery Ward: I.O. Snopes' son by first wife. 37-
     39, 104, 105, 107; canteen business, 112-116; atelier
     begun, 120-126, 150, 151; caught, 154, 156, 161-172;
     Flem gives key to G. Stevens, 176, 177, 257, 269, 347

Snopes, Vardaman: Twin of Bilbo Snopes; son of I.O. Snopes.
     37, 39, 129-131

Snopes, Virgil: Son of schoolmaster and brother of Byron
     Snopes. 41

Snopes, Wallstreet Panic: Older son of Eck Snopes. 32, 34,
     35, 39, 40, 110, 127-129, 143-150, 167, 279, 282, 347,
     362

Snopes, Mrs. Wallstreet Panic: Wife of Wall Snopes. 146-150,
     279, 282
  Her father: 148, 149

Spilmer, Mr.: Resident of Jefferson. 253

Stevens: Family name of early settlers in Yoknapatawpha County.
     316

Stevens, Gavin: Uncle of Chick Mallison; city attorney. 3-8,
     11, 13; Flem Snopes becomes power-plant supt., 15, 16,
     19, 20, 24, 27, 29-55; Cotillion Ball invitations, 56,

57; De Spain's cut-out, 58-65, 68-70; receives De Spain's "corsage," 71, 72; at Ball, 73, 74; fights De Spain, 75-78, 81, 82; suit against De Spain's Bonding Co., 83-88; refuses Eula V. Snopes, 89-96, 97-102; goes to Germany, 103-107, 111; returns from War, 112-116, 119-129; first sees Linda Snopes, 131-135; Flem Snopes becomes bank vice-president, 136-153; helps to catch Montgomery Ward Snopes, 154, 156, 161-182; Matt Levitt and Linda Snopes, 183-191, 192-195; graduation gift for Linda, 198-201, 202-218; visits Eula Snopes about Linda, 219-227, 228-230; Mannie Hait vs. I.O. Snopes, 231, 233, 244-248, 250-258; Flem's "respectability," 259-261; speculates about Flem's actions and motives, 262-295, 296, 298, 302-305, 309-318; Eula's last visit, 319-334, 335; Eula's death, 336-338, 340-343; Eula's funeral, 344, 345; lies to Linda about father, 346-348; plans for Linda to leave, 349-354; Eula's tombstone, 355-358; Byron Snopes' children, 359, 362, 364-366

Stevens, Gowan: Gavin Stevens' young cousin. 3, 11; joins night shift at power plant, 16, 22, 24-28, 45-53, 55-57; De Spain's cut-out, 59-69; Cotillion, 71-78, 81; eats ice cream with Ratliff, 105-107, 111, 112, 114, 116, 133, 186
  His mother: 3, 105, 111
  His father: 3, 105, 111
  His grandfather: 3

Stevens, Judge Lemuel: Father of Gavin Stevens and Maggie Mallison. 3, 4, 16, 41, 45, 46, 48, 49, 51, 52, 56; De Spain's cut-out, 58-61, 67, 78, 83, 86, 87; presides in Stevens vs. De Spain's Bonding Co., 97-99, 102, 113, 117, 181, 190, 344, 345

Sutpen: Name of early settler in Yoknapatawpha County. 316

Thorndyke, Mr.: Episcopal minister. 342, 343

Tom: Sartoris bank customer. 139

Top I: Husband of Guster; called "Big Top." 52

Top II: Aleck Sander's older brother; called "Top Little Top." 52, 64-68

Trumbull: Frenchman's Bend blacksmith. 36, 38

The Town

Tull, Vernon: Frenchman's Bend farmer. 39, 365-367

Tull, Mrs. Vernon: Wife of Vernon Tull whose sister's niece by marriage is wife of I.O. Snopes. 38

Varner: Family name of early settlers in Yoknapatawpha County. 271, 317

Varner, Eula: See Snopes, Eula Varner

Varner, Jody: Will Varner's son. 5, 6, 32, 227, 273, 294, 295, 299, 308, 328, 343, 344, 369

Varner, Will: Father of Jody Varner and Eula Varner Snopes. Flem Snopes' start, 5-8, 32; growth of Snopeses, 36-38, 79, 81, 82; Stock in bank, 117-119, 137, 147, 151; Eula and G. Stevens discuss Linda, 224, 225, 227, 228, 260, 261; Flem's motives according to G. Stevens, 263, 265, 271, 273-278, 283, 286, 288-295, 297-300, 303, 304, 308, 309, 311, 313; Eula's final talk with G. Stevens, 319-321, 326, 328, 333, 334; after Eula's death, 338, 339, 343, 351, 365

Varner, Mrs. Will: Wife of Will. 227, 276, 292-295, 297-300, 320, 329, 343, 344

Weddel, Grenier: Young bachelor whom Sally Hampton rejected for Maurice Priest. 70, 73, 77

Widrington, Mrs.: Wealthy newcomer to Jefferson. 362, 364

Wildermark: Dry-goods store owner in Jefferson who plays chess. 198, 200, 234, 306

Winbush, Grover Cleveland: Partner in restaurant with Flem Snopes. 3, 4, 8, 43, 88, 93, 124-126, 154, 156-163, 166, 167, 174, 195, 297
  His mother: 167

Wyott, Dr.: Atheist president emeritus of Jefferson Academy. 306
  His grandfather: 306

Wyott, Miss Vaiden: Second-grade teacher to whom Wallstreet Panic Snopes proposes. 127, 128, 143-146

UNNAMED

Young bonding man who checks for missing brass. 83, 87, 97, 98

Older bonding man. 83-87, 97, 98

Chinese laundryman in Jefferson. 306

Two Jewish brothers who live in Jefferson. 306

Tenant farmer who asks Flem Snopes about moving his money out of the bank. 268, 269, 277, 278, 280

Two strangers who rob Christian's. 154, 156-158, 160

Auditors who check for the missing brass. 21, 22, 31

Second group of auditors. 118, 119

Texan with spotted horses. 7, 34

Col. Bayard Sartoris' driver. 11

HISTORICAL

Attila (406?-453): King of the Huns. 35

Bach, Johann Sebastian (1685-1750): German composer. 103

[Barnes, Djuna (1892-)]: American poet and novelist. 317

Beethoven, Ludwig van (1770-1827): German composer. 103

Blackbeard (?-1718): English privateer who became pirate. 205

Bouillon, Godfrey de (1061?-1100): French crusade leader. 13

Brown, John (1800-1859): American abolitionist. 40

Burgoyne, John (1722?-1792): British general. 323

Caesar, Julius (100?-44 B.C.): Roman general and emperor. 12, 30, 49

Campion, Thomas (1567-1620): English poet and musician. 204

The Town 175

Capone, Al (1899-1947): American gangster. 178

Coolidge, Calvin (1872-1933): President of the United States, 1923-1929. 312, 313

Donne, John (1572-1631): English poet. 188, 189, 325

Einstein, Albert (1879-1955): German/American physicist. 159

Genghis Khan (1162-1227): Mongol leader. 35

Goethe, Johann Wolfgang von (1749-1832): German poet. 103

Grable, Betty (1916-1973): American film star. 14

Grant, Ulysses S. (1822-1885): Union general; President of United States, 1869-1877. 352

Handy, William C. (1873-1958): American Negro musician and composer. 72

Harlow, Jean (1911-1937): American film star. 14

Herrick, Robert (1591-1674): English poet. 204

Homer: Greek epic poet. 192

Horace (65-8 B.C.): Roman poet and satirist. 178

Jonson, Ben (1573?-1637): English dramatist. 204

Lao T'se (c.604-531 B.C.): Chinese philosopher. 362

Lee, Robert E. (1807-1870): Confederate general. 288

Messalina (?-48 A.D.): Third wife of Emperor Claudius. 205

Monroe, Marilyn (1926-1962): American film star. 14

Richard I (1157-1199): King of England. 13

Schiller, Johann (1759-1805): German poet. 103

Smith, Alfred E. (1873-1944): Governor of New York. 314

Stone, Phil (1893-1967): Oxford lawyer. 326-328
  His father: 327

Tamerlane (1336?-1405): Turkish conqueror. 35

Tancred (1078?-1112): Norman leader in First Crusade. 13

Virgil (70-19 B.C.): Roman poet. 178

Wagner, Richard (1813-1883): German composer. 89, 95

Webster, Noah (1758-1843): American lexicographer. 142

BIBLICAL

Adam: First man in Genesis. 44

Christ: 343

Devil: 350

Eve: Adam's wife in Genesis. 44

God: 11, 44, 88, 136, 168, 245, 270, 286, 316, 340, 364

Samson: Hebrew judge of great strength betrayed by Delilah in Judges. 278

LITERARY/MYTHIC

Guinevere: King Arthur's queen. 101

Helen: Wife of Menelaus. 44, 101-105, 114, 133, 205

Isolde: Tristram's beloved. 101

Juliet: Character in Shakespeare's *Romeo and Juliet*, 1594-1595. 101

Launcelot: Knight of King Arthur's Round Table. 101

Lilith: In medieval Jewish folklore the first wife of Adam. 44, 319

Paris: Prince of Troy. 101

Pistol: Follower of Falstaff in Shakespeare's *Merry Wives of Windsor*, 1599-1600; *Henry IV*, Part II (1597-98); *Henry V*, 1599. 205

Romeo: Character in Shakespeare's *Romeo and Juliet*, 1594-1595. 101

Santa Claus (Santy Claus): 352

Semiramis: Assyrian queen; legendary founder of Babylon. 44, 50, 133

Tristram: Knight sent to escort Isolde to her intended but who unwittingly falls in love with her. 101

THE UNVANQUISHED

[New York: Random House, 1938. 293 pp.]

Benbow: Jefferson family name. 229

Benbow, Judge: Jefferson lawyer. 259

Benbow, Cassius Q. (Uncle Cash): Former slave of Benbows who runs for marshal. 228, 229, 232, 234, 241, 253

Bowden, Matt: One of Grumby's gang who turns against Grumby. 189-193, 195, 203-209

Bowen, Captain: Union officer. 132

Breckbridge, Gavin: Fiancé of Drusilla Hawk who is killed at Shiloh. 101, 217-219, 227, 263

Bridger: One of Grumby's gang. 204-207, 209

Burdens: Two men killed by John Sartoris. 229, 232, 234, 236, 253, 257

Compson, General: Confederate officer in Civil War. 222, 282

Compson, Mrs.: Wife of General Compson; friend of Rosa Millard. 52, 80; Granny borrows hat, 87, 88, 92, 117, 120, 122, 127, 147, 148, 153, 155, 156, 178, 180, 211; helps to marry Drusilla Hawk to John Sartoris, 218, 220-224, 226, 227

Cook, Celia: Young girl who scratches her name on windowpane in Oxford. 17

Dick, Colonel Nathaniel G.: Union officer. 34-38, 88, 89, 120, 124, 125, 145, 146

Du Pre, Virginia Sartoris (Aunt Jenny): Younger sister of John Sartoris. 247, 251, 253, 254, 259; compared to Drusilla, 263, 265, 267, 268; her past, 270-273, 275-282, 291, 292
  Her husband: 263, 271

Fortinbride, Brother: Preacher who served in Col. John Sartoris' regiment. 152-158, 177-180

The Unvanquished   179

Grumby: Leader of renegade gang. 170-172; pursued by Bayard,
    Ringo, and Uncle Buck, 183, 184, 187, 191-193, 195, 198,
    201, 203; turned over to Bayard and Ringo, 204-210, 213,
    218, 248, 251, 254, 261, 283, 287

Habersham: Jefferson bank clerk. 253

Habersham, Martha: Wife of bank clerk. 215, 216, 223-225, 227,
    232, 234, 235, 241, 253

Harrison, Sergeant: Union soldier. 28-30, 32-37, 51, 251

Hawk, Dennison, I: Father of Drusilla and Denny Hawk. 15, 97,
    217, 219, 230, 231, 233

Hawk, Dennison, II (Cousin Denny): Drusilla Hawk's younger
    brother. 98-103, 105, 106, 113, 116, 147, 156, 219, 220,
    230, 232, 233, 236, 240; married, 292

Hawk, Drusilla: See Sartoris, Drusilla Hawk

Hawk, Louisa (Louise): Mother of Drusilla and Denny Hawk. At
    Hawkhurst, 98, 105, 106, 170, 215-224, 227; arrives at
    Sartoris, 230-236, 239-241

Hilliard: Livery-stable man in Oxford. 250

Holston, Mrs.: Jefferson lady. 237

Jingus: Hawk family slave. 98-101

Joby: Ringo's grandfather and Sartoris slave. 4, 8, 12-14,
    16; background, 18, 19, 22-27, 29; helps to dig up silver,
    42-50; drives wagon on aborted trip to Memphis, 51, 61-
    67, 80, 81, 84, 88-90, 135, 141, 162, 163, 165, 166, 174,
    183; Bayard and Ringo return home, 212, 213; War over,
    221, 224-227, 231; after John Sartoris' death, 251, 263,
    279

Loosh: Joby's son and Ringo's uncle; Sartoris slave. 4-6, 8-
    10, 12-14, 16, 19, 22-27; helps to dig up silver, 41-46,
    48-51; shows Yankees where silver is buried, 84, 85, 89,
    90, 104, 125, 142, 155, 246; at Sartoris, 279

Louvinia: Joby's wife and Sartoris slave. 8, 12, 13, 15, 16,
    19, 20; told to watch Loosh, 23-27, 29-31, 34-38, 42-
    48, 51, 58, 82; tells of John Sartoris' escape, 83, 84,
    86, 88-90, 99, 106, 133, 134, 141, 142, 155, 174, 211,

212; War over, 221, 226, 227, 236, 241; after John
Sartoris' death, 270, 273, 275, 276, 278, 279, 281, 293

McCaslin, Amodeus (Uncle Buddy): Twin of Theophilus McCaslin
who becomes sergeant in Tennant's Brigade in Virginia.
52-57

McCaslin, Theophilus (Uncle Buck): Twin of Amodeus who helps
Bayard and Ringo track Ab Snopes and Grumby. Sees Bayard
and Ringo in town, 52-61, 89, 159, 172; at Rosa Mallard's
funeral, 179-192; shot, 193-202, 207; Bayard and Ringo
return home, 211-213, 254, 259
  Their father: 52

Marengo (Ringo): Sartoris slave; companion of Bayard. 3-20;
helps to shoot Yankee's horse, 21-40; aborted trip to
Memphis, 41-52, 61-89; goes to get silver back, 90-103,
105-113, 116-136, 138, 139; as Granny's partner, 141-
149, 151-153, 156-163, 165-170, 172-175, 177-180; avenges
Granny's death with Bayard, 181-203; Grumby turned over
to them, 204-213, 216-220; War over, 221, 224-230, 232,
235, 236, 241; goes for Bayard after John Sartoris is
killed, 244-246, 248-252, 254, 267, 271, 279; rides with
Bayard into Jefferson, 282, 283, 289-291

Millard, Rosa (Granny): Mother-in-law of John Sartoris; sister
of Louisa Hawk. Ringo makes up names--Mary Harris, 146,
and Plurella Harris, 146, 149, for her to use. 7-12,
16-18, 20-22, 26-29; hides Bayard and Ringo, 30-39, 41-
50; aborted trip to Memphis, 51, 52, 61-67, 70-74, 77,
80-82, 84-86; goes after silver, mules, and Negroes,
87-99, 101, 103-106, 114, 117-134; partnership with Ab
Snopes, 135-175; her funeral, 177-181, 183, 184, 186,
187, 194, 198, 199, 203, 206, 209; her murder avenged,
211-213, 217-219, 221-223, 230, 233, 246-248, 250, 251
  Her sister in Memphis: 64

Missy Lena: Hawk family slave. 112

Mitchell, Unc Few: Man who is described by Louvinia as "loony."
83

Newberry, Col. G.W.: Union commander. 141, 145, 147, 149

Philadelphy: Loosh's wife and Sartoris slave. 4-6, 16, 24,
25, 27, 85, 86, 125

The Unvanquished   181

Redmond, Ben: Lawyer and former partner of Col. John Sartoris.
    251, 254, 258-260, 261, 266, 268, 276, 283-289

Ringo: See Marengo

Sartoris, Bayard, I: Brother of Col. John Sartoris and Virginia
    Du Pre. 271

Sartoris, Bayard, II: Son of Col. John Sartoris. 3-28; shoots
    Yankee's horse, 29, 30-50; aborted trip to Memphis, 51,
    52, 57-86; goes after silver, mules, and Negroes, 87-103,
    105-134; Granny's partnership with Ab Snopes, 135, 136,
    140-154, 156, 158-163, 165-170, 172-175; Granny's funeral,
    177-209; avenges Granny's murder, 210-213, 215-220; War
    over, 221, 223-241; after John Sartoris' death, 243-284;
    confronts Redmond, 285-293. Bayard is narrator of the
    seven sections of the novel.

Sartoris, Drusilla Hawk: Second wife of Col. John Sartoris.
    100; death of Gavin Breckbridge, 101, 102-106, 109-114;
    asks Bayard's help with joining troop, 115-118, 120-122;
    rides with John Sartoris' troop, 170, 212, 213, 215-219;
    War over, 220-222, 224-237; made voting commissioner,
    238-242, 247, 252-254, 256, 257, 261; kisses Bayard,
    262-265; after husband's death, 268-276, 278, 280, 281,
    284, 288, 291; leaves for Montgomery, 292, 293

Sartoris, Colonel John: Confederate officer; father of Bayard
    Sartoris II. 6-8; returns home after Vicksburg falls,
    9-21, 23, 25, 27, 30, 40, 42, 44, 45, 48, 49, 51, 52,
    54-61, 64, 69-74; captures Yankees, 75-80; escapes Yankees,
    81-85, 89, 91, 101, 103, 105, 107, 108, 112, 113, 115,
    116, 120, 136, 139, 140, 142, 145, 152-155; Drusilla
    with his troop, 170, 172, 174, 180, 212, 213, 215-217,
    219; War over, 220-235; kills Burdens, 236-242; after his
    death, 244-246, 249-257; his partnership with Redmond,
    258-268, 270-272, 276, 277, 279, 284, 285, 291
   His first wife and Bayard II's mother: 17, 219, 233

Simon: Ringo's father and son of Joby. 18, 19, 277-279

Snopes, Ab: Horse thief and Rosa Millard's "partner." 135;
    John Sartoris' orders, 136, 137-141, 143, 146-149, 151,
    152, 157-159, 161-169; convinces Rosa Millard to deal
    with Grumby, 170-173, 177, 180, 182-186, 192, 193, 195;
    discovered by Bayard, Ringo, and Uncle Buck, 197-201,
    211, 212

Sutpen, Colonel: Confederate officer who is elected by the
    regiment as Col. John Sartoris' successor. 58, 59, 255,
    256
  His son: 255
  His daughter: 255

Thorndyke, Ptolemy: Fictional Scottish author. 18

White, Jud: Man in Col. John Sartoris' old regiment. 288, 292

Wilkins, Mrs.: Wife of Professor Wilkins. 243-248, 281

Wilkins, Professor: Law instructor at Oxford with whom Bayard
    Sartoris II lives. 243-249, 266
  His son: 247

Worsham, Doctor: Minister at Sartoris' church before Civil
    War. 153, 154, 156

Wyatt, George: Man in Col. John Sartoris' old regiment. 237-
    239, 241, 254, 258, 260, 261, 267-270, 276, 283-285, 287-
    289

UNNAMED

Yankee lieutenant who looks for mules at Sartoris. 148-150,
    159-166

Confederate captain with Buck McCaslin in Jefferson. 52, 58-
    60, 159

Hill man whom John Sartoris killed. 254, 255
  His family: 255

Fiancé of Col. Sutpen's daughter. 255

HISTORICAL

Barksdale, William (1821-1863): Confederate general. 17

Coke, Edward (1552-1634): English jurist. 18

Cooper, James Fenimore (1789-1851): American novelist. 18

Crockett, David (1786-1836): Congressman and backwoodsman.
    281

The Unvanquished   183

Davis, Jefferson (1808-1889): President of Confederacy. 163

Dumas, Alexandre (1802-1870): French novelist. 18

Forrest, Nathan Bedford (1821-1877): Confederate general. 17,
    136, 145, 163, 171, 173, 207

Grant, Ulysses S. (1822-1885): Union general; President of
    United States, 1869-1877. 7, 140, 145, 159

Jackson, Thomas J. "Stonewall" (1824-1863): Confederate
    general. 58

Johnston, Joseph E. (1807-1891): Confederate general. 78

Josephus, Flavius (37-100?): Jewish historian. 18

Lee, Robert E. (1807-1870): Confederate general. 163

Lincoln, Abraham (1809-1865): President of United States, 1861-
    1865. 140, 145, 228

Littleton, Thomas (1407?-1481): English jurist. 18

Morgan, John Hunt (1825-1864): Confederate general. 17

Napoleon (1769-1821): Emperor of France. 14, 18

Pemberton, John C. (1818-1881): Confederate general. 7, 20

Scott, Walter (1771-1832): Scottish novelist. 18

Sevier, John (1745-1815): American pioneer and governor of
    Tennessee. 281

Sherman, William T. (1820-1891): Union general. 25, 26, 104,
    253

Smith, Andrew J. (1815-1897): Union general. 136, 137, 145-
    147

Taylor, Jeremy (1613-1667): English prelate and author. 18

Van Dorn, Earl (1820-1863): Confederate general. 7, 17

BIBLICAL

Cain: Son of Adam; slayer of Abel in Genesis. 246

Jesus: 96, 154, 249

Lord: 32, 39, 41, 54, 56, 85, 106, 128, 154, 155, 180, 254, 273

Lucifer: 274

THE WILD PALMS

[New York: Random House, 1939. 339 pp.]

Bledsoe: Man who works with livestock at Parchman. 326

Bradley: Neighbor of Harry Wilbourne and Charlotte Rittenmeyer at lake. 99, 106-109

Bradley, Mrs.: Wife of Bradley. 108

Buckner, Billie: Wife of Buck Buckner. 179-183, 190, 192-196, 203, 206, 209

Buckner, Buck: Utah mine manager. 179-181; meets Harry and Charlotte, 182, 183-194; Harry agrees to perform abortion, 195; leaves mine, 196-198, 200, 203; letter to Wilbourne, 204, 206, 209, 219

Buckworth, Warden: Deputy warden at Parchman. 76, 77, 79, 80, 325-331

Callaghan: Utah mine owner. 127-129, 182, 183, 195, 201

Cofer: Real estate agent. 6-8, 11, 17

Crowe: Host at party in New Orleans where Charlotte Rittenmeyer and Harry Wilbourne meet. 36, 44

De Montigny: Man from whom Flint borrows a dress suit. 35, 36

Doc: Part owner of McCord's lakeside cabin. 97

Flint: Harry Wilbourne's intern friend who loans him a dress suit. 34-37, 40, 44, 45

Gillespie: Part owner of McCord's lakeside cabin. 97

Gower, Mr.: District attorney. 317-320

Hamp: Man in warden's office whom Buckworth suggests could be judge in mock trial of Tall Convict. 328

Hogben: Man at Utah mine who runs ore train. 188, 202

Louisa: Maid in brothel where Harry Wilbourne goes to find help for Charlotte Rittenmeyer. 210-212

McCord: Chicago newspaperman who is friend of Harry Wilbourne
and Charlotte Rittenmeyer. 88-90, 96; offers cabin to
Harry and Charlotte, 97-104, 113, 116-118; Harry and
Charlotte back in Chicago, 120, 121, 123, 124, 129;
discussion with Harry, 130-141, 226

Martha: Physician's wife at beach. 3-10, 12, 14, 15, 19, 282,
283, 288-293

Pete: Mexican employee in brothel where Harry Wilbourne goes
to find medicine. 213, 214

Ralph: Charlotte Rittenmeyer's brother. 40, 48, 82, 223

Richardson, Dr.: Physician who attends Charlotte Rittenmeyer
when she dies. 294, 296, 298, 300, 301, 303, 307

Rittenmeyer, Ann: Younger daughter of Charlotte and Rat Rittenmeyer. 40, 42, 48, 124, 126, 221, 222, 227, 228, 311

Rittenmeyer, Charlotte (Charley): Wife of Rat Rittenmeyer.
At beach after abortion, 5-9, 11-18, 20-22; first meets
Harry, 31, 38-42; begins affair with Harry, 43, 44-50;
leaves with Harry for Chicago, 53-60; in Chicago, 81-98;
at lake, 99-118; back in Chicago, 119-137, 139-141; in
Utah at mine, 179-183, 191-203; tells Harry she is pregnant, 204-208; leaves mine, 209-211, 215-220; visits Rat,
221-228; at beach in Mississippi, 279, 284-291, 293,
294; in hospital, 296, 298, 301, 305, 306, 312, 314,
320, 323, 324
    Her father and brothers: 40, 82, 88

Rittenmeyer, Charlotte, II: Older daughter of Charlotte and
Rat Rittenmeyer. 40, 42, 48, 124, 126, 221, 222, 227,
228, 311

Rittenmeyer, Francis (Rat): Husband of Charlotte Rittenmeyer.
21, 38, 39; meets Harry Wilbourne, 40, 42-44, 47, 48;
with Charlotte at train station, 53-59, 82, 90, 95, 101;
visited by Charlotte, 221-226, 228, 288, 297, 298; pays
Harry's bond, 311-313; pleads for Harry at trial, 318-321; brings cyanide to Harry in jail, 322, 323

Waldrip, Mrs. Vernon: Tall Convict's ex-girlfriend. 338, 339

Wilbourne, Dr.: Harry's father. 31, 32

The Wild Palms

Wilbourne, Harry: Charlotte Rittenmeyer's lover. At beach
    after abortion, 5-12; asks doctor's help, 13-22; back-
    ground, 31-37; meets Charlotte, 38, 39-42; becomes Char-
    lotte's lover, 43, 44-50; discovers wallet, 51, 52;
    leaves for Chicago, 53-60; in Chicago, 81-98; at lake,
    99-118; back in Chicago, 119-129; discussion with McCord,
    130-141; in Utah at mine, 179-181; meets Buckners, 182,
    183-194; agrees to perform first abortion, 195; Buckners
    leave mine, 196, 197-203; Charlotte reveals her preg-
    nancy, 204-208; leaves mine, 209-220; in Louisiana, 221-
    228; in Mississippi, 279-294; in hospital, 295-307; in
    jail, 307-310; Rat pays bond, 311, 312-316; in court,
    317, 318, 320-321; visited by Rat in jail, 322-324
  His mother: 31
  His older half sister: 31-33, 50, 52, 86, 111, 208
  His brother-in-law: 33, 53, 111
  His younger half sister: 31

UNNAMED

Tall Convict. Background, 23-25, 27, 28; sent to help with flood,
    61-76; reported missing, 77-80; 143-146; rescues preg-
    nant woman, 147-163; meets people in other boat, 164,
    165-176; infant born, 177; on land, 229, 230-251; with
    Cajan, 252-278; discussion about his fate, 326-330; in
    jail, 331-339

Short, plump Convict at Parchman. Background, 25-29; sent to
    help with flood, 61-76; reports Tall Convict's disappear-
    ance, 77-80, 143, 145, 146, 150; listens to Tall Convict,
    161, 162, 165, 171, 172, 239, 240, 242, 247, 255, 260,
    275, 276; in jail, 331-339

Woman whom Tall Convict rescues. 75, 77, 78; rescued, 147-154,
    156, 161-172, 174-176; infant born, 177; with Tall Con-
    vict on land, 229-236, 239, 242, 243, 245, 246, 250;
    at Cajan's, 252-256, 260, 263, 265-272, 275, 276; Tall
    Convict surrenders, 278, 326, 332-337
  Her infant: 177, 231-233, 235, 239, 240, 243, 245, 246, 249,
    250, 252, 260, 263, 264, 270, 272, 276, 278, 332, 334,
    336

The Cajan with whom the Tall Convict hunts. 252-269, 275

Doctor married to Martha from whom Charlotte Rittenmeyer and
    Harry Wilbourne rent beach house. 3-22, 279-283, 285,
    288-294
  His father: 3, 4

Governor's young man/emissary. 325-330

Warden at Parchman. 77-80, 252, 325-330

Man on cottonhouse whom Tall Convict is sent to rescue. 75-79, 150, 152, 165, 326

Governor. 80, 325, 327, 330

Madam of brothel where Harry Wilbourne goes to find help for Charlotte Rittenmeyer. 211-213

HISTORICAL

Ahenobarbus: Name of plebeian Roman family which ended with Emperor Nero. 29

Alcott, Louisa May (1832-1888): American writer. 254

Anthony, Saint (c.250-350): First Christian monk. 103

Boone, Daniel (1734-1820): American backwoodsman. 122

Capone, Al (1899-1947): American gangster. 338

Carson, Kit (1809-1869): American trapper and frontiersman. 87

Crawford, Joan (1908-1977): American film actress. 209

Cyrano de Bergerac (1619-1655): French poet and soldier; central character in Rostand's *Cyrano*, 1898. 91

Dante (1265-1321): Italian poet. 187

Eisenstein, Sergei (1898-1948): Russian film producer and director. 187

Franz Josef (1830-1916): Emperor of Austria, 1848-1916. 98

Garbo, Greta (1906-): American film actress. 149

Gershwin, George (1898-1937): American composer. 36

Hoover, Herbert (1874-1964): President of United States, 1929-1933. 29

Jackson, Andrew (1767-1845): President of United States, 1829-1837. 277

The Wild Palms 189

James, Jesse (1847-1882): American outlaw. 23

Masters, Edgar Lee (1869-1950): American poet. 119

Napoleon (1769-1821): Emperor of France. 277

Nero (37-68): Roman emperor. 87

Nijinsky, Waslav (1890-1950): Russian dancer. 87

O'Leary, Mrs.: Woman whose cow supposedly started Chicago fire on 8 October 1871. 87

Roosevelt, Franklin D. (1882-1945): President of United States, 1933-1945. 211

Sandburg, Carl (1878-1967): American poet. 119

Schopenhauer, Arthur (1788-1860): German philosopher. 100

Teasdale, Sara (1884-1933): American poet. 100, 103

Vanderbilt, Cornelius (1794-1877): American transportation and finance magnate. 7

Whitman, Walt (1819-1892): American poet. 119

Wister, Owen (1860-1938): American writer. 287

BIBLICAL

Abraham: Old Testament patriarch in Genesis. 255

Adam: First man in Genesis. 109

God: 82, 93, 100, 114, 119, 136, 280

Isaiah: Hebrew prophet. 143

Moses: Old Testament patriarch. 35

Satan: 280

Solomon: King of Israel. 45

LITERARY/MYTHIC

Diamond Dick: Character in dime novels created by George Charles Jenks (1850-1929). 23

Don Juan: Legendary hero of Spain; subject of many authors, especially Byron. 45

Don Quixote: Central character in Cervantes' *Don Quixote*, 1605, 1615. 91

Falstaff: Character in Shakespeare's plays, *Merry Wives of Windsor*, 1599-1600; 1 & 2 *Henry IV*, 1597-1598. 91

Helen: Wife of Menelaus. 149

Hercules: Greek hero of great strength. 262

Lilith: Adam's first wife in Hebrew folklore. 115

Lothario: Character in Rowe's *The Fair Penitent*, 1703. 82

Medusa: Gorgon who could turn viewer into stone. 289

Micawber: Character in Dickens' *David Copperfield*, 1849-1850. 93

Roxane: Cyrano's beloved. 91

Santa Claus: 119

Venus: Goddess of love and beauty. 136

Short Fiction

"AD ASTRA"

In (I) *American Caravan IV*, ed. Alfred Kreymborg, Lewis Mumford, and Paul Rosenfeld (New York: Macaulay, 1931), pp. 164-181; (II) *These 13*, 1931; (III) *Collected Stories*, 1950.

Bland: American from the South who is in the Royal Flying Corps (World War I). (I) 164-171, 173-181; (II) 50-66, 68, 69, 71, 74-80; (III) 407-418, 420, 421, 423, 425-429

Comyn: Irishman in RFC. (I) 164-171, 173-179; (II) 50-56, 58-64, 67-69, 71-78; (III) 407-411, 413-416, 419-421, 423-427

Franz: Captured German flyer's brother who served in German army. (I) 171-174; (II) 64-67; (III) 417-420

Hume: Man who is reported to have said that Sartoris must have shot down the German who shot down his brother. (I) 169; (II) 60; (III) 414

Monaghan: American pilot in RFC. (I) 166-171, 174-179; (II) 54-64, 68-78; (III) 410-417, 420-427
  His father: (I) 170, 171; (II) 61-63; (III) 415-417
  His grandfather: (I) 170; (II) 61; (III) 415

Sartoris: American from the South who is in RFC. (I) 164-167, 169, 174-181; (II) 50-52, 54-56, 58-60, 63, 64, 69, 71-74, 79, 80; (III) 407-411, 413, 414, 421, 423-425, 428, 429
  His twin brother who was killed in war: (I) 169; (II) 59; (III) 414

UNNAMED

Narrator who is American in RFC. (I) 164-181; (II) 50-80; (III) 407-429

American military policeman with Monaghan and captured German flyer. (I) 168-171, 173-177; (II) 56, 60, 62, 66, 68-73; (III) 412, 414, 415, 419-424

The subadar who fought for the British in World War I. (I) 164-169, 173-175, 177-181; (II) 50-56, 58, 59, 63, 64, 66, 68, 69, 71-80; (III) 407-411, 413, 419-421, 423-429

Captured German flyer with Monaghan.   (I) 166-180; (II) 54-60, 63-70, 72-78; (III) 410-427
   His wife and child: (I) 168, 171, 172, 174, 179; (II) 58, 63, 65, 67, 76, 77; (III) 412, 417, 418, 420, 426
   His father: (I) 172; (II) 64, 65; (III) 417, 418
   His mother: (I) 174; (II) 67; (III) 420
   His brother in Berlin: (I) 171, 172; (II) 64, 65; (III) 417, 418
   His brother, a cadet: (I) 171-173; (II) 64, 67; (III) 417, 419

Waiter in restaurant. (I) 167, 170, 177; (II) 54, 60, 73; (III) 411, 414, 424

Patronne of restaurant. (I) 169, 170, 175, 176; (II) 59, 60, 70-72; (III) 414, 422, 423

HISTORICAL

Anthony (c.250-350): First Christian monk. (I) 167; (II) 56; (III) 412

Bishop, William Avery (1894-1956): Canadian aviator. (I) 173; (II) 67; (III) 419

Ur-Neill: Name of chief family of Ireland for over 1000 years; named for ancestor, Niall of the Nine Hostages. (I) 174; (II) 68; (III) 420

"ADOLESCENCE"

In *Uncollected Stories of William Faulkner*, ed. Joseph Blotner (New York: Random House, 1979).

Bundren, Alex: Father of Joe Bundren I; deceased. 467, 470

Bundren, Mrs. Alex: Mother of Joe Bundren I with whom Jule Bundren is sent to live. 460-462, 465-470, 472

Bundren, Bud: Son of Joe Bundren I and his first wife; becomes a Latin professor at a midwestern university. [459]-461, 470-472

Bundren, Cyril: Son of Joe Bundren I and his first wife; goes to state legislature. [459]-461, 470

Bundren, Jeff Davis: Son of Joe Bundren I and his first wife; is hanged for stealing a horse. [459]-461, 470

Bundren, Joe, I: Father of Jule, Cyril, Jeff Davis, Bud, and Joe II. [459]-461, 465, 467, 468, 470, 471
  First wife who is a small woman with large dark eyes: [459], 460
  Second wife who is a tall, angular shrew: 460, 468, 470-472

Bundren, Joe, II: Youngest son of Joe Bundren I and his first wife. 460, 461, 470

Bundren, Juliet (Jule): Daughter of Joe Bundren I and his first wife. [459]-473

Harvey, Deacon: Man who lives in town and sends revenuers to Lafe Hollowell's still where Lafe Hollowell and Joe Bundren I are killed. 470

Hollowell, Lafe: Lee Hollowell's father; bootlegger. 466, 470

Hollowell, Lee: Jule Bundren's friend. 461-468, 470, 471

HISTORICAL

Catullus, Gaius Valerius (84?-54 B.C.): Roman lyric poet. 460

LITERARY

Juliet: Character in Shakespeare's *Romeo and Juliet*, 1594-1595. 459

Romeo: Character in Shakespeare's *Romeo and Juliet*, 1594-1595. 459

"AFTERNOON OF A COW"

In (I) *Furioso*, 2 (Summer 1947), 5, 6, 8-17; (II) *Uncollected Stories of William Faulkner*, ed. Joseph Blotner (New York: Random House, 1979). First published in a French translation, "L'Après-midi d'une Vache," *Fontaine*, 27-28 (June-July 1943), 66-81.

Faulkner, Bill: Writer and farmer. (I) 5, 6, 8-17; (II) [424]-434

Faulkner, Mrs.: Wife of writer. (I) 8; (II) 426

Grover (Rover): Son of the Faulkners' Negro cook. (I) 5, 6, 15, 16; (II) [424], 425, 432, 433
 His mother: (I) 5; (II) [424]

James: Faulkner's nephew. (I) 5, 6, 10, 15, 16; (II) [424], 425, 428, 432, 433
 His father, Faulkner's brother: (I) 5; (II) [424]

Malcolm: Faulkner's son. (I) 5, 6, 10, 15, 16; (II) [424], 425, 428, 432, 433

Oliver: Negro who works for Faulkner. (I) 5, 6, 8-17; (II) [424]-434

Trueblood, Ernest V.: Story's narrator and ghost writer of Faulkner's fiction. (I) 5, 6, 8-17; (II) [424]-434

HISTORICAL

Rodin, Auguste (1840-1917): French sculptor. (I) 14; (II) 431

"AL JACKSON"

In *Uncollected Stories of William Faulkner*, ed. Joseph Blotner (New York: Random House, 1979).

Jackson, Al: The last Jackson descendent. [474]-479
 His mother: [474]
  Her father: [474]

Jackson, Claude: Second son of "Old Man" Jackson who is wild about women. 475-477

Jackson, Elenor (Perchie): Jackson daughter who eloped with a tin pedler. 476, 477
 Her husband: 477

Jackson, Herman: Jackson son with a "passion for education." 475, 478

"All the Dead Pilots"   197

Jackson, "Old Man": Father of Al, Claude, Elenor, and Herman.
     [474]-478
   His twelve sons: 475

Jackson, Sam: Man about whom Faulkner can get no information.
     478

Jackson, Spearhead: Man who was executed on British frigate
     in 1799. 477

Spearman, Jack: Bounty hunter in Minnesota. 478

UNNAMED

Pilot on boat who tells Faulkner about Al Jackson and his
     family. [474], 475
   His father: [474]

HISTORICAL

Anderson, Sherwood (1876-1941): American author. [474], 476-
     479

Faulkner, William (1897-1962): American author. [474]-479

Goethe, Johann Wolfgang von (1749-1832): German poet. 477

Jackson, Andrew (1767-1845): President of United States, 1829-
     1837. [474], 477, 478

Pershing, John Joseph (1860-1948): American general. 477

Scott, Walter (1771-1832): Scottish author. 478

Wagner, Richard (1813-1883): German composer. 477

Wilson, Woodrow (1856-1924): President of United States, 1913-
     1921. 477

"ALL THE DEAD PILOTS"

In (I) *These 13*, 1931; (II) *Collected Stories*, 1950.

Elnora: Negro servant of Sartorises. (I) 106; (II) 529

Ffollansbye: Member of John Sartoris' World War I squadron.
(I) 84, 85, 90; (II) 513, 514, 518

Isom: Negro servant of Sartorises. (I) 106; (II) 529

Kaye, Major C.: RAF officer who notifies Aunt Jenny Sartoris
of Johnny Sartoris' death. (I) 108; (II) 530

"Kitchener" (Kit): London girl friend of John Sartoris. (I)
85; (II) 514

Kyerling, R.: RAF pilot who saw John Sartoris shot down. (I)
108; (II) 530

Sartoris, John: American pilot in RAF. (I) 84-109; (II) 513-
531
  His grandfather: (I) 85, 106, 109; (II) 514, 529, 531

Sartoris, Mrs. Virginia (Aunt Jenny): Great aunt of John
    Sartoris. (I) 85, 89, 106-109; (II) 514, 517, 529, 530

Spoomer: Leader of RAF squadron. (I) 83-96, 101-105; (II)
    513-522, 525-528
  His uncle, British army corps commander: (I) 83, 84; (II)
    513

'Toinette: French girl. (I) 88-90, 98, 99; (II) 516, 517,
    523, 524

UNNAMED

Narrator, wounded soldier at RAF Wing Headquarters. (I) 81-
    109; (II) 512-531

Old woman who lives with 'Toinette. (I) 89, 93, 98, 100,
    101; (II) 516, 517, 519, 523-525

Gunnery sergeant with whom narrator talks. (I) 83, 86-92,
    103; (II) 513, 515-518, 526

Ambulance driver whom John Sartoris dresses in Spoomer's
    clothes. (I) 96, 101-103; (II) 522, 525-527

French corporal at bar. (I) 96, 100, 101; (II) 522, 524, 525

HISTORICAL

Gilbert, William S. (1836-1911): English playwright. (I) 101; (II) 525

Kitchener, Horatio Herbert (1850-1916): English general. (I) 85; (II) 514

Malbrouck: Legendary French crusader/soldier. (I) 107; (II) 529

Sullivan, Arthur (1842-1900): English composer. (I) 101; (II) 525

"AMBUSCADE"

In (I) *The Saturday Evening Post*, 207 (29 September 1934), 12, 13, 80, 81; (II) *Uncollected Stories of William Faulkner*, ed. Joseph Blotner (New York: Random House, 1979). Revised as first chapter of *The Unvanquished*, 1938.

Harrison: Yankee sergeant. (I) 80.3-81.2; (II) 12-14

Joby: Negro slave of Sartorises. (I) 12.3-13.3, 80.1, 80.2; (II) 5-10

Loosh: Negro slave of Sartorises. (I) 12.1-12.3, 13.2, 13.3, 80.1, 80.2; (II) [3]-9

Louvinia: Negro slave of Sartorises. (I) 12.3-13.3, 80.1-81.3; (II) 4-15

Marengo (Ringo): Negro companion of Bayard Sartoris. (I) 12.1-13.3, 80.1-81.3; (II) [3]-16

Millard, Rosa: Grandmother of Bayard Sartoris. (I) 12.3-13.2, 80.1-81.3; (II) 4-16

Philadelphy: Negro slave of Sartorises. (I) 12.1, 12.2, 13.3, 80.1, 80.2; (II) [3], 4, 8, 9

Sartoris, Bayard: Son of John Sartoris; narrator of story. (I) 12.1-13.3, 80.1-81.3; (II) [3]-16

Sartoris, John: Father of Bayard. (I) 12.2-13.2, 80.1-80.3, 81.3; (II) 4-9, 11, 16

UNNAMED

Yankee colonel who investigates shooting. (I) 81.1-81.2; (II)
    13-15
  His three sons: (I) 81.3; (II) 15

HISTORICAL

Pemberton, John C. (1818-1881): Confederate general. (I)
    12.2, 12.3; (II) 4

Sherman, William T. (1820-1891): Union general. (I) 80.1;
    (II) 8, 9

BIBLICAL

Lord: (I) 80.3, 81.3; (II) 12, 13

"AND NOW WHAT'S TO DO"

In (I) *The Mississippi Quarterly*, 26 (Summer 1973), 399-402;
(II) *A Faulkner Miscellany*, ed. James B. Meriwether (Jackson,
Miss.: University Press of Mississippi, 1974), 145-148.

Young man, central character: (I) 399-402; (II) 145-148
  His great-grandfather: (I) 399; (II) 145
  His grandfather: (I) 399; (II) 145
  His father: (I) 399, 400; (II) 145, 146

Girl in trouble: (I) 401; (II) 147

Man with pacing horse: (I) 401, 402; (II) 147, 148

"APPENDIX: COMPSON, 1699-1945"

In (I) *The Portable Faulkner*, ed. Malcolm Cowley (New York:
Viking, 1946), pp. 737-756; (II) as Foreword in *The Sound and
the Fury & As I Lay Dying* (New York: Modern Library, 1946),
pp. 3-22.

"Appendix: Compson, 1699-1945" 201

Beauchamp: Family name in Yoknapatawpha. (I) 742; (II) 8

Coldfield: Family name in Yoknapatawpha. (I) 742; (II) 8

Compson, Benjamin (Maury): Youngest child of Jason Compson III. (I) 743, 744, 751-753, 756; (II) 9, 10, 17-19, 22

Compson, Candace (Caddy): Daughter of Jason Compson III; mother of Quentin Compson IV. (I) 742-751, 753, 754; (II) 8-16, 18, 20
  Her first husband, young Indianian: (I) 744, 745, 747; (II) 11, 13
  Her second husband, moving picture magnate: (I) 745; (II) 11

Compson, Charles Stuart: Son of Quentin Compson I; father of Jason Compson I. (I) 738-740, 744, 747; (II) 4-8, 10, 13

Compson, Jason Lycurgus, I: Father of Quentin Compson II. (I) 737-741, 744, 747; (II) 3-7, 10, 13

Compson, Jason Lycurgus, II: Son of Quentin Compson II; father of Jason Compson III. (I) 741, 742, 747; (II) 7, 13

Compson, Jason Lycurgus, III: Son of Jason Compson II; father of Quentin III, Jason IV, Candace, and Benjamin Compson. His wife: (I) 743, 744, 750-754; (II) 9, 11, 17, 18
  Her brother: (I) 752, 753; (II) 18, 19

Compson, Jason Lycurgus, IV: Son of Jason Compson III. (I) 743, 745-752, 754, 755; (II) 9, 11-20

Compson, Quentin MacLachan, I: Father of Charles Stuart Compson. (I) 737-739, 744, 747; (II) 3-5, 7, 10, 13
  His father: (I) 738; (II) 4
  His mother: (I) 738; (II) 4

Compson, Quentin, II: Son of Jason Compson I; father of Jason Compson II. (I) 741, 742, 747; (II) 7, 8, 13

Compson, Quentin, III: Son of Jason Compson III. (I) 742-744, 747, 751, 753; (II) 8, 9, 13, 17, 19

Compson, Quentin, IV: Daughter of Caddy Compson. (I) 742, 744, 747, 748, 750, 751, 753-755; (II) 8-10, 13, 14, 16, 17, 19-21

Dilsey: Compsons' cook. (I) 742, 743, 747-753, 755, 756; (II) 8, 9, 13-18, 21, 22
  Her family: (I) 742; (II) 8

Doom: See Ikkemotubbe

Frony: Daughter of Dilsey; mother of Luster. (I) 748, 749, 755; (II) 14, 15, 21
  Her husband: (I) 755; (II) 21

Grenier: Family name in Yoknapatawpha. (I) 742; (II) 8

Holston: Family name in Yoknapatawpha. (I) 742; (II) 8

Ikkemotubbe (Doom): Chickasaw chief. (I) 737, 740; (II) 3, 6

Luster: Frony's son. (I) 753, 756; (II) 22

Maury: Brother of Jason III's wife. (I) 752, 753; (II) 18

Meek, Melissa: County librarian. (I) 745-750; (II) 11-16

Sartorises: Yoknapatawpha family. (I) 750; (II) 17

Snopeses: Yoknapatawpha family. (I) 741, 750; (II) 7, 16

Sutpen: Family name in Yoknapatawpha. (I) 742; (II) 8

T.P.: Dilsey's son. (I) 755; (II) 19, 21

UNNAMED

Chickasaw agent with whom Jason Compson I became a partner. (I) 737, 740; (II) 3, 6

Country man who buys Compson house. (I) 743, 751; (II) 9, 17

Ikkemotubbe's foster brother, a chevalier of France. (I) 737; (II) 3

German staff general with Candace Compson in photograph. (I) 746; (II) 12, 13

Pitchman at carnival with whom Quentin Compson IV, Caddy Compson' daughter, runs away. (I) 743, 748, 755; (II) 9, 14, 21

Memphis friend of Jason Compson IV. (I) 752; (II) 18

HISTORICAL

Boone, Daniel (1734-1820): American backwoodsman. (I) 738, 742; (II) 4, 8

Catullus, Gaius Valerius (84?-54 B.C.): Roman lyric poet. (I) 742; (II) 8

George II (1683-1760): King of England, 1727-1760. (I) 738; (II) 4

Horace (65-8 B.C.): Roman poet and satirist. (I) 742; (II) 8

Jackson, Andrew (1767-1845): President of United States, 1829-1837. (I) 737, 738; (II) 3, 4
His wife: (I) 738; (II) 4

Lincoln, Abraham (1809-1865): President of United States, 1861-1865. (I) 752; (II) 18

Livy (59 B.C.-17 A.D.): Roman historian. (I) 742; (II) 8

Napoleon (1769-1821): French emperor. (I) 737; (II) 3

Smith, Andrew J. (1815-1897): Union general. (I) 741; (II) 7

Smith, Thorne (1892-1934): American humorist. (I) 745; (II) 11

Stuart, Charles Edward (1720-1788): "Young Pretender" to British throne. (I) 738; (II) 3

Tarleton, Banastre (1754-1833): British officer in Revolutionary War. (I) 738; (II) 4

Wilkinson, James (1747-1825): American army officer in Revolutionary War. (I) 739; (II) 5

BIBLICAL

Lord: (I) 743, 750, 753; (II) 9, 16, 19

LITERARY

Crusoe, Robinson: Character in Defoe's *Robinson Crusoe*, 1719. (I) 742; (II) 8

"ARTIST AT HOME"

In (I) *Story*, 3 (August 1933), 27-41; (II) *Collected Stories*, 1950.

Blair, John: Poet, house guest of Howes. (I) 28-41; (II) 628-645
  His mother: (I) 33, 37; (II) 636, 640

Crain, Amos: Howes' farmer neighbor. (I) 30, 36, 37, 40, 41; (II) 631, 632, 638, 640, 644, 646

Crain, Mrs.: Amos Crain's wife. (I) 30, 40, 41; (II) 631, 644-646
  Their children: (I) 30, 41; (II) 631, 646

Howes, Ann: Wife of Roger Howes. (I) 27-41; (II) 627-646
  Her father: (I) 29, 40; (II) 630, 644
  Her mother: (I) 40; (II) 644
  Her two children: (I) 27, 28, 34, 36, 40, 41; (II) 627, 630, 633, 639, 640, 644

Howes, Roger: Author, husband of Ann Howes. (I) 27-41; (II) 627-646

Pinkie: Howes' Negro cook. (I) 29-32, 37; (II) 630, 632-634, 640, 641
  Her family: 633

UNNAMED

Narrator. (I) 27-41; (II) 627-646

Man at station. (I) 27, 28; (II) 628, 629

HISTORICAL

Pope, Alexander (1688-1744): English poet. (I) 39; (II) 643

Shelley, Percy Bysshe (1792-1822): English poet. (I) 32, 40; (II) 634, 644

BIBLICAL

Lord: (I) 41; (II) 645, 646

"BARN BURNING"

In (I) *Harper's*, 179 (June 1939), 86-96; (II) *Collected Stories*, 1950.

De Spain, Major: Landowner for whom Ab Snopes agrees to work.
(I) 89.1, 90.1-93.2, 95.2, 96.1; (II) 9, 11-13, 15-19, 23, 24

De Spain, Lula: Wife of Major de Spain. (I) 90.1-92.2; (II) 11, 12, 15, 16

Harris, Mr.: Man who accuses Ab Snopes of burning his barn. (I) 86.1-87.1; (II) 3-5

Lizzie: Sister of Lennie Snopes. (I) 87.2, 88.1, 89.1, 90.2, 91.2-92.2, 95.1, 95.2; (II) 6-9, 12, 14, 16, 17, 22

Sartoris, Colonel John: Commander of Confederate regiment. (I) 87.1, 96.2; (II) 4, 24

Snopes, Abner (Ab): Father of Sarty Snopes. (I) 86.1-96.2; (II) 3-22, 24
 His son; older brother of Sarty Snopes. (I) 86.2, 87.2, 88.1, 89.1, 91.1-95.1; (II) 4-9, 13, 14, 16, 17, 19-22

Snopes, Colonel Sartoris (Sarty): Younger son of Ab and Lennie Snopes. (I) 86.1-96.2; (II) 3-25

Snopes, Lennie: Wife of Ab Snopes. (I) 87.2, 88.1, 89.1, 90.2-92.2, 94.2, 95.1, 95.2; (II) 6-9, 12-14, 16, 17, 20-22

Snopes, Net: One of Sarty Snopes' twin sisters. (I) 87.2, 88.1, 89.1, 90.2-92.2, 95.1, 95.2; (II) 6-9, 12-14, 17, 22, 23
 Her sister: (I) 87.2, 88.1, 89.1, 90.2-92.2, 95.1, 95.2; (II) 6-9, 12-14, 17, 22, 23

UNNAMED

Justice of Peace at first trial.   (I) 86.1-87.1; (II) 3-5

Justice of Peace at second trial.   (I) 93.1; (II) 17, 18

Negro house servant who works for Major de Spain.   (I) 90.1, 90.2, 95.2, 96.1; (II) 11, 12, 23

Confederate provost's man who shoots Ab Snopes.   (I) 87.1; (II) 5

HISTORICAL

Malbrouck: Legendary French crusader/soldier.   (I) 96.2; (II) 25

"THE BEAR"

In (I) *The Saturday Evening Post*, 214 (9 May 1942), 30, 31, 74, 76, 77; (II) *Uncollected Stories of William Faulkner*, ed. Joseph Blotner (New York: Random House, 1979). Earlier version is Chapter 5 of *Go Down, Moses*, 1942; see also *Big Woods*, 1955.

Ash, Uncle: Negro cook.   (I) 31.1, 74.2, 74.4; (II) 283, 287, 288

Compson, General: Hunter at Major de Spain's camp.   (I) 30.1, 31.1, 31.2, 74.1, 74.2, 76.3; (II) [281], 282, 284, 286, 287, 293

De Spain, Major: Host of hunting camp.   (I) 30.1, 31.1-31.3, 74.1-74.3, 76.3; (II) [281], 282, 284-288, 293

Ewell, Walter: Hunter at Major de Spain's camp.   (I) 31.3, 74.2, 76.1-76.3; (II) 284, 287, 290, 291, 293

Fathers, Sam: Young boy's tutor in the woods.   (I) 31.1-31.3, 74.1-74.4, 76.1-76.3, 77.1, 77.2; (II) 282-295
  His mother: (I) 31.1, 77.1; (II) 282, 294
  His father: (I) 31.2, 77.1; (II) 282, 294

"A Bear Hunt" 207

Hogganbeck, Boon: Worker at hunting camp. (I) 74.2, 76.3;
    (II) 287, 293

Tennie's Jim: Negro at hunting camp. (I) 31.1, 74.2, 76.3;
    (II) 282, 287, 293

UNNAMED

Young boy at hunting camp; central character. (I) 30.1, 30.2,
    31.1-31.3, 74.1-74.4, 76.1-76.3, 77.1, 77.2; (II) [281]-
    295
  His father: (I) 30.1, 31.1, 31.2, 74.1, 74.2, 76.1, 76.3,
    77.1, 77.2; (II) [281], 282, 286, 287, 290-295
  His grandfather: (I) 74.4; (II) 289

MYTHIC

Priam: King of Troy. (I) 31.1; (II) 282

"A BEAR HUNT"

In (I) The Saturday Evening Post, 206 (10 February 1934), 8,
9, 74, 76; (II) Collected Stories, 1950; see also Big Woods,
1955.

Ash (Old Man Ash): See Bush (Old Man Bush)

Basket, John: One of Indians on mound. (I) 74.2, 74.3, 76.1,
    76.2; (II) 71-75, 77

Bonds, Jack: Contemporary of Provine brothers; does not appear
    in BW revision. (I) 8.1, 8.2, 76.3; (II) 63, 64, 79

Bush (Old Man Bush): Negro servant of Major de Spain; Old Man
    Ash in CS version; Ash Wylie in BW. (I) 8.3, 9.2, 74.1-
    74.3, 76.1-76.3; (II) 67, 68, 70-79

De Spain, Major: Host of hunting camp. (I) 8.1-8.3, 9.1, 9.2,
    74.1, 74.3, 76.1-76.3; (II) 63-71, 73-78

De Spain, Mrs.: Wife of Major de Spain. (I) 8.1; (II) 63.
  Her daughters: (I) 8.1; (II) 63

Fraser, Mr.: Member of hunting camp. (I) 74.3; (II) 73, 74

McCaslin, Uncle Ike: Member of hunting camp. (I) 9.3, 74.3; (II) 69, 74

Provine, Lucius: Worker for Major de Spain; Lucius Hogganbeck in *BW* revision. (I) 8.1-8.3, 9.1-9.3, 74.1-74.3, 76.1-76.3; (II) 63-79
  His brother: (I) 8.1, 8.2, 76.3; (II) 63, 64, 79

Provine, Mrs. Lucius: Wife of Lucius Provine. (I) 8.1, 8.2; (II) 63, 64
  Her three children: (I) 8.2; (II) 64

Ratliff: See Suratt

Suratt: Sewing machine salesman; Ratliff in *CS*, 1950, and *BW*. (I) 8.1, 8.3, 9.1-9.3, 74.1-74.3, 76.1-76.3; (II) 63, 65-79.

UNNAMED

Narrator, county inhabitant: (I) 8.1-76.3; (II) 63-79

HISTORICAL

Sherman, William T. (1820-1891): (I) 8.3; (II) 66

"BEYOND"

In (I) *Harper's*, 167 (September 1933), 394-403; (II) *Doctor Martino*, 1934; (III) *Collected Stories*, 1950.

Allison, Judge Howard: Central character who dies. (I) 394.1-403.2; (II) 201-222; (III) 781-798
  His aunts: (I) 399.1; (II) 212; (III) 790
  His wife: (I) 398.1, 398.2, 399.1; (II) 205, 211, 212; (III) 785, 789, 790, 796
    Her father: (I) 398.2; (II) 211; (III) 789

Allison, Howard, II: Judge's son. (I) 394.1, 396.1, 397.1, 398.1-399.2, 401.1-402.1; (II) 201, 206, 208, 211-213, 217, 218, 220; (III) 781, 785, 787, 789-791, 794, 795

"Beyond" 209

Allison, Sophia: Judge's mother. (I) 399.1; (II) 212; (III) 790

Chlory: Judge Allison's servant. (I) 394.1-395.1; (II) 201, 202, 204; (III) 781-783

Jake: Judge Allison's gardener. (I) 394.1-395.1, 402.2; (II) 201-203, 220; (III) 781-783, 797

Mothershed: Atheist friend of Judge Allison. (I) 396.2-397.2, 398.2, 399.2, 402.1, 402.2; (II) 207-212, 214, 219, 221; (III) 785-789, 791, 796, 797

Peabody, Lucius: Physician who attends Judge Allison. (I) 394.1, 394.2; (II) 201-203; (III) 781, 782

Pettigrew: Judge Allison's lawyer or executor. (I) 402.1, 402.2; (II) 219, 220; (III) 796, 797

UNNAMED

Young woman with child. (I) 399.2-401.2; (II) 213-218; (III) 791-795

Young man who is killed in automobile accident trying to miss child. (I) 395.2-396.2; (II) 204-206; (III) 783-785
  His fiancée. (I) 395.1; (II) 204, 205; (III) 783, 784

Author who wrote little women books. (I) 398.1; (II) 209; (III) 788

HISTORICAL

Ingersoll, Robert (1833-1897): American agnostic. (I) 396.2, 397.2-400.1, 402.1, 402.2; (II) 207, 209-215, 219, 221; (III) 786-792, 796, 797

Montesquieu, Charles Louis, Baron de (1689-1755): French philosopher. (I) 398.1; (II) 210; (III) 788

Paine, Thomas (1737-1809): Political and religious author. (I) 397.2, 398.1; (II) 209, 210; (III) 787, 788

Pilate, Pontius: Procurator of Judea under Tiberius, in first half of first century, A.D. (I) 400.2; (II) 216; (III) 793

Voltaire (1694-1778): French author and philosopher. (I) 396.2, 398.1, 398.2; (II) 207, 210, 211; (III) 786, 788, 789

BIBLICAL

God: (I) 398.1; (II) 210; (III) 788

Jesus: (I) 396.2; (II) 207; (III) 786

"THE BIG SHOT"

In *Uncollected Stories of William Faulkner*, ed. Joseph Blotner (New York: Random House, 1979).

Blount: Old family name in town. 512-516, 518

Blount, Doctor Harrison: Representative of town's old families who adds Martin's daughter to the list of debutantes after Martin offers to build an art gallery named for Blount's grandfather. 516-521
  His grandfather: 519
  His mother: 516

Govelli: Underworld figure with whom Dal Martin is involved. [504]-507, 514, 521, 522, 524

Heustace: Old family name in town. 512-516

Hickey: Policeman. 522, 523

Martin, Dal: The Big Shot. [504]-525
  His father: 508-510
  His two sisters: 508, 509
  His brothers: 508, 509
  His wife: 510-513

Martin, Wrennie: Dal Martin's daughter. 511-525

Monk: Type of man whom Martin wants his daughter to avoid. 518

Popeye: Gangster who works with Govelli and who kills Wrennie Martin. [504]-507, 518, 521, 522, 524, 525
  His mother: 505, 506

"Black Music"   *211*

Red: Type of man whom Martin wants his daughter to avoid. 518

Reeves, Don: Journalist who tells story of Martin to narrator.
     [504]-525

Sandeman: Old family name in town. 512-515, 518

Sandeman, Jerry: Scion of old family in town. 523

Tony: Italian who tends Martin's house. 512, 513
   His wife: 512, 513

Windham & Healy: Architects who design art museum. 519

UNNAMED

Town lady whom Blount visits to discuss museum offer. 519

Boss in big house where the young Dal Martin is turned away.
     508-511

Negro servant at big house. 508, 509, 513

Narrator to whom Don Reeves tells Martin's story. [504]-525

HISTORICAL

Forrest, Nathan Bedford (1821-1877): Confederate general. 519

Napoleon (1769-1821): Emperor of France. 505, 514, 516

Volstead, Andrew Joseph (1860-1946): U.S. legislator. 505

MYTHIC

Galahad: Knight of King Arthur's Round Table. 515

Launcelot: Knight of King Arthur's Round Table. 515

"BLACK MUSIC"

In (I) *Doctor Martino*, 1934; (II) *Collected Stories*, 1950.

Carter: Architect for whom Midgleston worked. (I) 276, 282; (II) 809, 810, 815

Harris, Elmer: Chief of Police. (I) 287, 288; (II) 819

Midgleston, Martha: Wildred Midgleston's wife. (I) 269, 270, 276, 277, 286-289; (II) 804, 810, 819-821
  Her second husband: (I) 289; (II) 821

Midgleston, Wilfred: Architect's draughtsman, husband of Martha Midgleston. (I) 263-290; (II) 799-821

Van Dyming, Mr. Carleton: Wealthy New Yorker. (I) 272-275, 283-285, 287; (II) 807-809, 815-819

Van Dyming, Mattie (Mathilda Lumpkin): Wife of Carleton Van Dyming. (I) 271-274, 276, 282-285, 287; (II) 806-810, 814-819

Widrington, Mr.: Manager of company which owns building where Midgleston sleeps in the attic. (I) 268; (II) 803

Widrington, Mrs.: Wife of manager. (I) 268; (II) 803

UNNAMED

Narrator, visitor in Rincon. (I) 263-290; (II) 799-821

Person who tells narrator about Midgleston. (I) 264-267; (II) 799-801

New England man who once owned the Van Dyming land. (I) 271, 272, 275; (II) 806, 809

Italian who also once owned land. (I) 272, 275; (II) 806, 807, 809

HISTORICAL

Ade, George (1866-1944): American humorist and playwright. (I) 264; (II) 800

Burns, William J. (1861-1932): American detective. (I) 265; (II) 801

BIBLICAL

Elijah: Old Testament prophet. (I) 263; (II) 799

Lord: (I) 286; (II) 818

MYTHIC

Pan: Greek god of shepherds and hunters. (I) 271; (II) 805

"THE BROOCH"

In (I) *Scribner's*, 99 (January 1936), 7-12; (II) *Collected Stories*, 1950.

Boyd, Mr.: Howard Boyd's father. (I) 7.1, 8.1, 12.3; (II) 647, 648, 650, 664

Boyd, Mrs.: Howard Boyd's mother. (I) 7.2-12.3; (II) 647-662, 664
  Her father: (I) 7.1; (II) 647, 648

Boyd, Amy: Howard Boyd's wife. (I) 7.2-12.3; (II) 648-662, 664
  Her father: (I) 7.2, 8.3; (II) 648, 652
  Her aunt: (I) 7.2; (II) 648
  Her child: (I) 8.3, 11.3, 12.2; (II) 652, 661, 663

Boyd, Howard: Amy Boyd's husband. (I) 7.1-12.3; (II) 647-665

Ross, Frank: Martha Ross' husband. (I) 9.2, 10.2, 11.1; (II) 655, 658, 660

Ross, Martha: Boyds' friend, wife of Frank Ross. (I) 9.2, 9.3, 10.2, 11.1; (II) 654, 655, 658, 660

HISTORICAL

Dante (1265-1321): Italian poet. (I) 7.2; (II) 648

LITERARY

Argensola, Abel de: Character in W.H. Hudson's *Green Mansions*, 1904. (I) 12.1, 12.2; (II) 663

Fauntleroy, Little Lord: Hero of novel by Frances Hodgson Burnett, 1886. (I) 7.2; (II) 648

Rima: Character in W.H. Hudson's *Green Mansions*, 1904. (I) 12.1, 12.2; (II) 663

"BY THE PEOPLE"

In *Mademoiselle*, 41 (October 1955), 86-89, 130, 131, 132, 133, 134, 135, 136, 137, 138, 139; incorporated in Chapter 13 of *The Mansion*, 1959.

Bookright: Man whom Eck Grier swapped a dog for half-a-day's work. 137.1

Charles: Nephew of Gavin Stevens; narrator. 86.1-139.1
  His father: 139.1

Devries: World War II hero running for Congress. 133.1, 134.1, 134.2, 135.1, 136.1, 137.1, 138.1, 138.2
  His sister: 137.1
    Her twin sons: 137.1, 138.1, 138.2

Grier, Eck: Dog owner in Frenchman's Bend. 137.1

Ratliff: Sewing machine salesman. 86.1, 86.2, 87.1, 87.2, 88.1, 88.2, 137.1, 138.1, 138.2, 139.1

Snopes: President of Farmers' and Merchants' Bank. 88.2

Snopes: Clarence Eggleston: Frenchman's Bend politician. 88.2, 89.1, 89.2, 130.1, 131.1, 132.1, 133.1, 134.1, 134.2, 135.1, 136.1, 137.1, 138.1, 138.2
  His grandmother's distant cousin by marriage. 130.1

Stevens, Uncle Gavin: Jefferson attorney. 88.1, 88.2, 89.2, 130.1, 133.1, 134.2, 135.1, 136.1, 137.1, 138.1, 138.2, 139.1
  His wife: 88.1

Varner, Uncle Billy: Frenchman's Bend landowner. 86.2, 88.2, 89.1, 130.1, 131.1, 134.2, 136.1, 137.1, 138.2

UNNAMED

Clarence Snopes' cohort. 89.2, 130.1

HISTORICAL

Cincinnatus, Lucius Quinctius (519?-439? B.C.): Roman statesman. 139.1

Long, Huey (1893-1935): Louisiana governor and senator. 130.1, 132.1, 136.1

BIBLICAL

God: 139.1

"CARCASSONNE"

In (I) *These 13*, 1931; (II) *Collected Stories*, 1950.

Luis: Cantina operator. (I) 355; (II) 897

Widdrington, Mrs.: Wealthy woman. (I) 355, 356; (II) 897, 898

UNNAMED

Narrator/Poet: (I) 352-358; (II) 895-900

HISTORICAL

Bouillon, Godfrey de (1061?-1100): French leader in First Crusade. (I) 354, 355; (II) 896, 897

Byron, Lord (1788-1824): British poet. (I) 356; (II) 898

Tancred (1078?-1112): Norman leader in First Crusade. (I) 354, 355; (II) 896, 897

BIBLICAL

Jesus: (I) 354, 357; (II) 896, 899

"CENTAUR IN BRASS"

In (I) *American Mercury*, 25 (February 1932), 200-210; (II) *Collected Stories*, 1950; incorporated in Chapter 1 of *The Town*, 1957.

Conner, Buck: Jefferson marshal. (I) 205.2, 209.2, 210.1; (II) 159, 167

Harker: Night engineer at power plant. (I) 200.1, 202.2, 203.1, 204.1, 204.2, 205.1, 205.2, 206.1, 206.2, 207.1, 207.2, 208.1, 208.2, 209.1; (II) 149, 153, 154, 156-158, 160-162, 165-168

Hoxey, Major: Jefferson bachelor, soon to be mayor of town. (I) 201.1, 201.2, 206.1; (II) 151, 152, 160

Snopes, Flem: Superintendent of municipal power plant. (I) 200.1-207.1, 208.2-210.2; (II) 149-162, 165-168
  His wife: (I) 200.1-201.2; (II) 149-152
    Her father: (I) 200.1; (II) 149
    Her daughter: (I) 200.1, 200.2; (II) 150

Suratt: Sewing machine salesman. (I) 200.1, 200.2, 204.1; (II) 149, 150, 157

Tom-Tom: Day fireman at power plant. (I) 200.1, 200.2-210.1; (II) 149, 152, 154-167
  His wife: (I) 201.2, 204.1, 206.1, 207.2, 208.1, 208.2, 209.1; (II) 152, 156, 160, 162, 163, 165

Turl: Negro night fireman at power plant. (I) 200.1, 202.2-210.1; (II) 149, 153-167

UNNAMED

Two auditors of power plant. (I) 204.2, 205.1, 209.2; (II) 157, 158, 162, 167

"Cheest"

City clerk.   (I) 204.2, 209.2; (II) 157, 158, 167

Texan with ponies.   (I) 200.2; (II) 150

Suratt's restaurant partner.   (I) 200.2; (II) 150

Narrator, Jefferson resident.   (I) 200.1-210.2; (II) 149-168

"CHANCE"

In (I) *William Faulkner: New Orleans Sketches*, ed. Carvel Collins (New York: Random House, 1968); (II) *Sinbad in New Orleans*, ed. Leland Cox (Spartanburg, S.C.: The Reprint Company, 1981). First printed in New Orleans *Times-Picayune* Sunday magazine section, 17 May 1925, p. 7.

UNNAMED

Man who is given five-dollar gold piece.   (I) 70-75; (II) 47-51

Beggar who tries to get money from hero.   (I) 70-72; (II) 47-49

Thief who takes five-dollar gold piece.   (I) 72, 73; (II) 49, 50

Policeman who catches thief.   (I) 72, 73; (II) 49, 50

Car salesman.   (I) 74, 75; (II) 51

"CHEEST"

In (I) *William Faulkner: New Orleans Sketches*, ed. Carvel Collins (New York: Random House, 1968); (II) *Sinbad in New Orleans*, ed. Leland Cox (Spartanburg, S.C.: The Reprint Company, 1981). First printed in New Orleans *Times-Picayune* Sunday magazine section, 5 April 1925, p. 4.

Potter, Jack: Narrator; man who works with horses.   (I) 41-45; (II) 53-56

UNNAMED

Girl Narrator meets at races. (I) 42-45; (II) 54-56

Girl's friend. (I) 42-44; (II) 54, 55

Horse owner. (I) 41, 42, 44, 45; (II) 53, 54, 56

HISTORICAL

Dempsey, William H. "Jack" (1895-): American boxer. (I) 41; (II) 53

"*THE COBBLER*"

In (I) *William Faulkner: New Orleans Sketches*, ed. Carvel Collins (New York: Random House, 1968); (II) *Sinbad in New Orleans*, ed. Leland Cox (Spartanburg, S.C.: The Reprint Company, 1981). First printed in New Orleans *Times-Picayune* Sunday magazine section, 10 May 1925, p. 7.

UNNAMED

Cobbler from Italy; narrator. (I) 66-69; (II) 69-71

Girl whom he loved. (I) 66-69; (II) 69-71

Man with gold rings. (I) 68; (II) 70, 71

BIBLICAL

Christ: (I) 67; (II) 70

"COUNTRY MICE"

In (I) *William Faulkner: New Orleans Sketches*, ed. Carvel Collins (New York: Random House, 1968); (II) *Sinbad in New Orleans*, ed. Leland Cox (Spartanburg, S.C.: The Reprint Company, 1981). First printed in New Orleans *Times-Picayune* Sunday magazine section, 20 September 1925, p. 7.

Gilman: Man who flies airplane. (I) 113-120; (II) 95-101
  His brother, the deputy: (I) 113-115, 117, 119, 120; (II) 95-97, 99-101
  His father, the justice of the peace: (I) 112, 118, 120; (II) 94, 95, 99, 101

Gus: Bootlegger's brother. (I) 111, 112, 114, 117-120; (II) 93, 94, 96, 99-101

Joe: Partner of Gus and Bootlegger. (I) 111-116, 118-120; (II) 93-97, 99-101

UNNAMED

Bootlegger who relates story to narrator. (I) 108-120; (II) 91-101

Narrator, Bootlegger's friend. (I) 108-120; (II) 91-101

"A COURTSHIP"

In (I) *Sewanee Review*, 56 (Autumn 1948), 634-653; (II) *Collected Stories*, 1950.

Basket, Herman: Chickasaw. (I) 634-644, 649, 651; (II) 361-372, 376, 379
  His sister: (I) 634-643, 649, 651, 652; (II) 361-368, 370, 371, 376, 379, 380
  His aunt: (I) 635-638, 640-644, 651; (II) 362-366, 368-370, 372, 379
  His uncle: (I) 641-643, 651; (II) 368-370, 379

Colbert, David: Chickasaw chief. (I) 636, 637, 646, 651; (II) 363, 365, 374, 379
  His wife: (I) 636, 637, 651; (II) 363, 365, 379
    Her niece: (I) 637; (II) 365
    Her grand-niece: (I) 636, 637, 651; (II) 363, 364, 379

Doom: See Ikkemotubbe

Hogganbeck, David: Riverboat pilot. (I) 634, 635, 638-652; (II) 361, 362, 365-380

Ikkemotubbe (Doom): Young Chickasaw, later chief. (I) 634-652; (II) 361-380
  His mother: (I) 635; (II) 362

Issetibbeha: Ikkemotubbe's uncle. (I) 634, 635, 637, 641-645, 651; (II) 361-363, 365, 368, 370, 372, 378

Log-in-the-Creek: Young Chickasaw. (I) 636-642, 644, 651, 652; (II) 363, 364, 366-371, 379, 380

Moketubbe: Issetibbeha's son. (I) 635; (II) 363
  His son: (I) 636; (II) 363

Owl-by-Night: Young Chickasaw. (I) 636-638, 642, 643, 645; (II) 363-365, 369, 370, 372, 373

Studenmare, Captain: Riverboat captain. (I) 639-641, 651, 652; (II) 366-368, 378, 380

Sylvester's John: Young Chickasaw. (I) 636, 638, 641-643; (II) 363, 365, 369, 370

Vitry, Chevalier Soeur-Blonde de: Doom's French companion. (I) 635, 651; (II) 363, 379

UNNAMED

Whiskey trader. (I) 637, 638, 642; (II) 364, 365, 369, 370

Eight slaves brought by Doom, among whom is Sam Fathers' mother. (I) 635, 651; (II) 363, 379

Narrator. (I) 634-653; (II) 361-380

Narrator's father. (I) 636-638, 641-647, 650, 651; (II) 363, 365, 369-374, 378

HISTORICAL

Jackson, Andrew (1767-1845): President of the United States, 1829-1837. (I) 634, 642; (II) 361, 370, 371

BIBLICAL

Solomon: King of Israel in 1 Kings. (I) 652; (II) 379

"CREVASSE"

In (I) *These 13*, 1931; (II) *Collected Stories*, 1950.

McKie, Mr.: British subaltern in World War I who is killed. (I) 110-119; (II) 465-472

UNNAMED

Captain: (I) 110-123; (II) 465-474

Sergeant: (I) 110-123; (II) 465-474

Wounded man: (I) 110-123; (II) 465-474

Other men: (I) 110-123; (II) 465-474

"DAMON AND PYTHIAS UNLIMITED"

In (I) *William Faulkner: New Orleans Sketches*, ed. Carvel Collins (New York: Random House, 1968); (II) *Sinbad in New Orleans*, ed. Leland Cox (Spartanburg, S.C.: The Reprint Company, 1981). First printed in New Orleans *Times-Picayune* Sunday magazine section, 15 February 1925, p. 7.

"Iowa": Narrator's friend. (I) 19; (II) 5

M Namara: Youth at racetrack. (I) 24-27; (II) 8-12

Morowitz: Shyster; McNamara's friend. (I) 20-27; (II) 5-12

UNNAMED

Narrator; stranger in New Orleans. (I) 19-27; (II) 5-12

HISTORICAL

Carnegie, Andrew (1835-1919): American industrialist. (I) 23; (II) 8

BIBLICAL

God: (I) 26; (II) 11

"A DANGEROUS MAN"

In *Uncollected Stories of William Faulkner*, ed. Joseph Blotner (New York: Random House, 1979).

Bowman, Mr.: Express agent; thick-built man who shows no age. [575]-582

Bowman, Mrs.: Bowman's wife who runs express office and looks like a washerwoman. [575], 577-582

Joe: Bowman's nephew who is married. 577-579

Minnie Maude: Woman who works at Rex theatre across from the express office. 578, 580, 581

Stowers, Zack: Bowman's friend who seeks help in avenging his wife's honor. [575]-577

Stowers, Mrs.: Zack's wife who has been insulted. 575, 577

Wall: Insurance salesman who Minnie Maude says is having an affair with Mrs. Bowman. 580, 581

Wiggins, Mrs.: Boarding house owner. 578

UNNAMED

Tall salesman who insults Mrs. Stowers. [575]-577

Short, fat companion of tall salesman. [575]-577

Narrator; town youth. [575]-582
  His aunt: 578

Bowmans' cook. 578, 579, 582

HISTORICAL

Balzac, Honoré de (1799-1850): French novelist. 582

LITERARY

Nucingen: Banker in several of Balzac's novels. 582

"DEATH-DRAG"

In (I) *Scribner's*, 91 (January 1932), 34-42; (II) *Doctor Martino* as "Death Drag," 1934; (III) *Collected Stories*, 1950.

Black, Mr.: Driver of car who takes aviators to town. (I) 35.2, 36.1; (II) 76-79; (III) 188-190

Ginsfarb ("Demon Duncan"): Man who jumps from plane on ladder. (I) 34.2-42.2; (II) 74-97; (III) 186-205

Harris: Man who owns car rented to flyers. (I) 39.2, 42.2; (II) 90, 97; (III) 199, 205

Jake: Driver of car in death drag. (I) 35.1, 35.2, 36.1, 37.2, 38.1, 38.2, 39.1, 40.1, 40.2, 41.2, 42.1; (II) 76-78, 82, 84-86, 88-93, 96, 97; (III) 188-190, 193-196, 198-201, 204, 205

Jock: Pilot of stunt plane. (I) 34.1-39.2, 40.2-42.1; (II) 72-97; (III) 185-191, 193-199, 201-205

Jones: Secretary of Fair Association. (I) 35.2, 36.1, 41.1; (II) 77-79, 94; (III) 188, 190, 203

Vernon: Restaurant man.   (I) 37.2, 38.2; (II) 83, 86; (III) 194, 196

Warren, Captain: RFC veteran.   (I) 34.1, 34.2, 36.2-39.1, 40.1-42.2; (II) 72-74, 81-88, 91-93, 95-97; (III) 185, 187, 192-198, 200-205

UNNAMED

Narrator, young boy.   (I) 34.1-42.2; (II) 72-97; (III) 185-205

Editor of paper.   (I) 36.1, 36.2; (II) 79, 80; (III) 190, 191

Taxi driver.   (I) 36.2, 37.1; (II) 80-82; (III) 190-193

Country woman who watches death drag.   (I) 39.2-40.2, 41.2; (II) 89-91, 93, 95; (III) 198-200, 202, 204

HISTORICAL

Coolidge, Calvin (1872-1933): President of United States, 1923-1929.   (I) 37.1; (II) 81; (III) 192

Fields, Lew (1867-1941): Member of American comedy team.   (I) 34.2; (II) 75; (III) 187

Weber, Joseph M. (1867-1942): Member of American comedy team.   (I) 34.2; (II) 75; (III) 187

BIBLICAL

Lord: (I) 39.2; (II) 89; (III) 199

"DELTA AUTUMN"

In (I) *Story*, 20 (May-June 1942), 46-55; (II) *Uncollected Stories of William Faulkner*, ed. Joseph Blotner (New York: Random House, 1979).   Revised as Chapter 6 of *Go Down, Moses*, 1942; see also *Big Woods*, 1955.

"Delta Autumn" 225

Boyd, Don: Young man on hunting trip with Ike McCaslin. (I)
 46.1-48.1, 49.1, 51.1, 51.2, 52.2-55.2; (II) 268-272,
 274, 276-280

De Spain, Major: Ike McCaslin's father's cavalry commander in
 Civil War and part owner of big bottom. (I) 50.2, 52.1;
 (II) 273, 275

Fathers, Sam: Ike McCaslin's tutor in the woods. (I) 50.2,
 52.1; (II) 273, 275
 His grandfather, a Chickasaw chief: (I) 50.2; (II) 273

Isham: Oldest Negro at hunting camp. (I) 50.1, 52.1, 53.1,
 54.1; (II) 273, 275, 277, 278

Legate, Will: Young man on hunting trip with Ike McCaslin.
 (I) 46.1-48.1, 49.1, 49.2, 51.1, 52.1, 52.2, 55.1, 55.2;
 (II) 268-272, 274-276, 280

McCaslin, Ike: Old hunter. (I) 46.1-48.1, 49.1-55.2; (II)
 [267]-280
 His father: (I) 48.1, 50.2; (II) 269, 273
 His wife and children: (I) 51.1; (II) 274
 His wife's niece and family: (I) 51.1; (II) 274

UNNAMED

Young Negro woman, Boyd's mistress. (I) 52.2-54.2; (II) 276-
 279
 Her father: (I) 54.1; (II) 278
 Her baby: (I) 53.1, 53.2; (II) 277, 278
 Her aunt: (I) 53.2, 54.1; (II) 278
 Her cousin: (I) 53.1, 54.1; (II) 277, 278

Youngest Negro on hunting trip. (I) 50.2, 51.1, 53.1; (II)
 273, 274, 277

HISTORICAL

Hitler, Adolf (1889-1945): German chancellor, 1933-1945. (I)
 47.2, 48.1; (II) 269

BIBLICAL

Lord: (I) 48.1, 54.1; (II) 270, 278

"DIVORCE IN NAPLES"

In (I) *These 13*, 1931; (II) *Collected Stories*, 1950.

Carl: Mess boy on merchant ship. (I) 330-340, 343-351; (II) 877-893
  His sister: (I) 334; (II) 880
  His father: (I) 334; (II) 880

George: Cook on merchant ship. (I) 330-351; (II) 877-893

Monckton: Crew member on merchant ship. (I) 330-332, 335-337, 343, 346-348; (II) 877-879, 881, 882, 886, 889, 890

UNNAMED

Bosun on merchant ship. (I) 330-332, 336, 337, 343, 346-348; (II) 877-879, 881, 882, 886, 889, 890

Narrator, crew member on merchant ship. (I) 330-351; (II) 877-893

Steward on merchant ship. (I) 337, 338, 342, 343, 347; (II) 882, 883, 887, 889

Cook on merchant ship. (I) 337, 344; (II) 882, 887

Old Man, captain of merchant ship. (I) 337, 346; (II) 882, 889

Woman with gold teeth in Naples. (I) 330-333, 339, 340, 343, 349, 350; (II) 877-879, 883, 884, 887, 891, 892

Two other women in Naples. (I) 330-333, 337; (II) 877-879, 882

HISTORICAL

Byron, Lord (1788-1824): English poet. (I) 336; (II) 882

"DOCTOR MARTINO"

In (I) *Harper's*, 163 (November 1931), 733-743; (II) *Doctor Martino*, 1934; (III) *Collected Stories*, 1950 as "Dr. Martino."

Charley, Uncle: Negro porter at summer resort. (I) 736.2, 741.1, 743.1, 743.2; (II) 10, 20, 24, 25; (III) 572, 584, 585

Cranston, Lily: Proprietress of summer resort. (I) 735.2, 736.1, 736.2, 737.1, 737.2, 738.1, 738.2, 739.2, 740.1, 740.2, 742.1, 743.1, 743.2; (II) 7-14, 17, 19, 22, 24-26; (III) 570-575, 578, 579, 582, 584, 585
Her father: (I) 735.2; (II) 8; (III) 571

Jarrod, Hubert: Wealthy Yale student. (I) 733.1-743.1; (II) 1-9, 11-24; (III) 565-573, 575-584
His mother: (I) 733.1; (II) 1; (III) 565

King, Alvina: Louise King's mother. (I) 733.2, 734.2, 735.1, 735.2, 736.1, 737.1, 737.2, 738.1, 738.2, 739.1, 740.1, 740.2, 741.1, 741.2, 742.1, 742.2; (II) 3-7, 9-15, 17-23; (III) 566-569, 571-576, 578-582

King, Louise: Hubert Jarrod's fiancée. (I) 733.1-743.1; (II) 1-24; (III) 565-584

Martino, Dr. Jules: Older man who visits summer resort each year. (I) 733.2, 734.1, 736.1-743.2; (II) 3, 4, 7-16, 18-26; (III) 566, 567, 569-585

HISTORICAL

Nightingale, Florence (1820-1910): English nurse. (I) 739.1; (II) 15; (III) 576

BIBLICAL

Lord: (I) 736.1, 740.2; (II) 9, 19; (III) 571, 579

"*DON GIOVANNI*"

In (I) *The Mississippi Quarterly*, 32 (Summer 1979), [484]-495; (II) *Uncollected Stories of William Faulkner*, ed. Joseph Blotner (New York: Random House, 1979).

Herb (Herbie): Wholesale buyer of women's clothes; widower.
    (I) 485-495; (II) [480]-488
  His wife: (I) 485; (II) [480]

Morrison: Herb's friend to whom he goes for advice about women.
    (I) 486-490, 494, 495; (II) 481-484, 488

Steinbauer, Miss: Girl who deserts Herb. (I) 486, 488, 489,
    491-493, 495; (II) 481-483, 485, 486, 488

UNNAMED

Writer who lives below Morrison; large collarless man. (I)
    487, 490-493; (II) 481, 482, 484-487

Man who dances with Miss Steinbauer. (I) 492-494; (II) 486,
    487

HISTORICAL

Balzac, Honoré de (1799-1850): French novelist. (I) 489; (II)
    483

Napoleon (1769-1821): Emperor of France. (I) 493; (II) 487

LITERARY

Don Giovanni: Lover in Mozart's *Don Giovanni*, 1787. (I) [484];
    (II) [480]

"DRY SEPTEMBER"

In (I) *Scribner's*, 89 (January 1931), 49-56; (II) *These 13*,
1931; (III) *Collected Stories*, 1950.

Butch: Youth who participates in lynching party. (I) 49.1-54.2;
    (II) 262-265, 270-274, 276; (III) 169-172, 176-178, 180

Cooper, Minnie: Spinster who accuses Will Mayes of assault.
    (I) 49.1-52.2, 55.1-56.1; (II) 261, 264, 267-271, 276-
    279; (III) 169-176, 180-182
  Her mother: (I) 51.2, 52.1; (II) 267, 269; (III) 173, 175
  Her aunt: (I) 51.2, 52.1; (II) 267, 269; (III) 173, 175

Hawkshaw, Henry: Barber. (I) 49.1-54.2; (II) 261-267, 270-276; (III) 169-173, 175, 176, 178, 179

McLendon: See Plunkett

Mayes, Will: Negro who is accused of assaulting Minnie Cooper. (I) 49.1-55.1; (II) 261-263, 270-277; (III) 169-173, 176-181

Plunkett, John: World War I veteran, leader of lynching party; John McLendon in *These 13* and *CS*. (I) 50.1-54.2, 56.1, 56.2; (II) 264-267, 270-276, 279, 280; (III) 171-173, 176-180, 182, 183
  His wife: (I) 56.1, 56.2; (II) 279, 280; (III) 182, 183

UNNAMED

Salesman who participates in lynching. (I) 49.1-54.2; (II) 261-266, 270-274, 276; (III) 169-172, 176-178, 180

Ex-soldier who participates in lynching. (I) 50.2, 51.1, 52.2-54.2; (II) 265, 266, 270-276; (III) 169, 171-173, 176, 178-180

Second barber. (I) 49.1, 50.2, 51.1; (II) 261, 265, 266; (III) 169, 172, 173

Third barber. (I) 49.1, 50.2, 51.1; (II) 261, 265, 266; (III) 169, 172, 173

Cashier in bank who courts Minnie Cooper. (I) 52.1; (II) 268, 269; (III) 174, 175

Clerk at soda fountain who buys whiskey for Minnie Cooper. (I) 52.1; (II) 269; (III) 175

"DULL TALE"

In *Uncollected Stories of William Faulkner*, ed. Joseph Blotner (New York: Random House, 1979).

Blount, Doctor Gavin: President of the Nonconnah Guards; bachelor physician. [526]-546

His grandfather killed in Civil War. 530, 533, 534, 540-542
His great-grandfather: 542
His grandmother, an invalid: 530, 532, 541, 544, 545
His spinster aunt: 530-532, 541, 545
His mother: 530
His successful physician father: 530-532

Coates, Harrison: Youth who dates Laverne Martin. 538, 539

Heustace: Youth who dates Laverne Martin. 538

Martin, Dal: Politician who wants his daughter to have her debut at ball given by Nonconnah Guards. [526]-529, 534-546
His wife: 527, 535, 537-539
His grandfather: 540, 541
His father: 536
His mother: 536
His brothers and sisters: 536

Martin, Laverne: Dal Martin's daughter. 527, 528, 534, 535, 537-546

Sandeman, Hack: Youth who dates Laverne Martin. 538, 539
His brother: 538, 539

Windham & Healy: Architects of Art Gallery. 541

UNNAMED

Lady with whom Blount discusses his dilemma. 534, 535, 539, 540, 542, 543

Negro who works for Martin and questions Blount. 543, 545

Owner of plantation where Martin's family worked. 536, 537

House Negro who turns Martin away from the front door. 536

HISTORICAL

Beauregard, P.G. (1818-1893): Confederate general. 534

Forrest, Nathan Bedford (1821-1877): Confederate general. 534, 540, 541

Goethe, Johann Wolfgang von (1749-1832): German poet. 534

Maltby, Jasper A. (1826-1867): Union general. 534

Van Dorn, Earl (1820-1863): Confederate general. 534

"ELLY"

In (I) *Story*, 4 (February 1934), 3-15; (II) *Doctor Martino*, 1934; (III) *Collected Stories*, 1950.

Ailanthia I: Elly's grandmother. (I) 3-15; (II) 243-248, 250-252, 254-256, 258-262; (III) 207-215, 217-223
  Her son: (I) 8, 10, 12; (II) 250, 251, 254, 257; (III) 214, 217, 220
    His wife: (I) 10, 11; (II) 254; (III) 217
    His daughter: (I) 10, 12; (II) 254, 256; (III) 217, 219

Ailanthia II (Elly): Young girl. (I) 3-15; (II) 242-262; (III) 207-224
  Her father: (I) 3, 6, 7, 11-13; (II) 243, 247, 248, 250, 254-256, 258; (III) 208, 211, 213, 217, 218, 220
  Her mother: (I) 3, 6-9, (II) 243, 248, 250-252, 254; (III) 208, 211-217

De Montigny, Paul: Elly's lover. (I) 3-15; (II) 242, 243, 245-249, 251-262; (III) 207-223
  His uncle: (I) 5; (II) 245; (III) 209

Philip: Elly's fiancé. (I) 7-9; (II) 249-252; (III) 213-216

UNNAMED

Elly's girlfriend. (I) 4, 5; (II) 245, 246; (III) 209, 210

"EPISODE"

In (I) *William Faulkner: New Orleans Sketches*, ed. Carvel Collins (New York: Random House, 1968); (II) *Sinbad in New Orleans*, ed. Leland Cox (Spartanburg, S.C.: The Reprint Company, 1981). First printed in New Orleans *Times-Picayune* Sunday magazine section, 16 August 1925, p. 2.

Joe: Old blind man.   (I) 104-107; (II) 87-89

Spratling: Artist friend of narrator.   (I) 104-107; (II) 87-89

UNNAMED

Old woman with Joe.   (I) 104-107; (II) 87-89

Narrator, a writer.   (I) 104-107; (II) 87-89

"AN ERROR IN CHEMISTRY"

In (I) *Ellery Queen's Mystery Magazine*, 7 (June 1946), 4-19; (II) *Knight's Gambit*, 1949.

Berry, Ben: Sheriff's deputy.   (I) 5.1, 6.2, 7.2, 8.1, 8.2, 10.2, 11.1, 11.2; (II) 109, 110, 112, 114, 117-120

Canova, Signor: See Flint, Joel

Ewell, Bryan: Sheriff's deputy protecting Wesley Pritchel. (I) 10.2, 11.1, 11.2, 12.1; (II) 117, 118

Flint, Ellie: Daughter of Wesley Pritchel; wife of Joel Flint. (I) 5.1-8.1, 9.2-10.2, 11.2-14.2, 15.2, 17.2-18.2; (II) 109-113, 115-117, 119-124, 126, 129, 130

Flint, Joel: Husband of Ellie Flint; previously known as Signor Canova. (I) 5.1-8.2, 9.2-11.2, 12.2-14.2, 15.2, 16.2-19.2; (II) 109-126, 128-131

Hub: Sheriff.   (I) 5.1, 6.2-17.1, 18.1-19.2; (II) 109-118, 120-131

Pritchel, Wesley: Father-in-law of Joel Flint.   (I) 5.1-6.2, 7.2-17.1, 18.1, 18.2; (II) 109-128, 130
  His wife and family: (I) 15.2; (II) 126

Stevens, Gavin: County attorney.   (I) 6.2-15.1, 16.1-17.2, 18.1-19.2; (II) 111-121, 123-131
  His father: (I) 16.2; (II) 127

Workman, Mr.: Insurance adjuster.   (I) 13.1-14.2, 18.1; (II) 121-124, 130

"Evangeline"   233

UNNAMED

Narrator, related to Gavin Stevens. (I) 5.1-19.2; (II) 109-131
  His father: (I) 16.2; (II) 127

Three northern men who want to buy land. (I) 9.1, 14.1-15.2; (II) 115, 123-125

"EVANGELINE"

In *Uncollected Stories of William Faulkner*, ed. Joseph Blotner (New York: Random House, 1979). First printed in *Atlantic*, 244 (November 1979), 68-80.

Abum: Female descendant of Raby. 585, 586

Bon, Charles: Judith Sutpen's husband from New Orleans who is an orphan and is same age as Henry Sutpen. 584-591, 598-603, 605, 606, 608, 609
  His guardian: 587, 588, 609

Bon, Mrs. Charles: Bon's mulatto wife. 599-603, 606, 608, 609
  Their son, nine years old: 602, 603, 606

Bon, Judith Sutpen: Sutpen's daughter who marries Charles Bon before he leaves for the war. 584-606, 608

Don: Architect friend of narrator who spends vacation in small Mississippi town. [583]-594, 596

Rose: Female descendent of Raby. 585, 586

Sibey: Female descendant of Raby. 585, 586

Sutpen, Col.: Planter who dies in 1870 when wagon overturns and throws him in a ditch. [583]-592, 595, 598, 600, 601, 603-606
  His wife who dies in 1863: 584, 587-591, 598, 601, 604

Sutpen, Henry: Sutpen's son who is never seen again after he brings Bon's body home. 584-591, 593, 595, 597-601, 603-607, 609

Sutpen, Judith: See Bon, Judith Sutpen

Sutpen, Raby: Old Negro, a great-grandmother. 585-587, 591-608
   Her daughter: 586, 587, 591, 592, 596, 607-609

UNNAMED

Narrator, a journalist. [583]-609

Negro with Bon's mulatto wife. 602, 603

Foreign architect brought in by Col. Sutpen. 584

HISTORICAL

Bayard, Pierre Terrail de (1473?-1524): French soldier-hero. 586

Sherman, William T. (1820-1891): Union general. 590

BIBLICAL

Lord: 600

"FOOL ABOUT A HORSE"

In (I) *Scribner's*, 100 (August 1936), 80-86; (II) *Uncollected Stories of William Faulkner*, ed. Joseph Blotner (New York: Random House, 1979). Incorporated in *The Hamlet*, Book One, Chapter 2, 1940.

Hoke: Man who owns pasture where Pat Stamper is camped. (I) 82.2, 82.3; (II) 123, 124

Holland, Anse: Owner of stock which Pap traded to Beasley Kemp for a horse. (I) 80.1, 80.2, 81.2, 86.3; (II) [118]-122, 134

Jim: Pat Stamper's Negro assistant. (I) 82.2-83.3, 84.2-85.3; (II) 123-127, 129-133

Kemp, Beasley: Man who traded Pap a horse. (I) 80.1-84.1, 85.3, 86.1; (II) [118]-127, 132, 133

McCaslin, Uncle Ike: Jefferson hardware store owner. (I) 81.3, 82.3, 84.1, 84.2, 85.2, 86.3; (II) 121, 124, 128, 129, 132, 134

Peabody, Doc: Yoknapatawpha store owner. (I) 84.2; (II) 129

Short, Herman: Man who swapped Pat Stamper a buckboard and a set of harness for horse. (I) 82.1, 82.3, 83.1, 85.3; (II) 122, 124, 125

Stamper, Pat: Horse trader. (I) 80.1, 80.3, 81.1, 81.2, 82.1-85.3, 86.3; (II) [118], 119, 122-132, 134

Tull, Odom: Man who takes Vynie to town for the separator. (I) 86.1, 86.2; (II) 133, 134

Varner, Jody: Son of Will Varner who manages Varner's store. (I) 82.1, 82.3, 83.2; (II) 122, 124, 126

Varner, Will: Frenchman's Bend store owner. (I) 81.1, 81.3, 82.1, 82.3, 83.3; (II) 120, 122, 124, 127

Vynie: Pap's wife; narrator's mother. (I) 80.1-81.3, 82.2-84.1, 85.1-86.3; (II) [118]-121, 123, 124, 128, 131-134

UNNAMED

Pap, narrator's father. (I) 80.1-86.3; (II) [118]-134

Narrator, young boy. (I) 80.1-86.3; (II) [118]-134

BIBLICAL

Lord: (I) 80.2, 81.1, 81.2; (II) [118]-120

"FOX HUNT"

In (I) *Harper's*, 163 (September 1931), 392-402; (II) *Doctor Martino*, 1934; (III) *Collected Stories*, 1950.

Adam: Wealthy young Indian, student at Yale; Allen in *DM* and
   CS. (I) 397.2, 398.1, 399.1; (II) 40, 41, 44, 45; (III)
   597, 598, 601, 602
 His wife: (I) 397.2, 399.2; (II) 40, 44; (III) 597, 601
 His father: (I) 398.1; (II) 41; (III) 598

Allen: See Adam

Andrews: Blair's servant. (I) 396.2; (II) 37; (III) 595

Blair, Harrison: Wealthy American. (I) 292.2-394.1, 395.1-
   402.2; (II) 29-32, 34-48, 50, 51; (III) 588-606
 His father: (I) 395.2, 397.1; (II) 35, 39; (III) 593, 597

Blair, Mrs. Harrison: Harrison Blair's wife. (I) 393.1, 394.2-
   401.2, 402.2; (II) 29, 33-47, 49-51; (III) 588, 589, 591-
   599, 601-603, 605-607
 Her mother: (I) 396.1, 397.1-398.1; (II) 37, 39-41; (III)
   594, 595, 597, 598
 Her father: (I) 396.1, 397.2; (II) 37, 40; (III) 595, 597

Burke: Blair's maid. (I) 397.2, 399.2, 400.2; (II) 40, 44, 45,
   47; (III) 597, 601-603

Callaghan: Riding instructor. (I) 397.1, 397.2, 399.1, 400.1,
   400.2; (II) 38-40, 43-46; (III) 596, 597, 600, 602, 603

Ernie: Blair's valet/bodyguard. (I) 395.2-401.1; (II) 35-47;
   (III) 593-604

Gawtrey, Steve: Mrs. Blair's lover. (I) 393.1, 394.2-400.2,
   401.2-402.2; (II) 29, 30, 33, 34, 43-47, 49-51; (III)
   588, 589, 591, 592, 599-603, 605-607

Mose, Unc: Negro who tends Blair's horses. (I) 392.1; (II)
   28; (III) 587

Van Dyming, Mr.: Man who is supposedly interested in buying
   Gawtrey's horse. (I) 399.1; (II) 43; (III) 600

Zigfield: Man who owns horses. (I) 397.1; (II) 39; (III) 596

UNNAMED

Blair's chauffeur. (I) 395.2-400.2; (II) 35-47; (III) 593-604

Older country man. (I) 392.2-395.1, 401.1-402.2; (II) 28-34,
    47-51; (III) 588-593, 604-607

Young country man. (I) 392.2, 393.1, 394.1-395.1, 401.1-402.2;
    (II) 28-35, 47-51; (III) 588-593, 604-607

Blair's groom. (I) 393.1, 393.2; (II) 30, 31; (III) 589, 590

HISTORICAL

Rockefeller, John D. (1839-1937): American oil magnate. (I)
    400.1; (II) 46; (III) 602

BIBLICAL

Lord: (I) 400.1; (II) 46; (III) 602

"FRANKIE AND JOHNNY"

In (I) *Sinbad in New Orleans*, ed. Leland Cox (Spartanburg, S.C.:
The Reprint Company, 1981); (II) *Uncollected Stories of William
Faulkner*, ed. Joseph Blotner (New York: Random House, 1979).
First printed in *The Mississippi Quarterly*, 31 (Summer 1978),
454-464.

Frances (Frankie): Young girl. (I) 105-115; (II) [338]-347
    Her mother: (I) 105, 109-115; (II) [338], 341-347
    Her father: (I) 105, 110, 115; (II) [338], 342, 343, 347

Johnny: Frankie's lover. (I) 105-109, 112, 113, 115; (II)
    339-342, 345-347
    His father: (I) 107; (II) 340

Ryan: Policeman. (I) 107, 108; (II) 340, 341

UNNAMED

Drunk who frightens Frankie. (I) 106-108; (II) 339-341

BIBLICAL

God: (I) 114; (II) 346

"GO DOWN, MOSES"

In (I) *Collier's*, 107 (25 January 1941), 19, 20, 24, 46; (II) *Uncollected Stories of William Faulkner*, ed. Joseph Blotner (New York: Random House, 1979). Revised as final chapter of *Go Down, Moses*, 1942.

Beauchamp, Luke: Mollie Beauchamp's husband. (I) 20.1, 45.1; (II) 259, 261

Beauchamp, Mollie Worsham: Old Negro woman, grandmother of Samuel Beauchamp. (I) 19.1, 19.3, 19.4, 20.1, 20.2, 45.1, 45.2, 46.1, 46.2; (II) [256]-266

Beauchamp, Samuel Worsham (Butch): Mollie Beauchamp's grandson. (I) 19.1-20.2, 45.1, 45.2, 46.1, 46.2; (II) [256]-262, 264-266
 His mother: (I) 19.1, 20.1, 20.2; (II) [256], 258, 261
 His father: (I) 19.1, 20.1, 20.2; (II) [256], 258, 260

Edmonds, Carothers: Landowner who sent Samuel Beauchamp away. (I) 19.1, 19.3, 20.1, 20.2, 45.1, 46.1; (II) 257-262, 264

Rouncewell: Store owner whom Samuel Beauchamp robbed. (I) 20.1; (II) 259

Stevens, Gavin: County attorney. (I) 19.2-20.2, 45.1, 45.2, 46.1, 46.2; (II) 257-266

Wilmoth, Mr.: Jefferson newspaper editor. (I) 20.1, 20.2, 45.1, 46.1; (II) 259, 260, 262, 263, 265, 266

Worsham, Miss Belle: Jefferson spinster. (I) 20.2, 45.1, 45.2, 46.1, 46.2; (II) 260-266
 Her father: (I) 20.2, 45.1; (II) 260, 261
 Her grandfather: (I) 20.2; (II) 260

Worsham, Hamp: Mollie Beauchamp's brother. (I) 19.4, 20.2, 45.2, 46.1; (II) 258, 260, 261, 263-265
 His parents: (I) 20.2; (II) 260
 His wife: (I) 20.2, 45.2, 46.1; (II) 260, 263-265

UNNAMED

Warden of prison where Samuel Beauchamp is executed. (I) 20.2, 45.1; (II) 260, 262

"Gold Is Not Always"   239

Census taker.   (I) 19.1; (II) [256], 257

                             BIBLICAL

Benjamin: Jacob's youngest son in Genesis.   (I) 19.3, 19.4,
     46.1; (II) 257, 264

                    "GOLD IS NOT ALWAYS"

In (I) *Atlantic*, 166 (November 1940), 563-70; (II) *Uncollected Stories of William Faulkner*, ed. Joseph Blotner (New York: Random House, 1979). Revised as Chapter 2 of "The Fire and the Hearth" in *Go Down, Moses*, 1942.

Beauchamp, Lucas: Old Negro who lives on Edmonds' plantation.
     (I) 563.1-565.1, 566.1-570.2; (II) [226]-229, 231-237
  His wife: (I) 570.2; (II) 237

Dan: Negro worker on Edmonds' plantation.   (I) 565.1-566.1,
     569.2; (II) 229-232, 237

Edmonds, Roth: Large landowner on whose land Lucas Beauchamp
        lives.   (I) 563.1-564.1, 565.1-567.1, 569.2-570.2; (II)
        [226], 227, 229-232, 236, 237
  His father: (I) 563.2, 570.1; (II) 227, 237

Oscar: Negro worker on Edmonds' plantation.   (I) 565.1, 565.2,
     566.1; (II) 229-231

Wilkins, George: Young Negro with Lucas Beauchamp.   (I) 564.1,
     564.2, 566.1-569.2, 570.2; (II) 227-229, 231-237

                             UNNAMED

Two white men who reportedly found gold in area.   (I) 563.2,
     564.2, 569.1, 570.1; (II) 227, 228, 237

Salesman of gold-finding machine.   (I) 563.1-564.2, 566.1-570.1;
     (II) [226]-229, 231-237

"GOLDEN LAND"

In (I) *American Mercury*, 35 (May 1935), 1-14; (II) *Collected Stories*, 1950.

Ewing, Ira, I: Father of Ira Ewing II; husband of Samantha
    Ewing I. (I) 1.2, 2.1, 2.2, 3.1, 6.1, 7.1, 12.2, 13.1,
    13.2; (II) 702-705, 710, 712, 722-724

Ewing, Ira, II: Son of Ira Ewing I; California businessman.
    (I) 1.1-14.1; (II) 701-725
  His wife: (I) 2.1, 2.2, 3.2, 4.1, 4.2, 5.1, 5.2, 6.1, 7.1,
    8.1, 8.2, 12.1, 12.2, 13.1, 14.1; (II) 703, 705-710,
    721, 723-725
  Her father: (I) 2.1; (II) 703

Ewing, Samantha, I: Mother of Ira Ewing II. (I) 2.1, 2.2, 3.1,
    4.1, 4.2, 5.1, 6.2, 7.1, 7.2, 8.1, 8.2, 10.2, 11.1, 12.1-
    14.2; (II) 702-704, 706-708, 711-715, 719-726

Ewing, Samantha, II (April Lalear): Ira Ewing II's daughter.
    (I) 2.1, 2.2, 3.2, 4.1, 5.1, 5.2, 6.2, 7.1, 7.2, 8.1,
    8.2, 9.1, 12.1, 12.2, 13.1, 13.2, 14.1; (II) 703, 705,
    706, 708, 709, 711, 713-715, 717, 721-725

Ewing, Voyd: Ira Ewing II's son. (I) 2.1, 2.2, 3.2, 4.1, 4.2,
    5.1, 5.2, 6.2, 7.1, 8.2, 12.1, 12.2, 13.1, 13.2, 14.1;
    (II) 703, 705-709, 711, 714, 717, 721-725

Kazimura: Japanese gardener. (I) 3.1, 6.2, 7.2, 11.1, 12.1;
    (II) 704, 711, 712, 719, 721

Philip: Filipino chauffeur for Ira Ewing II. (I) 2.2, 3.1,
    4.2, 6.1, 6.2, 8.2, 10.2, 11.1; (II) 703, 704, 707, 710,
    711, 715, 718, 720

UNNAMED

Ira Ewing II's mistress. (I) 9.2, 10.1-11.2; (II) 717-721
  Her daughter: (I) 9.2; (II) 717

Ira Ewing II's secretary. (I) 8.2, 9.1, 9.2; (II) 710, 715,
    716

HISTORICAL

Einstein, Albert (1879-1955): Mathematician and physicist. (I) 1.2; (II) 702

Rousseau, Jean Jacques (1712-1778): French philosopher. (I) 1.2; (II) 702

BIBLICAL

Lord: (I) 13.2; (II) 724

MYTHIC

Esculapius: Roman god of medicine and of healing. (I) 1.2; (II) 702

"HAIR"

In (I) *American Mercury*, 23 (May 1931), 53-61; (II) *These 13*, 1931; (III) *Collected Stories*, 1950.

Bidwell: Storekeeper. (I) 56.2, 60.1-61.2; (II) 226, 228-230; (III) 138, 145-147

Burchett: Man with whose family Susan Reed lives. (I) 53.1, 54.2, 55.1, 56.1; (II) 208, 212, 213, 215; (III) 131, 134-136

Burchett, Mrs.: Woman who watches after Susan Reed. (I) 53.1, 54.2, 55.1, 56.1, 58.2; (II) 208, 211-213, 215, 222; (III) 131, 134-136, 141
  Her children: (I) 53.1; (II) 208; (III) 131

Cowan, Mrs.: Hawkshaw's landlady in Jefferson. (I) 56.1, 59.1; (II) 215, 223, 224; (III) 136, 142

Ewing, Mitch: Freight agent in Jefferson. (I) 59.1; (II) 224; (III) 142, 143

Fox, "'"tt: Barber at Maxey's. (I) 53.2, 54.1, 54.2, 55.2, 56.1, 59.1, 59.2; (II) 209-212, 214, 215, 223, 225; (III) 131-136, 142-144

Hawkshaw: Barber whose name had been Henry Stribling. (I)
  53.1-61.2; (II) 208-229; (III) 131-148

Maxey: Barbershop owner. (I) 53.1, 53.2, 54.1, 55.2, 56.1,
  58.1-59.2; (II) 208-210, 215, 216, 221-225; (III) 131-
  133, 136, 137, 140-143
 His brother-in-law: (I) 58.2; (II) 222, 223; (III) 141, 142

Reed, Susan: Young girl who lives with the Burchetts. (I)
  53.1-55.2, 58.2-60.1, 61.2; (II) 208-215, 222, 224-227,
  230, 231; (III) 131-135, 141, 143, 144, 147, 148

Starnes, Sophie: Girl to whom Henry Stribling had been engaged.
  (I) 56.2, 57.1, 57.2, 60.2, 61.1; (II) 218-220, 228, 229;
  (III) 138-140, 146, 147

Starnes, Will: Sophie Starnes' father. (I) 56.2-58.1, 60.2;
  (II) 217-220, 228; (III) 138-140, 146

Starnes, Mrs. Will: Sophie Starnes' mother. (I) 56.2-57.2,
  60.1, 61.1, 61.2; (II) 218-220, 227, 229, 230; (III)
  138-140, 145-147

Stevens, Gavin: Jefferson District Attorney. (I) 60.1, 60.2,
  61.2; (II) 226-228, 230, 231; (III) 144, 145, 147, 148

Stribling, Henry: See Hawkshaw

UNNAMED

Narrator, a salesman. (I) 53.1-61.2; (II) 208-231; (III) 131-
  148

Starnes relatives in Alabama. (I) 58.1, 60.1, 60.2; (II) 226-
  228; (III) 140, 144-146

"HAND UPON THE WATERS"

In (I) *The Saturday Evening Post*, 212 (4 November 1939), 14,
15, 75, 76, 78, 79; (II) *Knight's Gambit*, 1949.

Ballenbaugh, Boyd: Younger brother of Tyler Ballenbaugh. (I)
  76.1, 76.2, 76.3, 78.1, 78.2, 79.1, 79.2; (II) 71, 72,
  74-80

Ballenbaugh, Tyler: Older brother of Boyd Ballenbaugh. (I) 76.1, 76.2, 76.3, 78.1, 78.2, 79.1, 79.2; (II) 70-80

Blake, Jim: Man who helps to carry Lonnie Grinnup's body. (I) 75.2, 76.1; (II) 68-70

Grenier, Louis: One of the three founders of Yoknapatawpha. (I) 15.2, 15.3; (II) 66

Grinnup, Lonnie: Descendent of Louis Grenier; real name also Louis Grenier. (I) 14.1, 14.2, 15.1, 15.2, 15.3, 75.1, 75.2, 76.1, 76.3, 78.2, 79.1, 79.2; (II) 63-68, 71-77, 80, 81

Holston: One of Yoknapatawpha's founders. (I) 15.2, 15.3; (II) 66

Ike: Man who helps to carry Lonnie Grinnup's body. (I) 75.2, 76.1; (II) 68-70

Joe: Deaf-mute raised by Lonnie Grinnup. (I) 14.1, 14.3, 15.1, 15.3, 75.1, 76.3, 78.1, 79.2; (II) 63-67, 72, 73, 79, 80

Matthew: Man who helps to carry Lonnie Grinnup's body. (I) 75.2, 76.1; (II) 68-70

Mitchell: Store owner. (I) 75.2; (II) 68

Nate: Negro man. (I) 78.1; (II) 74, 75

Pose: Man who helps to carry Lonnie Grinnup's body. (I) 75.2, 76.1; (II) 68-70

Stevens, Gavin: County attorney. (I) 15.1, 15.2, 15.3, 75.1, 75.2, 76.1, 76.2, 76.3, 78.1, 78.2, 79.1, 79.2; (II) 65-81
  His ancestor who helped to found Yoknapatawpha County: (I) 15.2, 15.3; (II) 66

UNNAMED

Older man who discovers Lonnie Grinnup's body. (I) 14.1, 14.2, 14.3, 15.1, 75.1, 76.1; (II) 63-65, 68, 69

Youth who discovers Lonnie Grinnup's body. (I) 14.1, 14.2, 14.3, 15.1, 75.1, 75.2, 76.1, 79.2; (II) 63-65, 68, 69, 81

Coroner. (I) 15.1, 75.1, 75.2; (II) 65, 67, 68

Sheriff. (I) 78.1, 79.2; (II) 79, 80

Insurance agent. (I) 76.3, 78.1; (II) 72-74

Woman with Nate. (I) 78.1; (II) 75

"THE HILL"

In *William Faulkner: Early Prose and Poetry*, ed. Carvel Collins (Boston: Little, Brown, 1962); first printed in *The Mississippian*, 10 March 1922, pp. 1, 2. This sketch was expanded into "Nympholepsy."

Laborer who lives in hamlet. 90-92

"HOG PAWN"

In *Uncollected Stories of William Faulkner*, ed. Joseph Blotner (New York: Random House, 1979); incorporated in Chapter 14 of Book Three of *The Mansion*, 1959.

Chick: Narrator. [311]-327

Gavin, Uncle: Lawyer uncle of Chick. 313-315, 317, 321-327

Meadowfill, Otis: Father of Essie Meadowfill Smith. [311]-327

Meadowfill, Mrs. Otis: Otis' wife. [311]-313, 316, 317, 319, 324, 325, 327

Smith, Essie Meadowfill: Daughter of Otis Meadowfill; wife of McKinley Smith. [311]-316, 318-320, 322, 323, 325-327

Smith, McKinley: Demobilized Korean War Marine sergeant. 312, 318-320, 323, 325-327

Snopes: Hog owner who tries to kill Meadowfill. 314-318, 320-327

HISTORICAL

Roosevelt, Franklin D. (1882-1945): President of United States, 1933-1945. 314

"HOME"

In (I) *William Faulkner: New Orleans Sketches*, ed. Carvel Collins (New York: Random House, 1968); (II) *Sinbad in New Orleans*, ed. Leland Cox (Spartanburg, S.C.: The Reprint Company, 1981). First printed in New Orleans *Times-Picayune* Sunday magazine section, 22 February 1925, p. 3.

Jean-Baptiste: Immigrant to New Orleans. (I) 28-33; (II) 13-17.
  His mother: (I) 29; (II) 14

Pete: Friend of Jean-Baptiste. (I) 29, 30, 32; (II) 13, 15, 16

Tony the Wop: Friend of Jean-Baptiste. (I) 29, 30, 32; (II) 13, 15, 16

UNNAMED

General, the: friend of Jean-Baptiste. (I) 29, 32; (II) 13, 16

HISTORICAL

Napoleon (1769-1821): Emperor of France. (I) 33; (II) 17

BIBLICAL

God: (I) 31, 32; (II) 16

"HONOR"

In (I) *American Mercury*, 20 (July 1930), 268-274; (II) *Doctor Martino*, 1934; (III) *Collected Stories*, 1950.

Harris: Owner of flying circus. (I) 272.1; (II) 365, 366;
    (III) 559, 560

Jack: Man who tells Monaghan about Harris. (I) 269.1; (II)
    357, 358; (III) 552, 553

John: Husband of woman for whom Monaghan demonstrates the car.
    (I) 274.1; (II) 370, 371; (III) 563

Monaghan, Buck: Narrator; World War I veteran; wing walker.
    (I) 268.1-274.2; (II) 355-371; (III) 551-564

Reinhardt: Car dealer for whom Monaghan works. (I) 268.1,
    274.1, 274.2; (II) 355, 356, 370, 371; (III) 551, 563,
    564

Rogers, Howard: Stunt pilot. (I) 269.1, 269.2, 270.1, 270.2,
    271.1, 271.2, 272.1, 272.2, 273.1, 273.2; (II) 357-368,
    370; (III) 552-563

Rogers, Mildred: Howard's wife. (I) 269.1, 269.2, 270.1, 270.2,
    271.1, 271.2, 273.2; (II) 357-365, 370; (III) 553-559,
    563
  Her mother: (I) 270.2; (II) 361; (III) 556
  Her child: (I) 273.2; (II) 370; (III) 563

Waldrip: Aviator who helped Monaghan learn wing walking. (I)
    268.1; (II) 356, 357; (III) 552

West, Miss: Reinhardt's secretary. (I) 268.1, 274.1, 274.2;
    (II) 355, 370, 371; (III) 551, 563, 564

White: Man from whom Monaghan wins money. (I) 268.1; (II)
    356, 357; (III) 552
  His wife: (I) 268.1; (II) 357; (III) 552

UNNAMED

Indian Subadar in British army whom Monaghan met in war. (I)
    273.2; (II) 369; (III) 562

German flyer who was taken prisoner. (I) 273.2; (II) 369;
    (III) 562

Idyll in the Desert 247

"THE HOUND"

In (I) *Harper's*, 163 (August 1931), 266-274; (II) *Doctor Martino*, 1934; (III) *Uncollected Stories of William Faulkner*, ed. Joseph Blotner (New York: Random House, 1979). Incorporated in Chapter 2 of Book Three in *The Hamlet*, 1940.

Cotton, Ernest: Man who kills Houston; bachelor who lives near Varner's store. (I) 266.1-274.2; (II) 52-71; (III) [152]-164

Houston: Man Cotton kills. (I) 266.2, 267.1, 268.1-272.2, 274.1, 274.2; (II) 53-62, 66, 67, 70; (III) [152]-158, 161, 162, 164

Joe: Driver of car which takes Cotton to jail. (I) 273.1, 273.2; (II) 68, 69; (III) 162, 163

Snopes: Clerk in Varner's store. (I) 271.1; (II) 63, 64; (III) 159

Tull, Vernon: Man who identifies Cotton's gun. (I) 271.1; (II) 63, 64; (III) 159

Varner: Store owner. (I) 266.2, 267.1, 268.2, 271.1; (II) 53, 54, 58, 63; (III) [152], 153, 156, 159

UNNAMED

Sheriff. (I) 268.2-270.2, 273.1, 273.2; (II) 58-62, 68; (III) 156-158, 162, 163

Five men at Varner's store. (I) 268.2-270.2; (II) 58-62; (III) 156-158

Deputy. (I) 270.2; (II) 62; (III) 158

Second deputy. (I) 273.1; (II) 68; (III) 162, 163

IDYLL IN THE DESERT

(I) New York: Random House, 1931; also in (II) *Uncollected Stories of William Faulkner*, ed. Joseph Blotner (New York: Random House, 1979).

Crump, Lucas: Mail carrier. (I) [3]-17; (II) [399]-411

Howes, Darrel (Dorry House): Young consumptive. (I) 6-17; (II) 402-411
  His mother: (I) 12; (II) 407
  His wife: (I) 15, 16; (II) 410, 411

Hughes, Manny: Postmaster in Blizzard, Arizona. (I) 13, 14; (II) 408, 409

Lewis, Matt: Livery stable owner. (I) 4, 10, 15, 17; (II) 400, 405, 410, 411

Painter: Rancher. (I) [3], 4, 10; (II) [399], 400, 405

Sharpses: People referred to by Lucas Crump. (I) [3]; (II) [399]

UNNAMED

Woman who tends to Howes. (I) 6-17; (II) 402, 403, 405-411.
  Her husband: (I) 7, 11-15, 17; (II) 403, 406-409, 411
  Her children: (I) 11; (II) 406

Narrator. (I) [3]-17; (II) [399]-411

BIBLICAL

Lord: (I) 8; (II) 404

Peter, Saint: Disciple of Christ. (I) [3]; (II) [399]

"JEALOUSY"

In (I) *William Faulkner: New Orleans Sketches*, ed. Carvel Collin (New York: Random House, 1968); (II) *Sinbad in New Orleans*, ed. Leland Cox (Spartanburg, S.C.: The Reprint Company, 1981). First printed in New Orleans *Times-Picayune* Sunday magazine section, 1 March 1925, p. 2.

Antonio: Italian restaurant owner. (I) 34-40; (II) 19-24
  His wife: (I) 34-39; (II) 19-23
    Her father: (I) 38; (II) 22, 23

"A Justice"

UNNAMED

Tall waiter. (I) 34, 36-40; (II) 19-24

BIBLICAL

God: (I) 35, 38; (II) 20, 22

"A JUSTICE"

In (I) *These 13*, 1931; (II) *Collected Stories*, 1950; see also *Big Woods*, 1955.

Basket, Herman: Indian, friend of Crawfishford. (I) 185-193, 195-206; (II) 345-359

Callicoat, David: Riverboat pilot. (I) 187, 188; (II) 346, 347

Compson, General: Narrator's grandfather. (I) 183, 184, 204, 206, 207; (II) 343, 344, 358-360

Compson, Caddy: Narrator's sister. (I) 183, 184, 204, 206, 207; (II) 343, 358, 360

Compson, Jason: Narrator's younger brother. (I) 183, 184, 204, 206, 207; (II) 343, 358, 360

Compson, Quentin: Narrator. (I) 183-207; (II) 343-360
  His great-grandfather: (I) 185; (II) 344

Crawfishford (Craw-ford): Father of Sam Fathers. (I) 186-205; (II) 345-359

Doom: See Ikkemotubbe

Fathers, Sam: Part-Indian, part-Negro worker on Compson farm. (I) 183-207; (II) 343-360
  His mother: (I) 185, 189, 190, 194-198, 200, 201, 204; (II) 344, 345, 347, 348, 350-356, 358
    Her Negro husband: (I) 195-198, 200-206; (II) 352-359
    Her second son: (I) 206; (II) 359

Ikkemotubbe (Doom): Nephew of the Man who becomes the Man.
(I) 185-200, 202-205; (II) 344-355, 357-359
His mother: (I) 186, 187, 190; (II) 346, 348
Her brother, the Man: (I) 186, 187, 190-193; (II) 346, 348-350
His son: (I) 186, 190-193; (II) 346, 348-350

Roskus: Negro worker for the Compsons. (I) 183, 206, 207; (II) 343, 360

Sometimes-Wakeup: Brother of the Man; uncle of Doom. (I) 186, 190-192; (II) 346, 348, 349

Stokes, Mr.: Manager of Compson farm. (I) 183, 184, 204, 206; (II) 343, 344, 358, 360

UNNAMED

The Willow-Bearer. (I) 191, 192; (II) 349

Whiskey trader. (I) 185, 187, 205; (II) 344, 346, 359

Three white men who take Negroes in exchange for the steamboat. (I) 194-196; (II) 351, 352

New Orleans French chief. (I) 190; (II) 348

"THE KID LEARNS"

In (I) *William Faulkner: New Orleans Sketches*, ed. Carvel Collins (New York: Random House, 1968); (II) *Sinbad in New Orleans*, ed. Leland Cox (Spartanburg, S.C.: The Reprint Company, 1981). First printed in New Orleans *Times-Picayune* Sunday magazine section, 31 May 1925, p. 2.

Gray, Johnny: Young man in New Orleans. (I) 86-91; (II) 81-85.

Little Sister Death: (I) 91; (II) 85

Mary: Girl whom Johnny rescues from the Wop. (I) 88-91; (II) 82-85

Otto: Johnny's friend. (I) 86-89; (II) 81-84

"Knight's Gambit" 251

Ryan: Policeman. (I) 90; (II) 84

Ryan, Mrs.: Policeman's wife. (I) 90; (II) 84, 85

UNNAMED

Wop, the. (I) 87-90; (II) 81-84

"THE KINGDOM OF GOD"

In (I) *William Faulkner: New Orleans Sketches*, ed. Carvel Collins (New York: Random House, 1968); (II) *Sinbad in New Orleans*, ed. Leland Cox (Spartanburg, S.C.: The Reprint Company, 1981). First printed in New Orleans *Times-Picayune* Sunday magazine section, 26 April 1925, p. 4.

Jake: Person with whom idiot sometimes stays. (I) 56; (II) 32

UNNAMED

Idiot. (I) 55-60; (II) 31-35

Idiot's brother. (I) 55-60; (II) 31-35

Companion of idiot and his brother. (I) 55-59; (II) 31-34

Policeman. (I) 56-60; (II) 32-35

Second policeman. (I) 58-60; (II) 33-35

"KNIGHT"S GAMBIT"

In *Knight's Gambit*, 1949.

Cayley, Miss: Young girl in whom Max Harriss is interested. 183-191, 194, 195, 226
  Her mother: 184

Cayley, Hence: Father of girl in whom Max Harriss is interested
    184, 185

Gualdres, Captain Sebastian: Argentinian officer. 136-138,
    142; returns with Harrisses, 163, 165-175; Miss Harriss
    discussed, 178-183, 185, 186, 189, 191, 193-195, 212-
    217; wager with Gavin Stevens, 218-224; married, 226,
    227; leaves, 228, 229, 238; sends message to G. Stevens,
    241-243
  His wife: see Harriss, Miss

Harriss: New Orleans bootlegger. 144-153, 155, 156, 160-163,
    165, 167, 210, 229, 230, 237, 241

Harriss, Miss: Daughter of bootlegger and wife of Sebastian
    Gualdres. 135-139, 141, 142, 146; born, 151-153, 159,
    160; moves to Yoknapatawpha County, 161-163, 166, 168,
    174, 175; talks with Gavin Stevens, 177-183; brings in
    Cayley girl, 184-191, 194, 195, 202, 203, 208, 216, 222,
    224; married, 226, 227; leaves, 228, 242

Harriss, Mrs.: Harriss' widow; Gavin Stevens' wife. 137, 138,
    142; background, 144, 145; marries Harriss, 146-154, 159;
    Harriss dead, 160-164, 166-169, 172-174; discussed by
    daughter, 179-182, 189, 193, 194, 216; Stevens' wager
    with Gualdres, 218, 219, 223, 227; relationship with
    Gavin Stevens, 233-236, 238; married to Gavin Stevens,
    241, 244, 245
  Her father: 143-145, 148, 149, 152, 153, 155, 166, 212,
    230, 233, 234
    His father: 166
  Her mother: 144

Harriss, Max: Son of bootlegger. 135-142, 146; born, 151-153,
    159, 160; moves to Yoknapatawpha County, 161-163, 172-
    175; discussed by sister and G. Stevens, 177-185, 188-
    190; discussed by Gavin Stevens and Robert Markey, 192-
    195, 198, 199, 202-205, 207; buys stallion, 208-212,
    216, 219, 221; returns from Memphis, 222-225; leaves to
    enlist, 226, 228, 229, 241, 242

Hogganbeck, Melissa: History teacher of Charles Mallison. 199,
    200, 205, 206

Killegrew, Hampton: Jefferson night marshal. 203, 204, 222,
    226

McCallum, Rafe: Farmer and horse breeder. 168, 200-202, 206,
    208-217, 219-221, 223

"Knight's Gambit"   253

McCallum nephews: Twins. 200

McWilliams, Mr.: Train conductor. 243, 245

Mallison, Charles: Nephew of Gavin Stevens. 135-145; history
    of Harrisses, 146-155, 159-166, 172-176; uncle talks with
    Miss Harriss, 177-191; uncle talks with Robert Markey,
    192-207; Harriss buys stallion, 208-217; uncle's wager
    with Gualdres, 218, 219, 221; uncle confronts Max Harriss,
    222-229, 231-233, 235-238; in military, 239-246
  His great aunt: 161
  His grandfather: 142
  His grandmother: 142-145, 147, 234
  His father: 142, 241

Mallison, Maggie: Mother of Charles; sister of Gavin Stevens.
    141-149, 151, 153, 154, 159-161, 163, 209, 213, 214, 233,
    240, 241

Markey, Robert: Memphis lawyer. 192-194, 198, 199, 204, 221,
    222

Mossop: Hence Cayley's wife's maiden name. 184

Pavoli: Italian fencing master. 162, 182

Sartoris, Benbow: Jefferson resident in World War II. 239, 240

Stevens, Gavin: County attorney. 135-144; background, 146-148,
    150, 152, 154, 155, 160, 161, 163-166, 173-176; talks
    with Miss Harriss, 177-191; talks with Robert Markey,
    192-195, 198-200, 202, 207; realizes Max Harriss has
    bought stallion, 208, 209-217; wager with Gualdres, 218,
    219, 221; confronts Max Harriss, 222-229, 231, 232; rela-
    tionship with young girl, 233-238; married, 241-246
  His wife: See Harriss, Mrs.

Warren, Captain: RFC pilot in World War I. 197, 198

UNNAMED

Russian woman whom Gavin Stevens had possibly known in Paris.
    236, 237

HISTORICAL

Catullus, Gaius Valerius (84?-54 B.C.): Roman lyric poet. 152, 155

Cervantes, Miguel de (1547-1616): Spanish novelist. 217

Conrad, Joseph (1857-1924): English novelist. 244

Hardy, Thomas (1840-1928): English novelist and poet. 183

Horace (65-8 B.C.): Roman poet and satirist. 146, 148, 230, 231

Long, Huey (1893-1935): Louisiana governor and senator. 229, 230

Ovid (43 B.C.-17? A.D.): Roman poet. 152

Shakespeare, William (1564-1616): English dramatist and poet. 183

BIBLICAL

God: 228

Judith: Jewish heroine who killed Assyrian general Holofernes in the Old Testament Apocrypha. 143

LITERARY/MYTHIC

Clarissa: Character in Samuel Richardson's *Clarissa Harlowe*, 1747-1748. 143

Crusoe: Character in Daniel Defoe's *Robinson Crusoe*, 1719. 241

Don Juan: Legendary hero of Spain; subject of many authors, especially Lord Byron. 167

Lothair: Norman knight in Monk Lewis's *Adelgitha*, 1806; also central character in Benjamin Disraeli's *Lothair*, 1870. 143

Marguerite: Character in Johann Wolfgang von Goethe's *Faust*, 1808, 1832. 143

Midas: Legendary Phrygian king who had touch of gold. 147, 148

Roland: Defender of Christians against Saracens in Charlemagne legends; hero of *Song of Roland*. 143

St. Elmo: Character in Augusta Jane Evans Wilson's *St. Elmo*, 1866. 143

Sampson, Batchelor: Character in Miguel de Cervantes' *Don Quixote*, 1605, 1615. 217

"LANDING IN LUCK"

In *William Faulkner: Early Prose and Poetry*, ed. Carvel Collins (Boston: Little, Brown, 1962); first printed in *The Mississippian*, 26 November 1919, pp. 2, 7.

Bessing: Flight instructor. 42-45, 47-50

Thompson, Cadet: Young barracks ace. 42-50

UNNAMED

Commanding Officer of flight unit. 43, 46, 47

"LEG"

In (I) *Doctor Martino*, 1934; (II) *Collected Stories*, 1950 as "The Leg."

Davy: Narrator; Young American who is wounded in World War I. (I) 291-311; (II) 823-842

George: Davy's friend killed in War. (I) 291-306, 314; (II) 823-835, 841, 842
  His people: (I) 306; (II) 835

Rust, Everbe Corinthia: Friend of Davy and George. (I) 291-295, 297, 300, 307-311, 314; (II) 823-826, 828, 830, 835-841

Rust, Jotham: Corinthia Rust's brother. (I) 293-295, 306-313; (II) 824-826, 835-841

Rust, Simon: Corinthia Rust's father. (I) 293-297, 306-308, 310-312; (II) 824-828, 836, 838-840

Sam'l: Man in yawl who rescues George. (I) 293, 295; (II) 824, 825

UNNAMED

Padre who brings picture to Davy. (I) 306-310, 312-314; (II) 835-838, 840-842

HISTORICAL

Campion, Thomas (1567-1620): English poet and musician. (I) 306; (II) 823

Jonson, Ben (1573?-1637): English dramatist. (I) 298; (II) 829

Keats, John (1795-1821): English poet. (I) 292; (II) 824

Marlowe, Christopher (1564-1593): English dramatist. (I) 306; (II) 835

Milton, John (1608-1674): English poet. (I) 291; (II) 823

Napier, John (1550-1617): Scottish mathematician. (I) 298; (II) 829

Shakespeare, William (1564-1616): English poet and playwright. (I) 306; (II) 835

Spenser, Edmund (1552?-1599): English poet. (I) 292; (II) 824

BIBLICAL

God: (I) 298, 307, 309, 313; (II) 828, 836, 838, 841

LITERARY/MYTHIC

Chloe: One of lovers in Greek pastoral romance. (I) 292; (II) 823

Circe: Enchantress in *Odyssey*. (I) 292, 294; (II) 824, 825

Comus: Young God of festivity and revelry. (I) 292; (II) 823

Hebe: Goddess of youth. (I) 292; (II) 823

Sabrina: Daughter of Locrine and Estreldis in British legend; goddess of river Severn. (I) 292; (II) 823

"THE LIAR"

In (I) *William Faulkner: New Orleans Sketches*, ed. Carvel Collins (New York: Random House, 1968); (II) *Sinbad in New Orleans*, ed. Leland Cox (Spartanburg, S.C.: The Reprint Company, 1981). First printed in New Orleans *Times-Picayune* Sunday magazine section, 26 July 1925, pp. 3, 6.

Ek: Man who tells yarns. (I) 92-103; (II) 117-126
  His father: (I) 95, 96; (II) 120

Gibson, Will: Man who owns store. (I) 92-97, 101-103; (II) 117-121, 125, 126

Haley, Lem: Man who owns dogs that treed Ek. (I) 96; (II) 120

Harmon, Mrs.: Woman through whose house a horse supposedly ran. (I) 93; (II) 118

Lafe: One of men at Gibson's store. (I) 92-97, 102; (II) 117-121, 125

Mitchell: Local resident. (I) 93; (II) 118

Rogers, Ken: Sheriff. (I) 95-97, 99, 100; (II) 120-124

Simpson boys: Men who make liquor. (I) 95; (II) 119

Starnes, Jim: Farmer in hill country. (I) 98-102; (II) 121-124

Starnes, Mrs.: Farmer's wife. (I) 97, 99-102; (II) 121-124

Tim: Sheriff's deputy. (I) 97, 98, 100; (II) 121, 123, 124

UNNAMED

Man who killed Starnes. (I) 92-95, 98-103; (II) 117-119, 122-126

"LION"

In (I) *Harper's*, 172 (December 1935), 67-77; (II) *Uncollected Stories of William Faulkner*, ed. Joseph Blotner (New York: Random House, 1979). Revised as Chapter 5, "The Bear," in *Go Down, Moses*, 1942.

Ad: Negro camp cook. (I) 68.1, 68.2, 69.1, 70.2, 71.1, 71.2, 72.1, 73.2, 75.1, 75.2, 76.2, 77.1; (II) 185-187, 189-191, 194-199

De Spain, Major: Large landowner near Jefferson. (I) 67.1-69.2, 70.2-72.2, 73.2, 74.2-77.1; (II) [184]-198

Hogganbeck, Boon: Man who works for Major de Spain. (I) 67.1-72.1, 73.2-77.2; (II) [184]-191, 193-200
  His grandmother: (I) 67.1; (II) [184]
  Her uncle, the Chickasaw chief: (I) 67.1; (II) [184]

McCaslin, Uncle Ike: Old hunter. (I) 68.2, 69.2, 71.2, 72.1, 72.2, 73.2, 75.1; (II) 186, 187, 190, 191, 193, 196

McCaslin, Theophilus: Uncle Ike McCaslin's grandson. (I) 73.2, 74.1; (II) 194

Quentin: Sixteen-year-old narrator. (I) 67.1-77.2; (II) [184]-200
  His father: (I) 73.1, 73.2, 74.1, 74.2, 76.1; (II) 193-195, 197

UNNAMED

Negro whom Boon killed. (I) 70.2, 77.2; (II) 189, 199

Conductor on train. (I) 69.1, 70.1; (II) 187, 189

Brakeman on train. (I) 69.1, 70.1, 70.2; (II) 187, 189

HISTORICAL

Dempsey, William H. "Jack" (1895-): American boxer. (I) 69.1; (II) 187

Kilrain, Jake (1859-1937): American boxer. (I) 69.1; (II) 187

Sullivan, John L. (1858-1918): American boxer. (I) 69.1; (II) 187

Tunney, James J. "Gene" (1898-1978): American boxer. (I) 69.1; (II) 187

"LIZARDS IN JAMSHYD'S COURTYARD"

In (I) *The Saturday Evening Post*, 204 (27 February 1932), 12, 13, 52, 57; (II) *Uncollected Stories of William Faulkner*, ed. Joseph Blotner (New York: Random House, 1979). Incorporated in Chapter 3 of Book One and Chapter 2 of Book Four of *The Hamlet*, 1940.

Armstid, Henry: Frenchman's Bend farmer. (I) 12.3, 13.1, 52.2, 52.3, 52.4, 57.1, 57.3, 57.4; (II) 136-138, 142-147, 149-151
  His wife: (I) 12.3, 13.1, 52.2, 57.3; (II) 137, 138, 142, 150
  Their children: (I) 13.1, 52.2; (II) 138, 142

Dick, Uncle: Old man with divining rod. (I) 52.3, 52.4, 57.1; (II) 143-147

Grimm, Eustace: Young farmer near Frenchman's Bend. (I) 57.1, 57.2, 57.3, 57.4; (II) 146-150

Littlejohn, Mrs.: Owner of boarding house in Frenchman's Bend. (I) 57.2, 57.3; (II) 147-149

Quick, Lon: Resident of Frenchman's Bend. (I) 57.1, 57.2; (II) 147
  His son: (I) 57.1; (II) 147

Snopes, Flem: Man who owns Old Frenchman's place. (I) 13.1, 13.2, 13.3, 52.1, 52.2, 52.3, 52.4, 57.1, 57.2, 57.3; (II) 138-143, 145, 147-149

Suratt: Sewing machine salesman. (I) 13.1, 13.2, 13.3, 52.1, 52.2, 52.3, 52.4, 57.1, 57.2, 57.3, 57.4; (II) 138-151
  His brother-in-law: (I) 52.1, 57.3; (II) 141, 150

Tull, Vernon: One of the men who buys Old Frenchman's place. (I) 52.2, 52.3, 52.4, 57.1, 57.3, 57.4; (II) 142-147, 149-151

Varner, Will: Landowner in Frenchman's Bend. (I) 12.3, 13.2, 13.3, 52.1; (II) 136-141

UNNAMED

Old Frenchman. (I) 12.2, 12.3, 13.3; (II) 136, 140

English architect who planned Old Frenchman's place. (I) 12.2; (II) 136

Northerner who wants to buy goats. (I) 13.2; (II) 138, 139

HISTORICAL

Grant, Ulysses S. (1822-1885): Union general; President of United States, 1869-1877. (I) 12.3; (II) 136

BIBLICAL

Lord: (I) 52.4; (II) 144, 145

LITERARY

Ben Hur: Central character in Lew Wallace's *Ben Hur*, 1880. (I) 12.1; (II) [135]

"*LO!*"

In (I) *Story*, 5 (November 1934), 5-21; (II) *Collected Stories*, 1950.

Weddel, Francis (Vidal): Indian chief from Mississippi. (I) 6, 11-21; (II) 383, 389-402
  His father: (I) 12; (II) 391
  His nephew: (I) 13-20; (II) 392-402
    Nephew's father: (I) 20; (II) 401

UNNAMED

Cabinet Secretary. (I) 9-19, 21; (II) 386-400, 402, 403
  His secretary: (I) 9-12, 18; (II) 386, 389, 390, 399

President of United States. (I) 5-21; (II) 381-403
  His wife: (I) 7, 10, 11; (II) 384, 388, 390

Horseman who meets with President and Secretary. (I) 9-12; (II) 386-390

Mayday 261

President's aide. (I) 7-12; (II) 384-386, 389, 390, 394

Two Indians who await President outside his door. (I) 5-7; (II) 382-384

President's secretary. (I) 19, 21; (II) 400, 402

First white man murdered by Francis Weddel's nephew. (I) 12-16, 18; (II) 391-393, 395, 396, 398

Chickasaw agent. (I) 14, 15, 20, 21; (II) 392, 393, 401, 402

HISTORICAL

Cornwallis, Charles (1738-1805): British general. (I) 19; (II) 399

Petrarch (1304-1373): Italian poet. (I) 19; (II) 399

Washington, George (1732-1799): President of United States, 1789-1797. (I) 19; (II) 399

BIBLICAL

God: (I) 20; (II) 399

MAYDAY

(I) [Notre Dame, Indiana]: University of Notre Dame Press, 1977; (II) Notre Dame, Indiana: University of Notre Dame Press, 1980.

Aelia, Princess: "Captive" princess. (I) 18, 29-34, 36, 41, 42; (II) 61, 62, 73-80, 85, 86

Aelian (Aelius): Father of Princess Aelia; Crown Marshall of Arles. (I) 18, 29, 36; (II) 61, 73, 80

Ambition: One of the faces in the water which Galwyn's companions show him at first. (I) 6; (II) 49

Boisgeclin, Constable du: Man at whose hand Galwyn is knighted.
(I) 23; (II) 66

Elys, Princess: "Captive" princess. (I) 17, 18, 28, 31, 32,
34, 41, 42; (II) 61, 62, 71, 72, 74-80, 85, 86

Experience: Condition discussed by Lord of Sleep. (I) 40; (II)
85

Fame: Condition discussed by Lord of Sleep. (I) 39; (II) 84

Fortitude: Face in water which Galwyn's companions show him at
first. (I) 5; (II) 49

Galwyn of Arthgyl: Knight who serves at hand of Constable du
Boisgeclin. (I) 3; joined by Hunger and Pain, 4, 5-9;
meets hermit, 10, 11-19; comes upon guard for Yseult, 20,
21-27; meets Princess Elys, 28; meets Princess Aelia, 29,
30-36; meets Lord of Sleep, 37, 38-43; (II) 47; joined by
Hunger and Pain, 48-50; meets hermit, 51, 52-62; comes
upon guard for Yseult, 63, 64-70; meets Princess Elys,
71, 72; meets Princess Aelia, 73, 74-80; meets Lord of
Sleep, 81, 82-87

Hunger: Small green design; one of Galwyn's companions. (I)
4-7, 9-11, 13-15, 19, 26, 27, 35-38, 41-43; (II) 48-53,
55, 57, 58, 62, 70, 71, 79-82, 85, 87

Little Sister Death: Girl in the water whom Galwyn decides
finally to embrace. (I) 6, 7, 15-19, 30, 36, 37, 42,
43; (II) 50, 51, 58-62, 74, 80, 81, 87

Morvidus, Earl Warwick: Knight in olden times who slays giant.
(I) 8, 9; (II) 52

Pain: Small red design, one of Galwyn's companions. (I) 4-7,
9-11, 13-15, 19, 26, 27, 35-38, 41-43; (II) 48-53, 55, 57,
58, 62, 70, 71, 79-82, 85, 87

Sethynnen ap Seydnn Seidi: King of Wales. (I) 17, 28, 36, 42;
(II) 61, 72, 80, 86

UNNAMED

Young Compassionate One. (I) 3; (II) 48

Paunchy little man, Lord of Sleep. (I) 37-42; (II) 81-86

"The Mirror of Chartres Street" 263

Hermit (Time). (I) 10-19; (II) 53-62
 His wife: (I) 13, 17; (II) 56, 60

BIBLICAL

God: (I) 21; (II) 65

Mary: Mother of Jesus. (I) 23; (II) 66

MYTHIC

Francis, Saint (1182-1226): Italian friar. (I) 6, 7, 43; (II)
 50, 87

Mark: King of Cornwall. (I) 20-23, 25, 30, 35; (II) 63-66,
 68, 74, 79

Menelaus: Greek king; Helen's husband. (I) 22; (II) 65

Tristram: Knight who tries to protect Yseult. (I) 21-25; (II)
 64-68

Uther Pendragon: Father of King Arthur. (I) 21; (II) 65

Yseult, Princess: King Mark's betrothed. (I) 20-27, 30, 35,
 36, 41, 42; (II) 63-70, 74, 79, 85, 86

"THE MIRROR OF CHARTRES STREET"

In (I) *William Faulkner: New Orleans Sketches*, ed. Carvel Collins
(New York: Random House, 1968); (II) *Sinbad in New Orleans*, ed.
Leland Cox (Spartanburg, S.C.: The Reprint Company, 1981).
First printed in New Orleans *Times-Picayune* Sunday magazine section, 8 February 1925, pp. 1, 6.

Ed: Man driving police wagon. (I) 18; (II) 3

UNNAMED

Narrator. (I) 15-18; (II) 1-3

Cripple. (I) 15-18; (II) 1-3

Policeman who arrests cripple. (I) 16-18; (II) 2, 3

HISTORICAL

Caesar, Julius (100?-44 B.C.): Roman general and emperor.
(I) 18; (II) 3

Gompers, Samuel (1850-1924): American labor leader. (I) 18;
(II) 3

Mendelssohn, Felix (1809-1847): German composer. (I) 16; (II) 2

Rameses II (c.1270): Egyptian pharoah. (I) 16; (II) 2

BIBLICAL

Jesus: (I) 16; (II) 1

Mary: Mother of Jesus. (I) 16; (II) 1

MYTHIC

King Arthur: King of the Britons. (I) 16; (II) 1

MISS ZILPHIA GANT

(I) Dallas: Book Club of Texas, 1932; also in (II) *Uncollected Stories of William Faulkner*, ed. Joseph Blotner (New York: Random House, 1979).

Gant, Jim: Stock trader. (I) 1-8, 13; (II) [368]-371, 373

Gant, Mrs. Jim: Wife of Jim Gant; Zilphia Gant's mother. (I)
2-22; (II) 369-378

Gant, Zilphia: Only child of Jim Gant and his wife. (I) 2-29;
(II) 369-379

Vinson, Mrs.: Woman at tavern with whom Jim Gant runs away.
(I) 2, 3, 5; (II) [368]-370

"Mississippi" 265

Zilphia, Little: Daughter of Zilphia Gant's beau/husband. (I) 28, 29; (II) 380, 381

UNNAMED

Zilphia Gant's beau/husband. (I) 15-26, 28; (II) 375-381
　　His second wife: (I) 25, 26, 28; (II) 379-381

Half-witted boy who tells Mrs. Gant that Jim has left. (I) 1, 3-6; (II) [368]-370

BIBLICAL

Christ: (I) 24; (II) 379

Mary: (I) 24; (II) 379

"MISSISSIPPI"

In *Essays, Speeches, & Public Letters* by William Faulkner, ed. James B. Meriwether (New York: Random House, 1966); first published in *Holiday*, 15 (April 1954), 33-47; see also *Big Woods*, 1955. In this account of his native state, Faulkner combines history with characters from his own fiction.

Arthur: Undergraduate at Harvard. 35, 36
　　His father, a physician: 35
　　His mother: 36

Caroline (Mammy): William's nurse and family servant. 16, 17, 39-42
　　Her grandson (or great-grandson): 17

Compson: Family name in Jefferson. 12

De Spain: Family name in Jefferson. 12

Ewell: Family name in Jefferson. 12

Habersham, Dr.: Drugstore owner in Jefferson. 19

Hestelle: Name which Mammy Caroline calls William's wife. 42

Hogganbeck: Family name in Jefferson. 12

Hogganbeck, Boon: Murry's stable foreman. 37

Holston: Family name in Jefferson. 12

Jim: Captain Joe Thoms's Negro. 37, 38

Knight, Newt: Principal proprietor in Jones County. 33

McCaslin: Family name in Jefferson. 12

Mary: William's first sweetheart. 38

Minnie: One of William's sweethearts. 38
  Her grandfather: 38

Moissant, John: Man who landed monoplane in Memphis. 38

Mulberry: Negro Federal Marshal in Jefferson. 19

Murry: William's father. 16, 17, 36, 37, 39, 42
  His wife, William's mother: 41, 42
  His brother and sister: 17

Ned: Servant of William's family. 39

Pete: Younger brother of bootlegger. 30, 31
  His brother, the bootlegger: 30, 31
  His and bootlegger's mother: 31

Redmond: Jefferson carpetbagger. 20

Sartoris: Family name in Jefferson. 12

Sartoris, Col.: Confederate officer killed by Redmond. 20

Snopes: Family name in Jefferson. 12-14, 18, 19, 25, 39

Thoms, Captain Joe: Delta planter. 37-39

Wales, Mr. Sells: Memphis millionaire. 22-24

William (Mr. Bill, Memmy, Pappy, the boy, the youth, the middle-
    aged): Writer of fiction. 11-17, 21-24, 28-33, 35-43
  His daughter: 40, 41
  His three younger brothers: 40, 42
  His grandfather: 16, 17, 39

"Mississippi"

His great-grandfather: 39
His bachelor kinsman: 33-35

Wylie: Owner of store at river crossing. 18, 19, 25

UNNAMED

Negro cook/deckhand/stevedore on bootlegger's boat. 30, 31

Captain of bootlegger's boat. 30, 31

Tall Baptist minister who converts people at Wylie's Crossing.
 18, 19

Taxi-driver companion of Arthur. 35, 36

Town clown companion of Arthur. 36

Fourth youth in taxi. 35, 36
 His father, the banker: 35, 36

Lawyer friend of William's. 21, 22, 28

HISTORICAL

Bilbo, Theodore G. (1877-1947): Mississippi senator and governor.
 13

Forrest, Nathan Bedford (1821-1877): Confederate general. 17

Hare, Joseph T. (?-1818): American bandit on Natchez Trace. 14

Harpe, Micajah (1768-1799): American bandit on Natchez Trace.
 14, 28

Harpe, Wiley (1770-1804): American bandit on Natchez Trace. 14,
 28

Johnston, Joseph E. (1807-1891): Confederate general. 17

Kosciusko, Thaddeus (1746-1817): Polish patriot. 32

Mason, Samuel (1750?-1804?): American bandit on Natchez Trace.
 14, 28

Murrell, John A. (1804?-1844): American bandit on Natchez Trace.
 14, 28

Napoleon (1769-1821): Emperor of France. 35

Pemberton, John C. (1818-1881): Confederate general. 17

Sherman, William T. (1820-1891): Union general. 15

Smith, Captain John (1580-1631): English colonist in America. 20

Vardaman, James K. (1861-1930): Mississippi senator and governor. 13

MYTHIC

Santa Claus: 16

"MISTRAL"

In (I) *These 13*, 1931; (II) *Collected Stories*, 1950.

Cavalcanti: Wine shop owner; Giulio Farinzale's uncle. (I) 290, 297, 321, 322, 328; (II) 848, 853, 870, 871, 875
  His wife: (I) 290, 298-300, 306, 321, 322; (II) 848, 853-856, 870, 871

Don: Young American with narrator. (I) 282-329; (II) 843-876

Farinzale, Giulio: Young soldier; lover of priest's ward. (I) 283, 284, 290-295, 297-300, 303, 305, 306, 308, 313, 319-323, 328; (II) 843, 844, 848-851, 853-857, 859, 861, 862, 865, 869-872, 875, 876

UNNAMED

Narrator, friend of Don's. (I) 283-329; (II) 843-876

Priest's ward. (I) 288-295, 300, 304, 307, 308, 313, 319, 320, 328; (II) 846-851, 858, 860, 861, 865, 869, 870, 875, 876
  Her mother: (I) 288, 289; (II) 847
  Her father: (I) 289; (II) 847

"Mistral" 269

Dead fiancé of priest's ward. (I) 288, 290-297, 300, 304, 324, 328; (II) 846-851, 853, 855, 858, 872

Priest. (I) 287-295, 297, 298, 300-302, 304, 305, 307-315, 317, 320, 321, 327, 328; (II) 846-852, 854-868, 870, 875, 876

Old man in corduroy whom narrator and Don meet. (I) 285-288, 291-293, 295, 296, 304; (II) 844-850, 852

Old woman to whom narrator and Don talk. (I) 285-296, 304; (II) 844-852
  Her daughters: (I) 293; (II) 850

Policeman. (I) 323, 324; (II) 871-873

Waiter to whom narrator and Don talk. (I) 318, 320-324; (II) 870-873

Peasant woman at priest's. (I) 307-314, 325; (II) 860, 861, 863-866, 873

HISTORICAL

Malbrouck: Legendary French crusader/soldier. (I) 298; (II) 853

Mussolini, Benito (1883-1945): Italian dictator. (I) 299, 306; (II) 854, 859

Nesbit (Nesbitt), Evelyn (1884-1967): Thaw's wife; former mistress of White. (I) 319; (II) 869

Thaw, Harry K. (1871-1947): Millionaire who killed White. (I) 319; (II) 869

White, Stanford (1853-1906): American architect. (I) 319; (II) 869

BIBLICAL

God: (I) 289, 292, 294, 314; (II) 849-851, 866

"MONK"

In (I) *Scribner's*, 101 (May 1937), 16-24; (II) *Knight's Gambit*, 1949.

Fraser: Whiskey maker. (I) 18.1, 19.2; (II) 42, 43, 45, 47

Gambrell, C.L.: Prison warden whom Monk kills. (I) 19.2, 21.1-22.2, 24.2; (II) 43, 44, 47, 48, 50, 53, 55, 57, 58
  His wife: (I) 19.2; (II) 47

Monk (Stonewall Jackson Odlethrop): Moron who kills Warden Gambrell. (I) 16.1, 16.2, 18.1-24.1; (II) 39-51, 53, 55-58

Odlethrop, Mrs.: Old lady with whom Monk lived. (I) 16.2, 18.1, 19.1; (II) 41, 42, 45
  Her son: (I) 16.2; (II) 41

Stevens, Gavin: County attorney. (I) 19.1-24.2; (II) 45-60

Terrel, Bill: Convict. (I) 21.2-24.2; (II) 52-59
  His children: (I) 23.1; (II) 56

UNNAMED

Narrator related to Gavin Stevens. (I) 16.1-24.2; (II) 39-60

Governor. (I) 19.2, 21.1-22.2, 24.2; (II) 47, 50-55, 59
  His grandfather: (I) 22.2; (II) 54

Guard at prison who guards Terrel. (I) 22.1, 23.1, 23.2, 24.2; (II) 55-57, 59

Man whom Monk was accused of killing. (I) 16.1, 18.2, 19.1; (II) 43, 44, 46

HISTORICAL

Jackson, Thomas J. "Stonewall" (1824-1863): Confederate general. (I) 19.1, 20.1; (II) 45, 46, 49

BIBLICAL

Lord: (I) 20.1, 22.1, 24.1, 24.2; (II) 49, 52, 57, 58, 60

"MOONLIGHT"

In *Uncollected Stories of William Faulkner*, ed. Joseph Blotner (New York: Random House, 1979); the index to another version of this story appears with the Unpublished Fiction.

Burchett, Mr.: Susan's guardian. 497-499

Burchett, Mrs. Etta: Susan's guardian. 497, 501

Hovis, Mr.: Man in town. 498

Skeet: Sixteen-year-old friend of youth. 497-501, 503

Susan: Young girl who has reed-thin body. 497-503

West, Doctor: Man in town. 498

UNNAMED

Sixteen-year-old boy who wants Susan. [495]-503
  His mother: 496, 497, 499, 500
  His father: 496, 497, 499
  His uncle: [495], 499, 502
  His aunt: [495], 499, 502

BIBLICAL

Delilah: Philistine mistress of Samson in Judges. 501

LITERARY

Ancient Mariner: Central figure in Coleridge's *The Ancient Mariner*, 1798. 498

"A MOUNTAIN VICTORY"

In (I) *The Saturday Evening Post*, 205 (3 December 1932), 6, 7, 39, 42, 44, 45, 46; (II) *Doctor Martino*, 1934, as "Mountain Victory"; (III) *Collected Stories*, 1950; (IV) *The Mississippi Quarterly*, 32 (Summer 1979), 482-483. This last appearance consists of only a previously unpublished episode from the original story.

Hule: Younger son of mountain family. (I) 6.1, 6.3, 7.1, 7.2,
  39.1, 39.3, 39.4, 42.2, 42.3, 42.4, 44.1, 44.2, 45.1,
  45.2, 46.1, 46.2, 46.3; (II) 315, 316, 320, 321, 325, 331,
  336, 338-347, 349-353; (III) 745, 746, 749, 750, 753, 754,
  755-758, 761-763, 767, 769, 770, 772, 774, 775; (IV) 482,
  483

Jubal: Negro servant of Saucier Weddel. (I) 6.1, 6.2, 6.3, 7.2,
  7.3, 39.1, 39.2, 39.3, 39.4, 42.1, 42.2, 42.3, 42.4, 44.1,
  44.2, 45.1, 45.2, 46.1, 46.2, 46.3; (II) 316-319, 322-
  331, 333, 336-341, 345-354; (III) 745-748, 750-758, 760,
  762-767, 769-777; (IV) 482, 483

Vatch: Older son of mountain family. (I) 6.1, 6.3, 7.1, 7.2,
  7.3, 39.1, 39.3, 39.4, 42.1, 42.2, 42.4, 44.1, 44.2, 45.1,
  46.2, 46.3; (II) 315, 316, 320-323, 325, 329, 331-337,
  341-346, 349-354; (III) 745, 746, 749-751, 753, 754, 756,
  758-763, 766-770, 773-777; (IV) 482, 483

Vidal, Francois: Saucier Weddel's grandfather. (I) 39.2, 39.4;
  (II) 327, 332; (III) 755, 759
 His wife: (I) 39.4; (II) 332; (III) 759

Weddel, Francis: Saucier Weddel's father. (I) 39.2, 39.4; (II)
  326, 328, 332, 333; (III) 754, 756, 759
 His wife: (I) 39.1, 39.3, 39.4, 42.1, 42.3, 44.1, 45.1; (II)
  324-326, 329, 333, 340, 348; (III) 752, 753, 756, 759,
  760, 765, 769, 772

Weddel, Saucier: Confederate major, son of Francis Weddel. (I)
  6.1, 6.2, 6.3, 7.1, 7.2, 7.3, 39.1, 39.2, 39.3, 39.4, 42.1,
  42.2, 42.3, 42.4, 44.1, 44.2, 45.1, 45.2, 46.1, 46.2, 46.3;
  (II) 315-327, 329-354; (III) 745-759, 762-777; (IV) 482,
  483

UNNAMED

Father of mountain family. (I) 6.1, 6.3, 7.1, 7.2, 7.3, 39.1,
  39.2, 39.3, 39.4, 42.1, 42.2, 42.3, 42.4, 44.2, 45.1,
  46.2, 46.3; (II) 315-319, 321-323, 325, 328, 331, 332,
  334-339, 341, 342, 345, 346, 349-353; (III) 745-748, 750,
  751, 753, 754, 756, 758, 759, 761-765, 767, 770, 773-777;
  (IV) 482

Mother of mountain family. (I) 6.1, 6.2, 6.3, 7.1, 7.3, 39.1,
  39.2, 39.3, 39.4, 42.1; (II) 315-320, 323, 325, 327-329,
  331, 335, 344; (III) 745-749, 751, 753, 754, 756, 758,
  761; (IV) 482

Daughter of mountain family. (I) 6.1, 6.3, 7.1, 7.2, 7.3, 39.1, 39.2, 39.3, 42.1, 42.2, 42.4, 44.1, 44.2, 45.2; (II) 315, 316, 319-323, 325, 328-331, 335-337, 342, 344-347, 350, 351; (III) 745, 746, 748-751, 753-758, 761-763, 767, 769, 770, 772, 774, 775; (IV) 482, 483

Rebel major killed by Vatch. (I) 42.1; (II) 334, 335; (III) 760, 761

The Man, head of Choctaw clan. (I) 39.2, 39.4, 42.3; (II) 328, 333, 338, 340; (III) 756, 759, 764, 765

HISTORICAL

Jackson, Andrew (1767-1845): President of United States, 1829-1837. (I) 39.2, 39.4, 42.3; (II) 328, 332; (III) 755, 756, 759

Longstreet, James (1821-1904): Confederate general. (I) 42.1; (II) 333; (III) 760

Napoleon (1769-1821): Emperor of France. (I) 39.4; (II) 332; (III) 759

"MR. ACARIUS"

In (I) The Saturday Evening Post, 238 (9 October 1965), 26, 27, 29, 31; (II) Uncollected Stories of William Faulkner, ed. Joseph Blotner (New York: Random House, 1979).

Acarius, Mr.: Successful Madison Avenue businessman. (I) 26.1-31.3; (II) [435]-448

Cochrane, Ab: Doctor of Mr. Acarius. (I) 26.1, 26.2, 27.1, 27.2, 27.3, 29.1, 29.2, 31.1, 31.3; (II) [435]-440, 442, 445, 448

Goldie: Hospital nurse. (I) 29.1, 29.2, 29.3, 31.1; (II) 440-445

Hill, Dr.: Director of hospital. (I) 27.3, 31.1, 31.2; (II) 439, 444, 446, 447

Lester, Judy: Girl friend of Watkins. (I) 29.1, 29.2, 29.3;
    (II) 442, 443

Miller: Patient at hospital. (I) 29.1, 29.2, 29.3, 31.1, 31.2,
    31.3; (II) 440-447

Watkins: Patient in hospital. (I) 29.2, 29.3, 31.1, 31.2, 31.3;
    (II) 442-448

HISTORICAL

Picasso, Pablo (1881-1977): Spanish artist. (I) 26.3; (II)
    [435]

BIBLICAL

Lord: (I) 31.3; (II) 447

"MULE IN THE YARD"

In (I) *Scribner's*, 96 (August 1934), 65-70; (II) *Collected Stories*, 1950; incorporated into Chapter 16 of *The Town*, 1957.

Hait: Man killed by train who worked for I.O. Snopes. (I) 65.1-
    66.2, 68.1, 68.2, 69.2, 70.1, 70.2; (II) 250, 252, 253,
    259, 261-264

Hait, Mannie: Wife of Hait. (I) 65.1-70.2; (II) 249-264

Het: Old Negro woman. (I) 65.1-66.1, 67.1-70.2; (II) 249-252,
    254-264

Snopes, I.O.: Mule owner. (I) 66.1-70.2; (II) 252-264

Spilmer: Man behind whose building Mannie Hait kills the mule.
    (I) 70.1; (II) 262

"My Grandmother Millard ..."   275

"MUSIC--SWEETER THAN THE ANGELS SING"

In (I) *The Freshman Theme Review* (University Press of Mississippi, April 1928); (II) *The Southern Review*, 12 (October 1976), 868-871. First published under name of Katharine Hargis; for an account of its publication see Dean Faulkner Wells and Laurence Wells, "The Trains Belonged to Everybody: Faulkner as Ghost Writer," *The Southern Review*, 12 (October 1976), 864-871.

Barr, Captain: Train engineer. (I) 1.2, 2.1, 2.2; (II) 868-871

I.C.: Man to whom ticket agent speaks. (I) 1.2; (II) 868

Joby: Negro who loves to hear Captain Barr blow train whistle. (I) 1.2, 2.1, 2.2, 3.1; (II) 868-871

Joe, Mister: Brakeman on train. (I) 1.2; (II) 868

Murray, Colonel: Man who owns the Birmingham cut-off road. (I) 2.1; (II) 869

Rastus: Negro friend of Joby. (I) 1.2, 2.1, 2.2; (II) 868-870

UNNAMED

Four brothers with whom Joby and Rastus sit on the train. (I) 1.2, 2.1; (II) 868, 869

BIBLICAL

David: King of Israel. (I) 2.1; (II) 869

Gabriel: Archangel. (I) 1.2; (II) 868

God: (I) 1.2, 2.1, 2.2, 3.1; (II) 868-871

"MY GRANDMOTHER MILLARD AND GENERAL BEDFORD FORREST AND THE BATTLE OF HARRYKIN CREEK"

In (I) *Story*, 22 (March-April 1943), 68-86; (II) *Collected Stories*, 1950.

Backhouse: Philip St-Just: Young Confederate officer; changes
    name to Backus. (I) 71.1, 73.2, 74.1, 74.2, 75.1, 75.2,
    76.1, 76.2, 77.1, 77.2, 80.1, 81.1, 82.1, 82.2, 83.1,
    83.2, 84.1, 84.2, 85.2, 86.1; (II) 672, 677-683, 688-699
  His grandfather: (I) 77.1; (II) 682
  His father: (I) 77.1; (II) 682
  His uncle: (I) 77.1, 83.1; (II) 682, 693

Backus, Cousin Melisandre: Bayard's cousin; wife of Philip
    Backus (Backhouse). (I) 68.1, 69.1, 70.1-72.2, 73.2-
    75.1, 76.1, 76.2, 77.2, 79.1-86.1; (II) 667, 668, 670,
    671, 674-684, 686-689, 693-699

Backus, Philip St-Just: See Backhouse, Philip St-Just

Compson, General: Confederate officer. (I) 73.1; (II) 675

Compson, Mrs.: General's wife. (I) 72.2, 73.1, 73.2; (II) 675,
    676

Holston, Dr.: Jefferson physician. (I) 73.1; (II) 675

Joby: Sartoris Negro slave. (I) 68.2, 70.2, 71.1, 72.1, 72.2,
    73.2, 74.1, 79.2, 81.2, 86.2; (II) 667, 668, 670, 671,
    674-677, 687, 691, 699

Louvinia: Joby's wife. (I) 68.2-72.2, 73.2, 74.2, 76.1, 77.2,
    79.2, 81.2, 85.2, 86.1, 86.2; (II) 667-671, 673, 675,
    676, 678, 683, 687, 690, 691, 698, 699

Lucius: Sartoris Negro slave. (I) 68.2-71.1, 72.1, 72.2, 73.2,
    74.1, 79.2, 80.1-81.2, 86.2; (II) 667-671, 673-677, 687-
    691, 699

Millard, Grandfather: Rosa Millard's husband. (I) 80.1, 83.2;
    (II) 688, 694

Millard, Rosa (Granny): Bayard Sartoris' grandmother. (I)
    68.1-71.1, 72.1-86.2; (II) 667-672, 674-699

Philadelphia: Lucius' wife. (I) 68.2, 69.1, 70.1-72.2, 73.2,
    74.2, 77.2, 79.1-80.2, 81.2, 85.2, 86.1, 86.2; (II) 668-
    671, 674-676, 678, 683, 686-689, 691, 697-699

Ringo: Bayard's Negro companion. (I) 68.1, 68.2, 69.2-71.1,
    72.1, 72.2, 73.2, 74.1, 75.1, 75.2, 76.2, 77.1, 77.2,
    79.1, 79.2, 80.1, 80.2, 81.1, 81.2, 84.1, 85.1, 85.2, 86.1
    86.2; (II) 667-672, 674-681, 683, 685-691, 695, 697-699

Roxanne, Aunt: Mrs. Compson's Negro slave. (I) 73.1; (II) 675

Sartoris, Bayard: Narrator; son of Col. John Sartoris. (I) 68.1-86.2; (II) 667-699

Sartoris, Colonel John: Confederate officer; narrator's father. (I) 68.1-72.1, 74.1, 77.2, 78.1, 79.2, 85.1, 85.2, 86.1; (II) 667-674, 677, 683, 684, 686, 697-699
  His mother: (I) 70.1; (II) 670
  His wife, Bayard's mother: (I) 86.1; (II) 698, 699

Savage: Confederate Battalion leader. (I) 76.1; (II) 680, 681

Snopes, Ab: Member of Col. John Sartoris's troop. (I) 72.1-73.1, 74.1, 75.1, 76.2-79.1, 80.1, 83.1; (II) 673-677, 679, 681-686, 688, 693

HISTORICAL

Bragg, Braxton (1817-1876): Confederate general. (I) 72.1, 83.1; (II) 673, 693

Early, Jubal A. (1816-1894): Confederate general. (I) 71.2; (II) 673

Forrest, Nathan Bedford (1821-1877): Confederate general. (I) 68.1, 72.1, 76.1, 78.1, 79.1, 80.1-85.2; (II) 667, 674, 680, 681, 684, 686, 688-698

Grant, Ulysses S. (1822-1885): Union general; President of United States, 1869-1877. (I) 71.2; (II) 673

Johnston, Joseph E. (1807-1891): Confederate general. (I) 83.1, 84.2, 85.1; (II) 693, 696, 697

Lee, Robert E. (1807-1870): Confederate general. (I) 71.2; (II) 673

Marion, Francis (1732?-1795): American Revolutionary War general. (I) 77.2; (II) 682

Smith, Andrew J. (1815-1897): Union general. (I) 80.2, 82.1, 82.2; (II) 689, 692

Wheeler, Joseph (1836-1906): Confederate general. (I) 71.2; (II) 673

"A NAME FOR THE CITY"

In *Harper's*, 201 (October 1950), 200, 201, 202, 204, 206, 208, 210, 212, 213, 214; revised as "The Courthouse (A Name for the City)" for *Requiem for a Nun*, 1951.

Compson: Man who traded Ikkemotubbe a racehorse for land.
    206.1, 206.2, 208.1, 208.2, 210.1, 210.2, 212.1, 212.2, 213.1, 213.2

Gavin, Uncle: Narrator's uncle. 200.1, 201.2

Grenier, Louis: One of founders of Yoknapatawpha county. 202.1, 202.2

Habersham, Dr. Samuel: One of founders of Yoknapatawpha county. 202.1, 202.2, 206.2
 His son: 202.1
 Son's wife, Issetibbeha's granddaughter: 202.1

Holston, Alexander: One of founders of Yoknapatawpha county.
    202.1, 202.2, 204.1, 204.2. 206.1, 206.2, 208.1, 208.2, 210.1, 210.2, 212.1, 212.2, 213.1, 213.2

Ikkemotubbe: Issetibbeha's successor as Chickasaw chief. 200.2, 206.1, 208.2, 210.2

Issetibbeha: Chickasaw chief; brother of Mohataha. 200.2, 202.1, 202.2, 206.1, 210.2

Mohataha: Mother of Ikkemotubbe; sister of Issetibbeha. 210.2, 213.2

Peabody, Doctor: Doctor Habersham's successor. 206.2, 210.1, 212.1, 212.2, 213.1, 213.2, 214.1, 214.2

Pettigrew, Thomas Jefferson: Mail rider for whom Jefferson is named. 204.1, 204.2, 208.1, 208.2, 210.1, 210.2, 212.1, 212.2, 213.1, 213.2, 214.1, 214.2
 His mother: 214.1

Ratcliffe: Owner of Jefferson trading post. 206.2, 210.1, 210.2, 212.1, 212.2, 213.1, 213.2, 214.1

Whitfield: Man whose cabin is church. 213.2, 214.1

UNNAMED

Gang of bandits. 201.1, 201.2, 202.1, 206.1, 206.2, 208.1, 208.2

Militia. 201.2, 206.1, 206.2

Narrator. 200.1-214.2

HISTORICAL

Dillinger, John (1902-1934): American gangster. 202.1

Harpe, Micajah (1768-1799): American bandit on Natchez Trace. 201.1, 201.2, 206.2, 208.1

Harpe, Wiley (1770-1804): American bandit on Natchez Trace. 201.1, 201.2, 206.2, 208.1

Homer: Greek epic poet. 200.1

Jackson, Andrew (1767-1845): President of United States, 1829-1837. 200.1

James, Jesse W. (1847-1882): American bandit. 202.1

Jefferson, Thomas (1743-1826): President of United States, 1801-1809. 214.1

Mason, Samuel (1750?-1804?): Natchez Trace bandit. 201.2

Murrell, John A. (1804?-1844): American bandit. 201.2

Napoleon (1769-1821): Emperor of France. 201.1

MYTHIC

Damocles: Courtier of ancient Syracuse. 201.1

"NEW ORLEANS"

In (I) *William Faulkner: New Orleans Sketches*, ed. Carvel Collins (New York: Random House, 1968); (II) *Sinbad in New Orleans*, ed. Leland Cox (Spartanburg, S.C.: The Reprint Company, 1981). First printed in *Double-Dealer*, 7 (January-February 1925), 102-107.

Frankie: Johnny's girl. (I) 5, 6; (II) 38, 39

Johnny: Man who protects Frankie. (I) 5, 6,; (II) 38, 39

Ryan: Policeman. (I) 6; (II) 39

UNNAMED

The Artist. (I) 12; (II) 43, 44

The Beggar. (I) 11, 12; (II) 43

The Cobbler. (I) 7, 8; (II) 40, 41
   His girl in Tuscany. (I) 8; (II) 41

The Cop. (I) 10, 11; (II) 42, 43
   His wife. (I) 11; (II) 43

The Longshoreman. (I) 9; (II) 41, 42

Magdalen. (I) 12, 13; (II) 44

The Priest. (I) 4, 5; (II) 38

The Sailor. (I) 7; (II) 40

The Tourist. (I) 13, 14; (II) 45

Wealthy Jew. (I) 3, 4; (II) 37, 38

HISTORICAL

Ahenobarbus: Name of plebeian Roman family which ended with Emperor Nero. (I) 4; (II) 37

Alexander (356-323 B.C.): King of Macedonia. (I) 4; (II) 37

Caesar, Julius (100?-44 B.C.): Roman general and emperor. (I) 4; (II) 37

Napoleon (1769-1821): Emperor of France. (I) 4; (II) 37

BIBLICAL

God: (I) 3, 5, 9; (II) 37, 38, 41, 42

Jesus: (I) 5, 9; (II) 38, 41

Maria (Mary): (I) 5; (II) 38

NOTES ON A HORSETHIEF

[Greenville, Miss.: Levee Press, 1951.]

Irey: Turnkey who holds Negro groom in custody. 22; recognizes Negro groom, 32-34; in judge's chamber, 35-37, 40-46; lawyer's plan to get Negro out of town, 47-52, 55, 57, 58, 64, 69, 70
His wife: 22, 32, 34, 41, 43, 44, 46, 48

UNNAMED

Sentry; English groom. 1, 2; train wreck, 3-6, 8-11; horse wins race, 12-17; deputy marshal resigns from case, 18, 19-29, 31, 36, 42, 44, 45, 51, 53, 54, 70

Negro groom. 3, 4, 7, 8; with English groom and horse after wreck, 9-11; horse wins race, 12-17; deputy marshal resigns from case, 18-22, 24, 25, 27-29, 32-34; in judge's chambers, 35-37, 40, 42, 44-47, 50-52; talks with lawyer, 53-55, 57, 64, 70, 71

Negro boy who rides horse. 13-15, 17, 19-22, 24, 27, 32, 42, 44, 64, 70

Federal deputy marshal. 3, 6, 13, 15-23, 25-27, 31
His father: 16, 17

Sheriff; relative of turnkey's wife. 22, 23, 34, 41, 43, 44, 46, 48, 49, 52

Deputy. 43, 52, 64

New Orleans lawyer. Sent by ex-deputy marshal, 21-31; in judge's
      chambers, 35-42, 45, 46; plan to get Negro out of town,
      47-52; talks with Negro, 53-65, 67
   His father: 60
   His son: 67
   His grandson: 67

U.S. oil baron. 2-4, 6, 8, 12, 17-19, 23, 25, 28, 44

Argentine prince. 1, 2

Sawmill owner who speaks to turnkey and Negro groom. 70, 71
   His mother: 70
   His three sisters: 70
   His two daughters: 70
   His wife: 70

HISTORICAL

Alexander (356-323 B.C.): King of Macedonia. 56

Blackstone, William (1723-1780): English jurist. 36

Booth, General William (1829-1912): Founder of Salvation Army.
      56

Brown, John (1800-1859): American abolitionist. 64

Bryan, William Jennings (1860-1925): American lawyer and
      political figure. 56

Caesar, Julius (100?-44 B.C.): Roman general and emperor. 36, 56

Calhoun, John C. (1782-1850): American statesman. 64

Capet: Family name of third dynasty of French kings from Hugh
      Capet (940?-996). 39

Charlemagne (742-814): King of the Franks. 39

Cicero, Marcus Tullius (106-43 B.C.): Roman orator and statesman.
      64

Coke, Edward (1552-1634): English jurist. 36

Demosthenes (385?-322 B.C.): Athenian orator. 64

Dickens, Charles (1812-1870): English novelist. 39

Ford, Henry (1863-1947): American automobile manufacturer. 65, 66

Genghis Khan (1162-1227): Mongol leader. 56, 64

Homer: Greek epic poet. 16

Hugo, Victor (1802-1885): French novelist. 39

Littleton, Thomas (1589-1645): English jurist. 36

Marlborough, First Duke of (John Churchill, 1650-1722): English military commander. 18

Mazarin, Jules (1602-1661): French cardinal and statesman. 56

Murat, Joachim (1767?-1815): French cavalry commander. 64

Murrell, John A. (1804?-1844): American bandit. 31

Napoleon (1769-1821): Emperor of France. 36, 56

Pitt, William (1759-1806): English statesman. 64

Prester John: Name of alleged Christian priest/king in Middle Ages. 56

Sunday, Billy (1862-1935): American evangelist. 56

Talleyrand-Perigord, Charles Maurice de (1754-1838): French statesman. 56

Warwick: Name of English earldom, created c.1088. 56

Webster, Daniel (1782-1852): American statesman. 64

BIBLICAL

Abraham: Old Testament patriarch in Genesis. 17

Adam: First man in Genesis. 15

Christ: 56

David: King of Israel. 20

Eve: Adam's wife in Genesis. 19

God: 38, 54

Goliath: Philistine giant killed by David in 1 Samuel. 20

Isaac: Old Testament patriarch; Abraham's son. 17

Mary: Mother of Jesus. 19

Moses: Old Testament patriarch. 64

Paul: Apostle of Christ. 64

Peter: Disciple of Christ. 56

Samson: Hebrew of great strength betrayed by Delilah in Judges. 41

Samuel's father: Elkanah; father of the first great prophet. 17

Satan: 54

LITERARY/MYTHIC

Ahab: Character in Herman Melville's *Moby Dick*, 1851. 19

Androcles: Roman slave saved by his kindness to lion. 19

Balzac's African deserter: Character in "A Passion in the Desert," 1832. 19

Helen: Wife of Menelaus. 15

Holmes, Sherlock: Central character in some of Arthur Conan Doyle's works. 54

Juliet: Character in William Shakespeare's *Romeo and Juliet*, 1594-1595, 15

Lilith: Adam's first wife in Hebrew folklore. 15

Lochinvar: Hero of ballad in Sir Walter Scott's *Marmion*, 1808. 15

Paris: Prince of Troy. 15

Pyramus: Babylonian lover of Thisbe. 15

Romeo: Character in William Shakespeare's *Romeo and Juliet*, 1594-1595. 15

Thisbe: Pyramus' lover. 15

"NYMPHOLEPSY"

In (I) *The Mississippi Quarterly*, 26 (Summer 1973), [403]-409; (II) *A Faulkner Miscellany*, ed. James B. Meriwether (Jackson, Miss.: University Press of Mississippi, 1974), pp. 149-155; (III) *Uncollected Stories of William Faulkner*, ed. Joseph Blotner (New York: Random House, 1979).

UNNAMED

Laborer. (I) [403]-409; (II) 149-155; (III) [331]-337

HISTORICAL

Thucydides (471?-400? B.C.): Greek historian. (I) 404; (II) 150; (III) [331]

"THE OLD PEOPLE"

In (I) *Harper's*, 181 (September 1940), 418-425; (II) *Uncollected Stories of William Faulkner*, ed. Joseph Blotner (New York: Random House, 1979). Revised as Chapter 4 of *Go Down, Moses*, 1942; see also *Big Woods*, 1955.

Ash, Uncle: Negro cook. (I) 421.1, 421.2; (II) 205-207

Baker, Joe (Jobaker): Chickasaw friend of Sam Fathers. (I) 420.1, 420.2, 424.1; (II) 204, 205, 210

De Spain, Major: Large landowner. (I) 418.2, 419.2, 420.2, 421.1, 421.2, 422.1, 422.2, 424.1, 424.2; (II) 202, 203, 205-207, 211

Ewell, Walter: Member of hunting group. (I) 418.2, 421.1, 421.2, 422.1, 422.2, 423.1, 423.2, 424.1, 424.2; (II) 202, 205-211

Fathers, Sam: Narrator's tutor in the woods. (I) 418.1-424.2, 425.2; (II) [201]-212
  His grandmother: (I) 419.1; (II) 202, 203
  Her husband, a slave: (I) 419.1; (II) 203

Hogganbeck, Boon: Worker for Major de Spain. (I) 418.2, 419.2, 421.1, 421.2, 422.1, 422.2, 423.1, 424.1; (II) 202, 203, 205-209, 211
  His grandmother: (I) 419.2; (II) 203

Ikkemotubbe (Doom): Grandfather of Sam Fathers. (I) 418.2, 419.1, 419.2; (II) 202, 203
  His mother: (I) 419.1; (II) 202
  His son: (I) 419.1; (II) 203

Issetibbeha: Ikkemotubbe's uncle. (I) 419.1; (II) 202

Jimbo: Negro worker for De Spain. (I) 418.2, 421.1, 421.2; (II) 202, 205-207

McCaslin, Uncle Ike: Old hunter. (I) 421.1-422.2, 424.1, 424.2; (II) 205-208, 211

Moketubbe: Doom's cousin. (I) 419.1; (II) 202, 203
  His son: (I) 419.1; (II) 202

Vitry, Chevalier Soeur-Blonde de: Doom's French companion. (I) 419.1; (II) 202, 203

UNNAMED

Narrator, young boy tutored by Sam Fathers in the woods. (I) 418.1-425.2; (II) [201]-212
  His father. (I) 418.2, 419.2-422.2, 424.1-425.2; (II) 202-208, 211, 212
  His grandfather. (I) 418.2, 420.1; (II) 202, 204
  His great-grandfather. (I) 419.1; (II) 203

"'ONCE ABOARD THE LUGGER--'"

In (I) *Contempo*, 1 (1 February 1932), 1, 4; (II) *Uncollected Stories of William Faulkner*, ed. Joseph Blotner (New York: Random House, 1979).

Joe: Pete's older brother. (I) 1.2; (II) [352]

Pete: One of four men on the boat. (I) 1.2, 4.1, 4.3; (II) [352]-354, 357, 358

UNNAMED

Captain of boat. (I) 1.2, 4.1, 4.2, 4.3; (II) [352]-358

Negro on boat. (I) 1.2, 4.1, 4.2, 4.3; (II) [352]-358

Narrator, one of four men on boat. (I) 1.2, 4.1, 4.2, 4.3; (II) [352]-358

HISTORICAL

Conrad, Joseph (1857-1924): English novelist. (I) 4.3; (II) 358

LITERARY

Conrad's centaur: Reference to tugboat captain in "Falk" by Joseph Conrad. (I) 4.3; (II) 358

"ONCE ABOARD THE LUGGER -----"

In *Uncollected Stories of William Faulkner*, ed. Joseph Blotner (New York: Random House, 1979); the first part of this story, also in *Uncollected Stories*, was first published in *Contempo*, 1 (1 February 1932), 1, 4; see above.

Cap'm: Man whom Ed's companion threatens to tell that Ed killed the Negro. 363

Ed: Italian who kills Pete. [359]-365

Joe: Owner of boat. [359], 363

Pete: Joe's brother, a bootlegger. [359]-361, 363-367

UNNAMED

Negro on boat killed by man with Alabama drawl. [359], 360, 362-364, 366

Narrator on boat. [359]-367

The priest whom Ed's companion threatens to tell that Ed killed the Negro. 363

Captain of boat knocked out by Ed and his companion. [359]-361, 365, 366

Man with Ed who has red hair and an Alabama drawl; kills Negro. [359]-365

HISTORICAL

Conrad, Joseph (1857-1924): English novelist. 365

Dewey, Admiral George (1837-1917): American naval officer. 360

Houdini, Harry (1874-1926): American magician. 360, 361, 363, 365

Rickard, Tex (1871-1929): American prize-fight promoter. 359

Swanson, Gloria (1898-   ): American film actress. 359

BIBLICAL

God: 364

LITERARY

Conrad's centaur: Reference to tugboat captain in "Falk" by Joseph Conrad. 365

"OUT OF NAZARETH"

In (I) *William Faulkner: New Orleans Sketches*, ed. Carvel Collins (New York: Random House, 1968); (II) *Sinbad in New Orleans*, ed. Leland Cox (Spartanburg, S.C.: The Reprint Company, 1981). First printed in New Orleans *Times-Picayune* Sunday magazine section, 12 April 1925, p. 4.

Spratling: Artist friend of Narrator. (I) 46-50, 53, 54; (II) 57-60, 63

UNNAMED

Narrator, a writer. (I) 46-54; (II) 57-60, 63

Youth who looks like David. (I) 47-50, 53, 54; (II) 57-60, 63

Narrator in Youth's story. (I) 50-53; (II) 60-63

HISTORICAL

Browning, Elizabeth (1806-1861): English poet. (I) 49; (II) 59

Cezanne, Paul (1839-1906): French artist. (I) 46; (II) 57

Frost, Robert (1874-1963): American poet. (I) 49; (II) 59

Housman, A.E. (1859-1936): English poet. (I) 49; (II) 59

Jackson, Andrew (1767-1845): President of United States, 1829-1837. (I) 46; (II) 57

BIBLICAL

David: King of Israel. (I) 47, 53; (II) 58, 63

Jonathan: Son of Saul. (I) 47; (II) 58

MYTHIC

Diana: Goddess of the hunt. (I) 46; (II) 57

"PANTALOON IN BLACK"

In (I) *Harper's*, 181 (October 1940), 503-513; (II) *Uncollected Stories of William Faulkner*, ed. Joseph Blotner (New York: Random House, 1979). Revised as Chapter 3 of *Go Down, Moses*, 1942.

Acey: Negro at sawmill. (I) 503.2, 504.1; (II) 239

Alec, Uncle: Husband of Rider's aunt. (I) 507.1, 507.2, 509.1, 509.2, 510.1; (II) 245, 248, 249
  His wife, Rider's aunt: (I) 503.1, 503.2, 504.2, 507.1, 507.2, 509.1-510.1, 513.1; (II) [238]-240, 245, 248, 249, 254, 255

Beauchamp, Lucas: Negro tenant on Edmonds plantation. (I) 504.2; (II) 240

Birdsong: White night watchman at sawmill. (I) 510.2, 511.1, 511.2, 512.1; (II) 250, 251, 253, 254
  His family: (I) 511.2, 512.1, 513.1, 513.2; (II) 252-255

Edmonds, Carothers: Landowner on whose land Rider lives. (I) 504.1, 504.2; (II) 240

Ketcham: Jailor. (I) 513.1, 513.2; (II) 254, 255

McAndrews: Foreman at sawmill. (I) 507.1, 508.1, 512.1, 512.2; (II) 244, 246, 253

Mannie: Rider's wife. (I) 503.1-506.1, 507.2, 510.1, 512.1; (II) [238]-242, 245, 250, 253

Mayfield: Sheriff. (I) 512.1, 512.2, 513.1; (II) 252-254

Rider (Spoot): Negro sawmill worker. (I) 503.1-513.2; (II) [238]-255
  His parents: (I) 503.2; (II) [238]

UNNAMED

Sheriff's deputy. (I) 511.2-513.2; (II) 252-255
  His wife. (I) 511.2, 512.1, 513.2; (II) 252, 253, 255

White bootlegger. (I) 508.1, 508.2; (II) 246, 247

Fireman at sawmill. (I) 506.2, 512.1; (II) 243, 244, 253

BIBLICAL

Lord: (I) 507.2, 510.1; (II) 245, 249

"PENNSYLVANIA STATION"

In (I) *American Mercury*, 31 (February 1934), 166-174; (II) *Collected Stories*, 1950.

Gihon, Danny: Old man's nephew; son of Margaret Gihon. (I) 167.1, 167.2, 168.2-171.2, 172.2-174.1; (II) 610-612, 614, 615, 617-625

Gihon, Mrs. Margaret Noonan: Danny's mother; old man's sister. (I) 167.1-174.2; (II) 611-625

Pinckski, Mr.: Man who sells coffins. (I) 167.2-171.2, 172.2-173.2, 174.2; (II) 612-617, 620, 622, 623

Zilich, Mrs. Sophie: Neighbor of Mrs. Gihon. (I) 169.1, 169.2, 170.2-173.2, 174.2; (II) 614, 615, 617, 618, 620-625

UNNAMED

Old man who sits on bench; Mrs. Gihon's brother. (I) 166.1-174.2; (II) 609-625

Young man who sits on bench. (I) 166.1-167.2, 168.2, 170.1, 171.1-173.1, 174.1, 174.2; (II) 609-614, 616, 617, 619-622, 624, 625

Lawyer who defends Danny Gihon. (I) 171.1-172.2; (II) 611, 618-621

Man who clears station of derelicts. (I) 166.2, 172.1, 172.2, 173.2, 174.1; (II) 610, 620, 621, 623-625

BIBLICAL

Lord: (I) 170.1; (II) 616

"PETER"

In *Uncollected Stories of William Faulkner*, ed. Joseph Blotner (New York: Random House, 1979).

Eagle Beak: Man who sleeps with Peter's mother. 490

Euphrosy: Prostitute who has sense according to Peter's mother. 491

Imogene: Prostitute. 493

Joe Lee: Man with Imogene. 493

Mable: Peter's mother; a prostitute. [489]-491, 493

Peter: Young boy; Mable's son. [489]-494
   His brother: [489]

Spratling: Artist drawing Peter; friend of narrator. [489]-494

UNNAMED

Negro whom Peter calls the "Baptis'." 490, 491

Chinese who visits Peter's mother. [489]-492

Narrator; Spratling's friend. [489]-494

BIBLICAL

God: 492

MYTHIC

Hercules: Greek hero of great strength. 490

"POINT OF LAW"

In (I) *Collier's*, 105 (22 June 1940), 20, 21, 30, 32; (II) *Uncollected Stories of William Faulkner*, ed. Joseph Blotner (New York: Random House, 1979). Revised as first section of "The Fire and the Hearth," Chapter 2, of *Go Down, Moses*, 1942.

Beauchamp, Lucas: Negro who lives on Edmonds' plantation. (I) 20.1-20.4, 21.1-21.4, 30.1-30.3, 32.1, 32.2; (II) [213]-225
  His older daughter: (I) 20.4; (II) 214
  His grandchildren: (I) 20.4; (II) 214
  His wife: (I) 20.1, 20.4, 21.1, 21.2, 32.1, 32.2; (II) [213], 215-217, 222-224

Beauchamp, Nat: See Wilkins, Nat Beauchamp

Edmonds, Carothers (Roth): Son of Zack Edmonds; owner of Edmonds' plantation. (I) 20.1-20.4, 21.1-21.4, 30.1-30.3, 32.1, 32.2; (II) [213]-222, 224

Edmonds, Zack: Roth Edmonds' father. (I) 20.4, 30.2, 32.1; (II) 214, 220, 222

Gowan, Judge: Judge who tries Lucas Beauchamp and George Wilkins. (I) 30.1, 30.3, 32.1; (II) 218, 220-223

Henry: Jefferson marshal. (I) 32.1; (II) 222

Tom: Deputy. (I) 21.1-21.3; (II) 216-218

Wilkins, George: Young Negro, Nat Beauchamp's husband. (I) 20.2-20.4, 21.1-21.4, 30.1-30.3, 32.1, 32.2; (II) [213]-225

Wilkins, Nathalie Beauchamp (Nat): Lucas Beauchamp's daughter; George Wilkins' wife. (I) 20.1-20.4, 21.1-21.4, 30.1-30.3, 32.1, 32.2; (II) [213]-224

UNNAMED

Commissioner. (I) 21.1-21.4; (II) 216-218

Sheriff. (I) 20.4, 21.1, 21.3, 21.4, 30.1, 30.2, 32.2; (II) 215-220, 224

LITERARY

Capulet: Family in Shakespeare's *Romeo and Juliet*, 1594-1595.
    (I) 21.1; (II) 216

Montague: Family in Shakespeare's *Romeo and Juliet*, 1594-1595.
    (I) 21.1; (II) 216

"A PORTRAIT OF ELMER"

In *Uncollected Stories of William Faulkner*, ed. Joseph Blotner (New York: Random House, 1979). First printed in *The Georgia Review*, 33 (Fall 1979), 534-564.

Angelo: Man with Elmer in Paris. [610]-612, 622, 623, 631, 632, 635-640

Ethel: Woman who bears Elmer's bastard child. 612, 623, 624, 626
  Her family: 624
  Her bastard son: 612, 623

Gloria: Woman Mr. Monson knows who performs in a New Orleans nightclub. 614

Grover: Ethel's husband. 624

Hodge, Mr.: Elmer's father. [610], 614-616, 620-622, 632-634, 637

Hodge, Mrs.: Elmer's mother. [610], 614-616, 620-622, 625, 632-634, 637

Hodge, Elmer (Elly): Young artist. [610]-641
  His two brothers: 614-616, 625, 633

Hodge, Jo: Elmer's sister. 614-616, 621, 622, 625, 629-631, 633

Merridew, Mrs.: Velma's mother. 619

Merridew, Velma: Girl from whom Elmer borrows sugar. 619, 620

Monson, Mr.: Myrtle's father. 613, 614

"A Portrait of Elmer"

Monson, Mrs.: Myrtle's mother. 611, 613, 614, 635, 640

Monson, Myrtle: Girl Elmer loves. 611-614, 622, 632, 634, 635, 638, 640, 641

UNNAMED

Teacher on whom Elmer develops a crush. 616-618

Boy like god whom Elmer admires. 616

Man who makes Liberty Loan speech. 629-631

HISTORICAL

Cezanne, Paul (1839-1906): French artist. 637

Chopin, Frédéric (1810-1849): Polish composer. 640

Hals, Frans (1580?-1666): Dutch artist. 637

Joan of Arc (1412-1431): French leader. 615

Manet, Édouard (1832-1883): French artist. 637

Matisse, Henri (1869-1954): French artist. 637

Monet, Claude (1840-1926): French artist. 637

Morgan, J.P. (1837-1913): American financier. 622
  His wife: 622

Picasso, Pablo (1881-1973): Spanish artist. 637

Rembrandt (1606-1669): Dutch artist. 637

Swanson, Gloria (1898-   ): American film actress. 622

Verlaine, Paul (1844-1896): French poet. 640

BIBLICAL

Adam: First man in Genesis. 622

Eve: Adam's wife in Genesis. 622

Job: Old Testament patriarch. 620

Samuel: Hebrew judge and prophet. 640

"THE PRIEST"

In (I) *Sinbad in New Orleans*, ed. Leland Cox (Spartanburg, S.C.: The Reprint Company, 1981); (II) *Uncollected Stories of William Faulkner*, ed. Joseph Blotner (New York: Random House, 1979). First printed in *The Mississippi Quarterly*, 29 (Summer 1976), 446-450.

Gianotti, Father: Priest's instructor of whom he did not
    approve. (I) 27; (II) 349

UNNAMED

Priest. (I) 25-29; (II) [348]-351

HISTORICAL

Becket, St. Thomas à (1118?-1170): Archbishop of Canterbury.
    (I) 25; (II) [348]

Bembo, Pietro (1470-1574): Cardinal-Deacon of St. Ciriaco.
    (I) 26; (II) 349

Savonarola, Girolamo (1452-1498): Italian martyr and reformer.
    (I) 25; (II) [348]

BIBLICAL

God: (I) 25, 28, 29; (II) [348], 351

Maria (Mary): (I) 26, 29; (II) 349, 351

"RACE AT MORNING"

In (I) *The Saturday Evening Post*, 227 (5 March 1955), 26, 27, 103, 104, 106; (II) *Uncollected Stories of William Faulkner*, ed. Joseph Blotner (New York: Random House, 1979). Also see *Big Woods*, 1955.

Edmonds, Roth: Member of hunting group. (I) 27.1-27.3, 103.1, 106.2-106.4; (II) [296]-299, 308, 310

Ernest, Mister: Narrator's guardian. (I) 27.1-27.3, 103.1, 103.2, 104.1-104.3, 104.5, 106.1-106.4; (II) [296]-310
  His wife: (I) 106.3; (II) 308

Ewell, Walter: Member of hunting group. (I) 27.1, 106.2, 106.4; (II) [296], 308, 310

Legate, Willy: Member of hunting group. (I) 27.1, 27.2, 103.1, 103.2, 106.2, 106.4; (II) [296], 297, 299-301, 308, 310

McCaslin, Uncle Ike: Old member of hunting group. (I) 27.2, 27.3, 103.1, 103.2, 106.2, 106.3, 106.4; (II) 297-300, 308, 310

Simon: Negro cook. (I) 27.2, 27.3, 103.1, 106.2; (II) 297-299, 307, 308

UNNAMED

Narrator, young boy. (I) 27.1-106.4; (II) [296]-310
  His mother. (I) 106.2; (I) 307, 308
  His father. (I) 106.2; (II) 307, 308

Vicksburg roadhouse man with whom narrator's mother ran away. (I) 106.2; (II) 307, 308

"RAID"

In (I) *The Saturday Evening Post*, 207 (3 November 1934), 18, 19, 72, 73, 75, 77, 78; (II) *Uncollected Stories of William Faulkner*, ed. Joseph Blotner (New York: Random House, 1979). Revised as Chapter 3 of *The Unvanquished*, 1938.

Bowen, Captain: Union army officer. (I) 78.2; (II) 56

Breckbridge, Gavin: Dead fiancé of Drusilla Hawk. (I) 72.2; (II) 44

Compson, Mrs.: Jefferson friend of Rosa Millard. (I) 18.1, 19.1, 75.2, 77.1, 77.2; (II) [37]-39, 48-51, 53

Dick, Col. Nathaniel G.: Union army officer. (I) 18.1, 18.2, 75.2, 77.1, 77.2; (II) [37], 38, 49, 51

Hawk, Uncle Denny: Drusilla Hawk's father. (I) 72.1; (II) 42

Hawk, Cousin Denny: Drusilla Hawk's brother. (I) 72.1, 72.2, 73.1, 73.2; (II) 42-44

Hawk, Cousin Drusilla: Daughter of Denny and Louise Hawk. (I) 72.2, 73.1, 73.2, 75.1, 75.2, 75.3; (II) 43-50

Hawk, Aunt Louise: Drusilla Hawk's mother. (I) 72.1, 73.2; (II) 42, 46

Jingus: Hawk Negro slave. (I) 72.1, 72.2; (II) 42.44

Joby: Sartoris Negro slave. (I) 18.1, 18.2, 18.3; (II) [37]-39

Loosh: Joby's son. (I) 18.2, 18.3, 73.1, 77.1; (II) 38, 45, 52

Louvinia: Joby's wife. (I) 18.1, 18.2, 18.3, 72.1, 78.3; (II) [37]-39, 42, 57

McCaslin, Uncle Buck: Old Yoknapatawpha resident. (I) 18.2; (II) 38

Millard, Rosa: Bayard Sartoris' grandmother. (I) 18.1-18.3, 19.1-19.3, 72.1, 73.1, 73.2, 75.1-75.3, 77.1-77.3, 78.1-78.3; (II) [37]-42, 44-57

Philadelphy: Loosh's wife. (I) 77.1; (II) 52

Ringo: Bayard Sartoris' Negro companion. (I) 18.1-18.3, 19.1-19.3, 72.1, 72.2, 73.1, 73.2, 75.1, 75.2, 77.1, 77.2, 77.3, 78.1, 78.2, 78.3; (II) [37]-46, 48-57

Sartoris, Bayard: Young narrator, Col. John Sartoris' son. (I) 18.1-78.3; (II) [37]-57

Sartoris, Col. John: Confederate officer, Bayard's father. (I) 18.2, 72.2, 73.1, 73.2, 75.1, 75.2; (II) 38, 44-49

HISTORICAL

Sherman, William T. (1820-1891): Union general. (I) 73.1, 77.1, 77.2, 77.3, 78.2; (II) 45, 52-54, 56

BIBLICAL

God: (I) 73.2, 77.3; (II) 41, 49

Jesus: (I) 19.3, 75.2; (II) 46, 47, 54

"RED LEAVES"

In (I) *The Saturday Evening Post*, 203 (25 October 1930), 6, 7, 54, 56, 58, 60, 62, 64; (II) *These 13*, 1931; (III) *Collected Stories*, 1950; see also *Big Woods*, 1955.

Berry, Louis: Chickasaw. (I) 6.1-6.3, 7.1, 7.2, 56.1, 56.2, 58.1, 60.1, 60.2, 62.1, 62.2, 64.1-64.3; (II) 127-131, 140-142, 144-147, 151-153, 155, 158-162; (III) 313-317, 322-327, 331-333, 337

Doom: Father of Issetibbeha. (I) 6.1, 7.1-7.3, 54.1, 54.2, 56.1, 58.1, 62.2; (II) 127, 131-135, 142, 145, 146, 159; (III) 313, 316-319, 322, 324, 326, 327, 336
  His mother: (I) 7.2; (II) 133; (III) 317
  His uncle: (I) 7.3, 54.2; (II) 134, 139; (III) 318, 322
  His cousin: (I) 7.3; (II) 134; (III) 318

Had-Two-Fathers: See John Had-Two-Fathers

Issetibbeha: Moketubbe's father; Doom's son. (I) 6.1-6.3, 7.1, 7.2, 54.1, 54.2, 56.1, 56.2, 58.1, 58.2, 60.1, 60.2, 62.1, 62.2, 64.2, 64.3; (II) 127-130, 132, 134-141, 143, 145-149, 151, 152, 155, 159, 160, 163-165; (III) 313-328, 330, 331, 333, 336, 337, 339, 340
  His newest wife: (I) 54.2, 56.2; (II) 138, 143; (III) 321, 325
  His maternal uncle: (I) 54.1; (II) 136; (III) 320
  His uncles and cousins: (I) 54.1; (II) 135, 136; (III) 319, 320

John Had-Two-Fathers: Chickasaw. Had-Two-Fathers in *These 13* and *CS*. (I) 62.2; (II) 158; (III) 336

Moketubbe: Issetibbeha's son. (I) 6.3, 7.1, 7.2, 54.2, 56.1,
    56.2, 58.1, 62.1, 62.2, 64.1, 64.2; (II) 131, 132, 137-
    141, 143-147, 156-161, 163; (III) 315-317, 320-323, 325-
    327, 334-339
  His mother: (I) 54.2; (II) 137; (III) 320, 321

Three Basket: Chickasaw. (I) 6.1-6.3, 7.1, 7.2, 56.1, 56.2,
    58.1, 60.2, 62.1, 62.2, 64.1, 64.2, 64.3; (II) 127-131,
    140-142, 144-147, 152, 153, 155, 158-166; (III) 313-317,
    322-327, 331-333, 336, 338-341

Vitry, Chevalier Soeur Blonde de: Doom's French companion.
    (I) 7.2, 7.3, 54.1; (II) 133, 136, 137; (III) 317, 318,
    320

UNNAMED

Negro, Issetibbeha's servant. (I) 6.3, 7.1, 56.1, 58.1, 58.2,
    60.1, 60.2, 62.1, 62.2, 64.1, 64.2, 64.3; (II) 130, 131,
    141, 144-157, 159-166; (III) 315, 316, 322, 324, 326-341

West Indian woman, Issetibbeha's mother. (I) 7.3, 54.1, 54.2;
    (II) 134, 137; (III) 318, 321
  Her brother: (I) 7.3, 54.1; (II) 134; (III) 318

Young man who attends Moketubbe. (I) 56.2, 58.1, 62.2; (II)
    144-146, 158; (III) 325-327, 335

Negro head man who offers Issetibbeha's servant food. (I)
    58.2, 60.2; (II) 147, 154; (III) 332, 333

HISTORICAL

Carondelet, Francisco (1748?-1807?): Spanish governor of
    Louisiana. (I) 7.3; (II) 133; (III) 318

Louis XV (1710-1774): King of France. (I) 54.2; (II) 137;
    (III) 320

Pompadour, Marquise de (1721-1764): Mistress of Louis XV.
    (I) 54.2; (II) 137; (III) 320

Wilkinson, James (1757-1825): American general. (I) 7.3; (II)
    133; (III) 318

"RETREAT"

In (I) *The Saturday Evening Post*, 207 (13 October 1934), 16, 17, 82, 84, 85, 87, 89; (II) *Uncollected Stories of William Faulkner*, ed. Joseph Blotner (New York: Random House, 1979). Revised as Chapter 2 of *The Unvanquished*, 1938.

Compson, Mrs.: Jefferson friend of Rosa Millard. (I) 17.2, 82.1, 87.1; (II) 20, 23, 32

Joby: Sartoris Negro slave. (I) 16.1-16.3, 17.1, 82.1-82.3, 84.1, 87.2, 87.3; (II) [17]-20, 23-27, 32-35

Loosh: Joby's son. (I) 16.1-16.3, 17.1, 87.3, 89.1; (II) [17]-19, 34, 35

Louvinia: Joby's wife. (I) 16.1-16.3, 17.1, 17.2, 87.2, 87.3, 89.1; (II) [17]-21, 33-35

Marengo (Ringo): Bayard's Negro companion. (I) 16.1-16.3, 17.1, 17.2, 82.1-82.3, 84.1, 84.2, 85.1, 85.2, 87.1-87.3, 89.1, 89.2; (II) [17]-36

McCaslin, Uncle Buck: Old Yoknapatawpha resident. (I) 17.2, 17.3, 82.1; (II) 20-22

Millard, Rosa: Bayard Sartoris' grandmother. (I) 16.1-16.3, 17.1, 17.2, 82.1-82.3, 84.1, 84.2, 85.1, 85.2, 87.1-87.3, 89.1, 89.2; (II) [17]-36
  Her sister: (I) 82.2; (II) 24

Mitchell, Unc Few: Man who is described by Louvinia as "loony." (I) 87.3; (II) 34

Philadelphy: Loosh's wife. (I) 87.3, 89.1; (II) 35

Sartoris, Bayard: Young narrator; Col. John Sartoris' son. (I) 16.1-89.2; (II) [17]-36

Sartoris, Col. John: Confederate officer; Bayard Sartoris' father. (I) 16.1, 16.2, 17.1-17.3, 82.1, 82.2, 84.1, 84.2, 85.1, 85.2, 87.1-87.3; (II) [17], 19-22, 24, 27-35

UNNAMED

Man who replaced Col. John Sartoris as colonel of his regiment. (I) 17.3, 82.1; (II) 21, 22

Captain of Confederate company in Jefferson. (I) 17.2, 17.3, 82.1; (II) 20-22

HISTORICAL

Jackson, Thomas J. "Stonewall" (1824-1863): Confederate general. (I) 17.3; (II) 21

Johnston, Joseph E. (1807-1870): Confederate general. (I) 87.1; (II) 31

BIBLICAL

Lord: (I) 16.1, 17.3, 87.3; (II) [17], 19, 21, 35

"A RETURN"

In *Uncollected Stories of William Faulkner*, ed. Joseph Blotner (New York: Random House, 1979).

Awce: Negro servant of the Randolphs. 554, 555, 558, 560, 563-565

Blount, Gavin, I: Chairman of the Committee and major in the Confederacy. 548-550, 553, 566, 567, 574

Blount, Gavin, II: Great nephew of Gavin Blount I; physician who is bachelor and lives with two maiden aunts. 556, 557, 565-574
  His father: 566, 567
  His two maiden aunts: 566

Gillman, Mrs.: Lewis Randolph Gordon's friend with whom she went to school. 565

Gordon, Charles: Lewis Randolph Gordon's husband who is killed in chicken house in Civil War. [547], 550, 551, 558, 561, 566, 568, 569, 573
  His father: 555, 558-564
  His mother: 555, 558-563

"A Return"

Gordon, Lewis Randolph: Charles Gordon's wife, Randolph's
    mother. [547]-574
  Her mother who dies from pneumonia after trying to bury
    silver: [547], 550-554, 557
  Her father who disappears after being in prison: [547], 553-
    555, 557-559

Gordon, Randolph: Lewis Randolph Gordon's son; successful
    businessman. 548-574
  His son: 563, 570, 571
  His daughter: 563, 570, 571

Heustace: Chairman of Guards who inherited it from Gavin Blount I.
    567

Heustace, Henry: Friend of Randolph Gordon who is invited to
    dinner. 569-573

Heustace, Mrs. Henry: Henry Heustace's wife. 569, 571-573

Joanna: Negro nurse of Randolph Gordon during War. 553-555,
    558, 560, 562, 564, 572

Lucius: Randolph's chauffeur. 565, 573, 574

Melissandre (Lissy): Daughter of Joanna and Awce who helps
    Lewis Randolph Gordon after Joanna dies. 564-566

Mullen: Man who had been in Forrest's cavalry command. 550

Sandeman: Chairman of Guards before Gavin Blount II. 567

Will: Negro man of Randolphs. 554, 555

                            UNNAMED

Yankees who entered Lewis Randolph Gordon's house. 557, 558,
    572, 573

Yankee whom Lewis Randolph Gordon perhaps killed; Gavin Blount
    II imagines scene which Randolph Gordon does not remember
    happening. 557, 558

Couple about Randolph Gordon's age at dinner. 570-573

Young woman and man who are Randolph Gordon's son and daughter's
    guests at dinner. 570-573

HISTORICAL

Davis, Jefferson (1808-1889): President of Confederacy. 549

Forrest, Nathan Bedford (1821-1877): Confederate general. 550

Johnston, Albert S. (1803-1862): Confederate general. 553

Lucullus, Lucius Licinius (c.70 B.C.): Roman general. 555

Shields, James (1806?-1879): United States senator and army officer. 550

Van Dorn, Earl (1820-1863): Confederate general. 555

BIBLICAL

God: 562

"THE ROSARY"

In (I) *William Faulkner: New Orleans Sketches*, ed. Carvel Collins (New York: Random House, 1968); (II) *Sinbad in New Orleans*, ed. Leland Cox (Spartanburg, S.C.: The Reprint Company, 1981). First printed in New Orleans *Times-Picayune* Sunday magazine section, 3 May 1925, p. 2.

Harris: Man who hates "The Rosary" and his neighbor. (I) 61-65; (II) 65-68
    His family: (I) 61, 65; (II) 65, 68

Venturia, Juan: Shopkeeper who hates Harris, his neighbor. (I) 61-65; (II) 65-68

"A ROSE FOR EMILY"

In (I) *Forum*, 83 (April 1930), 233-238; (II) *These 13*, 1931; (III) *Collected Stories*, 1950.

"Royal Street"

Barron, Homer: Yankee road builder. (I) 234.2, 236.1, 236.2, 237.1, 238.2; (II) 170, 174, 176-178, 182; (III) 122, 124, 126, 127, 130

Grierson, Mr.: Emily's father. (I) 233.1, 234.1, 235.1, 235.2, 237.1, 238.1; (II) 168-175, 178, 181; (III) 120, 122-125, 129

Grierson, Emily: Jefferson spinster. (I) 233.1-238.2; (II) 167-181; (III) 119-129

Sartoris, Colonel: Jefferson mayor. (I) 233.2, 234.1, 234.2, 237.2; (II) 168, 170, 179; (III) 119-121, 128

Stevens, Judge: Jefferson mayor. (I) 234.2, 235.1; (II) 171, 172; (III) 122

Tobe: Negro servant of Griersons. (I) 233.1, 234.1-235.1, 237.1-238.1; (II) 167, 169-171, 178, 180, 181; (III) 119-122, 127-129

Wyatt, old lady: Relative of Griersons. (I) 235.1, 236.2; (II) 172, 175; (III) 123, 125

UNNAMED

Narrator, Jefferson resident. (I) 233.1-238.2; (II) 167-182; (III) 119-130

"ROYAL STREET"

In *Sinbad in New Orleans*, ed. Leland Cox (Spartanburg, S.C.: The Reprint Company, 1981). "Hong Li" first printed in *The Mississippi Quarterly*, 26 (Summer 1973), 395.

Frankie: Johnny's girl. 139, 140

Hong Li: New Orleans Chinese. 146, 147

Johnny: Man who protects Frankie. 139, 140

Ryan: Policeman. 139

UNNAMED

The Artist. 144, 145

The Beggar. 144

The Cobbler. 142
  His girl in Tuscany. 142

The Cop. 143, 144
  His wife. 144

The Longshoreman. 141

Magdalen. 145, 146

The Priest. 138, 139

The Sailor. 140, 141

Wealthy Jew. 137, 138

HISTORICAL

Ahenobarbus: Name of plebeian Roman family which ended with
    Emperor Nero. 138

Alexander (356-323 B.C.): King of Macedonia. 138

Caesar, Julius (100?-44 B.C.): Roman general and emperor. 138

Napoleon (1769-1821): Emperor of France. 138

BIBLICAL

God: 137-139, 141

Jesus: 139, 141

Maria (Mary): 138, 139

"SEPULTURE SOUTH: GASLIGHT"

In (I) *Harper's Bazaar*, 88 (December 1954), 84, 140, 141; (II) *Uncollected Stories of William Faulkner*, ed. Joseph Blotner (New York: Random House, 1979).

Alice, Aunt: Uncle Charley's wife. (I) 84, 140.1, 140.3; (II) 450-452

Arthur: Liddy's husband. (I) 84; (II) [449], 450

Charley, Uncle: Brother of narrator's father. (I) 84, 140.1-140.3; (II) 450-452

Florence: Maid's name. (I) 140.1; (II) 451

Julia: Maid's name. (I) 140.1; (II) 451

Liddy: Cook of narrator's family. (I) 84, 140.1; (II) [449]-

Julia: Cook of narrator's family. (I) 84, 140.1; (II) [449]-451

Maggie: Narrator's sister. (I) 140.1, 140.2, 140.4, 141.1; (II) 451, 452, 454, 455

Rodney, Uncle: Youngest brother of narrator's father. (I) 140.1, 140.3; (II) 451, 452

Sarah: Simon's wife. (I) 140.2; (II) 452

Simon: Narrator's family servant. (I) 140.2; (II) 452

Wedlow, Mr.: Jeweler. (I) 84; (II) 450

UNNAMED

Narrator. (I) 84-141.2; (II) [449]-455
  His grandfather. (I) 84, 140.1-140.4, 141.1; (II) [449]-455
  His father: (I) 140.1; (II) 451
  His grandmother. (I) 84, 140.4, 141.1; (II) [449], 454, 455
  His father. (I) 84, 140.1-140.4, 141.1; (II) [449]-455
  His mother. (I) 84, 140.1-140.4, 141.1; (II) 450-455
    Her sister and her husband: (I) 84; (II) 450
    Her children in addition to Narrator: (I) 140.1, 140.2; (II) 451

Three honorary pallbearers. (I) 140.3, 140.4; (II) 452, 454

HISTORICAL

Bee, Barnard E. (1824-1861): Confederate general. (I) 140.3; (II) 452

McDowell, Irvin (1818-1885): Union general. (I) 140.3; (II) 453

BIBLICAL

God: (I) 140.2; (II) 452

"SHALL NOT PERISH"

In (I) *Story*, 23 (July-August 1943), 40-47; (II) *Collected Stories*, 1950.

Bookwright, Homer: Cattle truck owner. (I) 40.2, 41.1; (II) 102

De Spain, Major: Wealthy Jefferson resident. (I) 41.1, 42.1, 43.1-45.2; (II) 103, 104, 106-110
  His son, the aviator: (I) 41.1, 43.2, 44.1, 44.2; (II) 103, 107, 108
  His father: (I) 43.2; (II) 107

Grier: Young narrator; Pete Grier's brother. (I) 40.1-47.2; (II) 101-115

Grier: Father of Pete Grier and narrator. (I) 40.1-44.1, 45.1-47.2; (II) 101-114
  His grandfather: (I) 46.1-47.2; (II) 111-114

Grier, Mrs.: Mother of Pete Grier and narrator. (I) 40.1-46.1; (II) 101-114
  Her brother: (I) 44.2; (II) 109
  Her mother: (I) 44.2; (II) 109
  Her grandfather: (I) 44.2; (II) 109
  Her great-grandmother: (I) 44.2; (II) 109

Grier, Pete: Narrator's brother. (I) 40.1-42.2, 43.2, 44.2, 45.1, 46.2-47.2; (II) 101-114

"Shall Not Perish" 309

Killegrew, "Old Man": Griers' neighbor. (I) 41.2; (II) 103

Millard, Mrs. Rosa: Mother-in-law of Col. Sartoris. (I) 46.2; (II) 112

Quick, Solon: Bus driver. (I) 43.1, 45.1, 45.2; (II) 106, 110, 111

Quick, Mrs. Solon: Wife of bus driver. (I) 45.2; (II) 111

Sartoris, Col. John: Confederate officer from Yoknapatawpha. (I) 46.2; (II) 112

UNNAMED

De Spain's Negro servant. (I) 42.1, 43.1, 44.2-45.2; (II) 104, 106, 109, 110

Wealthy Jefferson lady who left money for museum. (I) 45.2; (II) 110, 111

HISTORICAL

Forrest, Nathan Bedford (1821-1877): Confederate general. (I) 47.1; (II) 112, 113

Grant, Ulysses S. (1822-1885): Union general; President of United States, 1869-1877. (I) 46.2; (II) 112

Lincoln, Abraham (1809-1865): President of United States, 1861-1865. (I) 46.2; (II) 112

Morgan, John Hunt (1825-1864): Confederate general. (I) 46.2; (II) 112

Van Dorn, Earl (1820-1863): Confederate general. (I) 46.2; (II) 112

BIBLICAL

God: (I) 46.1; (II) 111

"SHINGLES FOR THE LORD"

In (I) *The Saturday Evening Post*, 215 (13 February 1943), 14, 15, 68, 70, 71; (II) *Collected Stories*, 1950.

Armstid: Farmer who lives near Whitfield's church. (I) 68.1, 68.4, 70.1, 70.2, 71.2; (II) 34, 38-43

Armstid, Mrs.: Armstid's wife. (I) 70.1, 70.2; (II) 39-41

Bookwright, Homer: Volunteer workman on church. (I) 14.1, 15.1-15.3, 68.1-68.3, 70.2, 71.2; (II) 27-31, 34-37, 40-43

Grier: Young narrator; son of Res Grier. (I) 14.1-71.2; (II) 27-43

Grier, Res (Pap): Narrator's father. (I) 14.1, 15.1-15.3, 68.1-68.4, 70.1, 70.2, 71.1, 71.2; (II) 27-43
 His wife; narrator's mother. (I) 14.1, 15.3, 68.4, 70.1, 70.2, 71.1, 71.2; (II) 27, 32, 38, 39, 41-43

Killegrew, "Old Man": Farmer who lives near Griers. (I) 14.1, 15.1, 68.4; (II) 27, 28, 30, 38

Killegrew, Mrs.: Wife of "Old Man" Killegrew. (I) 14.1; (II) 28

Quick, Solon: Volunteer workman on church. (I) 14.1, 15.1-15.3, 68.1-68.4, 70.1, 70.2, 71.2; (II) 27-38, 40-43

Snopes: Volunteer workman on church. (I) 15.2, 68.4, 70.2, 71.2; (II) 31, 38, 40-43

Tull, Vernon: Volunteer workman on church. (I) 15.2, 15.3, 68.1-68.4, 70.2, 71.2; (II) 31-34, 36, 37, 40-43
 His family: (I) 70.2; (II) 41

Varner, Will: Man who gave Tull puppy which he and Grier raised. (I) 15.3; (II) 32

Whitfield, Rev.: Minister whose church is burned. (I) 14.1, 15.1, 68.4, 70.1, 70.2, 71.2; (II) 27-30, 38, 40-43

"Skirmish at Sartoris" 311

BIBLICAL

Archangel Michael: (I) 70.2; (II) 40

God: (I) 14.1, 70.2; (II) 28, 29, 41

"SKIRMISH AT SARTORIS"

In (I) *Scribner's*, 97 (April 1935), 193-200; (II) *Uncollected Stories of William Faulkner*, ed. Joseph Blotner (New York: Random House, 1979). Revised as Chapter 6 of *The Unvanquished*, 1938.

Benbow: Jefferson family. (I) 197.2; (II) 66

Benbow, Cassius Q.: Former Benbow slave; acting marshal of Jefferson. (I) 197.2, 198.1, 199.1, 200.2; (II) 66, 68, 69, 73

Breckbridge, Gavin: Drusilla Hawk Sartoris' dead fiancé. (I) 194.1, 194.2, 196.2; (II) 59-61, 65

Burdens: Two men killed by John Sartoris. (I) 197.2-199.2; (II) 66, 68-71

Compson, General: Confederate officer. (I) 195.1, 195.2; (II) 62

Compson, Mrs.: General Compson's wife. (I) 195.1, 195.2, 196.2, 197.1; (II) 61-65

Habersham, Martha: Wife of bank clerk. (I) 193.1, 195.2, 196.1, 197.1, 198.1, 198.2, 199.1, 200.2; (II) [58], 63-65, 68-70, 72, 73

Hawk, Dennison, I: Drusilla Hawk's father. (I) 194.1, 194.2, 198.1, 198.2; (II) 59-61, 67, 69

Hawk, Dennison, II (Denny): Drusilla Hawk's brother. (I) 194.1, 194.2, 197.2, 198.2, 199.1, 199.2, 200.1; (II) 59-61, 66, 68-70, 72

Hawk, Drusilla: Daughter of Dennison I and Louisa Hawk. (I) 193.1-200.2; (II) [58]-73

Hawk, Louisa: Drusilla Hawk's mother. (I) 193.1-195.2, 197.1-200.2; (II) [58]-63, 65, 67-70, 72, 73

Holston, Mrs.: Jefferson lady. (I) 199.2; (II) 71

Joby: Sartoris Negro slave. (I) 195.1, 196.1-197.1, 198.1; (II) 61, 62, 64, 65, 68

Louvinia: Joby's wife. (I) 195.1, 196.2, 197.1, 199.1, 199.2, 200.2; (II) 62, 65, 70, 73

Millard, Rosa: Grandmother of Bayard/narrator. (I) 193.2, 194.1-195.2, 198.1, 198.2; (II) 59-63, 67, 69

Ringo: Bayard Sartoris' Negro companion. (I) 193.2-195.1, 196.1-198.1, 199.1, 200.2; (II) 59-62; 64-68, 70, 73

Sartoris, Bayard: Colonel John Sartoris' son; narrator. (I) 193.1-200.2; (II) [58]-73

Sartoris, Colonel John: Confederate officer; Bayard Sartoris' father. (I) 193.1-200.2; (II) [58]-73
  His first wife; Bayard Sartoris' mother: (I) 194.2, 198.2; (II) 61, 68

Wyatt, George: Man in Col. John Sartoris' old regiment. (I) 199.2-200.2; (II) 71-73

UNNAMED

Mrs. Holston's porter. (I) 199.2; (II) 71

HISTORICAL

Lincoln, Abraham (1809-1865): President of United States, 1861-1865. (I) 197.1; (II) 65

BIBLICAL

God: (I) 194.2, 198.1; (II) 61, 67

"SMOKE"

In (I) *Harper's*, 164 (April 1932), 562-578; (II) *Doctor Martino*, 1934; (III) *Knight's Gambit*, 1949.

"Smoke" 313

Dodge, Granby: Cousin of Holland twins. (I) 563.2, 564.2, 565.2, 567.1, 570.1, 571.1, 573.1, 573.2, 575.1, 577.1-578.2; (II) 124-126, 128, 129, 132, 138-140, 146, 149, 150, 155-158; (III) 6, 7, 9, 10, 13, 19-25, 28, 29, 33-36

Dukinfield, Judge: Jefferson judge. (I) 565.2-568.1, 569.1-571.1, 572.1, 572.2, 574.1, 574.2, 576.1-577.1; (II) 128-133, 136-140, 143-145, 147, 149, 152-155; (III) 10-14, 16-20, 22-24, 26, 28, 31, 32

Dukinfield, Emma: Judge Dukinfield's daughter. (I) 572.2, 576.2, 577.1; (II) 144, 153, 154; (III) 24, 31, 32

Holland, Anselm, I: Father of Anse and Virginius Holland. (I) 562.1-566.1, 567.1, 568.1-573.1, 577.2, 578.1; (II) 120-130, 132, 134-140, 142-144, 146, 156, 157; (III) 3-11, 13, 15-23, 25, 34, 35

Holland, Anselm, II: One of twin sons of Anselm Holland I. (I) 562.1-564.2, 565.2, 566.1, 567.1, 568.1-570.1, 571.1-573.1, 575.1, 575.2, 577.2; (II) 120-126, 128, 129, 132-138, 141-144, 146, 149, 151, 156; (III) 3-11, 13-23, 25, 28, 34

Holland, Cornelia Mardis: Anselm Holland's wife; mother of twins. (I) 562.1, 562.2, 563.2-565.1, 568.1-569.2, 571.2, 572.1-573.1; (II) 120-123, 125, 127, 134-137, 142-144, 146; (III) 3, 4, 6, 7, 9, 15-17, 22, 23, 25
  Her father: (I) 562.1; (II) 120, 121; (III) 3

Holland, Virginius: One of twin sons of Anselm Holland I. (I) 562.1-566.1, 567.1, 568.1-570.1, 571.1, 573.1, 574.2-575.2, 576.2, 577.2-578.2; (II) 120-129, 132-138, 140, 146, 149-151, 153-158; (III) 3-11, 13-19, 21, 25, 28-30, 32-36

Job, Uncle: Negro janitor. (I) 566.2-567.2, 571.1, 572.1, 574.1, 575.2, 576.1-577.1; (II) 130-133, 140, 143, 147, 151-154; (III) 12-14, 21, 22, 26, 30-33

Stevens, Gavin: County attorney. (I) 567.1-577.2; (II) 132-157; (III) 13-36

West: Drugstore owner. (I) 574.1, 574.2, 576.1, 577.1, 577.2; (II) 147-149, 152, 155, 156; (III) 26-28, 31, 33, 34

UNNAMED

Man who murders Judge Dukinfield.   (I) 574.1-576.2; (II) 147-153; (III) 27-31

Foreman in court room.   (I) 567.1, 569.2, 573.2, 576.1; (II) 132, 133, 137, 138, 145, 151; (III) 13, 14, 18, 26

Narrator, one of jury.   (I) 562.1-577.2; (II) 120-158; (III) 3-36

Sheriff.   (I) 564.2, 565.1; (II) 126, 127, 141; (III) 8, 9, 21

HISTORICAL

Einstein, Albert (1879-1955): Mathematician-physicist.   (I) 569.1; (II) 136; (III) 16

BIBLICAL

God: (I) 566.1, 572.1; (II) 130, 143; (III) 11, 22

"SNOW"

In *Uncollected Stories of William Faulkner*, ed. Joseph Blotner (New York: Random House, 1979).

Brix: Swiss guide who dies to save wife.   667, 668, 670, 672-675
  His wife who later kills German: [665], 666, 669, 670, 672-676
  Married daughter of wife's mother's half-sister with whom she lived: 673, 674
  Married daughter's husband: 674

Don: Narrator's companion from California.   666-677

Grignon, Papa: Mayor of Swiss village.   669, 670, 672

Hiller, Emil: Swiss guide.   667-670, 672-676

Ploeckner, General von: German governor killed by Swiss woman; the "Big Shot."   [665], 666, 672-675

"Spotted Horses" 315

                              UNNAMED

Waiter with rotten teeth. 671-675

Priest in Swiss village. 667-669, 673, 674

Narrator who had been successful architect and is now subaltern
    of engineers. [665]-677
  His child. [665], 666

                          "SPOTTED HORSES"

In (I) Scribner's, 89 (June 1931), 585-597; (II) Uncollected
Stories of William Faulkner, ed. Joseph Blotner (New York:
Random House, 1979). Incorporated into Chapter 1 of Book Four
of The Hamlet, 1940.

Armstid, Henry: Frenchman's Bend farmer. (I) 587.2-591.2,
    592.2-594.1, 595.2-596.2; (II) 168-174, 176-179, 181, 182

Armstid, Mrs. Henry: Henry's wife. (I) 588.1-592.1, 593.1,
    594.1, 594.2, 595.2-597.1; (II) 169-175, 177-179, 181-
    183
  Their children: (I) 588.2, 589.1, 594.1, 596.2; (II) 170, 171,
    178, 179, 182

Armstid, Ina May: Armstids' oldest daughter. (I) 588.2, 589.1,
    594.1, 596.2; (II) 170, 171, 178, 179, 182

Buck: Texan with spotted horses. (I) 586.2-591.1, 594.1, 594.2,
    596.1, 596.2; (II) 167-174, 178-182

Bundren, Mrs.: Woman to whom Suratt tried to sell a sewing
    machine. (I) 591.1, 595.1; (II) 174, 180

Durley: One of the men who carries Henry Armstid into Little-
    john's. (I) 593.1; (II) 176, 177

Ernest: One of the men who carries Henry Armstid into Little-
    john's. (I) 593.1-594.1; (II) 176-178

Freeman: Frenchman's Bend resident. (I) 595.1, 596.2; (II)
    180, 182

Littlejohn, Mrs.: Boarding house owner. (I) 586.2, 587.1, 588.1, 589.2, 591.1-592.1, 593.1-596.1, 597.1; (II) 167-169, 171, 173-181, 183

Quick: One of the men who carries Henry Armstid into Littlejohn's. (I) 593.1, 593.2; (II) 176-178

Quick, Lon: One of the men who bought horses. (I) 595.1; (II) 180

Snopes, Ad: Eck Snopes' son. (I) 590.2-592.2, 595.1, 596.1, 596.2; (II) 173-176, 180-183

Snopes, Eck: Flem Snopes' cousin. (I) 587.1, 587.2, 588.2, 589.1, 590.2-592.2, 593.2, 595.1-596.2; (II) 168, 170, 171, 174-176, 178, 180-183

Snopes, Eula Varner: Flem Snopes' wife. (I) 586.1, 586.2; (II) 166, 167
 Her baby: (I) 586.2; (II) 167

Snopes, Flem: Clerk in Varner's store. (I) 585.1-587.2, 590.1-591.1, 594.1-597.2; (II) [165]-168, 170, 172-174, 178-183

Snopes, I.O.: Flem Snopes' cousin. (I) 591.1, 595.1-597.2; (II) 174, 180-183

Suratt: Narrator, sewing machine salesman. (I) 585.1-597.2; (II) [165]-183

Tull, Vernon: Frenchman's Bend farmer. (I) 592.1, 592.2, 596.1; (II) 175, 176, 181

Tull, Mrs.: Vernon Tull's wife. (I) 592.1, 592.2; (II) 175, 176
 Her aunt: (I) 592.2; (II) 176
 Her three daughters: (I) 592.1, 592.2; (II) 176

Varner, "Uncle Billy": Eula Varner Snopes' father. (I) 585.2, 586.1, 586.2, 593.1-594.1; (II) [165]-167, 177, 178

Varner, Eula: See Snopes, Eula Varner

Varner, Jody: Eula Varner Snopes' brother. (I) 585.2, 586.1, 595.1, 596.2; (II) [165], 166, 180, 182

Winterbottom: One of the men who carries Henry Armstid into
    Littlejohn's.   (I) 593.1-594.1, 595.1, 595.2, 596.2,
    597.1, 597.2; (II) 176-178, 180-183

"SUNSET"

In (I) *William Faulkner: New Orleans Sketches*, ed. Carvel Collins
(New York: Random House, 1968); (II) *Sinbad in New Orleans*, ed.
Leland Cox (Spartanburg, S.C.: The Reprint Company, 1981).
First printed in New Orleans *Times-Picayune* Sunday magazine
section, 24 May 1925, pp. 4, 7.

Bob, Mister: Negro's employer.   (I) 78, 83, 85; (II) 74, 79, 80
    His family: (I) 78; (II) 74

Wallace, Capt.: Officer in State National Guard unit.   (I) 76;
    (II) 73

UNNAMED

Negro who wants to go to Africa.   (I) 76-85; (II) 73-80

"THE TALL MEN"

In (I) *The Saturday Evening Post*, 213 (31 May 1941), 14, 15,
95, 96, 98, 99; (II) *Collected Stories*, 1950.

Gombault, Mr.: Deputy marshal.   (I) 14.1, 14.2, 15.1-15.3,
    95.1, 96.1, 96.2, 98.1, 98.2, 99.1, 99.2; (II) 45-50,
    53-61

McCallum, Old Anse: Father of Jackson, Stuart, Rafe, Lee, and
    Buddy McCallum.   (I) 96.1, 96.2, 98.1, 98.2, 99.1; (II)
    54-57, 60

McCallum, Mrs. Anse: Old Anse McCallum's wife.   (I) 98.2; (II)
    60

McCallum, Anse, II: One of Buddy McCallum's twin sons. (I)
14.1, 14.2, 15.2, 15.3, 95.1, 95.2, 95.3, 96.1, 96.2,
98.1, 98.2, 99.2; (II) 45, 47-50, 52-55, 57, 58, 60

McCallum, Buddy: Old Anse McCallum's youngest son. (I) 15.1-
15.3, 95.1-95.3, 96.1, 96.2, 98.1, 98.2, 99.2; (II) 47-58,
60
 His wife; mother of twins: (I) 96.2, 98.2; (II) 55, 60

McCallum, Jackson: Old Anse McCallum's oldest son. (I) 95.1-
95.3, 96.1, 96.2, 98.1, 98.2, 99.2; (II) 49-52, 54-58,
60

McCallum, Lee: One of Old Anse McCallum's sons. (I) 15.3, 95.1,
95.3, 96.1, 96.2, 98.1, 98.2, 99.2; (II) 45, 49, 52, 54-
58, 60

McCallum, Lucius: One of Buddy McCallum's twin sons. (I) 14.1,
14.2, 15.2, 15.3, 95.1-95.3, 96.1, 96.2, 98.1, 98.2, 99.2;
(II) 45, 47-50, 52-55, 57, 58, 60

McCallum, Rafe: One of Old Anse McCallum's sons. (I) 15.1-
15.3, 95.1-95.3, 96.1, 96.2, 98.1, 98.2, 99.2; (II) 47-
49, 51, 52, 54-58, 60

McCallum, Stuart: One of Old Anse McCallum's sons. (I) 15.3,
95.1-95.3, 96.1, 96.2, 98.1, 98.2, 99.2; (II) 49-52, 54-
58, 60

Pearson, Mr.: State draft investigator. (I) 14.1, 14.2, 15.1-
15.3, 95.1, 95.3, 96.1, 98.1, 98.2, 99.1, 99.2; (II) 45-
55, 58-61
 His grandfather: (I) 15.3; (II) 49

Schofield, Dr.: Physician who amputates Buddy McCallum's leg.
(I) 14.1, 15.1-15.3, 95.1-95.3; (II) 45, 47-49, 51, 52

Stevens, Gavin: County attorney. (I) 98.1; (II) 56

HISTORICAL

Jackson, Thomas J. "Stonewall" (1824-1863): Confederate general.
(I) 96.1; (II) 54

Sheridan, Phillip H. (1831-1888): Union general. (I) 96.1;
(II) 54

"THAT EVENING SUN GO DOWN"

In (I) *American Mercury*, 22 (March 1931), 257-267; (II) *These 13*, 1931, as "That Evening Sun"; (III) *Collected Stories*, 1950.

Compson, Caddy: Narrator's (Quentin) sister. (I) 257.2-267.2;
    (II) 233, 236, 238-242, 244-260; (III) 290-309

Compson, Mr. Jason: Father of Quentin, Caddy, and Jason Compson. (I) 257.2-261.1, 262.1-264.1, 265.1-267.2; (II) 233, 234, 236-246, 248, 249, 255-260; (III) 290, 292-296, 298-301, 303, 305-309
  His wife; mother of Quentin, Caddy, and Jason Compson. (I) 259.1, 259.2, 260.2-263.1, 264.1, 265.1; (II) 237-239, 241, 242, 245-247; (III) 292-296, 299, 300, 303, 305

Compson, Jason: Quentin Compson's younger brother. (I) 257.2-267.2; (II) 233, 234, 236, 238-241, 243-260; (III) 290-295, 297-309

Compson, Quentin: Narrator; older son of Compsons. (I) 257.1-267.2; (II) 232-260; (III) 289-309

Dilsey: Compsons' Negro cook. (I) 257.2, 258.2, 259.1, 260.2, 261.1-262.2; (II) 233, 236, 241, 243-247, 254; (III) 290, 292, 295, 297-300, 305

Frony: Dilsey's daughter. (I) 260.1, 262.1; (II) 240, 245; (III) 294, 298

Jesus: See Jubah; named changed to Jesus in *These 13*

Jubah: Negro with whom Nancy lived. (I) 257.2-262.2, 266.1, 267.1; (II) 233, 236, 238-244, 246, 247, 256, 257, 259; (III) 290, 292-300, 306, 307, 309

Lovelady, Mr.: Insurance agent. (I) 266.1, 267.1; (II) 258; (III) 308
  His wife: (I) 266.1, 267.1; (II) 258; (III) 308
  Their daughter: (I) 267.1; (II) 258; (III) 308

Nancy: Negro woman who cooks for Compsons when Dilsey is ill. (I) 257.2-267.2; (II) 233-260; (III) 289-307

Rachel, Aunt: Old Negro woman. (I) 260.1, 266.1, 266.2; (II) 239, 240, 256, 257; (III) 294, 306, 307

Stovall: Deacon in the Baptist church. (I) 258.1; (II) 234, 235; (III) 291

T.P.: Negro youth. (I) 260.1; (II) 240; (III) 294

Versh: Negro who lives near Compsons. (I) 262.2; (II) 247; (III) 300

UNNAMED

Jailor. (I) 258.2; (II) 235; (III) 291

Marshal who arrests Nancy. (I) 258.1, 262.1; (II) 234, 245; (III) 291, 298

BIBLICAL

God: (I) 261.1; (II) 243, 258; (III) 297, 308

Jesus: (I) 261.1; (II) 242; (III) 296, 297

"THAT WILL BE FINE"

In (I) *American Mercury*, 35 (July 1935), 264-276; (II) *Collected Stories*, 1950

Church, Mrs.: Jefferson lady. (I) 269.1; (II) 274

Emmeline: Nurse of Aunt Louisa's baby. (I) 269.1, 271.1, 272.1; (II) 274, 279

Fred I: Georgie's uncle. (I) 265.1, 267.1, 269.1-271.2, 272.2, 274.2; (II) 267, 271, 274-276, 278-280

Fred II: Georgie's cousin. (I) 265.1, 269.2, 270.1, 271.2; (II) 267, 275, 276, 279

George: Georgie's father. (I) 264.2-265.2, 266.2-270.2, 271.2, 272.2, 274.2, 275.2, 276.1; (II) 266-276, 278-280, 286, 287

Georgie: Narrator; son of George and Sarah. (I) 264.1-276.2; (II) 265-288

"That Will Be Fine"

His grandfather: (I) 264.1-273.2, 274.2-275.2; (II) 265-279, 282, 285-288
His grandmother: (I) 265.1, 268.1, 269.1; (II) 272-274

John Paul: Negro servant. (I) 266.2, 267.1; (II) 269, 270

Jordan, Mrs.: Mottstown lady who lives near Grandpa. (I) 276.1, 276.2; (II) 287

Louisa I: Georgie's aunt; Fred's wife. (I) 265.1, 266.2-269.2, 271.1, 271.2, 275.2; (II) 267, 269-275, 278, 279, 287
Her baby: (I) 265.1, 269.1, 271.2; (II) 267, 274, 279

Louisa II: Georgie's cousin; daughter of Fred and Louisa. (I) 265.1, 269.2, 270.1, 271.2; (II) 267, 275, 276, 279

Mandy: Grandpa's Negro cook. (I) 265.1, 269.1-270.1, 274.1, 274.2; (II) 267, 274-276, 284

Pruitt, Mr.: President of Compress Association. (I) 267.2, 268.1, 268.2, 271.2; (II) 271, 273, 274, 278, 279

Pruitt, Mrs.: Pruitt's wife. (I) 269.1; (II) 274

Rodney, Uncle: Georgie's uncle; brother of Sarah and Louisa. (I) 264.1-276.2; (II) 265-288

Rosie: Negro cook for Georgie's family. (I) 264.1-265.1, 266.1, 267.1, 270.1, 271.1, 275.2, 276.1, 276.2; (II) 265-267, 269, 270, 276, 278, 286, 287

Sarah: Georgie's mother; George's wife. (I) 264.1-269.2, 270.2-271.2, 275.2, 276.1; (II) 265-275, 277-279, 287

Tucker, Mr.: Mottstown man. (I) 265.2, 266.1, 270.1; (II) 268, 276

Tucker, Mrs.: Woman with whom Uncle Rodney had an affair. (I) 264.2, 272.2, 274.2; (II) 266, 281, 285

Watts: Jefferson sheriff. (I) 270.2; (II) 277

UNNAMED

Mottstown sheriff. (I) 267.2, 270.2, 271.1, 272.1; (II) 271, 277, 278, 280

Mottstown woman whose husband kills Uncle Rodney. (I) 273.2-274.2; (II) 283, 284

Mottstown man who kills Uncle Rodney. (I) 273.2-274.2; (II) 283, 284

BIBLICAL

God: (I) 270.2; (II) 277

MYTHIC

Santa Claus: (I) 270.2; (II) 277

"THERE WAS A QUEEN"

In (I) *Scribner's*, 93 (January 1933), 10-16; (II) *Doctor Martino*, 1934; (III) *Collected Stories*, 1950.

Benbow, Narcissa: See Sartoris, Narcissa Benbow

Caspey: Elnora's husband. (I) 10.1; (II) 99; (III) 727

Du Pre, Virginia: Col. John Sartoris' sister. (I) 10.1-16.1; (II) 99-119; (III) 727-744
  Her father: (I) 12.1; (II) 105; (III) 732
  Her mother: (I) 12.1; (II) 105; (III) 732
  Her husband: (I) 12.1; (II) 105; (III) 732

Elnora: Sartoris cook. (I) 10.1-12.2, 15.2-16.2; (II) 98-107, 117-119; (III) 727-734, 743, 744
  Her mother: (I) 10.1, 12.1; (II) 99, 105; (III) 727, 733

Isom: Elnora's son. (I) 10.1, 11.2-12.2, 13.2, 15.2; (II) 99, 104-107, 110, 117, 118; (III) 728, 731-734, 737, 743

Joby: Elnora's son living in Memphis. (I) 10.1; (II) 99; (III) 727

Saddie: Elnora's daughter. (I) 10.1-11.2, 15.2; (II) 99, 101, 104, 106, 111, 118; (III) 728, 729, 732, 733, 737, 743

Sartoris, Bayard: Son of Col. John Sartoris. (I) 10.1, 10.2, 12.2, 13.1, 14.1, 14.2; (II) 98, 99, 107, 109, 113; (III) 727, 728, 734-736, 739

Sartoris, Bayard: Grandson of old Bayard Sartoris; husband of
    Narcissa Benbow Sartoris. (I) 10.1, 11.1, 12.2, 13.1,
    14.1, 14.2; (II) 98-100, 102, 107-109, 112-114; (III)
    727, 728, 730, 734-736, 738-740

Sartoris, Benbow (Bory): Son of young Bayard and Narcissa
    Sartoris. (I) 10.1-11.2, 12.2-15.2, 16.2; (II) 99-104,
    107-112, 114-117, 119; (III) 727-731, 734-738, 740-742,
    744

Sartoris, Colonel John: Confederate officer; father of old
    Bayard Sartoris and of Elnora. (I) 10.1, 12.1, 12.2;
    (II) 98-100, 105-107; (III) 727, 728, 732-734

Sartoris, John: Old Bayard's son; father of young Bayard. (I)
    10.1, 12.2, 15.1; (II) 98, 99, 107, 117; (III) 727, 728,
    742

Sartoris, John: Young Bayard's twin brother. (I) 10.1, 12.2;
    (II) 99, 108, 110; (III) 728, 734-736

Sartoris, Narcissa Benbow: Wife of young Bayard; mother of
    Benbow. (I) 10.1-15.2, 16.2; (II) 99-119; (III) 727-
    744
  Her brother: (I) 13.1; (II) 109; (III) 735

Simon: Husband of Elnora's mother. (I) 10.1; (II) 99; (III)
    727

UNNAMED

Bookkeeper who wrote obscene letters to Narcissa Benbow. (I)
    13.1, 14.1, 14.2; (II) 113-115; (III) 735, 736, 739, 740

Federal agent; Yankee Jew. (I) 13.1, 13.2, 14.2, 15.1; (II)
    110, 114-116; (III) 736, 737, 740, 741

"THRIFT"

In (I) *The Saturday Evening Post*, 203 (6 September 1930), 16,
17, 78, 82; (II) *Uncollected Stories of William Faulkner*, ed.
Joseph Blotner (New York: Random House, 1979).

Ffollansbye: Man who first recommended Mac for promotion. (I)
    16, 17.1-17.3, 78.1, 82.1; (II) 384-388, 394

MacWyrglinchbeath (Mac): Scot in British army. (I) 16, 17.1-
    17.3, 78.1-78.4, 82.1-82.3; (II) [382]-398

Robinson: Officer in Mac's unit. (I) 78.2-78.4; (II) 389-392

Whiteley: Officer who questions Mac. (I) 17.1, 17.2; (II)
    385

UNNAMED

Whiteley's sergeant. (I) 17.1, 17.2; (II) 385

Mac's Scottish neighbor. (I) 17.3, 78.1, 82.3; (II) 386, 387,
    389, 397, 398

HISTORICAL

Caesar, Julius (100?-44 B.C.): Roman general and emperor. (I)
    78.4; (II) 393

LITERARY

Shylock: Character in Shakespeare's *The Merchant of Venice*,
    1596. (I) 78.2; (II) 390

"TOMORROW"

In (I) *The Saturday Evening Post*, 213 (23 November 1940), 22,
23, 32, 35, 37, 38, 39; (II) *Knight's Gambit*, 1949.

Bookwright: Frenchman's Bend farmer who kills Buck Thorpe. (I)
    22.1, 23.1, 23.2, 23.3, 32.1, 39.2; (II) 85-90, 104, 105
  His daughter: (I) 22.1, 23.1, 23.2, 23.3; (II) 86-89

Chick; Charley: Narrator; Gavin Stevens' nephew. (I) 22.1-
    39.2; (II) 85-105
  His mother: (I) 23.3; (II) 90

Fentry, G.A.: Father of Stonewall Jackson Fentry. (I) 32.1,
    32.2, 35.1-35.3, 37.1, 38.2, 39.1; (II) 90-96, 101, 103
  His father: (I) 35.1; (II) 92
  His mother: (I) 35.1; (II) 92
  His wife: (I) 35.1; (II) 92

"Tomorrow" 325

Fentry, Jackson and Longstreet: See Buck Thorpe

Fentry, Stonewall Jackson: Farmer who raised Buck Thorpe as a child. (I) 23.1, 23.3, 32.1, 32.2, 35.1-35.3, 37.1, 37.2, 38.1, 38.2, 39.1, 39.2; (II) 86-105

Frazier, Judge: Jefferson judge. (I) 23.2, 23.3; (II) 88, 89

Holland: Foreman of jury. (I) 23.3; (II) 89

Pruitt, Mrs.: Rufus Pruitt's mother. (I) 32.2, 35.1-35.3, 37.1; (II) 91-95, 97
  Her husband: (I) 35.1; (II) 92

Pruitt, Rufus: Man who tells Gavin Stevens about Fentrys. (I) 32.2, 35.1-35.3, 37.1, 38.2, 39.1; (II) 91-97, 103

Quick, Ben (Old Man): Sawmill owner. (I) 35.1, 37.2, 38.1; (II) 93, 98, 100

Quick, Isham: Ben Quick's son. (I) 23.1, 37.1, 37.2, 38.1, 38.2, 39.1, 39.2; (II) 86, 97-103

Rouncewell, Mrs.: Boarding house owner. (I) 23.2; (II) 89

"Smith, Miss": Jackson Fentry's "wife"'s fictional maiden name. (I) 35.3, 37.2, 38.1, 38.2; (II) 95, 99-102
  Her husband: (I) 37.2, 38.1, 38.2; (II) 99-102
  Her father: (I) 37.2; (II) 99

Stevens, Captain: Gavin Stevens' father. (I) 22.1, 23.2, 32.2, 38.2; (II) 85, 88, 91, 103

Stevens, Gavin: County attorney. (I) 22.1, 23.1-23.3, 32.1, 32.2, 37.1, 37.2, 38.1, 39.2; (II) 85-94, 96-100, 104, 105

Thorpe, Buck: Man killed by Bookwright; under name Jackson and Longstreet Fentry raised by Jackson Fentry. (I) 22.1, 23.1, 35.1-35.3, 37.1, 37.2, 38.1, 38.2, 39.1, 39.2; (II) 85-87, 89, 93-97, 100-105
  His wife: (I) 23.1, 23.3; (II) 86, 89

Thorpes: "Miss Smith"'s two brothers. (I) 37.2, 38.1, 38.2; (II) 99-102

Varner, Will: Store owner and justice of peace. (I) 23.1, 37.1; (II) 86, 97

Whitfield, Preacher: Frenchman's Bend preacher. (I) 38.1; (II) 100, 101

"TURN ABOUT"

In (I) *The Saturday Evening Post*, 204 (5 March 1932), 6, 7, 75, 76, 81, 83; (II) *Doctor Martino*, 1934; (III) *Collected Stories*, 1950, as "Turnabout."

Agatha: Hope's aunt. (I) 81.2; (II) 186; (III) 497

Albert: British military policeman. (I) 7.1-7.3; (II) 163-166; (III) 478-480

Beatty: Name which Hope mentions. (I) 6.2; (II) 161; (III) 476

Bogard, Captain H.S.: American flying officer. (I) 6.1-6.3, 7.1-7.3, 75.1-75.4, 76.1-76.4, 81.1-81.4, 83.1-83.4; (II) 159-200; (III) 475-509

Burt: Boatswain's mate on torpedo boat with Hope and Smith. (I) 75.2, 76.3, 81.1, 81.2, 83.1, 83.2, 83.4; (II) 169, 170, 181, 185, 186, 194-196, 199; (III) 483, 493, 496-499, 502-505, 507, 508

Collier: American pilot. (I) 76.2, 76.4; (II) 178, 182; (III) 491, 494

Harper: Gunner of Bogard's plane. (I) 75.2, 83.4; (II) 170, 200; (III) 484, 509

Hope, L.C.W. (Claude): British midshipman on torpedo boat. (I) 6.1-6.3, 7.1-7.3, 75.1-75.4, 76.1-76.4, 81.1-81.4, 83.1-83.4; (II) 160-180, 182-199; (III) 475-492, 494-508
  His father: (I) 75.3; (II) 171; (III) 485

Jerry: American flying officer. (I) 75.1-75.3; (II) 168-170; (III) 481-484

McGinnis, Lt. Darrell (Mac): American flying officer. (I) 6.2, 6.3, 7.1, 7.3, 75.3, 75.4, 76.1-76.4, 83.1, 83.4; (II) 161, 162, 166, 167, 172-180, 182, 194, 200; (III) 476, 477, 480, 481, 485-492, 494, 504, 509

Reeves: Seaman on torpedo boat with Hope and Smith. (I) 75.2, 76.3, 81.1, 81.2, 83.1, 83.2, 83.4; (II) 169, 170, 181, 185, 186, 194-196, 199; (III) 483, 493, 496-499, 502-505, 507, 508

Smith, R. Boyce: British midshipman on torpedo boat. (I) 75.1-75.4, 76.1-76.4, 81.1-81.4, 83.1-83.4; (II) 168-173, 175, 179, 180, 182-194, 196-199; (III) 482-486, 488, 491, 492, 494-508

Watts: Gunner on Bogard's plane. (I) 83.4; (II) 200; (III) 509

Wutherspoon, Jamie: Hope's friend. (I) 7.2; (II) 164; (III) 479

UNNAMED

American military policeman. (I) 6.1-6.3, 7.1, 7.2; (II) 160-165; (III) 475-479

HISTORICAL

Machiavelli, Niccolò (1469-1527): Italian statesman and author. (I) 83.3; (II) 198: (III) 507

LITERARY

Alice: Character in Lewis Carroll's *Alice in Wonderland*, 1865. (I) 81.2; (II) 186; (III) 497

"TWO DOLLAR WIFE"

In (I) *College Life*, 18 (January 1936), 8-10, 85, 86, 88, 90; (II) *Uncollected Stories of William Faulkner*, ed. Joseph Blotner (New York: Random House, 1979).

Carberry, Doc: Physician who gets needle out of baby's throat. (I) 90.1, 90.2; (II) 422

Houston, Mr.: Doris's father. (I) 10.2; (II) 415

Houston, Mrs.: Doris's mother. (I) 8.1, 9.1, 90.2; (II) [412], 413, 422
  Her baby: (I) 90.1-90.3; (II) 422

Houston, Doris: See Johns, Doris Houston

Joe, Little: Crap shooter. (I) 85.2; (II) 416

Johns, Doris Houston: Girl who elopes with Maxwell Johns. (I) 8.1, 8.2, 9.1, 9.2, 10.1, 10.2, 85.3, 88.2, 88.3, 90.1-90.3; (II) [412]-415, 417, 420-422

Johns, Maxwell: Young man suspended from Sewanee. (I) 8.1, 8.2, 9.1, 9.2, 10.1, 10.2, 85.1-85.3, 86.1-86.3, 88.1-88.3, 90.1-90.3; (II) [412]-423
  His father: (I) 10.1; (II) 414

Jornstadt: Princeton student. (I) 10.2, 85.1-85.3, 86.1-86.3, 88.2, 88.3, 90.1; (II) 415-421
  His aunt: (I) 10.2; (II) 415

Lucille: Walter Mitchell's date. (I) 9.2, 10.1, 10.2, 88.2, 88.3, 90.1; (II) 413-415, 420, 421

Mitchell, Walter: Maxwell Johns's friend. (I) 9.2, 10.1, 10.2, 85.1-85.3, 86.2, 88.2, 88.3; (II) 413-419

Peter: Negro crap shooter. (I) 86.1, 86.3, 88.1; (II) 418, 419

White, Hap: Fat youth at party. (I) 10.2, 85.1-85.3, 86.1-86.3, 88.2, 88.3, 90.1; (II) 415-421

UNNAMED

Justice of peace. (I) 88.2, 88.3, 90.1; (II) 420, 421

Houstons' maid. (I) 8.1, 90.2, 90.3; (II) [412], 422

"TWO SOLDIERS"

In (I) *The Saturday Evening Post*, 214 (28 March 1942), 9-11, 35, 36, 38, 40; (II) *Collected Stories*, 1950.

"Two Soldiers" 329

Foote, Mr.: Jefferson policeman. (I) 11.3, 35.1, 35.2, 36.1;
    (II) 89-92

Grier: Narrator, Pete's younger brother. (I) 9.1-40.2; (II)
    81-98

Grier, Pete: Narrator's older brother. (I) 9.1-9.3, 10.1-
    10.3, 11.1-11.3, 35.1, 35.2, 36.1-36.3, 38.1, 38.2; (II)
    81-98
  Father of Pete and narrator: (I) 9.1, 9.2, 10.1-10.3, 11.1-
    11.3; (II) 81, 82, 84-88
  Mother of Pete and narrator: (I) 9.1, 10.2, 11.1-11.3, 38.1,
    38.2; (II) 81, 84-88, 96, 98
    Her mother: (I) 10.3; (II) 84

Habersham, Mrs.: Jefferson lady. (I) 35.1, 35.2, 36.1; (II)
    89-92

Killegrew, "Old Man": Neighbor of Griers with radio. (I) 9.1-
    9.3; (II) 81, 82
  His wife: (I) 9.1; (II) 81

McKellogg, Colonel: Army officer in Memphis. (I) 38.2; (II) 98

McKellogg, Mrs.: The Colonel's wife. (I) 38.1, 38.2; (II)
    97-99
  Their son: (I) 38.2; (II) 98

Marsh: Brother of narrator's (Grier's) mother. (I) 10.3, 11.2;
    (II) 84, 85, 87

Tull: Farmer who lives near Griers. (I) 10.1; (II) 83
  His daughters: (I) 10.1; (II) 83

UNNAMED

Young lady with Mrs. Habersham. (I) 35.2, 36.1; (II) 90-92

Jefferson ticket agent. (I) 11.3, 35.1, 35.2, 36.1; (II) 89-
    92

HISTORICAL

MacArthur, General Douglas (1880-1964): American general. (I)
    9.3; (II) 82

"UNCLE WILLY"

In (I) *American Mercury*, 36 (October 1935), 156-168; (II) *Collected Stories*, 1950.

Barbour, Mr.: Sunday school teacher. (I) 157.1, 157.2; (II) 227

Barger, Sonny: Negro storekeeper. (I) 161.1; (II) 234

Bean, Captain: Pilot in Jefferson. (I) 164.2; (II) 241

Billie: Name in Uncle Willy Christian's black book. (I) 162.1; (II) 236

Bundren, Darl: Country man taken to state asylum. (I) 158.1; (II) 228, 229

Callaghan, Miss: School teacher. (I) 157.2; (II) 228

Christian, Hoke: Uncle Willy Christian's father. (I) 156.2, 160.2; (II) 226, 233

Christian, Uncle Willy: Drugstore owner; son of Hoke Christian. (I) 156.1-168.2; (II) 225-245
  His sister: (I) 156.1, 158.2-159.2, 160.2, 161.2, 162.2, 163.1, 164.2; (II) 225, 229, 230, 232, 233, 235, 237, 238, 241
    Her husband: (I) 156.1; (II) 225

Christian, Mrs. Willy: Willy Christian's wife. (I) 162.1, 162.2, 163.1; (II) 236-238

Hovis, Mrs.: Jefferson lady. (I) 158.2; (II) 229

Jack: Name in Uncle Willy Christian's black book. (I) 162.1; (II) 236

Lorine: Name in Uncle Willy Christian's black book. (I) 162.1; (II) 236

Merridew, Mrs.: Jefferson lady. (I) 158.1-163.2, 164.2, 166.2-167.2; (II) 228-239, 241, 244-246

Miller, Brother: Teacher of men's Bible class. (I) 157.2, 159.1; (II) 227, 228, 230

Robert, Uncle: Narrator's uncle. (I) 163.2; (II) 239

"The Unvanquished"

Schultz, Rev.: Jefferson minister. (I) 157.2-159.1, 160.1-161.1, 162.2; (II) 227-232, 234, 237

Schultz, Mrs.: The Reverend's wife. (I) 158.1; (II) 229

Secretary: Negro chauffeur for Uncle Willy Christian. (I) 161.2, 162.1, 163.2, 164.2, 165.1-167.2; (II) 235, 236, 239, 241-247

Wylie, Job: Negro worker in Christian's drugstore. (I) 156.2, 160.1-161.1, 162.1, 163.2-167.2; (II) 226, 232-234, 236, 239-247

UNNAMED

Narrator, fourteen-year-old boy in Jefferson. (I) 156.1-168.2; (II) 225-247
  His father. (I) 156.2, 158.1, 162.1-163.2, 166.2-168.2; (II) 226, 228, 236-239, 244-247
  His mother. (I) 162.1; (II) 236

New clerk in Christian's drugstore. (I) 159.2-162.1; (II) 231-236

BIBLICAL

God (Maker): (I) 159.2; (II) 232

"THE UNVANQUISHED"

In (I) *The Saturday Evening Post*, 209 (14 November 1936), 12, 13, 121, 122, 124, 126, 128, 130; (II) *Uncollected Stories of William Faulkner*, ed. Joseph Blotner (New York: Random House, 1979). Revised as Chapter 4, "Riposte in Tertio," of *The Unvanquished*, 1938.

Compson, Mrs.: Jefferson friend of Rosa Millard. (I) 122.2, 124.2, 124.3; (II) 80, 81, 84, 85

Dick, Col. Nathaniel G.: Union army officer. (I) 122.1; (II) 79, 80

Fortinbride, Brother: Preacher who served in Col. Sartoris'
    regiment. (I) 124.2, 124.3, 126.1; (II) 83-86

Grumby: Leader of renegade gang. (I) 128.3; (II) 93

Hawk, Cousin Denny: Drusilla Hawk's brother. (I) 122.2,
    124.3; (II) 81, 85

Hawk, Drusilla: Bayard Sartoris' cousin. (I) 128.3; (II) 93

Hawk, Aunt Louisa: Mother of Drusilla and Denny Hawk. (I)
    128.3; (II) 93

Joby: Sartoris Negro slave. (I) 12.1, 13.2, 126.3, 128.1, 130.2;
    (II) [74], 77, 89-91, 95

Loosh: Joby's son. (I) 124.3; (II) 85

Louvinia: Joby's wife. (I) 13.2, 13.3, 124.3, 130.2; (II)
    77, 78, 85, 95

McCaslin, Uncle Buck: Old Yoknapatawpha resident. (I) 126.1,
    130.1; (II) 87, 94

Millard, Rosa: Bayard Sartoris' grandmother. (I) 12.1-12.3,
    13.1-13.3, 121.1-121.3, 122.1, 122.2, 124.1-124.3, 126.1,
    126.3, 128.1-128.3, 130.1, 130.2; (II) [74]-96

Newberry, Col. G.W.: Union officer. (I) 13.2, 122.1, 122.2;
    (II) 77, 79-82

Ringo: Bayard Sartoris' Negro companion. (I) 12.1-12.3, 13.2,
    13.3, 121.1-121.3, 122.1, 122.2, 124.1-124.3, 126.1-
    126.3, 128.1-128.3, 130.1, 130.2; (II) [74]-96

Sartoris, Bayard: Young narrator; Col. John Sartoris' son.
    (I) 12.1-130.2; (II) [74]-96

Sartoris, Colonel John: Confederate officer; Bayard Sartoris'
    father. (I) 12.1, 12.2, 13.1, 122.1, 124.2, 126.1, 128.3,
    130.1, 130.2; (II) [74], 76, 77, 79, 83-85, 93-95

Snopes, Ab: Horse thief; Rosa Millard's "partner." (I) 12.1-
    12.3, 13.1, 13.2, 121.2, 122.1, 122.2, 124.1, 124.2,
    126.1, 126.3, 128.1-128.3, 130.1; (II) [74]-78, 80-83,
    86-95

Worsham, Dr.: Minister at Sartoris church before War. (I)
    124.2, 124.3; (II) 84-86

"Vendée"   333

UNNAMED

Captain of Confederate company in Jefferson. (I) 126.1; (II)
    87

Yankee lieutenant who seizes mules from Rosa Millard. (I)
    122.2, 124.1, 126.1-126.3, 128.1, 128.2; (II) 81, 82, 87-
    91

HISTORICAL

Davis, Jefferson (1808-1889): President of Confederacy. (I)
    126.3; (II) 89

Forrest, Nathan Bedford (1821-1877): Confederate general. (I)
    12.2, 122.1, 126.3, 128.3, 130.1; (II) 75, 79, 89, 93-
    95

Grant, Ulysses S. (1822-1885): Union general; President of
    United States, 1869-1877. (I) 13.1, 13.2, 122.1; (II)
    77, 87

Lee, Robert E. (1807-1870): Confederate general. (I) 126.3;
    (II) 89

Lincoln, Abraham (1809-1865): President of United States, 1861-
    1865. (I) 13.1, 122.1; (II) 77, 79

Smith, Andrew J. (1815-1897): Union general. (I) 13.1, 13.2,
    122.1; (II) 75, 79, 80

BIBLICAL

Jesus: (I) 124.2; (II) 84

Lord: (I) 124.3, 126.3, 128.2; (II) 84, 85, 89, 91, 92

"VENDÉE"

In (I) *The Saturday Evening Post*, 209 (5 December 1936), 16,
17, 86, 87, 90, 92, 93, 94; (II) *Uncollected Stories of William
Faulkner*, ed. Joseph Blotner (New York: Random House, 1979).
Revised as Chapter 5 of *The Unvanquished*, 1938.

Bowden, Matt: Member of Grumby's gang who turns against Grumby.
(I) 87.1, 87.2, 90.1, 92.2-93.2; (II) 103-107, 111-114

Bridger: Member of Grumby's gang. (I) 92.2, 93.1, 93.2; (II) 111-113

Compson, Mrs.: Jefferson friend of Rosa Millard. (I) 16.1, 16.3, 94.1; (II) [97], 98, 115

Fortinbride, Brother: Preacher who served in Col. John Sartoris' regiment. (I) 16.1, 16.2; (II) [97], 98

Grumby: Leader of renegade gang. (I) 17.2, 86.1, 87.1, 87.2, 90.1, 90.2, 92.1, 92.2, 93.1, 93.2, 94.1, 94.2; (II) 100, 102, 104, 105, 108, 110-117

Hawk, Drusilla: Bayard Sartoris' cousin. (I) 94.2; (II) 116, 117

Joby: Sartoris' Negro slave. (I) 90.2, 94.2; (II) 109, 116, 117

Louvinia: Joby's wife. (I) 90.2, 94.1, 94.2; (II) 109, 116

McCaslin, Uncle Buck: Old Yoknapatawpha resident who helps Bayard Sartoris and Ringo. (I) 16.2, 16.3, 17.1-17.3, 86.1, 86.2, 87.1, 87.2, 90.1, 90.2, 92.1, 93.2, 94.1, 94.2; (II) 98-110, 113, 115-117

Millard, Rosa: Bayard Sartoris' grandmother. (I) 16.1-16.3, 17.1, 17.2, 86.1, 90.1, 90.2, 93.1, 93.2, 94.1, 94.2; (II) [97]-102, 106, 108, 109, 111, 113-117

Ringo: Bayard's Negro companion. (I) 16.1-16.3, 17.1-17.3, 86.1, 86.2, 87.1, 87.2, 90.1, 90.2, 92.1, 92.2, 93.1, 93.2, 94.1, 94.2; (II) [97]-117

Sartoris, Bayard: Narrator; Col. John Sartoris' son. (I) 16.1-94.2; (II) [97]-117

Sartoris, Colonel John: Confederate officer; Bayard Sartoris' father. (I) 16.3, 90.2, 94.2; (II) 98, 109, 116, 117

Snopes, Ab: Horse thief; Rosa Millard's "partner." (I) 16.1-16.3, 17.1-17.3, 87.2, 90.1, 90.2, 92.1, 94.1, 94.2; (II) [97]-102, 105-110, 116

"*Victory*"

Yance: Sartoris Negro slave. (I) 17.1; (II) 100

HISTORICAL

Forrest, Nathan Bedford (1821-1877): Confederate general. (I) 93.1; (II) 113.

BIBLICAL

God: (I) 16.2; (II) 98

"*VICTORY*"

In (I) *These 13*, 1931; (II) *Collected Stories*, 1950.

Cunningham, Sergeant: British sergeant who tries to help Alec Gray II. (I) 12, 13, 15, 16; (II) 438-441

Gray, Alec, I: Alec Gray II's grandfather. (I) 17-21, 24-26; (II) 441-444, 447, 448

Gray, Alec, II: Young Scot who joins British army. (I) 3-11, 13-42, 45-47; (II) 431-459, 461-464

Gray, Annie: Alec Gray II's mother. (I) 19-21, 24-26, 32, 34, 35, 38; (II) 443, 444, 447, 448, 452-454, 456

Gray, Elizabeth: Youngest child of Annie and Matthew Gray. (I) 21, 25, 27, 34, 35, 37, 38; (II) 444, 447, 448, 454, 456

Gray, Jessie: Alec Gray II's sister. (I) 20, 21, 24, 25, 27, 35, 37; (II) 443, 444, 447, 448, 454, 456

Gray, John Wesley: Alec Gray II's brother. (I) 17, 20, 21, 24, 25, 27, 34, 35, 37, 38; (II) 442, 444, 447, 448, 454, 456

Gray, Matthew, I: Alec Gray II's father; Annie Gray's husband. (I) 17-21, 24-26, 32-36; (II) 441-444, 447, 448, 452-455

Gray, Matthew, II: Alec Gray II's brother. (I) 17, 20, 21, 24, 25, 27, 34, 35, 37, 38; (II) 442, 444, 447, 448, 454, 456

Gray, Uncle Simon: Alec Gray I's brother. (I) 18; (II) 442

McLan: Soldier disciplined by Capt. Alec Gray II. (I) 28; (II) 449

Walkley: Subaltern who meets Alec Gray II during and after the war. (I) 32, 33, 47-49; (II) 452, 453, 463, 464

Whiteby: Man who was in British army and committed suicide after war. (I) 39; (II) 457

UNNAMED

Sergeant major who disciplines Alec Gray II and is killed later by Gray. (I) 12-16, 21-24; (II) 437-441, 444-446

Alec Gray II's sergeant. (I) 27-30; (II) 449-451

Colonel with sergeant major who disciplines Alec Gray II. (I) 12-14, 17; (II) 437-439

Alec Gray II's corporal. (I) 16, 20, 21; (II) 441, 443, 444

BIBLICAL

God: (I) 36; (II) 455

Peter: Disciple of Christ. (I) 26; (II) 448

"WASH"

In (I) *Harper's*, 168 (February 1934), 258-266; (II) *Doctor Martino*, 1934; (III) *Collected Stories*, 1950; incorporated into Chapter 7 of *Absalom, Absalom!*, 1936.

Dicey: Old Negro midwife. (I) 258.1, 261.2-263.2; (II) 223, 224, 231, 233-236; (III) 535, 536, 542-546

"Wash" 337

Jones, Milly: Wash Jones's granddaughter. (I) 258.1, 258.2,
    259.2, 261.1-265.2; (II) 223-225, 227, 230, 232, 233,
    235-241; (III) 535, 536, 538, 540-547, 549
  Her daughter: (I) 258.1, 262.1, 262.2, 263.2-264.2; (II)
    223, 224, 233, 234, 236, 238; (III) 535, 536, 543-548

Jones, Wash: Man who lives on Sutpen's property. (I) 258.2-
    266.2; (II) 224-241; (III) 536-550
  His wife: (I) 263.2; (II) 236; (III) 546
  His daughter: (I) 258.2, 259.1, 263.2; (II) 225, 236; (III)
    536, 537, 546

Sutpen, Colonel: Confederate officer; landowner. (I) 258.1-
    264.1, 265.1, 265.2; (II) 223-235, 237, 239; (III) 535-
    545, 547, 548

Sutpen, Mrs.: Col. Sutpen's wife. (I) 258.2, 259.1, 260.1,
    262.1; (II) 225, 226, 228, 232; (III) 536, 537, 539,
    542
  Sutpen's son: (I) 260.1, 262.1; (II) 227, 228, 232; (III)
    538, 542

Sutpen, Judith: Col. Sutpen's daughter. (I) 260.1-261.1; (II)
    228-230; (III) 539-541

UNNAMED

Major; sheriff who comes for Wash. (I) 265.2, 266.2; (II)
    240, 241; (III) 549, 550

Negro woman who turns Wash away from front door. (I) 259.2;
    (II) 226; (III) 537

HISTORICAL

Lee, Robert E. (1807-1870): Confederate general. (I) 260.1,
    261.2, 265.1; (II) 228, 231, 239; (III) 539, 541, 548

Lincoln, Abraham (1809-1865): President of United States, 1861-
    1865. (I) 260.2; (II) 229; (III) 540

Sherman, William T. (1820-1891): Union general. (I) 259.1,
    260.2; (II) 226, 229; (III) 537, 540

BIBLICAL

God: (I) 259.2, 260.1; (II) 227, 228; (III) 538

THE WISHING TREE

(I) New York: Random House, 1967; also in (II) *The Saturday Evening Post*, 240 (8 April 1967), 48, 50, 51, 52, 53, 57, 58, 60, 61, 62, 63.

Alice: Negro maid. (I) 7, 9, 11-17; meets Egbert, 20-27; discovers tree, 28, 29, 32-34; wishes for food, 35-41; sees Exodus, 42-52, 54-58; becomes small, 59, 62, 63, 65, 66, 68-73; meets St. Francis, 74, 76-80; (II) 48.1, 48.2, 50.1, 50.2; meets Egbert, 51.1-51.4, 52.1; discovers tree, 52.2-52.4; wishes for food, 53.1-53.4; sees Exodus, 57.1, 57.2, 58.1, 58.2, 60.1, 60.2; becomes small, 60.3, 61.1-61.4, 62.1; meets St. Francis, 62.2, 63.1

Dicky: Dulcie's younger brother. (I) 7, 9, 11-17; meets Egbert, 18, 20-27; discovers tree, 28, 29, 32-34; wishes for food, 35-37, 39-41; soldier appears, 42, 43, 45, 48-50, 55-58; becomes small, 59, 62, 63, 65, 66, 68-73; meets St. Francis, 74, 76-81; (II) 48.1, 48.2, 50.1, 50.2; meets Egbert, 51.1-51.4, 52.1; discovers tree, 52.2-52.4; wishes for food, 53.1, 53.3, 53.4; soldier appears, 57.1, 57.2, 58.1, 58.2, 60.1, 60.2; becomes small, 60.3, 61.1-61.4, 62.1; meets St. Francis, 62.2, 63.1-63.3

Dulcie: Young girl. (I) 5-17; meets Egbert, 20-27; discovers tree, 28, 29, 32-34; wishes for food, 35-41, 44, 45, 47-50, 55-58; becomes small, 59, 62, 63, 65, 66; separated from others, 68-73; meets St. Francis, 74, 76-79; awakens, 80-82; (II) 48.1, 48.2, 50.1, 50.2; meets Egbert, 51.1-51.4, 52.1; discovers tree, 52.2-52.4; wishes for food, 53.1-53.4, 57.1, 57.2, 58.1, 58.2, 60.1, 60.2; becomes small, 60.3, 61.1, 61.2; separated from others, 61.3, 61.4, 62.1; meets St. Francis, 62.2, 63.1; awakens, 63.2-63.4
  Her mother: (I) 7, 13, 20, 23, 27, 81; (II) 48.1, 50.1, 51.1, 51.4, 63.2, 63.3

Egbert: Little old man. (I) 18, 20, 21; joins group, 22-26; discovers tree, 28, 29, 32-34; wishes for food, 35-41; joined by Exodus, 44-52, 54-59; becomes little, 62, 63,

      65, 66; Dulcie alone visits him, 68-73, 78; (II) 51.1,
      51.2; joins group, 51.3, 51.4, 52.1; discovers tree,
      52.2-52.4; wishes for food, 53.1-53.4; joined by Exodus,
      57.1, 57.2, 58.1, 58.2, 60.1, 60.2; becomes small, 60.3,
      61.1-61.4; Dulcie alone visits him, 62.1, 62.2, 63.1
His father: (I) 47; (II) 58.1

Exodus: Alice's Negro husband who is soldier. (I) 41-44; joins
      group, 45-52, 54-59; becomes small, 62, 63, 65, 66; carries
      group in his hat, 68-73; meets St. Francis, 74, 76-80;
      (II) 57.1; joins group, 57.2, 58.1, 58.2, 60.1, 60.2;
      becomes small, 60.3, 61.1; carries group in hat, 61.2-
      61.4, 62.1; meets St. Francis, 62.2, 63.1

Genesis: Ten-year-old killed by "meanness" according to Alice.
      (I) 45; (II) 57.2

George: Dulcie's neighbor. (I) 9, 11, 12, 14-17; meets Egbert,
      18, 20-23, 25, 26; discovers tree, 28, 29, 32; wishes
      for food, 35-41; joined by Exodus, 45, 47-52, 54; wishes
      for lion, 55-59; disappears, 61, 62, 78; (II) 48.2, 50.1,
      50.2; meets Egbert, 51.1-51.4, 52.1; discovers tree, 52.2-
      52.4; wishes for food, 53.1, 53.4; joined by Exodus,
      57.1, 57.2, 58.1, 58.2; wishes for lion, 60.1, 60.2;
      disappears, 60.3, 63.1

Maggie: Egbert's wife. (I) 21, 22, 36, 73, 78; (II) 51.1-
      51.4, 52.1, 62.2, 63.1

Maurice: Red-haired boy. (I) Described, 6-10, 12-17; meets
      Egbert, 18, 20-23, 25; discovers tree, 28, 29, 32-34;
      wishes for food, 35-41; joined by Exodus, 45, 48-50, 55-
      59, 61; becomes small, 62, 63, 65, 66, 68-73; meets St.
      Francis, 74, 76-80, 82; (II) Described, 48.1, 48.2, 50.1,
      50.2; meets Egbert, 51.1-51.4, 51.1; discovers tree,
      52.2-52.4; wishes for food, 53.1, 53.2, 53.4; joined by
      Exodus, 57.1, 57.2, 58.1, 58.2, 60.1, 60.2; becomes
      small, 60.3, 61.1-61.4, 62.1; meets St. Francis, 62.2,
      63.1, 63.4

HISTORICAL

Francis, Saint (1182-1226): Italian friar. (I) 74, 76-79, 82;
      (II) 62.2, 63.1, 63.4

"WITH CAUTION AND DISPATCH"

In *Uncollected Stories of William Faulkner*, ed. Joseph Blotner (New York: Random House, 1979). First printed in *Esquire*, 92 (September 1979), 51-61.

Atkinson: Aviator in Sartoris's squadron. 644, 661, 662

Britt: One of three flight commanders in RAF squadron. 643-646, 648, 653, 657-659, 663, 664

Harry: Captain/adjutant in office after Sartoris's "crash." 646

Sartoris, John: Aviator from Mississippi; twenty years old. [642]-664

Sibleigh: Flight Commander in squadron with Sartoris. 645, 658, 660, 663

Tate: Flight Commander in squadron with Sartoris. 645, 658

UNNAMED

Private who meets Sartoris on field after Sartoris is forced to land. 646.

Colonel to whom Sartoris speaks on telephone after "crash." 647

Officer on ship. 654-656

HISTORICAL

Edward, Prince of Wales (1330-1376): Eldest son of Edward III; called the "Black Prince." [642]

Haig, Douglas (1861-1928): English general. 644

Johnson, Jack (1878-1946): American Negro boxer. [642]

Kitchener, Horatio Herbert (1850-1916): English general. 654

Ludendorff, Erich Friedrich Wilhelm (1865-1937): German general. 664

"YO HO AND TWO BOTTLES OF RUM"

In (I) *William Faulkner: New Orleans Sketches*, ed. Carvel Collins (New York: Random House, 1968); (II) *Sinbad in New Orleans*, ed. Leland Cox (Spartanburg, S.C.: The Reprint Company, 1981). First printed in New Orleans *Times-Picayune* Sunday magazine section, 27 September 1925, pp. 1, 2.

Ayers, Freddie: Mate aboard the *Diana*. (I) 122-131; (II) 128-135

Bucky: Name uttered by engineer's assistant. (I) 129; (II) 133

Yo Ho: Chinese messboy. (I) 123-129; (II) 129-133

UNNAMED

Captain of *Diana*. (I) 122-126, 128; (II) 128-132

Chief engineer. (I) 122-124, 126, 128-131; (II) 128, 129, 132-135

Engineer's assistant. (I) 128-131; (II) 132-135

Bosun. (I) 124, 125, 128, 131; (II) 129, 130, 132, 135

Second mate. (I) 128-131; (II) 132-135

Unpublished Fiction

"THE DEVIL BEATS HIS WIFE"

[University of Virginia. MS., 3 pp.]

Brian: Man with whom Doris discusses her marriage. [1]

Della: Doris's Negro maid. [1-3]

Dick: Man Doris knows who, she says, would give her "one." [1]

Harry: Man Della speaks to at train station. [1]

Semmes, Doris: Hubert's wife. [1, 3]

Semmes, Hubert: Doris's husband who leaves wife and stays in New Orleans. [1, 3]

HISTORICAL

Edward VIII (1894-1972): King of England, 1936; Prince of Wales, 1911-1936. [1]

Washington, George (1732-1799): President of United States, 1789-1797. [1]

"ELMER"

[University of Virginia. TS., 123 pp. Because the typescript is not numbered consecutively, the page numbers have been supplied for the index. See note on page 348.]

Andrew: Man who works for Lord Wysbroke. 105

Bingham, Mister: Mate on boat. 69

Bleyth, George: Son of Lord Wysbroke. 102-105, 110, 112-117, 121, 122
  His remote female connection: 104, 110
  His mother: 114, 116
  His grandfather: 114, 115

Bryan, Mr.: Man whom Mrs. Monson knows. 90

Charles: Man with Lord Wohledon. 109

Ethel: Woman who has Elmer Hodge's bastard child. 42-59
  Their son: 23, 42, 46, 49, 51-53, 58, 59

Gloria: New Orleans lady; friend of Mr. Monson. 24
  Her daughter: 24

Grover: Ethel's husband. 44-50, 52-55, 57

Harris, Mr.: Lord Wysbroke's steward. 106

Henry: Servant at Wysbroke Hall. 105

Hodge, Mr.: Elmer Hodge's father. 4-12, 16-18, 26-30, 35-41

Hodge, Mrs.: Elmer Hodge's mother. 4-8, 16-18, 26-30, 34-40

Hodge, Elmer: An artist. On freighter, 1-3; remembers family's past, 4-18; back on ship, 19-24; returns to Houston after World War I, 26-30; remembers past, 31-40; affair with Ethel and has bastard son, 42-54; meets Myrtle, 55; visits Ethel, 56-60; on ship, 61-67; in Venice, 68-76, 80-89
  His brother who deserted family at Paris, Tenn.: 4-8, 11, 12, 16-18, 31, 38
  His oldest brother who leaves Memphis for St. Louis: 4-8, 11, 12, 16-18, 31, 34, 38

Hodge, Jo-Addie: Elmer's sister. 5-18, 29-31, 34, 35, 38, 64-66

Jessop, Farmer: Man who has Lord Wysbroke's horses. 105

Jock: Man with Lord Wohledon. 109

Joe: Seaman; former college football player. 21, 22

Lafe: One of men who watch Hodges' house burn. 6

Marina, Angelo: Prisoner with spaniel eyes. 71, 83-85, 87-89

Monson, Mr.: Myrtle Monson's father. 24, 25, 90, 93, 101

Monson, Mrs.: Myrtle Monson's mother. 20, 24-26, 85; in Europe, 90-96, 99-104, 110, 111; reflects upon trip to Rapallo, 117-120; Myrtle joins her in Rome, 121-123

"Elmer" 347

Monson, Myrtle: Girl with whom Elmer Hodge becomes involved. 20, 23-26, 30, 55, 60, 67, 90-99, 117, 120-123

Ray, Mister: Second officer on ship. 1, 20-22, 73-76, 80, 82, 84, 85

Wohledon, Lord Ivor: Son of Lord Wynsbroke; George Bleyth's brother. 103, 108-112, 115-117, 121, 122

Wysbroke, Lord: English nobleman. 102-112, 115, 116

UNNAMED

Captain on ship. 1, 2, 20, 69

Older boy who looks like a god whom Elmer Hodge admires. 31-33

Chief Engineer on ship. 1-3, 70, 85

Ship's officer on Monsons' ship. 93, 96-99

Captain on Monsons' ship. 93, 96-98

Figures in Elmer Hodge's dream after he passes out. 76-80

Three people Mrs. Monson saw in Rapallo: woman, man, and hulking lad who remind her of "an heritage of an old and splendid thing worn out with time ..." 117-119

HISTORICAL

Anthony, Saint (c.250-350): First Christian monk. 63

Belasco, David (1854-1931): American playwright and theatrical producer. 84

Bell, Clive (1881-1964): English critic. 3

Bouguereau, Adolphe William (1825-1905): French artist. 60

Cezanne, Paul (1839-1906): French artist. 60

Charles I (1600-1649): King of England, 1625-1649. 114

Columbus, Christopher (1451-1506): Italian explorer. 76

D'Annunzio, Gabriele (1863-1938): Italian author. 84

Degas, Edgar (1834-1917): French artist. 60

Faure, Elie (1873-1937): French historian and critic. 3

James, Henry (1843-1916): American novelist. 23

Joan of Arc (1412-1431): French leader. 6, 7

Kipling, Rudyard (1865-1936): English author. 21

Manet, Édouard (1832-1883): French artist. 60

Matisse, Henri (1869-1954): French artist. 60

Moore, George (1852-1933): Irish novelist. 60

Morgan, J.P. (1837-1913): American financier. 30

Napoleon (1769-1821): Emperor of France. 121

Peter the Hermit (1050?-1115?): French hermit and monk. 79

Picasso, Pablo (1881-1973): Spanish artist. 60

Richard I (1157-1199): King of England, 1189-1199. 86

Swanson, Gloria (1898-): American film actress. 30

Victor Emmanuel III (1869-1947): King of Italy. 83

BIBLICAL

Adam: First man in Genesis. 30, 76

Eve: Adam's wife in Genesis. 30

MYTHIC

Diana: Goddess of the hunt. 37, 45, 55, 56, 74

Leda: Maiden ravished by Zeus in form of a swan. 73

Note: Pages 1-33 (numbered 1-33)
          34-41 (numbered 44-51)
          42-60 (no page numbers)

Pages 61-85 (numbered 66-90; 73 and 74 have deleted
    page numbers)
86 (no page number)
87-89 (numbered 92-94)
90-123 (numbered 73-106)

"A LETTER"

[Rowanoak papers. TS., 13 pp. This story and "A Letter to Grandmama" are essentially the same; neither is complete. I was unable to determine the order of composition and have indexed both of them.]

Railroad agent, bachelor of forty, who has lived in boarding
    house for twelve years. 1-6

Woman whose husband has deserted her, leaving her with two
    children. 3-7, 10-13
  Her older son, about six years old. 3-6
  Her husband who is still supported by his mother. 3, 4, 6,
    12, 13
  Her father who became contactor; partner of wife's father.
    7-13
  Her mother-in-law who continues to support her son and does
    not know he has deserted his family. 3, 4
  Her mother, only child of planter, who marries her father's
    partner and dies not long after daughter is born. 6-12
  Her grandfather, a planter who commits suicide after daughter
    marries his partner. 8-10
  Her second child, three years old, who always sleeps and has
    not learned to walk. 3-6

"A LETTER TO GRANDMAMA"

[Rowanoak papers. TS., 6 pp.]

Jane: Small, young woman who walks up and down railroad platform with her children and jumps in front of train which is carrying her husband. 1-6

Her three-year-old child, killed instantly when Jane jumps in
    front of train: 1, 2, 5
Her husband who deserted Jane for a Spanish woman and fled
    to Mexico: 1-6
  His father: 4
  His mother, an invalid, who sends money believing her son
    is with Jane: 2-4, 6

Johnny: Six-year-old son of Jane. 1-6

UNNAMED

Rail agent, bachelor of forty who once asked Jane to marry him.
    1-6

Spanish woman with whom Jane's husband ran away. 2

"LOVE"

[University of Virginia. TS., 49 pp.]

Ed: Gorhams' butler. 6, 30-33

Ernest (Ernie): Gorhams' footman. 3-6, 23, 30-35, 41, 43, 48,
    49

Ethel: Name mentioned by footman as he turns up lights. 3

Gorham, Mr.: Beth Gorham Jeyfus' father. 11, 12, 16-23

Gorham, Beth: See Jeyfus, Beth Gorham

Gorham, Clara: Beth Gorham Jeyfus' mother. 12, 16-18

Grass, Das: Major's oriental servant. 5, 6, 8-11, 13-15, 23-
    34, 36, 44-47, 49

Hamilton: Local man. 21, 37, 39, 40

Howard: Man who tells Hugh about plane incident with Jeyfus.
    38

Hugh: The Major. 1-5, 7-27, 30, 33, 36-38, 40-48

"Moonlight"

Jeyfus, Beth Gorham: Girl who marries Bob Jeyfus. 1-4, 7, 8, 12, 15-23, 36-44, 48

Jeyfus, Bob: Young man who fought in World War I; once a pilot under the Major. 16, 19-23, 36-44

Joe: Name mentioned by footman as he turns up lights. 3

Mac: Local man who dated Beth Gorham. 37-40

UNNAMED

Italian maid who jealously reacts to Beth Gorham's flirtation with the Major. 1-9, 18, 19, 30, 31, 33-36, 45, 46, 48, 49

HISTORICAL

Nightingale, Florence (1820-1910): English nurse. 4

BIBLICAL

God: 32

MYTHIC

Diana: Goddess of the hunt. 1

"MOONLIGHT"

[University of Virginia. TS., 16 pp. There are two versions of this story with different characters; see published version in Short Fiction.]

Binford, Robert: Youth who dates Cecily but leaves her with George. 1-12

Cecily: Girl who dates Robert Binford and George. 8-16
  Her mother: 9

George: Youth who dates Cecily and is friend of Robert Binford.
    1-16
  His uncle: 6

Jody: Soda clerk in drugstore. 1-5

Mac: Person in drugstore from whom Robert Binford borrows coat. 1

William, Walter: Boy whom Cecily tells her mother she is dating.

UNNAMED

Negro who is trying to ride bicycle on back wheel. 1, 5

"ROSE OF LEBANON"

[Rowanoak papers. TS., 33 pp.]

Awce, Unk: Gordons' Negro. [21]

Blount, Doctor Gavin: Bachelor physician with impractical face
    who is obsessed with Lewis Randolph Gordon. 1-3, [4-31]
  His grandmother: 1, 2, [4, 5, 12, 13, 18]
  His father: 1, [9]
  His grandfather: 2, [10-13]

Blount, Miss Levinia: Blount's aunt. 2, [4]

Gordon, Charley: Lewis Randolph Gordon's husband killed at
    Holly Springs in chicken roost. [12-15, 17, 19, 20, 31-33]
  His father who wandered away after War: [16, 19-21]
  His mother who fell down stairs and died: [15, 16, 18-20]

Gordon, Lewis Randolph: Charley Gordon's wife. [5, 12-33]
  Her mother: [18]
  Her father: [17, 18]

Gordon, Ran: Lewis Randolph Gordon's son; successful banker.
    3, [5, 19-31]
  His wife: [23]
  Their son and daughter: [23]

Mymie: One of Lewis Randolph Gordon's Negroes when Yankees invade house. [27,28]

Ned: Old Negro who works for lady whom Gavin Blount visits. 1-[5]

UNNAMED

Elderly woman who has known Blount all his life. 3-[6, 13-15, 17, 18, 22, 24]

Five Yankees who invade Gordon home and whom Lewis Randolph Gordon curses. [27-29, 31]

HISTORICAL

Becque, Henry François (1837-1899): French dramatist. [4]

Bragg, Braxton (1817-1876): Confederate general. [19]

Davis, Jefferson (1808-1889): President of Confederacy. [11]

Fort, Paul (1872-1960): French poet. [4]

Grant, Ulysses S. (1822-1885): Union general; President of United States, 1869-1877. [19]

Mallarmé, Stéphane (1842-1898): French poet. [4]

Van Dorn, Earl (1820-1863): Confederate general. [19]

"WILD PALMS"

[Rowanoak papers. TS., 22 pp.]

Charlotte: Young, thin, dark-haired woman. 3-16, 18-21

Harry: Young man with Charlotte; a painter. 3-22

John: Name Charlotte calls. 19

Krootz, Hype: Bootlegger who delivers from house to house on beach. 7

Martha: Doctor's wife. 1-4, 6-13, 17, 22

Martin: Real estate man who rents cottage to Charlotte and
    Harry. 4-6, 9, 20

UNNAMED

Doctor; Martha's husband who checks Charlotte. 1-22
  His father: 1, 2, 22

HISTORICAL

Vanderbilt, Cornelius (1794-1877): American transportation and
    finance magnate. 5

Indices

TITLE INDEX

Absalom, Absalom! 3
"Ad Astra" 193
"Adolescence" 194
"Afternoon of a Cow" 195
"Al Jackson" 196
"All the Dead Pilots" 197
"Ambuscade" 199
"And Now What's to Do" 200
"Appendix: Compson, 1699-1945" 200
"Artist at Home" 204
As I Lay Dying 12

"Barn Burning" 205
"The Bear" 206
"A Bear Hunt" 207
"Beyond" 208
"The Big Shot" 210
Big Woods 17
"Black Music" 211
"The Brooch" 213
"By the People" 214

"Carcassonne" 215
"Centaur in Brass" 216
"Chance" 217
"Cheest" 217
"The Cobbler" 218
"Country Mice" 219
"A Courtship" 219
"Crevasse" 221

"Damon and Pythias Unlimited" 221
"A Dangerous Man" 222
"Death-Drag" 223
"Delta Autumn" 224

"The Devil Beats His Wife" 345
"Divorce in Naples" 226
"Doctor Martino" 226
"Don Giovanni" 227
"Dry September" 228
"Dull Tale" 229

"Elly" 231
"Elmer" 345
"Episode" 231
"An Error in Chemistry" 232
"Evangeline" 233

A Fable 22
Flags in the Dust 34
"Fool About a Horse" 234
"Fox Hunt" 235
"Frankie and Johnny" 237

Go Down, Moses 55
"Go Down, Moses" 238
"Gold Is Not Always" 239
"Golden Land" 240

"Hair" 241
The Hamlet 65
"Hand Upon the Waters" 242
"The Hill" 244
"Hog Pawn" 244
"Home" 245
"Honor" 245
"The Hound" 247

Idyll in the Desert 247

357

Intruder in the Dust 74

"Jealousy" 248
"A Justice" 249

"The Kid Learns" 250
"The Kingdom of God" 251
"Knight's Gambit" 251

"Landing in Luck" 255
"Leg" 255
"A Letter" 349
"A Letter to Grandmama" 349
"The Liar" 257
Light in August 81
"Lion" 257
"Lizards in Jamshyd's Courtyard" 259
"Lo!" 260
"Love" 350

The Mansion 89
Mayday 261
"The Mirror of Chartres Street" 263
Miss Zilphia Gant 264
"Mississippi" 265
"Mistral" 268
"Monk" 270
"Moonlight" 271
"Moonlight" (Unpublished) 351
Mosquitoes 104
"A Mountain Victory" 271
"Mr. Acarius" 273
"Mule in the Yard" 274
"Music--Sweeter Than the Angels Sing" 275
"My Grandmother Millard and General Bedford Forrest and the Battle of Harrykin Creek" 275

"A Name for the City" 278
"New Orleans" 280
Notes on a Horsethief 281
"Nympholepsy" 285

"The Old People" 285
"'Once Aboard the Lugger--'" 287
"Once Aboard the Lugger -----" 287
"Out of Nazareth" 289

"Pantaloon in Black" 290
"Pennsylvania Station" 291
"Peter" 292
"Point of Law" 293
"A Portrait of Elmer" 294
"The Priest" 296
Pylon 112

"Race at Morning" 297
"Raid" 297
"Red Leaves" 299
The Reivers 117
Requiem for a Nun 127
"Retreat" 301
"A Return" 302
"The Rosary" 304
"A Rose for Emily" 304
"Rose of Lebanon" 352
"Royal Street" 305

Sanctuary 135
Sanctuary (Original version) 141
Sartoris 46
"Sepulture South: Gaslight" 307
"Shall Not Perish" 308
"Shingles for the Lord" 310
"Skirmish at Sartoris" 311
"Smoke" 312
"Snow" 314
Soldiers' Pay 147
The Sound and the Fury 154
"Spotted Horses" 315
"Sunset" 317

Title Index

"The Tall Men" 317
"That Evening Sun Go Down" 319
"That Will Be Fine" 320
"There Was a Queen" 322
"Thrift" 323
"Tomorrow" 324
The Town 162
"Turn About" 326
"Two Dollar Wife" 327
"Two Soldiers" 328

"Uncle Willy" 330
The Unvanquished 178
"The Unvanquished" 331

"Vendée" 333
"Victory" 335

"Wash" 336
The Wild Palms 185
"Wild Palms" 353
The Wishing Tree 338
"With Caution and Dispatch" 340

"Yo Ho and Two Bottles of Rum" 341

MASTER CHARACTER INDEX

Abe
  Flags 34
  Sartoris 46
Abum
  "Evangeline" 233
Acarius, Mr.
  "Mr. Acarius" 273
Acey
  Go Down, Moses 55
  "Pantaloon" 290
Ad (see also Ash, Uncle;
  Wylie, Ash)
  "Lion" 258
Adam (also Allen)
  "Fox Hunt" 236
Adams, Mayor
  Town 162
Adams, "Miss Eve"
  Town 162
Adams, Theron
  Town 162
Aelia, Princess
  Mayday 261
Aelian (Aelius)
  Mayday 261
Agatha
  "Turn About" 326
Ailanthia I
  "Elly" 231
Ailanthia II (Elly)
  "Elly" 231
Akers
  Absalom 3
Albert
  As I Lay Dying 12
Albert
  Mansion 89

Albert
  "Turn About" 326
Alec, Unc
  Go Down, Moses 55
  "Pantaloon" 290
Aleck Sander
  Intruder 74
  Town 162
Alford, Doctor
  As I Lay Dying 12
  Flags 34
  Sartoris 46
Alice
  Light in August 81
Alice
  Reivers 117
Alice
  Soldiers' Pay 147
Alice
  Wishing Tree 338
Alice, Aunt
  "Sepulture South" 307
Allan
  Flags 34
  Sartoris 46
Allanovna, Myra
  Mansion 89
Allen (see Adam)
Allen, Bobbie
  Light in August 81
Allison, Miss
  Mansion 89
Allison, Mrs.
  Mansion 89
Allison, Judge Howard
  "Beyond" 208
Allison, Howard, II
  "Beyond" 208

Allison, Sophia
  "Beyond" 208
Ambition
  Mayday 261
Ames, Dalton
  Sound and Fury 154
Andrew
  "Elmer" 345
Andrews
  "Fox Hunt" 236
Angélique
  Fable 22
Angelo
  "Portrait of Elmer" 294
Anse
  Sound and Fury 154
Antonio
  "Jealousy" 248
Armstead
  Intruder 74
Armstid
  As I Lay Dying 12
Armstid
  Hamlet 65
Armstid
  Light in August 81
Armstid
  "Shingles" 310
Armstid, Mrs.
  "Shingles" 310
Armstid, Henry
  Hamlet 65
  Mansion 89
  Town 162
  "Lizards" 259
  "Spotted Horses" 315
Armstid, Mrs. Henry
  Hamlet 65
  "Spotted Horses" 315
Armstid, Ina May
  "Spotted Horses" 315
Armstid, Lula
  As I Lay Dying 12
Armstid, Martha
  Light in August 81
Arthur
  "Mississippi" 265
Arthur
  "Sepulture South" 307

Ash, Uncle (see also Ad;
    Bush, Old Man)
  Go Down, Moses 55
  "The Bear" 206
  "Old People" 285
Atkins, Miss
  Light in August 81
Atkinson
  Pylon 112
Atkinson
  "With Caution and Dispatch"
    340
Avant, Jim
  Reivers 117
Awce
  "A Return" 302
Awce, Unk
  "Rose of Lebanon" 352
Ayers, Major
  Mosquitoes 104
Ayers, Freddie
  "Yo Ho" 341

Backhouse, Philip St-Just
    (Backus)
  "My Grandmother Millard"
    276
Backus, Mr.
  Mansion 89
  Town 162
Backus, Melisandre
  "My Grandmother Millard"
    276
Backus, Melisandre (see
    also Harriss, Melisandre;
    Stevens, Melisandre)
  Town 162
Baddrington, Harold (Plex)
  Mansion 89
Baird, Dr.
  Soldiers' Pay 147
Baker, Joe (Jobaker)
  Big Woods 17
  Go Down, Moses 55
  "Old People" 285
Ballenbaugh I
  Reivers 117
Ballenbaugh II
  Reivers 117

Master Character Index 363

Ballenbaugh, Miss
  Reivers 117
Ballenbaugh, Boyd
  "Hand Upon the Waters" 242
Ballenbaugh, Tyler
  "Hand Upon the Waters" 243
Ballott, Mr.
  Reivers 117
Barbour, Mr.
  "Uncle Willy" 330
Barger, Sonny
  "Uncle Willy" 330
Barr, Captain
  "Music--Sweeter" 275
Barron, Homer
  "Rose for Emily" 305
Barron, Jake
  Mansion 89
Bascomb
  Sound and Fury 154
Bascomb, Maury
  Sound and Fury 154
Basket, Herman
  Big Woods 17
  "Courtship" 219
  "Justice" 249
Basket, John
  Big Woods 17
  "Bear Hunt" 207
Basket, Three
  Big Woods 17
Beale, Colonel
  Fable 22
Bean, Captain
  "Uncle Willy" 330
Beard
  Sound and Fury 154
Beard, Virgil
  Flags 34
  Sartoris 46
Beard, Will C.
  Flags 34
  Sartoris 46
Beard, Mrs. Will C.
  Flags 34
  Sartoris 46
  Light in August 81
Beatty
  "Turn About" 326

Beauchamp
  Town 162
  "Appendix: Compson" 201
Beauchamp, Amodeus McCaslin
  Go Down, Moses 55
Beauchamp, Bobo
  Reivers 117
Beauchamp, Callina McCaslin
  Go Down, Moses 55
Beauchamp, Fonsiba
  Go Down, Moses 55
Beauchamp, Henry
  Go Down, Moses 55
Beauchamp, Hubert
  Go Down, Moses 55
Beauchamp, James Thucydus
  (see also Tennie's Jim)
  Go Down, Moses 55
  Reivers 117
Beauchamp, Lucas Quintus
  Carothers McCaslin
  Go Down, Moses 55
  Intruder 74
  Reivers 117
  "Go Down, Moses" 238
  "Gold Is Not Always" 239
  "Pantaloon" 290
  "Point of Law" 293
Beauchamp, Molly (Mollie)
  Go Down, Moses 56
  Intruder 74
  "Go Down, Moses" 238
Beauchamp, Nat (see Wilkins,
  Nathalie Beauchamp)
Beauchamp, Philip Manigault
  Fable 22
Beauchamp, Samuel Worsham
  Go Down, Moses 56
  "Go Down, Moses" 238
Beauchamp, Sophonsiba (see
  McCaslin, Sophonsiba)
Beauchamp, Tennie
  Go Down, Moses 56
  Reivers 117
Beauchamp, Tomey's Turl
  Go Down, Moses 56
Beauchamp, Tomey's Turl
  Town 162
Bedenberry, Brother
  Light in August 81

Benbow
  Town 162
  Unvanquished 178
  "Skirmish" 311
Benbow, Judge
  Absalom 3
  Unvanquished 178
Benbow, Judge
  Hamlet 65
Benbow, Belle Mitchell
  Flags 34
  Sartoris 46
  Sanctuary 135
  Sanctuary (original) 141
Benbow, Cassius Q. (Uncle Cash)
  Unvanquished 178
  "Skirmish" 311
Benbow, Francis
  Flags 34
  Sartoris 46
Benbow, Horace
  Flags 34
  Sartoris 46
  Sanctuary 135
  Sanctuary (original) 141
Benbow, Julia
  Flags 34
  Sartoris 46
Benbow, Narcissa (see also Sartoris, Narcissa)
  Mansion 89
Benbow, Percy
  Absalom 3
Benbow, Will
  Flags 35
  Sartoris 46
Berry, Ben
  "Error in Chemistry" 232
Berry, Louis
  "Red Leaves" 299
Bessing
  "Landing in Luck" 255
Best, Henry
  Town 162
Beth
  Sanctuary 135
  Sanctuary (original) 141

"Bidet"
  Fable 22
Bidwell
  "Hair" 241
Biglin, Luther
  Mansion 89
Biglin, Mrs. Luther
  Mansion 89
Billie
  "Uncle Willy" 330
Binford, Dewitt
  Town 162
Binford, Mrs. Dewitt
  Town 162
Binford, Lucius
  Mansion 89
  Reivers 117
  Sanctuary 135
  Sanctuary (original) 141
Binford, Robert
  "Moonlight" (Unpub.) 351
Binfords
  Mansion 89
Bingham, Mister
  "Elmer" 345
Bird, Tom Tom (see also Tom-Tom)
  Town 162
Bird, Uncle
  Flags 35
  Sartoris 46
Birdsong
  Go Down, Moses 56
  "Pantaloon" 290
Birdsong, Preacher
  Town 163
Bishop
  Town 163
Bishop, Ephriam (Eef)
  Mansion 89
Black, Mr.
  "Death-Drag" 223
Blair, Harrison
  "Fox Hunt" 236
Blair, Mrs. Harrison
  "Fox Hunt" 236

Master Character Index 365

Blair, John
  "Artist at Home" 204
Blake, Jim
  "Hand Upon the Waters" 243
Bland
  "Ad Astra" 193
Bland, Mrs.
  Sound and Fury 154
Bland, Gerald
  Sound and Fury 154
Bledsoe
  Wild Palms 185
Bledsoe, Sgt.
  Fable 22
Bleyth, Captain
  Soldiers' Pay 147
Bleyth, George
  "Elmer" 345
Blount
  "Big Shot" 210
Blount, Gavin, I
  "A Return" 302
Blount, Gavin, II
  "Dull Tale" 229
  "A Return" 302
  "Rose of Lebanon" 352
Blount, Harrison
  "Big Shot" 210
Blount, Levinia
  "Rose of Lebanon" 352
Blum
  Fable 22
Bob, Mister
  "Sunset" 317
Bogard, H.S.
  "Turn About" 326
Boggan
  Fable 22
Boisgeclin, Constable du
  Mayday 262
Bolivar, Uncle Dick (see also Dick, Uncle)
  Hamlet 65
Bon, Charles
  Absalom 3
  "Evangeline" 233
Bon, Mrs. Charles
  "Evangeline" 233

Bon, Charles Etienne Saint-Valery
  Absalom 3
Bon, Eulalia (see Sutpen, Eulalia Bon)
Bon, Judith Sutpen
  "Evangeline" 233
Bond, Jim
  Absalom 3
Bonds, Jack
  "Bear Hunt" 207
Bookwright
  Intruder 74
Bookwright
  "Tomorrow" 324
Bookwright, Calvin (Uncle Cal)
  Mansion 89
  Reivers 117
  Town 163
Bookwright, Herman
  Mansion 90
Bookwright, Homer
  Mansion 90
  "By the People" 214
  "Shall Not Perish" 308
  "Shingles" 310
Bookwright, Odom
  Hamlet 65
  Mansion 90
Bookwrights
  Mansion 89
Bouc, Pierre
  Fable 22
Bowden, Matt
  Unvanquished 178
  "Vendée" 334
Bowen, Captain
  Unvanquished 178
  "Raid" 298
Bowman, Mr.
  "Dangerous Man" 222
Bowman, Mrs.
  "Dangerous Man" 222
Boyd, Mr.
  "Brooch" 213
Boyd, Mrs.
  "Brooch" 213
Boyd, Amy
  "Brooch" 213

Boyd, Don
  "Delta Autumn" 225
Boyd, Howard
  "Brooch" 213
Bradley
  Wild Palms 185
Bradley, Mrs.
  Wild Palms 185
Brandt, Dr.
  Flags 35
  Sartoris 46
Breckbridge, Gavin
  Unvanquished 178
  "Raid" 298
  "Skirmish" 311
Brian
  "Devil Beats His Wife" 345
Bridesman, Captain
  Fable 22
Bridger
  Unvanquished 178
  "Vendée" 334
Briggins, Lycurgus
  Reivers 117
Briggins, Mary
  Reivers 117
Britt
  "With Caution and Dispatch" 340
Brix
  "Snow" 314
Broussard, George
  Mosquitoes 104
Brown, Joe (see Burch, Lucas)
Brownlee, Percival
  Go Down, Moses 56
Brummage, Judge
  Mansion 90
Bryan, Mr.
  "Elmer" 346
Brzewski
  Fable 22
Buchwald
  Fable 22
Buck
  Flags 35
  Sartoris 46

Buck
  "Spotted Horses" 315
Buckner, Billie
  Wild Palms 185
Buckner, Buck
  Wild Palms 185
Buckworth
  Wild Palms 185
Bucky
  "Yo Ho" 341
Buffaloe
  Mansion 90
  Reivers 117
  Town 163
Buford (Bufe)
  Light in August 81
Bullitt, R.Q.
  Pylon 112
Bullitt, Sharlie
  Pylon 112
Bunch, Byron
  Light in August 81
Bundren, Mrs.
  "Spotted Horses" 315
Bundren, Addie
  As I Lay Dying 12
Bundren, Alex
  "Adolescence" 194
Bundren, Mrs. Alex
  "Adolescence" 194
Bundren, Anse
  As I Lay Dying 12
Bundren, Mrs. Anse
  As I Lay Dying 12
Bundren, Bud
  "Adolescence" 194
Bundren, Cash
  As I Lay Dying 12
Bundren, Cyril
  "Adolescence" 195
Bundren, Darl
  As I Lay Dying 13
  "Uncle Willy" 330
Bundren, Dewey Dell
  As I Lay Dying 13
Bundren, Jeff Davis
  "Adolescence" 195

Bundren, Jewel
  As I Lay Dying 13
Bundren, Joe, I
  "Adolescence" 195
Bundren, Joe, II
  "Adolescence" 195
Bundren, Juliet (Jule)
  "Adolescence" 195
Bundren, Vardaman
  As I Lay Dying 13
Burch, Lucas (Joe Brown)
  Light in August 81
Burchett
  "Hair" 241
Burchett, Mrs.
  "Hair" 241
Burchett, Mr.
  "Moonlight" 271
Burchett, Etta
  "Moonlight" 271
Burden, Beck
  Light in August 82
Burden, Calvin, I
  Light in August 82
Burden, Calvin, II
  Light in August 82
Burden, Evangeline
  Light in August 82
Burden, Joanna
  Light in August 82
  Mansion 90
Burden, Juana
  Light in August 82
Burden, Nathaniel
  Light in August 82
Burden, Sarah
  Light in August 82
Burden, Vangie
  Light in August 82
Burdens (see also Burden, Calvin I and Calvin II)
  Unvanquished 178
  "Skirmish" 311
Burgess
  Sound and Fury 154
Burgess, Mrs.
  Sound and Fury, 154

Burk
  Fable 22
Burke
  "Fox Hunt" 236
Burney, Mr.
  Soldiers' Pay 147
Burney, Mrs.
  Soldiers' Pay 147
Burney, Dewey
  Soldiers' Pay 147
Burnham, Frank
  Pylon 112
Burrington, Nathaniel
  Light in August 82
Burrington, Nathaniel, II
  Light in August 82
Burt
  "Turn About" 326
Bush, Lem
  Light in August 82
Bush, Old Man (see also Ash; Wylie, Ash)
  "Bear Hunt" 207
Butch
  "Dry September" 228
"Butler, Joe"
  Flags 35
  Sartoris 46

Cain
  Hamlet 65
Caldwell, Sam
  Reivers 118
Callaghan
  Wild Palms 185
Callaghan
  "Fox Hunt" 236
Callaghan, Miss
  "Uncle Willy" 330
Callicott, David
  "Justice" 249
Callie, Aunt
  Reivers 118
Canova, Signor (see Flint, Joel)
Cap'm
  "Once Aboard Lugger" 287

Carberry, Doc
  "Two Dollar Wife" 327
Carl
  "Divorce in Naples" 226
Caroline (Mammy)
  "Mississippi" 265
Carruthers, Miss
  Light in August 82
Carter
  "Black Music" 212
Caspey (see also Strother,
    Caspey)
  "There Was a Queen" 322
Casse-tête
  Fable 22
Cavalcanti
  "Mistral" 268
Cayley, Miss
  "Knight's Gambit" 251
Cayley, Hence
  "Knight's Gambit" 252
Cecily
  "Moonlight" (Unpub.) 351
Chance, Vic
  Pylon 112
Charles (see also Mallison,
    Charles, Jr.)
  "By the People" 214
Charles
  "Elmer" 346
Charley
  Light in August 82
Charley
  Reivers 118
Charley, Uncle
  "Doctor Martino" 227
Charley, Uncle
  "Sepulture South" 307
Charlie
  Sound and Fury 154
Charlotte (see also Ritten-
    meyer, Charlotte)
  "Wild Palms" 353
Chick; Charley (see also Mal-
    lison, Charles, Jr.)
  "Hog Pawn" 244
  "Tomorrow" 324

Chlory
  "Beyond" 209
Christian, Hoke
  "Uncle Willy" 330
Christian, Walter
  Town 163
Christian, Uncle Willy
  Mansion 90
  Reivers 118
  Town 163
  "Uncle Willy" 330
Christian, Mrs. Willy
  "Uncle Willy" 330
Christmas, Joe
  Light in August 83
Church, Mrs.
  "That Will Be Fine" 320
Cinthy
  Light in August 83
Clapp, Walter
  Reivers 118
Clay, Sis Beulah
  Sound and Fury 154
Clefus
  Town 163
Clytemnestra (Clytie)
  Absalom 3
Coates, Harrison
  "Dull Tale" 230
Cochrane, Ab
  "Mr. Acarius" 273
Cofer
  Wild Palms 185
Colbert, David
  "Courtship" 220
Coldfield
  Requiem 127
  "Appendix: Compson" 201
Coldfield, Ellen (see Sut-
    pen, Ellen Coldfield)
Coldfield, Goodhue
  Absalom 4
Coldfield, Rosa
  Absalom 4
Coleman, Mrs.
  Soldiers' Pay 147
Collier
  "Turn About" 326

Collyer
  Fable 22
Compson
  Requiem 127
  Sound and Fury 154
  Town 163
  "Mississippi" 265
Compson, Benjamin
  Mansion 90
  Sound and Fury 154
  "Appendix: Compson" 201
Compson, Candace
  Mansion 90
  Sound and Fury 155
  "Appendix: Compson" 201
  "Justice" 249
  "That Evening Sun" 319
Compson, Caroline
  Sound and Fury 155
Compson, Charles Stuart
  "Appendix: Compson" 201
Compson, Jason Lycurgus, I
  Requiem 127
  "Appendix: Compson" 201
  "Name for the City" 278
Compson, Jason Lycurgus, II
  Absalom 4
  Big Woods 17
  Go Down, Moses 56
  Intruder 74
  Reivers 118
  Requiem 127
  Town 163
  Unvanquished 178
  "Appendix: Compson" 201
  "Bear" 206
  "Justice" 249
  "My Grandmother Millard" 276
  "Skirmish" 311
Compson, Mrs.
  Absalom 4
  Town 163
  Unvanquished 178
  "My Grandmother Millard" 276
  "Raid" 298
  "Retreat" 301

  "Skirmish" 311
  "Unvanquished" 331
  "Vendée" 334
Compson, Jason Lycurgus, III
  Absalom 4
  Sound and Fury 155
  "Appendix: Compson" 201
  "That Evening Sun" 319
Compson, Jason Lycurgus, IV
  Mansion 90
  Sound and Fury 156
  Town 163
  "Appendix: Compson" 201
  "Justice" 249
  "That Evening Sun" 319
Compson, Quentin MacLachan, I
  "Appendix: Compson" 201
Compson, Quentin, II
  Mansion 90
  "Appendix: Compson" 201
Compson, Quentin, III
  Absalom 5
  Big Woods 17
  Mansion 90
  Sound and Fury 156
  "Appendix: Compson" 201
  "Justice" 249
  "That Evening Sun" 319
Compson, Quentin, IV
  Mansion 90
  Sound and Fury 156
  "Appendix: Compson" 201
Comyn
  Flags 35
  Sartoris 47
  "Ad Astra" 193
Confrey, Mame
  Light in August 83
Confrey, Max
  Light in August 83
Conner, Buck (see also Connors, Buck)
  Light in August 83
  "Centaur in Brass" 216

Connors, Buck
  Town 163
Connors, Buck, II
  Town 163
Conventicle
  Fable 22
Cook, Celia
  Unvanquished 178
Cooper
  Pylon 112
Cooper, Minnie
  "Dry September" 228
Corporal (see Stefan)
Cotton, Ernest (see also
    Snopes, Mink)
  "Hound" 247
Cowan, Mrs.
  "Hair" 241
Cowrie
  Fable 23
Crack
  Mansion 90
Crain, Amos
  "Artist at Home" 204
Crain, Mrs. Amos
  "Artist at Home" 204
Cranston, Lily
  "Doctor Martino" 227
Crawfishford
  "Justice" 249
Crawford, Dr.
  Big Woods 17
  Go Down, Moses 56
Crenshaw, Jack
  Town 163
Crowe
  Wild Palms 185
Crump, Lucas
  Idyll in the Desert 248
Cunningham, Sergeant
  "Victory" 335

Dad
  Mansion 90
Daingerfield, Miss
  Sound and Fury 157
Daisy (see also Wylie, Daisy)
  Go Down, Moses 56

Damuddy
  Sound and Fury 157
Dan
  Go Down, Moses 57
  "Gold Is Not Always" 239
Dandridge, Maggie (see
    Stevens, Maggie Dandridge)
Davy
  "Leg" 255
Deacon
  Sound and Fury 157
Della
  "Devil Beats His Wife"
    345
Demarchi
  Fable 23
Demont
  Fable 23
Demont, Marthe (Magda)
  Fable 23
De Montigny
  Fable 23
De Montigny
  Wild Palms 185
De Montigny, Paul
  "Elly" 231
Depre, Virginia (see also
    Du Pre, Virginia)
  Requiem 127
De Spain
  Town 163
  "Mississippi" 265
De Spain, Major
  Absalom 5
  Big Woods 17
  Go Down, Moses 57
  Hamlet 65
  Intruder 74
  Mansion 90
  Reivers 118
  Town 163
  "Barn Burning" 205
  "Bear" 206
  "Delta Autumn" 225
  "Lion" 258
  "Old People" 285
De Spain, Major
  Big Woods 17
  "Bear Hunt" 207

De Spain, Mrs.
  Big Woods 17
  "Bear Hunt" 207
De Spain, Major
  "Shall Not Perish" 308
De Spain, Lula
  Hamlet 65
  "Barn Burning" 205
De Spain, Manfred
  Mansion 90
  Reivers 118
  Town 163
Despleins, Jules
  Pylon 112
Devries, Colonel
  Mansion 91
  "By the People" 214
Dicey
  "Wash" 336
Dick
  "Devil Beats His Wife" 345
Dick, Uncle (see also Bolivar, Uncle Dick)
  "Lizards" 259
Dick, Colonel Nathaniel G.
  Unvanquished 178
  "Raid" 298
  "Unvanquished" 331
Dicky
  Wishing Tree 338
Dilazuck
  Mansion 91
Dilsey (see also Gibson, Dilsey)
  "Appendix: Compson" 201
  "That Evening Sun" 319
Doc
  Sanctuary 135
  Sanctuary (original) 141
Doc
  Wild Palms 185
Dodge, Granby
  "Smoke" 313
Dollar
  Light in August 83
Don
  "Evangeline" 233
  "Mistral" 268
  "Snow" 314

Doom (see also Ikkemotubbe)
  Reivers 118
  "Red Leaves" 299
Doshey
  Hamlet 65
Dough, James
  Soldiers' Pay 147
Downs, Mrs.
  Intruder 75
Drake, Judge
  Sanctuary 135
  Sanctuary (original) 141
Drake, Hubert (Buddy)
  Sanctuary 135
  Sanctuary (original) 141
Drake, Temple (see also Stevens, Temple Drake)
  Sanctuary 135
  Sanctuary (original) 141
Dukinfield, Judge
  Mansion 91
  Town 164
  "Smoke" 313
Dukinfield, Emma
  "Smoke" 313
Dulcie
  Wishing Tree 338
Du Pre, Virginia (see also Depre, Virginia; Sartoris, Virginia; Jenny, Miss)
  Flags 35
  Sartoris 47
  Mansion 91
  Town 164
  Unvanquished 178
  "There Was a Queen" 322
Durley
  "Spotted Horses" 315

Eagle Beak
  "Peter" 292
Earl (see also Triplett, Earl)
  Sound and Fury 157
Ed
  Mosquitoes 104
Ed
  Reivers 118

Ed (see also Walker, Ed)
　Sanctuary (original)　142
Ed
　Soldiers' Pay　147
Ed
　"Mirror of Chartres Street"
　　263
Ed
　"Love"　350
Ed
　"Once Aboard Lugger"　288
Edmonds
　Big Woods　18
　Town　164
Edmonds, Alice
　Go Down, Moses　57
Edmonds, Carothers (Roth)
　Big Woods　18
　Go Down, Moses　57
　Intruder　75
　Reivers　118
　Town　164
　"Go Down, Moses"　238
　"Gold Is Not Always"　239
　"Pantaloon"　290
　"Point of Law"　293
　"Race at Morning"　297
Edmonds, Louisa
　Reivers　118
Edmonds, McCaslin (Cass)
　Big Woods　19
　Go Down, Moses　57
　Reivers　118
　Town　164
Edmonds, Zachary (Zack)
　Go Down, Moses　57
　Reivers　118
　"Point of Law"　293
Egbert
　Wishing Tree　338
Ek
　"Liar"　257
Elly (see Ailanthia II)
Elma, Miss
　Town　164
Elnora
　Flags　35
　Sartoris　47

Sanctuary (original)　142
"All the Dead Pilots"
　　198
"There Was a Queen"　322
Elys, Princess
　Mayday　262
Emmeline
　"That Will Be Fine"　320
Emmy
　Soldiers' Pay　147
Ephraim
　Intruder　75
Ephum
　Reivers　118
Ernest
　"Spotted Horses"　315
Ernest (Ernie)
　"Love"　350
Ernest, Mister
　Big Woods　18
　"Race at Morning"　297
Ernie
　"Fox Hunt"　235
Ethel
　"Portrait of Elmer"　294
　"Elmer"　346
Ethel
　"Love"　350
Eunice
　Flags　35
　Sartoris　47
Eunice
　Go Down, Moses　57
Euphrony (see Strother,
　　Euphrony)
Euphrosy
　"Peter"　292
Eustace
　Flags　35
　Sartoris　47
Ewell
　"Mississippi"　265
Ewell, Bryan
　"Error in Chemistry"　232
Ewell, Walter, I
　Big Woods　18
　Go Down, Moses　57

Master Character Index 373

Mansion 91
Reivers 118
"Bear" 206
"Old People" 286
Ewell, Walter, II
  Big Woods 18
  "Race at Morning" 297
Ewing, Ira, I
  "Golden Land" 240
Ewing, Ira, II
  "Golden Land" 240
Ewing, Mitch (see also
    Mitch)
  "Hair" 241
Ewing, Samantha, I
  "Golden Land" 240
Ewing, Samantha, II (April
    Lalear)
  "Golden Land" 240
Ewing, Voyd
  "Golden Land" 240
Exodus
  Wishing Tree 339
Experience
  Mayday 262

Fairchild, Dawson
  Mosquitoes 104
Falls, Will
  Flags 35
  Sartoris 47
Fame
  Mayday 262
Farinzale, Giulio
  "Mistral" 268
Farmer
  Requiem 127
Farmer, Cecilia
  Requiem 127
Farr, Cecily Saunders
  Soldiers' Pay 147
Farr, George
  Soldiers' Pay 148
Fathers, Sam
  Big Woods 18
  Go Down, Moses 58
  Intruder 75
  Reivers 119

"Bear" 206
"Delta Autumn" 225
"Justice" 249
"Old People" 286
Faulkner
  Mosquitoes 104
Faulkner, Bill
  "Afternoon of a Cow" 196
Faulkner, Mrs.
  "Afternoon of a Cow" 196
Feinman, Col. H.I.
  Pylon 112
Fentry, G.A.
  "Tomorrow" 324
Fentry, Jackson and Long-
    street (see Thorpe,
    Buck)
Fentry, Stonewall Jackson
  "Tomorrow" 325
Ffollansbye
  "All the Dead Pilots"
    198
  "Thrift" 323
Fittie, Aunt
  Reivers 119
Flint
  Wild Palms 185
Flint, Ellie
  "Error in Chemistry" 232
Flint, Joel (Signor Canova)
  "Error in Chemistry" 232
Florence
  "Sepulture South" 307
Fonzo (see also Winbush,
    Fonzo)
  Sanctuary 136
  Sanctuary (original) 142
Foote, Mr.
  "Two Soldiers" 329
Fortinbride, Brother
  Unvanquished 178
  "Unvanquished" 332
  "Vendée" 334
Fortitude
  Mayday 262
Fothergill, Zeb
  Flags 36
  Sartoris 47

Fox, Matt
  "Hair" 241
Frances (Frankie)
  "Frankie and Johnny" 237
Frank
  Sanctuary 136
  Sanctuary (original) 142
Frankie
  Flags 36
  Sartoris 47
Frankie
  "New Orleans" 280
  "Royal Street" 305
Franz
  "Ad Astra" 193
Fraser
  Intruder 75
Fraser
  "Monk" 270
Fraser, Mr.
  Big Woods 18
  "Bear Hunt" 208
Fraser, Squire Adam
  Intruder 75
Fraser, Doyle
  Intruder 75
Frazier
  Town 164
Frazier, Judge
  "Tomorrow" 325
Fred I
  "That Will Be Fine" 320
Fred II
  "That Will Be Fine" 320
Freeman
  Hamlet 65
Freeman, Mrs.
  Hamlet 66
Freeman
  "Spotted Horses" 315
Frony
  Sound and Fury 157
  "Appendix: Compson" 202
  "That Evening Sun" 319
Frost, Mark
  Mosquitoes 104

Gabe
  Reivers 119
Galwyn of Arthgyl
  Mayday 262
Gambrell, C.L.
  "Monk" 270
Gant, Eunice
  Town 164
Gant, Jim
  Miss Zilphia Gant 264
Gant, Mrs. Jim
  Miss Zilphia Gant 264
Gant, Zilphia
  Miss Zilphia Gant 264
Gargne, Monsieur
  Fable 23
Garroway, Mr.
  Town 164
Gary, Doctor
  Soldiers' Pay 148
Gatewood, Jabbo
  Town 164
Gatewood, Uncle Noon
  Town 164
Gavin, Uncle (see also
    Stevens, Gavin)
  "Hog Pawn" 244
  "Name for the City" 278
Gawtrey, Steve
  "Fox Hunt" 236
Gene
  Sanctuary 136
  Sanctuary (original) 142
Genesis
  Wishing Tree 339
George
  Hamlet 66
George
  Sanctuary 136
  Sanctuary (original) 142
George
  "Divorce in Naples" 226
George
  "Leg" 255
George
  "That Will Be Fine" 320
George
  Wishing Tree 339

Master Character Index 375

George
  "Moonlight" (Unpub.) 352
Georgie
  "That Will Be Fine" 320
Gianotti, Father
  "The Priest" 296
Gibson, Dilsey (see also
    Dilsey)
  Sound and Fury 157
Gibson, Roskus (see also
    Roskus)
  Sound and Fury 157
Gibson, T.P. (see also T.P.)
  Sound and Fury 157
Gibson, Versh (see also Versh)
  Sound and Fury 158
Gibson, Will
  "Liar" 257
Gihon
  Mansion 91
Gihon, Danny
  "Pennsylvania Station" 291
Gihon, Margaret Noonan
  "Pennsylvania Station" 291
Gillespie
  Wild Palms 185
Gillespie, Mr.
  As I Lay Dying 14
Gillespie, Mack
  As I Lay Dying 14
Gilligan, Joe (Yaphank)
  Soldiers' Pay 148
Gillman, Mr.
  Light in August 83
Gillman, Mrs.
  "A Return" 302
Gilman
  "Country Mice" 219
Ginotta, Mr.
  Mosquitoes 104
Ginotta, Mrs.
  Mosquitoes 105
Ginotta, Joe
  Mosquitoes 105
Ginotta, Pete
  Mosquitoes 105
Ginsfarb
  "Death-Drag" 223

Gloria
  "Portrait of Elmer" 294
  "Elmer" 346
Goldie
  "Mr. Acarius" 273
Gombault, Mr.
  Town 164
  "Tall Men" 317
Gombault, Uncle Pete
  Requiem 127
Goodwin, Lee
  Sanctuary 136
  Sanctuary (original) 142
Goodyhay, Brother Joe C.
  Mansion 91
Gordon
  Mosquitoes 105
Gordon, Charles (Charley)
  "A Return" 302
  "Rose of Lebanon" 352
Gordon, Lewis Randolph
  "A Return" 303
  "Rose of Lebanon" 352
Gordon, Randolph
  "A Return" 303
  "Rose of Lebanon" 352
Gorham, Mr.
  "Love" 350
Gorham, Beth (see Jeyfus,
    Beth Gorham)
Gorham, Clara
  "Love" 350
Govelli
  "Big Shot" 210
Gowan, Judge
  Go Down, Moses 58
  "Point of Law" 293
Gower
  Wild Palms 185
Gowrie
  Intruder 75
  Town 164
Gowrie, Amanda W.
  Intruder 75
Gowrie, Bilbo
  Intruder 75
Gowrie, Bryan
  Intruder 75
Gowrie, Crawford
  Intruder 75

Gowrie, Forrest
    Intruder 75
Gowrie, N.B. Forrest (Nub)
    Intruder 75
    Mansion 91
    Town 164
Gowrie, Vardaman
    Intruder 75
Gowrie, Vinson
    Intruder 76
Grady
    Pylon 112
Gragnon, General Charles
    Fable 23
Graham, Eustace
    Sanctuary 136
    Sanctuary (original) 142
Grant, Joe
    Pylon 112
Grass, Das
    "Love" 350
Gratton, Mr.
    Flags 36
    Sartoris 47
Gray, Alec, I
    "Victory" 335
Gray, Alec, II
    "Victory" 335
Gray, Annie
    "Victory" 335
Gray, Elizabeth
    "Victory" 335
Gray, Jessie
    "Victory" 335
Gray, John Wesley
    "Victory" 335
Gray, Johnny
    "Kid Learns" 250
Gray, Matthew, I
    "Victory" 335
Gray, Matthew, II
    "Victory" 336
Gray, Uncle Simon
    "Victory" 336
Green, Captain
    Soldiers' Pay 148
Greenleaf
    Intruder 76

Grenier
    Town 164
    "Appendix: Compson" 202
Grenier, Louis
    Intruder 76
    Reivers 119
    Requiem 127
    Town 164
    "Hand Upon the Waters" 243
    "Name for the City" 278
Grier
    "Shall Not Perish" 308
    "Shingles for the Lord" 310
    "Two Soldiers" 329
Grier, Eck (see also Grier, Res)
    "By the People" 214
Grier, Pete
    "Shall Not Perish" 308
    "Two Soldiers" 329
Grier, Res
    Mansion 91
    "Shall Not Perish" 308
    "Shingles for the Lord" 310
Grier, Mrs. Res
    "Shall Not Perish" 308
Grierson, Mr.
    "Rose for Emily" 305
Grierson, Emily
    "Rose for Emily" 305
Grignon, Papa
    "Snow" 314
Grimm, Eustace
    As I Lay Dying 14
    Hamlet 66
    "Lizards" 259
Grimm, Percy
    Light in August 83
Grinnup, Dan (Dan Grenier)
    Reivers 119
Grinnup, Lonnie (Louis Grenier)
    Intruder 76
    "Hand Upon the Waters" 243

Grove, Lena
  Light in August   83
Grove, McKinley
  Light in August   84
Grover
  "Afternoon of a Cow"   196
Grover
  "Portrait of Elmer"   294
  "Elmer"   346
Grumby, Major
  Hamlet   66
  Unvanquished   179
  "Unvanquished"   332
  "Vendée"   334
Grummet
  As I Lay Dying   14
Gualdres, Captain
  "Knight's Gambit"   252
Gus
  "Country Mice"   219
Guster
  Town   165

Habersham
  Town   165
Habersham
  Unvanquished   179
Habersham, Dr.
  "Mississippi"   265
Habersham, Mrs.
  "Two Soldiers"   329
Habersham, Emily
  Town   165
Habersham, Eunice
  Intruder   76
  Town   165
Habersham, Martha
  Unvanquished   179
  "Skirmish"   311
Habersham, Dr. Samuel
  Intruder   76
  Requiem   127
  Town   165
  "Name for the City"   278
Had-Two-Fathers (see John Had-Two-Fathers)
Hagood
  Pylon   112

Hait (see also Hait, Lonzo)
  "Mule in the Yard"   274
Hait, Lonzo
  Mansion   91
  Town   165
Hait, Mannie
  Town   165
  "Mule in the Yard"   274
Haley
  Hamlet   66
Haley, Lem
  "Liar"   257
Halladay, Jim
  Intruder   76
Halliday
  Light in August   84
Hamblett, Jim
  Absalom   5
Hamilton
  "Love"   350
Hamp
  Wild Palms   185
Hampton, Hub or Hope
  Hamlet   66
  Intruder   76
  Mansion   91
  Reivers   119
  Town   165
Hampton, Mrs. Hope
  Intruder   76
Hampton, Hub, II
  Mansion   91
  Reivers   119
Hank
  Pylon   112
Hanley
  Fable   23
Harker
  Town   165
  "Centaur in Brass"   216
Harker, Otis
  Town   165
Harmon, Mrs.
  "Liar"   257
Harper
  "Turn About"   326
Harris
  Hamlet   66
  "Barn Burning"   205

Harris
  "Death-Drag" 223
Harris
  "Honor" 246
Harris
  "Rosary" 304
Harris, Mr.
  Sanctuary 136
  Sanctuary (original) 142
Harris, Mr.
  "Elmer" 346
Harris, Elmer
  "Black Music" 212
Harris, Meloney
  Flags 36
  Sartoris 47
Harrison
  Unvanquished 179
  "Ambuscade" 199
Harriss
  Mansion 91
  "Knight's Gambit" 252
Harriss, Miss
  "Knight's Gambit" 252
Harriss, Max
  "Knight's Gambit" 252
Harriss, Melisandre Backus
  (see also Stevens, Melisandre Backus)
  "Knight's Gambit" 252
Harry
  Fable 23
Harry
  "With Caution and Dispatch"
  340
Harry
  "Devil Beats His Wife" 345
Harry (see also Wilbourne, Harry)
  "Wild Palms" 353
Harvey, Deacon
  "Adolescence" 195
Hatcher, Louis
  Sound and Fury 158
Hatcher, Martha
  Sound and Fury 158
Hawk, Dennison, I
  Unvanquished 179

"Raid" 298
"Skirmish" 311
Hawk, Dennison, II
  Unvanquished 179
  "Raid" 298
  "Skirmish" 311
  "Unvanquished" 332
Hawk, Drusilla (see also Sartoris, Drusilla Hawk)
  "Raid" 298
  "Skirmish" 311
  "Unvanquished" 332
  "Vendée" 334
Hawk, Louisa (Louise)
  Unvanquished 179
  "Raid" 298
  "Skirmish" 311
  "Unvanquished" 332
Hawkshaw, Henry (Henry Stribling)
  "Dry September" 229
  "Hair" 242
Head, Herbert
  Sound and Fury 158
Henderson, Mrs.
  Soldiers' Pay 148
Henri
  Fable 23
Henry
  Go Down, Moses 58
  "Point of Law" 293
Henry
  Mansion 91
Henry
  Requiem 127
Henry
  Soldiers' Pay 148
Henry
  Sound and Fury 158
Henry
  "Elmer" 346
Henry, Uncle
  Flags 36
  Sartoris 47
Heppleton, Joan
  Flags 36
Herb (Herbie)
  "Don Giovanni" 228

Hestelle
  "Mississippi" 265
Het
  Town 165
  "Mule in the Yard" 274
Heustace
  "Big Shot" 210
Heustace
  "Dull Tale" 230
Heustace
  "A Return" 303
Heustace, Henry
  "A Return" 303
Heustace, Mrs. Henry
  "A Return" 303
Hickey
  "Big Shot" 210
Hightower, Gail, I
  Light in August 84
Hightower, Gail, II
  Light in August 84
Hightower, Hiram
  Reivers 119
Hill, Dr.
  "Mr. Acarius" 273
Hiller, Emil
  "Snow" 314
Hilliard
  Unvanquished 179
Hines, Eupheus (Doc)
  Light in August 84
Hines, Mrs. Eupheus
  Light in August 84
Hines, Milly
  Light in August 84
Hipps, Buck
  Hamlet 66
Hoake
  Hamlet 66
Hodge, Mr.
  "Portrait of Elmer" 294
  "Elmer" 346
Hodge, Mrs.
  "Portrait of Elmer" 294
  "Elmer" 346
Hodge, Elmer
  "Portrait of Elmer" 294
  "Elmer" 346

Hodge, Jo
  "Portrait of Elmer" 294
Hodge, Jo-Addie
  "Elmer" 346
Hogben
  Wild Palms 185
Hogganbeck
  "Mississippi" 266
Hogganbeck, Boon
  Big Woods 18
  Go Down, Moses 58
  Intruder 76
  Reivers 119
  Town 165
  "Bear" 207
  "Lion" 258
  "Mississippi" 266
  "Old People" 286
Hogganbeck, David
  "Courtship" 220
Hogganbeck, Everbe Corinthia
    (Miss Corrie)
  Reivers 119
Hogganbeck, Lucius (see also
    Provine, Lucius)
  Big Woods 18
  Mansion 91
  Reivers 120
  Town 165
Hogganbeck, Mrs. Lucius
  Big Woods 18
Hogganbeck, Melissa
  Town 165
  "Knight's Gambit" 252
Hoke
  "Fool About a Horse" 234
Holcomb, Ashley
  Town 165
Holcomb, Beth
  Mansion 91
Holland
  "Tomorrow" 325
Holland, Mr.
  Mansion 91
Holland, Anse
  Hamlet 66
  "Fool About a Horse" 234

Holland, Anselm, I
    "Smoke" 313
Holland, Anselm, II
    "Smoke" 313
Holland, Cornelia Mardis
    "Smoke" 313
Holland, Virginius
    "Smoke" 313
Hollowell, Lafe
    "Adolescence" 195
Hollowell, Lee
    "Adolescence" 195
Holmes, Miss
    Sound and Fury 158
Holmes, Jack
    Pylon 112
Holston
    Town 165
    "Appendix: Compson" 202
    "Hand Upon the Waters" 243
    "Mississippi" 266
Holston, Dr.
    "My Grandmother Millard" 276
Holston, Mrs.
    Unvanquished 179
    "Skirmish" 312
Holston, Alexander
    Absalom 5
    Intruder 77
    Mansion 91
    Requiem 128
    Town 165
    "Name for the City" 278
Hong Li
    "Royal Street" 305
Hood, Uncle Parsham
    Reivers 120
Hooper, Mr.
    Mosquitoes 105
Hope, L.C.W. (Claude)
    "Turn About" 326
Hopkins
    Sound and Fury 158
Horn
    Fable 23

Houston
    As I Lay Dying 14
Houston
    Flags 36
    Sartoris 47
Houston, Mr.
    "Two Dollar Wife" 327
Houston, Mrs.
    "Two Dollar Wife" 328
Houston, Doris (see Johns, Doris Houston)
Houston, Jack or Zack
    Hamlet 66
    Mansion 92
    Town 166
    "Hound" 247
Houston, Lucy Pate or Letty Bookwright
    Hamlet 66
    Town 165
Hovis, Mr.
    Town 166
Hovis, Mrs.
    "Uncle Willy" 330
Hovis, Mr.
    "Moonlight" 271
Howard
    "Love" 350
Howes, Anne
    "Artist at Home" 204
Howes, Darrel (Dorry House)
    Idyll in the Desert 248
Howes, Roger
    "Artist at Home" 204
Hoxey, Major (see also De Spain, Manfred)
    "Centaur in Brass" 216
Hub
    Flags 36
    Sartoris 47
Hub
    "Error in Chemistry" 232
Hugh
    "Love" 350
Hughes, Manny
    Idyll in the Desert 248

Hule
  "Mountain Victory" 272
Hulett
  Go Down, Moses 58
Hume
  "Ad Astra" 193
Hunger
  Mayday 262
Hurtz
  Pylon 113

I.C.
  "Music--Sweeter" 275
Ike
  "Hand Upon the Waters" 243
Ikkemotubbe (see also Doom)
  Absalom 5
  Big Woods 18
  Go Down, Moses 58
  Requiem 128
  Town 166
  "Appendix: Compson" 202
  "Courtship" 220
  "Justice" 250
  "Name for the City" 278
  "Old People" 286
Imogene
  "Peter" 292
Ingraham (see Ingrum)
Ingrum
  Intruder 77
Ingrum, Willy
  Intruder 77
Iowa
  "Damon and Pythias" 221
Irey
  Fable 23
  Notes on a Horsethief 281
Isham
  Big Woods 19
  Go Down, Moses 58
  "Delta Autumn" 225
Isom
  Flags 36
  Sartoris 47
  Sanctuary 136
  Sanctuary (original) 142
  "All the Dead Pilots" 198
  "There Was A Queen" 322
Isaac, Uncle
  Pylon 115

Issetibbeha
  Big Woods 19
  Go Down, Moses 58
  Reivers 120
  Requiem 128
  Town 166
  "Courtship" 220
  "Name for the City" 278
  "Old People" 286
  "Red Leaves" 299

Jabbo, Cap'm
  Mansion 92
Jack
  "Honor" 246
Jack
  "Uncle Willy" 330
Jackie
  Reivers 120
Jackson, Al
  Mosquitoes 105
  "Al Jackson" 196
Jackson, Arthur (Art)
  Pylon 113
Jackson, Claude
  Mosquitoes 105
  "Al Jackson" 196
Jackson, Elenor (Perchie)
  "Al Jackson" 196
Jackson, Herman
  "Al Jackson" 196
Jackson, "Old Man"
  Mosquitoes 105
  "Al Jackson" 197
Jackson, Sam
  "Al Jackson" 197
Jackson, Spearhead
  "Al Jackson" 197
Jake
  "Beyond" 209
Jake
  "Death-Drag" 223
Jake
  "Kingdom of God" 251
James
  "Afternoon of a Cow" 196
James, Lt. Col.,
  Fable 23
Jameson, Dorothy
  Mosquitoes 105

Jane
  "Letter to Grandmama" 349
Jarrod, Hubert
  "Doctor Martino" 227
Jean
  Fable 23
Jean-Baptiste
  "Home" 245
Jenny, Miss (see also Du Pre, Jenny)
  Sanctuary 136
  Sanctuary (original) 142
Jerks
  Soldiers' Pay 148
Jerry
  "Turn About" 326
Jessop, Farmer
  "Elmer" 346
Jesus (see Jubah)
Jeyfus, Beth Gorham
  "Love" 351
Jeyfus, Bob
  "Love" 351
Jiggs
  Pylon 113
Jim
  Hamlet 66
Jim
  Hamlet 66
  "Fool About a Horse" 234
Jim
  "Mississippi" 266
Jimbo (see also Tennie's Jim; Beauchamp, Tennie's Jim)
  "Old People" 286
Jingus
  Unvanquished 179
  "Raid" 298
Joanna
  "A Return" 303
Job
  Town 166
Job, Uncle
  Sound and Fury 158
Job, Uncle
  "Smoke" 313
Jobaker (see Baker, Joe)

Joby
  Flags 36
  Sartoris 48
  Unvanquished 179
  "Ambuscade" 199
  "My Grandmother Millard" 276
  "Raid" 298
  "Retreat" 301
  "Skirmish" 312
  "Unvanquished" 332
  "Vendée" 334
Joby
  "Music--Sweeter" 275
Joby
  "There Was a Queen" 322
Jock
  "Death-Drag" 223
Jock
  "Elmer" 346
Jody
  As I Lay Dying 14
Jody
  "Moonlight" (Unpub.) 352
Joe
  Flags 36
  Sartoris 48
Joe
  Intruder 77
Joe
  Pylon 113
Joe
  Sanctuary 136
  Sanctuary (original) 142
Joe
  "Country Mice" 219
Joe
  "Dangerous Man" 222
Joe
  "Episode" 232
Joe
  "Hand Upon the Waters" 243
Joe
  "Hound" 247
Joe
  "Once Aboard Lugger" 287
  "Once Aboard Lugger" 288

Master Character Index 383

Joe
  "Two Dollar Wife" 328
Joe
  "Elmer" 346
Joe
  "Love" 351
Joe, Mister
  "Music--Sweeter" 275
Joe Lee
  "Peter" 292
John
  "Honor" 246
John
  "Wild Palms" 353
John Had-Two-Fathers
  "Red Leaves" 299
John Henry
  Flags 36
  Sartoris 48
John Paul
  "That Will Be Fine" 321
Johnny
  "Frankie and Johnny" 237
  "New Orleans" 280
  "Royal Street" 305
Johnny
  "Letter to Grandmama" 350
Johns, Doris Houston
  "Two Dollar Wife" 328
Johns, Maxwell
  "Two Dollar Wife" 328
Jonas
  Go Down, Moses 58
Jones
  Sanctuary (original) 142
Jones
  "Death-Drag" 223
Jones, Doctor
  Flags 36
  Sartoris 48
Jones, Hershall
  Sanctuary 136
  Sanctuary (original) 143
Jones, Januarius
  Soldiers' Pay 148
Jones, Melicent
  Absalom 5

Jones, Milly
  Absalom 5
  "Wash" 337
Jones, Wash
  Absalom 5
  "Wash" 337
Jordan, Mrs.
  "That Will Be Fine" 321
Jornstadt
  "Two Dollar Wife" 328
Joseph
  Big Woods 19
Jubah
  "That Evening Sun" 319
Jubal
  "Mountain Victory" 272
Jug
  Pylon 113
Julia
  "Sepulture South" 307
Julio
  Sound and Fury 158
Junkin, Professor
  Sound and Fury 158
Jupe
  Light in August 84

Kauffman, Julius, I
  Mosquitoes 105
Kauffman, Julius, II
  Mosquitoes 105
Kaye, Major C.
  "All the Dead Pilots" 198
Kazimura
  "Golden Land" 240
Kemp, Beasley
  Hamlet 66
  "Fool About a Horse" 235
Kennedy, Wat
  Light in August 84
Kenny
  Sound and Fury 158
Ketcham
  Go Down, Moses 58
  "Pantaloon" 290
Killebrew, Miss
  Town 166

Killegrew, Hampton
  "Knight's Gambit" 252
Killegrew, Hunter
  Mansion 92
Killegrew, "Old Man"
  "Shall Not Perish" 309
  "Shingles for the Lord"
    310
  "Two Soldiers" 329
Killegrew, Mrs.
  "Shingles for the Lord"
    310
King, Alvina
  "Doctor Martino" 227
King, Louise
  "Doctor Martino" 227
Kitchener (Kit)
  "All the Dead Pilots" 198
Kneeland, Mr.
  Town 166
Knight, Newt
  "Mississippi" 266
Kohl, Barton
  Mansion 92
Kohl, Linda Snopes (see also
    Snopes, Linda)
  Mansion 92
Krootz, Hype
  "Wild Palms" 353
Kyerling, R.
  "All the Dead Pilots"
    198
Kyrilytch, Vladimir (see
    Ratcliffe, V.K.)

Labove
  Hamlet 67
Labove
  Hamlet 67
Lafe
  As I Lay Dying 14
Lafe
  "Liar" 257
Lafe
  "Elmer" 346
Lallemont
  Fable 24
Lamar, Ruby (see also Ruby)
  Sanctuary 136

Landry
  Fable 24
Lapin
  Fable 24
Laura, Miss
  Sound and Fury 158
Laverne (see Shumann, La-
    verne)
Lawington, Miss
  As I Lay Dying 14
Leblanc
  Pylon 113
Ledbetter, Mrs.
  Mansion 92
  Town 166
Legate, Bob
  Reivers 120
Legate, Willy
  Big Woods 19
  Go Down, Moses 58
  Intruder 77
  "Delta Autumn" 225
  "Race at Morning" 297
Legendre, Dr.
  Pylon 113
Leonard
  Hamlet 67
Leonora
  Pylon 113
Lessep, Grandfather
  Reivers 120
Lessep, Grandmother
  Reivers 120
Lester, Judy
  "Mr. Acarius" 274
Levine, Gerald David
  Fable 24
Levitt, Matt
  Town 166
Lewis, Matt
  Idyll in the Desert 248
Liddy
  "Sepulture South" 307
Lilly, Mr.
  Intruder 77
Linscomb, Colonel
  Reivers 120
Little Chicago
  Reivers 120

Master Character Index 385

Little Sister Death
  Sound and Fury 158
  "Kid Learns" 250
  Mayday 262
Littlejohn
  As I Lay Dying 14
Littlejohn
  Hamlet 67
  Intruder 77
Littlejohn
  Mansion 92
Littlejohn, Mrs.
  Flags 36
  Hamlet 67
  Town 166
  "Lizards" 259
  "Spotted Horses" 316
Lizzie
  "Barn Burning" 205
Log-in-the-Creek
  "Courtship" 220
Long, Judge
  Mansion 92
  Town 166
Loosh (see also Lucius)
  Unvanquished 179
  "Ambuscade" 199
  "Raid" 298
  "Retreat" 301
  "Unvanquished" 332
Lorine
  "Uncle Willy" 330
Lorraine
  Sound and Fury 158
Lorraine, Miss
  Sanctuary 137
  Sanctuary (original) 143
Louisa
  Wild Palms 185
Louisa I
  "That Will Be Fine" 321
Louisa II
  "That Will Be Fine" 321
Louvinia
  Flags 37
  Sartoris 48
  Unvanquished 179
  "Ambuscade" 199
  "My Grandmother Millard" 276
  "Raid" 298
  "Retreat" 301
  "Skirmish" 312
  "Unvanquished" 332
  "Vendée" 334
Lovelady
  "That Evening Sun" 319
Lovemaiden, Butch
  Reivers 120
Lowe, Julian
  Soldiers' Pay 148
Lucille
  "Two Dollar Wife" 328
Lucius (see also Loosh)
  "My Grandmother Millard" 275
Lucius
  "A Return" 303
Ludus
  Mansion 92
Ludus
  Reivers 120
Luis
  "Carcassonne" 215
Luke
  Sanctuary 137
  Sanctuary (original) 143
Luluque
  Fable 24
Luster
  Absalom 6
  Sound and Fury 158
  "Appendix: Compson" 202
Luster
  Reivers 120
Lytle, Horace
  Reivers 120

McAndrews
  Go Down, Moses 58
  "Pantaloon" 290
MacCallum (see also MacCallum, Stuart)
  As I Lay Dying 14
McCallum
  Hamlet 67
  Intruder 77
  Town 166

McCallum, Anse, I (see also
    MaCallum, Virginius, I)
  Hamlet 67
  "Tall Men" 317
McCallum, Mrs. Anse
  "Tall Men" 317
McCallum, Anse, II
  Town 166
  "Tall Men" 318
McCallum, Buddy (see also
    MaCallum, Virginius, II)
  Intruder 77
  Town 166
  "Tall Men" 318
MacCallum, Henry
  Flags 37
  Sartoris 48
MacCallum, Jackson
  Flags 37
  Sartoris 48
  "Tall Men" (as McCallum)
    318
MacCallum, Lee
  Flags 37
  Sartoris 48
  "Tall Men" (as McCallum)
    318
McCallum, Lucius
  "Tall Men" 318
McCallum, "Old Man Hundred-
    and-One"
  Hamlet 67
MacCallum, Raphael Semmes
    (Rafe)
  As I Lay Dying 14
  Flags 37
  Sartoris 48
  Mansion (as McCallum) 92
  "Knight's Gambit" (as McCal-
    lum) 252
  "Tall Men" (as McCallum)
    318
MacCallum, Stuart
  Flags 37
  Sartoris 48
  "Tall Men" (as McCallum)
    318
MacCallum, Virginius, I
  Flags 37
  Sartoris 48

McCallum, Virginius, II
    (Buddy)
  Flags 37
  Sartoris 48
McCallum twins
  "Knight's Gambit" 253
McCannon, Shrevlin (see
    also Mackenzie, Shreve)
  Absalom 6
McCarron
  Hamlet 67
McCarron, Alison Hoake
  Hamlet 67
  Mansion 92
McCarron, Hoake
  Hamlet 67
  Mansion 92
  Town 166
McCaslin
  Requiem 128
  Town 166
  "Mississippi" 266
McCaslin, Amodeus (Uncle
    Buddy)
  Big Woods 19
  Go Down, Moses 58
  Unvanquished 180
McCaslin, Delphine
  Reivers 120
McCaslin, Isaac (Ike; Uncle
    Ike)
  Big Woods 19
  Go Down, Moses 59
  Hamlet 67
  Intruder 77
  Mansion 93
  Reivers 120
  Town 166
  "Bear Hunt" 208
  "Delta Autumn" 225
  "Fool About a Horse" 235
  "Lion" 258
  "Old People" 286
  "Race at Morning" 297
McCaslin, Lucius Quintus
    Carothers
  Big Woods 19
  Go Down, Moses 59
  Intruder 77
  Reivers 121

McCaslin, Ned
  Reivers 121
McCaslin, Sophonsiba Beauchamp
  Go Down, Moses 59
McCaslin, Theophilus (Uncle Buck)
  Absalom 6
  Big Woods 19
  Go Down, Moses 59
  Hamlet 67
  Reivers 121
  Unvanquished 180
  "Raid" 298
  "Retreat" 301
  "Unvanquished" 332
  "Vendée" 334
McCaslin, Theophilus
  "Lion" 258
McCord
  Wild Palms 186
McDiarmid, Mr.
  Reivers 121
McEachern, Simon
  Light in August 84
McEachern, Mrs. Simon
  Light in August 85
McGinnis, Lt. Darrell
  "Turn About" 326
McGowan, Skeets
  As I Lay Dying (as Skeet MacGowan) 14
  Intruder 77
  Mansion 93
  Town 166
McKellogg, Colonel
  "Two Soldiers" 329
McKellogg, Mrs.
  "Two Soldiers" 329
MacKenzie, Shreve (see also McCannon, Shreve)
  Sound and Fury 159
McKie, Mr.
  "Crevasse" 221
McLan
  "Victory" 336
McLendon, Capt. Jackson (see also Plunkett)

  Light in August 85
  Mansion 93
  Town 167
McNamara
  "Damon and Pythias" 221
McWilliams, Mr.
  "Knight's Gambit" 253
McWillie
  Reivers 121
MacWyrglinchbeath
  "Thrift" 324
Mable
  "Peter" 292
Mac
  Pylon 113
Mac
  Sound and Fury 158
Mac
  "Love" 351
Mac
  "Moonlight" (Unpub.) 352
Madden, Rufus
  Soldiers' Pay 149
Maggie (see also Mallison, Margaret)
  Requiem 128
Maggie
  "Sepulture South" 307
Maggie
  Wishing Tree 339
Mahon, Reverend (Uncle Joe)
  Soldiers' Pay 149
Mahon, Donald
  Soldiers' Pay 149
Mahon, Margaret Powers
  Soldiers' Pay 149
Malcolm
  "Afternoon of a Cow" 196
Mallison, Charles, Sr.
  Intruder 77
  Mansion 93
  Town 167
Mallison, Charles, Jr. (see also Charles; Chick)
  Intruder 77
  Mansion 93
  Town 167
  "Knight's Gambit" 253

Mallison, Margaret Stevens
  (see also Maggie)
  Intruder 78
  Mansion 93
  Town 167
  "Knight's Gambit" 253
Mandy
  Flags 37
  Sartoris 48
Mandy
  "That Will Be Fine" 321
Mannie
  Go Down, Moses 59
  "Pantaloon" 290
Mannigoe, Nancy (see also
    Nancy)
  Requiem 128
Marchand
  Pylon 114
Marders, Mrs.
  Flags 37
  Sartoris 48
Marengo (see also Ringo)
  Unvanquished 180
  "Ambuscade" 199
  "Retreat" 301
Marge
  Sanctuary 137
  Sanctuary (original) 143
Marina, Angelo
  "Elmer" 346
Markey, Robert
  "Knight's Gambit" 253
Marsh
  "Two Soldiers" 329
Martel, General
  Fable 24
Martha
  Wild Palms 186
  "Wild Palms" 354
Marthe
  Fable 24
Martin
  "Wild Palms" 354
Martin, Dal
  "Big Shot" 210
  "Dull Tale" 230

Martin, Laverne
  "Dull Tale" 230
Martin, Wrennie
  "Big Shot" 210
Martino, Dr. Jules
  "Doctor Martino" 227
Mary
  "Kid Learns" 250
Mary
  "Mississippi" 266
Marya
  Fable 24
Matthew
  "Hand Upon the Waters"
    243
Maurice
  Wishing Tree 339
Maurier
  Mosquitoes 106
Maurier, Harrison
  Soldiers' Pay 149
Maurier, Mrs. Patricia
  Mosquitoes 106
Maury
  "Appendix: Compson" 202
Maxey
  Light in August 85
  "Hair" 242
Maycox, Judge
  Intruder 78
Maydew (see also Mayfield)
  Go Down, Moses 59
Mayes, Will
  "Dry September" 229
Mayfield (see also Maydew)
  "Pantaloon" 290
Meadowfill, Essie (see
    Smith, Essie Meadowfill)
Meadowfill, Otis
  Mansion 93
  "Hog Pawn" 244
Meadowfill, Mrs. Otis
  Mansion 93
  "Hog Pawn" 244
Meek, Melissa
  "Appendix: Compson" 202
Meeks, Doc
  Mansion 93

Melissandre (Lissy)
  "A Return" 303
Merridew, Mrs.
  "Uncle Willy" 330
Merridew, Mrs.
  "Portrait of Elmer" 294
Merridew, Velma
  "Portrait of Elmer" 294
Metcalf
  Light in August 85
Middleton, Capt.
  Fable 24
Midgleston, Mrs. Martha
  "Black Music" 212
Midgleston, Wilfred
  "Black Music" 212
Mike
  Sound and Fury 159
Milhaud, Madame
  Fable 24
Millard, Grandfather
  "My Grandmother Millard" 276
Millard, Rosa (Granny)
  Hamlet 67
  Unvanquished 180
  "Ambuscade" 199
  "My Grandmother Millard" 276
  "Raid" 298
  "Retreat" 301
  "Shall Not Perish" 309
  "Skirmish" 312
  "Unvanquished" 332
  "Vendée" 334
Miller
  "Mr. Acarius" 274
Miller, Brother
  "Uncle Willy" 330
Miller, Mrs.
  Soldiers' Pay 149
Millingham
  Intruder 78
Mink
  Sound and Fury 159
Minnie
  Mansion 93
  Reivers 121

Sanctuary 137
Sanctuary (original) 143
Minnie
  "Mississippi" 266
Minnie Maude
  "Dangerous Man" 222
Missy Lena
  Unvanquished 180
Mitch (see also Ewing, Mitch)
  Flags 37
  Sartoris 48
Mitchell
  "Hand Upon the Waters" 243
Mitchell
  "Liar" 257
Mitchell, Mrs.
  Soldiers' Pay 149
Mitchell, Belle (see Benbow, Belle Mitchell)
Mitchell, "Little" Belle
  Flags 37
  Sartoris 48
  Sanctuary 137
  Sanctuary (original) 143
Mitchell, Harry
  Flags 37
  Sartoris 48
  Sanctuary 137
  Sanctuary (original) 143
Mitchell, Hugh
  Hamlet 68
Mitchell, Unc Few
  Unvanquished 180
  "Retreat" 301
Mitchell, Walter
  "Two Dollar Wife" 328
Mohataha
  Mansion 93
  Requiem 128
  "Name for the City" 278
Moissant, John
  "Mississippi" 266
Moketubbe
  Big Woods 19
  Go Down, Moses 59
  Reivers 121

Moketubbe (cont.)
  "Courtship" 220
  "Old People" 286
  "Red Leaves" 300
Monaghan, Buck
  Fable 24
  Flags 38
  Sartoris 49
  "Ad Astra" 193
  "Honor" 246
Monckton
  "Divorce in Naples" 226
Monk
  Pylon 114
Monk (Stonewall Jackson
    Odlethrop)
  "Monk" 270
Monk
  "Big Shot" 210
Monson, Mr.
  "Portrait of Elmer" 294
  "Elmer" 346
Monson, Mrs.
  "Portrait of Elmer" 295
  "Elmer" 346
Monson, Myrtle
  "Portrait of Elmer" 295
  "Elmer" 347
Montgomery, Jake
  Intruder 78
Mooney
  Light in August 85
Moore, Brother
  Flags 38
  Sartoris 49
Morache
  Fable 25
Morowitz
  Damon and Pythias 220
Morrison
  "Don Giovanni" 228
Morvidus, Earl Warwick
  Mayday 262
Mosby, Uncle Hogeye
  Intruder 78
Mose, Unc
  "Fox Hunt" 236

Moseley
  As I Lay Dying 14
Mossop
  "Knight's Gambit" 253
Mothershed
  "Beyond" 209
Muir
  Town 167
Mulberry
  Requiem 128
Mulberry
  "Mississippi" 266
Mullen
  "A Return" 303
Murray
  Hamlet 68
Murray, Colonel
  "Music--Sweeter" 275
Murry
  "Mississippi" 266
Myers, Al
  Pylon 114
Mymie
  "Rose of Lebanon" 353
Myrtle
  Flags 38
  Sartoris 49
Myrtle
  Sound and Fury 159
Myrtle, Miss
  Sanctuary 137
  Sanctuary (original) 143

Nancy (see also Mannigoe,
    Nancy)
  "That Evening Sun" 319
Natalie
  Sound and Fury 159
Nate
  "Hand Upon the Waters"
    243
Ned
  "Mississippi" 266
Ned
  "Rose of Lebanon" 353
Nelson, Cal'line (Callie)
  Soldiers' Pay 150

Nelson, Loosh
  Soldiers' Pay 150
Newberry, Col. G.W.
  Unvanquished 180
  "Unvanquished" 332
Nightingale, Mr.
  Mansion 93
Nightingale, Tug
  Mansion 93
Nunnery, Mrs.
  Town 167
Nunnery, Cedric
  Town 167

Odlethrop, Mrs.
  "Monk" 270
Odlethrop, Stonewall Jackson
  (see Monk)
Odum, Cliff
  Hamlet 68
Oliver
  "Afternoon of a Cow" 196
Ord, Matt
  Pylon 114
Ord, Mrs. Matt
  Pylon 114
Oscar
  Go Down, Moses 60
  "Gold Is Not Always" 239
Osgood
  Fable 25
Otis
  Reivers 121
Ott, Jimmy
  Pylon 114
Otto
  "Kid Learns" 250
Owl-by-Night
  "Courtship" 220

Pain
  Mayday 262
Painter
  Idyll in the Desert 248
Pap
  Sanctuary 137
  Sanctuary (original) 143

Paralee
  Intruder 78
Parker
  Sound and Fury 159
Parsham
  Reivers 122
Patch, Dan
  Reivers 122
Patterson
  Sound and Fury 159
Patterson, Mrs.
  Sound and Fury 159
Patterson boy
  Sound and Fury 159
Paul
  Fable 25
Pavoli
  "Knight's Gambit" 253
Peabody
  Town 167
Peabody, Dr.
  Requiem 128
  "Name for the City" 278
Peabody, Lucius Quintus, I
  As I Lay Dying 14
  Flags 38
  Sartoris 49
  Hamlet 68
  Reivers 122
  Sound and Fury 159
  Town 167
  "Beyond" 209
  "Fool About a Horse" 235
Peabody, Lucius Quintus, II
  Flags 38
  Sartoris 49
Pearson, Mr.
  "Tall Men" 318
Peebles, E.E.
  Light in August 85
Pete
  Pylon 114
Pete
  Requiem 128
Pete
  Wild Palms 186
Pete
  "Home" 245

Pete
  "Mississippi" 266
Pete
  "Once Aboard Lugger" 287
  "Once Aboard Lugger" 288
Peter
  "Two Dollar Wife" 328
Peter
  "Peter" 292
Pettibone
  Absalom 6
Pettigrew
  "Beyond" 209
Pettigrew, Thomas Jefferson
  Requiem 128
  "Name for the City" 278
Peyton, George
  Reivers 122
Philadelphia (Philadelphy)
  Unvanquished 180
  "Ambuscade" 199
  "My Grandmother Millard" 276
  "Raid" 298
  "Retreat" 301
Philip
  "Elly" 231
Philip
  "Golden Land" 240
Phoebe (Fibby)
  Go Down, Moses 60
Picklock
  Fable 25
Pinckski, Mr.
  "Pennsylvania Station" 291
Pinkie
  "Artist at Home" 204
Piotr
  Fable 25
Ploeckner
  Flags 38
  Sartoris 49
Ploeckner, Gen. von
  "Snow" 314
Plunkett, John (see also McLendon, John)
  "Dry September" 229

Polchek
  Fable 25
Poleymus
  Reivers 122
Pomp
  Light in August 85
Popeye (see also Vitelli, Popeye)
  Sanctuary 137
  Sanctuary (original) 143
Popeye
  "Big Shot" 210
Pose
  "Hand Upon the Waters" 243
Potter, Jack
  "Cheest" 217
Powell, John
  Reivers 122
Powers, Margaret (see Mahon, Margaret Powers)
Powers, Richard
  Soldiers' Pay 150
Priest, Alexander
  Reivers 122
Priest, Alison Lessep
  Reivers 122
Priest, Lessep
  Reivers 122
Priest, Lucius, I
  Reivers 122
Priest, Lucius, II
  Reivers 122
Priest, Lucius, III
  Reivers 123
Priest, Maurice (Maurice Parsons)
  Town 168
Priest, Maury, I
  Reivers 123
Priest, Maury, II
  Reivers 123
Priest, Sally Hampton (Sally Hampton Parsons)
  Town 168
Priest, Sarah Edmonds
  Reivers 123

Master Character Index 393

Pritchel, Wesley
  "Error in Chemistry" 232
Provine
  Big Woods 19
Provine, Lucius (see also
    Hogganbeck, Lucius)
  "Bear Hunt" 208
Provine, Mrs. Lucius
  "Bear Hunt" 208
Provine, Wilbur
  Town 168
Pruitt, Mr.
  "That Will Be Fine" 321
Pruitt, Mrs.
  "That Will Be Fine" 321
Pruitt, Mrs.
  "Tomorrow" 325
Pruitt, Rufus
  "Tomorrow" 325

Quentin
  "Lion" 258
Quick
  "Spotted Horses" 316
Quick, Ben
  Hamlet 68
  "Tomorrow" 325
Quick, Isham
  "Tomorrow" 325
Quick, Lon
  As I Lay Dying 14
  Hamlet 68
  "Lizards" 259
  "Spotted Horses" 316
Quick, Lon, II
  As I Lay Dying 14
Quick, Solon
  Mansion 93
  "Shall Not Perish" 309
  "Shingles" 310
Quick, Mrs. Solon
  "Shall Not Perish" 309
Quick, Theron
  Mansion 93
Quinn, Dr.
  Sanctuary 138
  Sanctuary (original) 143

Quistenberry, Dink
  Town 168

Rachel
  Flags 38
  Sartoris 49
Rachel, Aunt
  "That Evening Sun" 319
Rainey, Paul
  Reivers 123
Ralph
  Wild Palms 186
Rastus
  "Music--Sweeter" 275
Ratcliffe
  Requiem 128
  "Name for the City" 278
Ratcliffe, Nelly
  Mansion 94
Ratcliffe, V.K.
  Mansion 94
Ratliff, V.K. (see also
    Suratt)
  Big Woods 19
  Hamlet 68
  Mansion 94
  Town 168
  "By the People" 214
Ray, Mister
  "Elmer" 347
Reba, Miss (see also Rivers,
    Miss Reba)
  Reivers 123
Red
  Requiem 128
  Sanctuary 138
  Sanctuary (original) 143
Red
  "Big Shot" 211
Redlaw (see also Redmond)
  Flags 38
  Sartoris 49
Redmond (see also Redlaw)
  Requiem 128
  Unvanquished 181
  "Mississippi" 266
Reed, Susan
  "Hair" 242

Reeves
  "Turn About" 327
Reeves, Don
  "Big Shot" 211
Reichman, Mr.
  Mosquitoes 106
Reinhardt
  "Honor" 246
Renaud
  Pylon 114
Renfrow
  Town 168
Reno
  Flags 38
  Sartoris 49
Res
  Flags 38
  Sartoris 49
Rhodes, Miss
  Reivers 123
Richard
  Flags 38
  Sartoris 49
Richardson, Dr.
  Wild Palms 186
Riddell
  Town 168
Riddey
  Hamlet 68
Rideout
  Hamlet 68
Rideout, Doctor
  Go Down, Moses 60
Rideout, Aaron (see also Winbush, Grover Cleveland)
  Hamlet 68
Rider
  Go Down, Moses 60
  "Pantaloon" 290
Ringo (see also Marengo)
  "My Grandmother Millard" 276
  "Raid" 298
  "Skirmish" 312
  "Unvanquished" 332
  "Vendée" 334

Rittenmeyer, Ann
  Wild Palms 186
Rittenmeyer, Charlotte
  Wild Palms 186
Rittenmeyer, Charlotte, II
  Wild Palms 186
Rittenmeyer, Francis (Rat)
  Wild Palms 186
Rivers, Lee
  Soldiers' Pay 150
Rivers, Miss Reba (see also Reba, Miss)
  Mansion 94
  Sanctuary 138
  Sanctuary (original) 143
Robert, Uncle
  "Uncle Willy" 330
Robinson
  "Thrift" 324
Robyn, Henry
  Mosquitoes 106
Robyn, Patricia
  Mosquitoes 106
Robyn, Theodore (Josh)
  Mosquitoes 106
Rodney, Uncle
  "Sepulture South" 307
Rodney, Uncle
  "That Will Be Fine" 321
Roebuck, John Wesley
  Town 168
Rogers, Deacon
  Flags 38
  Sartoris 49
  Sound and Fury 159
Rogers, Howard
  "Honor" 246
Rogers, Ken
  "Liar" 257
Rogers, Mildred
  "Honor" 246
Roscius
  Go Down, Moses 60
Rose
  "Evangeline" 233
Rosie
  "That Will Be Fine" 321

Roskus (see also Gibson,
    Roskus)
  "Justice" 250
Ross, Frank
  "Brooch" 213
Ross, Martha
  "Brooch" 213
Rouncewell
  Go Down, Moses 60
  "Go Down, Moses" 238
Rouncewell
  Mansion 94
Rouncewell, Mr.
  Reivers 123
Rouncewell, Mrs.
  Mansion 94
  Reivers 123
  Town 168
  "Tomorrow" 325
Rouncewell, Whit
  Town 168
Roxanne, Aunt
  "My Grandmother Millard"
    277
Roy
  Mosquitoes 107
Ruby (see also Lamar, Ruby)
  Sanctuary (original) 143
Russell
  Light in August 85
Russell, Ab
  Sound and Fury 159
Rust, Everbe Corinthia
  "Leg" 255
Rust, Jotham
  "Leg" 255
Rust, Simon
  "Leg" 255
Ryan
  "Frankie and Johnny" 237
  "Kid Learns" 251
  "New Orleans" 280
  "Royal Street" 305
Ryan, Mrs.
  "Kid Learns" 251

Saddie (see also Saturday)
  "There Was a Queen" 322

Sales, Mac
  Pylon 114
Salmon
  Light in August 85
Sam
  Hamlet 68
Sam'l
  "Leg" 255
Samson
  As I Lay Dying 15
Samson
  Town 168
Samson, Rachel
  As I Lay Dying 15
Sande, Earl
  Reivers 123
Sandeman
  "Big Shot" 211
Sandeman
  "A Return" 303
Sandeman, Hack
  "Dull Tale" 230
Sandeman, Jerry
  "Big Shot" 211
Sarah
  "Sepulture South" 307
Sarah
  "That Will Be Fine" 321
Sartoris
  Big Woods 19
  Requiem 128
  Town 169
  "Appendix: Compson" 202
  "Mississippi" 266
Sartoris
  "Ad Astra" 193
Sartoris, Bayard, I
  Flags 38
  Sartoris 49
  Unvanquished 181
Sartoris, Bayard, II
  Big Woods 19
  Flags 38
  Sartoris 49
  Go Down, Moses 60
  Hamlet 68
  Mansion 94
  Reivers 124

Sartoris, Bayard, II (cont.)
  Requiem 129
  Town 169
  Unvanquished 181
  "Ambuscade" 199
  "My Grandmother Millard" 277
  "Raid" 298
  "Retreat" 301
  "Rose for Emily" 305
  "Skirmish" 312
  "There Was a Queen" 322
  "Unvanquished" 332
  "Vendée" 334
Sartoris, Bayard, III
  Flags 39
  Sartoris 50
  Mansion 94
  Sanctuary (original) 144
  Town 169
  "There Was a Queen" 323
Sartoris, Benbow
  Flags 39
  Sartoris 50
  Mansion 94
  Sanctuary 138
  Sanctuary (original) 144
  Town 169
  "Knight's Gambit" 253
  "There Was a Queen" 323
Sartoris, Caroline White
  Flags 39
  Sartoris 50
Sartoris, Drusilla Hawk
  (see also Hawk, Drusilla)
  Unvanquished 181
Sartoris, John, I
  Absalom 6
  Big Woods 19
  Flags 39
  Sartoris 50
  Go Down, Moses 60
  Hamlet 68
  Light in August 85
  Mansion 94
  Reivers 124
  Requiem 129
  Sound and Fury 159

  Town 169
  Unvanquished 181
  "Ambuscade" 199
  "Barn Burning" 205
  "Mississippi" 266
  "My Grandmother Millard" 277
  "Raid" 298
  "Retreat" 301
  "Shall Not Perish" 309
  "Skirmish" 312
  "There Was a Queen" 323
  "Unvanquished" 332
  "Vendée" 334
Sartoris, John, II
  Flags 39
  Sartoris 50
  "There Was a Queen" 323
Sartoris, John, III (Johnny)
  Flags 39
  Sartoris 50
  Mansion 94
  Sanctuary (original) 144
  "All the Dead Pilots" 198
  "There Was a Queen" 323
  "With Caution and Dispatch" 340
Sartoris, Lucy Cranston
  Flags 40
  Sartoris 50
Sartoris, Narcissa Benbow
  (see also Benbow, Narcissa)
  Flags 40
  Sartoris 50
  Mansion 94
  Sanctuary 138
  Sanctuary (original) 144
  Town 169
  "There Was a Queen" 323
Sartoris, Virginia (see also Du Pre, Virginia)
  "All the Dead Pilots" 198
Saturday (see also Saddie)
  Sanctuary (original) 144
Saunders, Cecily (see Farr, Cecily Saunders)

Saunders, Minnie
   Soldiers' Pay 150
Saunders, Robert, I
   Soldiers' Pay 150
Saunders, Robert, II
   Soldiers' Pay 150
Savage
   "My Grandmother Millard" 277
Schluss
   Soldiers' Pay 150
Schofield, Dr.
   "Tall Men" 318
Schultz, Rev.
   "Uncle Willy" 331
Schultz, Mrs.
   "Uncle Willy" 331
Secretary
   "Uncle Willy" 331
Semmes, Mr.
   Big Woods 19
   Go Down, Moses 60
Semmes, Doris
   "Devil Beats His Wife" 345
Semmes, Hubert
   "Devil Beats His Wife" 345
Sethynnen ap Seydnn Seidi
   Mayday 262
Shack
   Sanctuary 138
   Sanctuary (original) 144
Sharpses
   Idyll in the Desert 248
Shegog, Reverend
   Sound and Fury 159
Short, Herman
   Hamlet 68
   "Fool About a Horse" 235
Shumann, Dr. Carl
   Pylon 114
Shumann, Mrs.
   Pylon 114
Shumann, Jack
   Pylon 114
Shumann, Laverne
   Pylon 114
Shumann, Roger
   Pylon 115

Sibey
   "Evangeline" 233
Sibleigh
   Fable 25
   Flags 40
   Sartoris 51
   "With Caution and Dispatch" 340
Sickymo
   Go Down, Moses 60
Simmons
   Sound and Fury 159
Simms
   Light in August 85
Simon
   Big Woods 19
   "Race at Morning" 297
Simon (see also Strother, Simon)
   Unvanquished 181
   "There Was a Queen" 323
Simon
   "Sepulture South" 307
Simpson boys
   "Liar" 257
Skeet
   "Moonlight" 271
Skipworth
   Intruder 78
Smith, Lieutenant
   Fable 25
"Smith, Miss"
   "Tomorrow" 325
Smith, Mrs.
   Flags 40
   Sartoris 51
Smith, Essie Meadowfill
   Mansion 94
   "Hog Pawn" 244
Smith, McKinley
   Mansion 95
   "Hog Pawn" 244
Smith, R. Boyce
   "Turn About" 327
Smitty
   Pylon 115
Snopes
   As I Lay Dying 15

Snopes
  Big Woods 19
  Hamlet 68
  Town 169
  "Appendix: Compson" 202
  "Mississippi" 266
Snopes (see also Snopes,
    Launcelot)
  "Hound" 247
Snopes
  "Shingles" 310
Snopes (see also Snopes,
    Orestes)
  "Hog Pawn" 244
Snopes, Abner (Ab)
  Hamlet 69
  Mansion 95
  Town 169
  Unvanquished 181
  "Barn Burning" 205
  "My Grandmother Millard"
    277
  "Unvanquished" 332
  "Vendée" 334
Snopes, Mrs. Ab
  Hamlet 69
Snopes, Ad (see also Snopes,
    Wallstreet P.)
  "Spotted Horses" 316
Snopes, Admiral Dewey
  Mansion 95
  Town 169
Snopes, Bilbo
  Mansion 95
  Town 169
Snopes, Byron
  Flags 40
  Sartoris 51
  Mansion 95
  Town 169
Snopes, Clarence
  Flags 40
  Mansion 95
  Sanctuary 138
  Sanctuary (original) 144
  Town (see also Snopes,
    Doris) 170
  "By the People" 214

Snopes, Colonel Sartoris
    (Sarty)
  "Barn Burning" 205
Snopes, Doris
  Mansion 95
  Town (see Snopes, Clar-
    ence)
Snopes, Eckrum (Eck)
  Hamlet 69
  Mansion 95
  Town 170
  "Spotted Horses" 316
Snopes, Mrs. Eck
  Town 170
Snopes, Eula Varner
  Hamlet 69
  Mansion 95
  Town 170
  "Spotted Horses" 316
Snopes, Flem
  As I Lay Dying 15
  Flags 40
  Sartoris 51
  Hamlet 69
  Mansion 95
  Reivers 124
  Town 170
  "By the People" 214
  "Centaur in Brass" 215
  "Lizards" 259
  "Spotted Horses" 316
Snopes, I.O.
  Flags 40
  Hamlet 69
  Mansion 96
  Sound and Fury 159
  Town 170
  "Mule in the Yard" 274
  "Spotted Horses" 316
Snopes, Mrs. I.O.
  Town 171
Snopes, Mrs. I.O. (second
    wife)
  Flags 40
  Town 171
Snopes, Isaac
  Hamlet 69

Snopes, Launcelot (see also
    Snopes, Lump)
  Hamlet 70
Snopes, Lennie
  "Barn Burning" 205
Snopes, Linda (see also
    Kohl, Linda Snopes)
  Town 171
Snopes, Lump (see also Snopes,
    Launcelot)
  Mansion 96
Snopes, Mink (see also Cot-
    ton, Ernest)
  Hamlet 70
  Mansion 96
  Town 171
Snopes, Mrs. Mink (see also
    Snopes, Yettie)
  Hamlet 70
Snopes, Montgomery Ward
  Flags 40
  Sartoris 51
  Mansion 96
  Town 171
Snopes, Net
  "Barn Burning" 205
Snopes, Orestes (Res)
  Mansion 96
Snopes, Saint Elmo
  Hamlet 70
Snopes, "Schoolmaster"
  Town 169
Snopes, Vardaman
  Mansion 96
  Town 171
Snopes, Virgil
  Mansion 96
  Sanctuary 138
  Sanctuary (original) 144
  Town 171
Snopes, Vynie (see also
    Vynie)
  Hamlet 70
Snopes, Wallstreet Panic
    (Wall)
  Hamlet 70
  Mansion 96
  Town 171

Snopes, Mrs. Wallstreet
    Panic
  Town 171
Snopes, Watkins Products
  Mansion 96
Snopes, Wesley
  Mansion 96
Snopes, Yettie (see also
    Snopes, Mrs. Mink)
  Mansion 96
Sol
  Flags 41
  Sartoris 51
Sometimes-Wakeup
  "Justice" 250
Son Thomas
  Reivers 124
Spearman, Jack
  "Al Jackson" 197
Spilmer, Mr.
  Town 171
  "Mule in the Yard" 274
Spoade I
  Mansion 97
  Sound and Fury 159
Spoade II
  Mansion 97
Spoomer
  "All the Dead Pilots"
    198
Spratling
  "Episode" 232
  "Out of Nazareth" 289
  "Peter" 292
Stamper, Pat
  Hamlet 70
  "Fool About a Horse" 235
Starnes, Jim
  "Liar" 257
Starnes, Mrs. Jim
  "Liar" 257
Starnes, Sophie
  "Hair" 242
Starnes, Will
  "Hair" 242
Starnes, Mrs. Will
  "Hair" 242
Stefan (the Corporal)
  Fable 25

Steinbauer, Miss
  "Don Giovanni" 228
Steinbauer, Genevieve
  Mosquitoes 107
Stevens
  Requiem 129
  Town 171
Stevens [infant]
  Requiem 129
Stevens, Bucky
  Requiem 129
Stevens, Gavin (see also
    Gavin, Uncle)
  Go Down, Moses 60
  Intruder 78
  Light in August 85
  Mansion 97
  Requiem 129
  Town 171
  "By the People" 214
  "Error in Chemistry" 232
  "Go Down, Moses" 238
  "Hair" 242
  "Hand Upon the Waters" 243
  "Knight's Gambit" 253
  "Monk" 270
  "Smoke" 313
  "Tall Men" 318
  "Tomorrow" 325
Stevens, Gowan
  Requiem 129
  Sanctuary 138
  Sanctuary (original) 144
  Town 172
Stevens, Judge/Captain Lemuel
  Intruder 78
  Mansion 97
  Reivers 124
  Town 172
  "Rose for Emily" 305
  "Tomorrow" 325
Stevens, Maggie Dandridge
  Intruder 78
Stevens, Melisandre Backus
    (see also Harriss, Mrs.
    Melisandre Backus)
  Mansion 97

Stevens, Temple Drake (see
    also Drake, Temple)
  Requiem 129
Stillwell, Shuford H.
  Mansion 97
Stokes, Mr.
  "Justice" 250
Stovall, Mr.
  "That Evening Sun" 320
Stowers, Zack
  "Dangerous Man" 222
Stowers, Mrs. Zack
  "Dangerous Man" 222
Straud, Dr.
  Flags 41
  Sartoris 51
Strother, Caspey (see also
    Caspey)
  Flags 41
  Sartoris 51
Strother, Euphrony
  Flags 41
  Sartoris 51
Strother, Simon (see also
    Simon)
  Flags 41
  Sartoris 51
Strutterbuck, Captain
  Mansion 97
Strutterbuck, Q'Milla
  Mansion 97
Studenmare, Captain
  "Courtship" 220
Sue
  Flags 41
  Sartoris 51
Sunday (Sundy)
  Sanctuary (original)
    144
Suratt (see also Ratliff,
    V.K.)
  As I Lay Dying 15
  Flags 41
  Sartoris 51
  "Bear Hunt" 208
  "Centaur in Brass" 216
  "Lizards" 259
  "Spotted Horses" 316

Susan
  "Moonlight" 271
Sutpen
  Requiem 129
  Town 172
  "Appendix: Compson" 202
Sutpen, Colonel (see also
    Sutpen, Thomas)
  "Evangeline" 233
  "Wash" 337
Sutpen, Mrs. (see also Sutpen, Ellen Coldfield)
  "Wash" 337
Sutpen, Ellen Coldfield
  Absalom 6
Sutpen, Eulalia Bon
  Absalom 6
Sutpen, Henry
  Absalom 7
  "Evangeline" 233
Sutpen, Judith (see also
    Bon, Judith Sutpen)
  Absalom 7
  "Wash" 337
Sutpen, Raby
  "Evangeline" 234
Sutpen, Thomas (see also
    Sutpen, Colonel)
  Absalom 7
  Big Woods 19
  Go Down, Moses 60
  Reivers 124
  Requiem 129
  Unvanquished 182
Sutterfield, Tobe
  Fable 26
Sylvester's John
  "Courtship" 220

Talliaferro, Ernest
  Mosquitoes 107
Tate
  "With Caution and Dispatch"
    340
Tennie (see Beauchamp, Tennie)
Tennie's Jim (see also Beauchamp, Tennie's Jim)
  Big Woods 20
  "Bear" 207

Terrel, Bill
  "Monk" 270
Thelma
  Mansion 97
Thelma Frances
  Mosquitoes 107
Theodule
  Fable 26
Thisbe, Aunt
  Go Down, Moses 60
Thompson
  Sound and Fury 159
Thompson, Cadet
  "Landing in Luck" 255
Thompson, Pappy
  Light in August 85
Thompson, Roz
  Light in August 85
Thoms, Captain Joe
  "Mississippi" 266
Thorndyke, Mr.
  Town 172
Thorndyke, Ptolemy
  Unvanquished 182
Thorpe
  Fable 26
Thorpe, Buck
  "Tomorrow" 325
Thorpes
  "Tomorrow" 325
Three Basket
  "Red Leaves" 300
Thucydides
  Go Down, Moses 60
Tim
  "Liar" 257
Tobe
  Flags 41
  Sartoris 52
Tobe
  Soldiers' Pay 150
Tobe
  "Rose for Emily" 305
'Toinette
  "All the Dead Pilots"
    198
Tom
  Go Down, Moses 60
  "Point of Law" 293

Tom
  Town 172
Tomasina (Tomey)
  Go Down, Moses 60
Tomey's Turl (see Beauchamp, Tomey's Turl)
Tommy
  Sanctuary 139
  Sanctuary (original) 145
Tom-Tom (see also Bird, Tom Tom)
  "Centaur in Brass" 216
Tony the Wop
  "Home" 245
Tony
  "Big Shot" 211
Top I
  Town 172
Top II
  Town 172
T.P. (see also Gibson, T.P.)
  "Appendix: Compson" 202
  "That Evening Sun" 320
Triplett, Earl (see also Earl)
  Mansion 97
Trueblood, Ernest V.
  "Afternoon of a Cow" 196
Trumbull
  Hamlet 70
  Town 172
Tubbs, Mr. Euphus
  Intruder 79
  Mansion 97
  Requiem 130
Tubbs, Mrs. Euphus
  Intruder 79
  Mansion 97
  Requiem 130
Tucker, Mr.
  "That Will Be Fine" 321
Tucker, Mrs.
  "That Will Be Fine" 321
Tull, Cora
  As I Lay Dying 15
  Hamlet 70
  Mansion 97
  Town 173
  "Spotted Horses" 316

Tull, Eula
  As I Lay Dying 15
Tull, Kate
  As I Lay Dying 15
Tull, Odum (see also Odum, Cliff)
  "Fool About a Horse" 235
Tull, Vernon
  As I Lay Dying 15
  Hamlet 70
  Mansion 97
  Sanctuary 139
  Town 173
  "Hound" 247
  "Lizards" (see also Bookwright, Odom) 259
  "Shingles" 310
  "Spotted Horses" 316
  "Two Soldiers" 329
Tulls
  Mansion 97
Turl (see also Beauchamp, Tomey's Turl)
  "Centaur in Brass" 216
Turpin
  Flags 41
Turpin
  Mansion 98
Turpin, Buck
  Sound and Fury 159
Turpin, Minnie Sue
  Flags 41
Turpins
  Mansion 97

Uncle Bud
  Sanctuary 139
  Sanctuary (original) 145
Urquhart
  Intruder 79

Van
  Sanctuary 139
  Sanctuary (original) 145
Van Dyming, Mr.
  "Fox Hunt" 236
Van Dyming, Carleton
  "Black Music" 212

Master Character Index

Van Dyming, Mattie
  "Black Music" 212
Van Tosch, Mr.
  Reivers 124
Varner
  Town 173
Varner, Eula (see Snopes,
  Eula Varner)
Varner, Jody
  As I Lay Dying 15
  Hamlet 71
  Light in August 85
  Mansion 98
  Town 173
  "Fool About a Horse" 235
  "Spotted Horses" 316
Varner, Maggie
  Hamlet 71
Varner, Will (Uncle Billy)
  As I Lay Dying 15
  Flags 41
  Hamlet 71
  Intruder 79
  Light in August 85
  Mansion 98
  Town 173
  "By the People" 215
  "Fool About a Horse" 235
  "Hound" 247
  "Lizards" 259
  "Shingles" 310
  "Spotted Horses" 316
  "Tomorrow" 325
Varner, Mrs. Will
  Mansion 98
  Town 173
Vatch
  "Mountain Victory" 272
Venturia, Juan
  "Rosary" 304
Vera
  Reivers 124
Vernon
  Sound and Fury 160
Vernon
  "Death-Drag" 224
Versh (see also Gibson, Versh)
  "That Evening Sun" 320

Vidal, Francois
  "Mountain Victory" 272
Vines, Deacon
  Light in August 85
Vinson, Mrs.
  Miss Zilphia Gant 264
Virgil
  Reivers 124
Vitelli, Popeye (see also
  Popeye)
  Requiem 130
Vitry, Chevalier Soeur-
  Blonde de
  Big Woods 20
  Go Down, Moses 61
  "Courtship" 220
  "Old People" 286
  "Red Leaves" 300
Vynie (see also Snopes,
  Vynie)
  "Fool About a Horse" 235

"Wagner, Hal"
  Flags 41
  Sartoris 52
Waldrip
  "Honor" 246
Waldrip, Mrs. Vernon
  Wild Palms 186
Wales, Mr. Sells
  "Mississippi" 266
Walker, Ed
  Sanctuary 139
Walker, Mrs. Ed
  Sanctuary 139
Walkley
  "Victory" 336
Wall
  "Dangerous Man" 222
Wallace, Capt.
  "Sunset" 317
Waller, Hamp
  Light in August 86
Walter
  Mosquitoes 107
Walter
  Mosquitoes 107
Walthall, Parson
  Sound and Fury 160

Wardle, Mrs.
  Soldiers' Pay 150
Warren, Captain
  "Death-Drag" 224
  "Knight's Gambit" 253
Watkins
  "Mr. Acarius" 274
Wattman, Jakeleg
  Mansion 98
Watts
  Flags 41
  Sartoris 52
Watts
  "That Will Be Fine" 321
Watts
  "Turn About" 327
Watts, Birdie
  Reivers 124
Weddel, Francis
  "Lo" 260
  "Mountain Victory" 272
Weddel, Grenier
  Town 173
Weddel, Saucier
  "Mountain Victory" 272
Wedlow, Mr.
  "Sepulture South" 307
West
  "Smoke" 313
West, Doctor
  "Moonlight" 271
West, Miss
  "Honor" 246
West, David
  Mosquitoes 107
White
  "Honor" 246
White, Hank
  Soldiers' Pay 151
White, Hap
  "Two Dollar Wife" 328
White, Jed
  Unvanquished 182
Whiteby
  "Victory" 336
Whiteley
  "Thrift" 324

Whitfield
  Requiem 130
  "Name for the City" 278
Whitfield, Rev.
  As I Lay Dying 15
  Hamlet 71
  "Shingles" 310
  "Tomorrow" 326
Whittington
  Hamlet 71
Widdrington, Mrs.
  "Carcassonne" 215
Widrington, Mr.
  "Black Music" 212
Widrington, Mrs.
  Town 173
Widrington, Mrs.
  "Black Music" 212
Wiggins, Mrs.
  "Dangerous Man" 222
Wilbourne, Dr.
  Wild Palms 186
Wilbourne, Harry (see also
  Harry)
  Wild Palms 187
Wildermark
  Town 173
Wilkie
  Sound and Fury 160
Wilkins, Professor
  Unvanquished 182
Wilkins, Mrs.
  Unvanquished 182
Wilkins, George
  Go Down, Moses 61
  "Gold Is Not Always" 239
  "Point of Law" 293
Wilkins, Nathalie Beauchamp
  Go Down, Moses 61
  "Point of Law" 293
Will
  "A Return" 303
Willard
  Soldiers' Pay 151
William
  "Mississippi" 266
William, Walter
  "Moonlight" (Unpub.) 352

Willow, Col.
  Absalom 8
Wilmoth, Mr.
  Go Down, Moses 61
  "Go Down, Moses" 238
Wilson, Sergeant
  Fable 26
Winbush, Fonzo (see also Fonzo)
  Mansion 98
Winbush, Grover Cleveland (see also Rideout, Aaron)
  Mansion 98
  Town 173
Winbush, Mrs. G.C.
  Mansion 98
Winbush, Mack
  Reivers 124
Windham & Healy
  "Big Shot" 211
  "Dull Tale" 230
Winterbottom
  Hamlet 71
Winterbottom
  Light in August 86
Winterbottom
  "Spotted Horses" 317
Winterbottom, Mrs.
  Flags 41
  Sartoris 52
Wiseman, Eva
  Mosquitoes 107
Witt
  Fable 26
Wohledon, Lord Ivor
  "Elmer" 347
Wordwin, Mr.
  Reivers 124
Workitt
  Intruder 79
Workitt, Uncle Sudley
  Intruder 79
Workman, Mr.
  "Error in Chemistry" 232
Worsham, Doctor
  Unvanquished 182
  "Unvanquished" 332

Worsham, Belle
  Go Down, Moses 61
  "Go Down, Moses" 238
Worsham, Hamp
  Go Down, Moses 61
  "Go Down, Moses" 238
Worsham, Samuel
  Go Down, Moses 61
Worthington, Mrs.
  Soldiers' Pay 151
Wright, Doc
  Sound and Fury 160
Wutherspoon, Jamie
  "Turn About" 327
Wyatt
  "Rose for Emily" 305
Wyatt, Captain
  Flags 41
Wyatt, George
  Unvanquished 182
  "Skirmish" 312
Wyatt, Henry
  Go Down, Moses 61
Wyatt, Sally
  Flags 42
  Sartoris 52
Wyatt, Sophia
  Flags 42
  Sartoris 52
Wylie
  "Mississippi" 267
Wylie, Captain
  Sartoris 52
Wylie, Ash, I (see also Ash)
  Big Woods 20
Wylie, Ash, II
  Big Woods 20
Wylie, Daisy
  Big Woods 20
Wylie, Job
  "Uncle Willy" 331
Wyott I
  Reivers 124
Wyott II
  Reivers 124
Wyott, Dr.
  Town 173

Wyott, Vaiden
  Town 173
Wysbroke, Lord
  "Elmer" 347

Yance (see also Joby)
  "Vendée" 335
Yo Ho
  "Yo Ho" 341

Zigfield
  "Fox Hunt" 236
Zilich, Mrs. Sophia
  "Pennsylvania Station"
    291
Zilphia, "Little"
  Miss Zilphia Gant 265

HISTORICAL/BIBLICAL/LITERARY/MYTHIC

Abraham
  Absalom 10
  Fable 32
  Flags 45
  Sartoris 54
  Go Down, Moses 63
  Wild Palms 189
  Notes on a Horsethief
    283
Achilles
  Soldiers' Pay 153
Adam
  Fable 32
  Sanctuary 140
  Sanctuary (original) 146
  Town 176
  Wild Palms 189
  Notes on a Horsethief
    283
  "Portrait of Elmer" 295
  "Elmer" 348
Ade, George (1866-1944)
  "Black Music" 212
Aelia
  Soldiers' Pay 151
Agamemnon
  Absalom 10
Ahab
  Fable 32
  Notes on a Horsethief
    284
Ahenobarbus
  Flags 43

  Wild Palms 188
  "New Orleans" 280
  "Royal Street" 306
Alcott, Louisa May (1832-
    1888)
  Wild Palms 188
Alexander (356-323 B.C.)
  Fable 28
  Requiem 131
  Soldiers' Pay 151
  "New Orleans" 280
  Notes on a Horsethief
    282
  "Royal Street" 306
Alice
  "Turn About" 327
Ancient Mariner
  Soldiers' Pay 153
  "Moonlight" 271
Anderson, Sherwood (1876-
    1941)
  "Al Jackson" 197
Androcles
  Fable 32
  Notes on a Horsethief
    284
Andromeda
  Fable 32
Anthony, Saint (c.250-350)
  Fable 28
  Wild Palms 188
  "Ad Astra" 194
  "Elmer" 347

Antipas, Herod (d. after 40
    A.D.)
  Fable 28
Antony (83?-30 B.C.)
  Pylon 116
Aramis
  Go Down, Moses 64
Archimedes (287?-212 B.C.)
  Fable 28
Argensola, Abel de
  "Brooch" 214
Arlen, Michael (1895-1956)
  Flags 43
  Sartoris 53
Armistead, Lewis A. (1817-
    1863)
  Intruder 79
Arthur, King
  "Mirror of Chartres Street"
    264
Ashby, Turner (1828-1862)
  Go Down, Moses 62
Ashur-bani-pal (669-626 B.C.)
  Mosquitoes 108
Astor, John Jacob, II (1822-
    1890)
  Light in August 87
  Mansion 99
Atalanta
  Flags 45
  Soldiers' Pay 153
Atthis
  Soldiers' Pay 153
Attila (406?-453)
  Town 174
Austen, Jane (1775-1817)
  Soldiers' Pay 151

Bacchus
  Fable 32
Bach, Johann Sebastian
    (1685-1750)
  Mansion 99
  Town 174
Bacon, Francis (1561-1626)
  Mansion 99
Ball, Albert (1896-1917)
  Fable 28

Balzac, Honoré de (1799-
    1850)
  Mosquitoes 108
  "Dangerous Man" 223
  "Don Giovanni" 228
Balzac's African deserter
  Fable 32
  Notes on a Horsethief
    284
Barcas
  Fable 28
Barker, William G. (?-?)
  Fable 28
Barksdale, William (1821-
    1863)
  Requiem 131
  Unvanquished 182
Barnes, Djuna (1892-   )
  Intruder 79
  Town 174
Bayard, Pierre Terrail de
    (1473?-1524)
  Absalom 8
  "Evangeline" 234
Beardsley, Aubrey V. (1872-
    1898)
  Absalom 8
  Light in August 87
  Soldiers' Pay 151
Beatrice
  Mosquitoes 110
Beauregard, Pierre G. de
    (1818-1893)
  Flags 43
  Sartoris 53
  "Dull Tale" 230
Beckett, St. Thomas à (1118?-
    1170)
  "Priest" 296
Becque, Henry Francis (1837-
    1899)
  "Rose of Lebanon" 353
Bee, Barnard E. (1824-1861)
  Requiem 131
  "Sepulture South" 308
Beelzebub
  Absalom 10

Beethoven, Ludwig van (1770-1827)
  Mansion 99
  Town 174
Belasco, David (1853-1931)
  Soldiers' Pay 151
  "Elmer" 347
Bell, Clive (1881-1964)
  "Elmer" 347
Bembo, Pietro (1470-1574)
  "Priest" 296
Ben Hur
  Absalom 10
  "Lizards" 260
Benjamin
  Go Down, Moses 64
  "Go Down, Moses" 239
Berlioz, Louis Hector (1803-1869)
  Mosquitoes 108
  Sanctuary 140
  Sanctuary (original) 146
Bernhardt, Sarah (1845?-1923)
  Requiem 131
Bilbo, Theodore G. (1877-1947)
  Mansion 99
  "Mississippi" 267
Bishop, William Avery (1894-1956)
  Fable 29
  "Ad Astra" 194
Blackbeard (?-1718)
  Town 174
Blackstone, William (1723-1780)
  Absalom 9
  Fable 29
  Hamlet 72
  Sanctuary 140
  Sanctuary (original) 146
  Notes on a Horsethief 282
Bluebeard
  Absalom 10
  Mosquitoes 110
Boelcke, Oswald (1891-1916)
  Fable 29

Boone, Daniel (1734-1820)
  Wild Palms 188
  "Appendix: Compson" 203
Booth, William (1829-1912)
  Fable 29
  Flags 43
  Notes on a Horsethief 282
Bouillon, Godfry de (1061?-1100)
  Town 174
  "Carcassonne" 215
Bouguereau, Adolphe William (1825-1905)
  "Elmer" 347
Bovary
  Sanctuary 140
  Sanctuary (original) 146
Bragg, Braxton (1817-1876)
  "My Grandmother Millard" 277
  "Rose of Lebanon" 353
Brown, John (1800-1859)
  Fable 29
  Go Down, Moses 62
  Intruder 79
  Town 174
  Notes on a Horsethief 282
Browning, Elizabeth (1806-1861)
  "Out of Nazareth" 289
Brunhilde
  Hamlet 73
Bryan, William Jennings (1860-1925)
  Fable 29
  Notes on a Horsethief 282
Burgoyne, John (1722?-1792)
  Mansion 99
  Town 174
Burns, William J. (1861-1932)
  "Black Music" 212
Burnside, Ambrose E. (1824-1881)
  Requiem 131

Master Character Index   *409*

Burr, Aaron (1756-1836)
    Mansion 99
Butler, Benjamin F. (1818-1893)
    Mosquitoes 108
Byron, Lord (1788-1824)
    Fable 29
    Flags 43
    Sartoris 53
    Mosquitoes 108
    Sound and Fury 160
    "Carcassonne" 215
    "Divorce in Naples" 226

Caesar, Julius (100?-44 B.C.)
    Fable 29
    Flags 43
    Sartoris 53
    Hamlet 72
    Mosquitoes 108
    Reivers 125
    Requiem 131
    Soldiers' Pay 151
    Town 174
    "Mirror of Chartres Street"
        264
    "New Orleans" 281
    Notes on a Horsethief 282
    "Royal Street" 306
    "Thrift" 324
Cain
    Unvanquished 184
Calhoun, John C. (1782-1850)
    Fable 29
    Notes on a Horsethief 282
Campion, Thomas (1567-1620)
    Town 174
    "Leg" 256
Capet
    Fable 29
    Notes on a Horsethief 282
Capone, Al (1899-1947)
    Town 175
    Wild Palms 188
Capulet
    Go Down, Moses 64
    "Point of Law" 294
Carnegie, Andrew (1835-1919)
    "Damon and Pythias" 222

Carondelet, Francisco
        (1748?-1807?)
    "Red Leaves" 300
Carson, Kit (1809-1869)
    Wild Palms 188
Carver, George Washington
        (1864-1943)
    Mansion 99
Casanova, Giovanni Jacopo
        (1725-1798)
    Light in August 87
Cassandra
    Absalom 10
Castle, Irene (1893-1969)
    Soldiers' Pay 151
Catullus, Gaius Valerius
        (84?-54 B.C.)
    Mansion 99
    "Adolescence" 195
    "Appendix: Compson" 203
    "Knight's Gambit" 254
Cellini, Benvenuto (1500-
        1571)
    Soldiers' Pay 151
Cervantes, Miguel de (1547-
        1616)
    "Knight's Gambit" 254
Cezanne, Paul (1839-1906)
    "Out of Nazareth" 288
    "Portrait of Elmer" 295
    "Elmer" 347
Chaplin, Charles (1889-1977)
    Mansion 99
Charlemagne (742-814)
    Fable 29
    Notes on a Horsethief
        282
Charles I (1600-1649)
    "Elmer" 347
Chloe
    "Leg" 256
Chopin, Frédéric (1810-
        1849)
    Mosquitoes 108
    "Portrait of Elmer" 295
Christ (see Jesus)
Churchill, Winston (1874-
        1965)
    Mansion 99

Cicero, Marcus Tullius (106–43 B.C.)
  Fable 29
  Notes on a Horsethief 282
Cincinnatus, Lucius Quinctius (519?–439? B.C.)
  Flags 43
  Sartoris 53
  Mansion 100
  Requiem 131
  "By the People" 215
Cinderella
  Soldiers' Pay 153
Circe
  "Leg" 256
Claiborne, William C.C. (1775–1817)
  Requiem 131
Clarissa
  "Knight's Gambit" 254
Clay, Henry (1777–1852)
  Requiem 131
Clemens, Samuel (see Twain, Mark)
Cleopatra (69–30 B.C.)
  Pylon 116
Cleveland, Grover (1837–1908)
  Go Down, Moses 62
Clovis (466?–511)
  Fable 29
Cobb, Ty (1886–1961)
  Reivers 125
Coke, Edward (1552–1634)
  Absalom 9
  Fable 29
  Hamlet 72
  Requiem 131
  Unvanquished 182
  Notes on a Horsethief 282
Columbus, Christopher (1451–1506)
  Sound and Fury 160
  "Elmer" 347
Comus
  "Leg" 256
Conrad, Joseph (1857–1924)
  "Knight's Gambit" 254

"Once Aboard Lugger" 287
"Once Aboard Lugger" 288
Conrad's centaur
  "Once Aboard Lugger" 287
  "Once Aboard Lugger" 288
Coolidge, Calvin (1872–1933)
  Sanctuary 140
  Town 175
  "Death-Drag" 224
Cooper, James Fenimore (1789–1851)
  Unvanquished 182
Cornwallis, Charles (1738–1805)
  "Lo" 261
Corot, Jean B. (1796–1875)
  Flags 43
  Sartoris 53
Crane, Ichabod
  Hamlet 73
Crawford, Joan (1908–1977)
  Wild Palms 188
Crockett, David (1786–1836)
  Unvanquished 182
Crusoe, Robinson
  Mansion 103
  "Appendix: Compson" 203
  "Knight's Gambit" 254
Cyrano de Bergerac (1619–1655)
  Fable 29
  Mosquitoes 108
  Wild Palms 188

Damocles
  Requiem 134
  "Name for the City" 279
D'Annunzio, Gabriele (1863–1938)
  "Elmer" 348
Dante (1265–1321)
  Mosquitoes 108
  Wild Palms 188
  "Brooch" 213
Darwin, Charles (1809–1882)
  Mosquitoes 108
David
  Fable 32

"Music--Sweeter" 274
Notes on a Horsethief 284
"Out of Nazareth" 289
Davis, Jacques Louis (1748-1825)
  Requiem 131
Davis, Jefferson (1808-1889)
  Absalom 9
  Requiem 131
  Unvanquished 183
  "A Return" 304
  "Unvanquished" 333
  "Rose of Lebanon" 353
Debs, Eugene V. (1855-1926)
  Flags 43
  Sartoris 53
  Mansion 100
Debussy, Claude (1862-1918)
  Mosquitoes 108
DeFrance, Abraham (?-?)
  Requiem 131
Degas, Edgar (1834-1917)
  "Elmer" 348
Delilah
  Flags 45
  Sartoris 54
  Mansion 102
  "Moonlight" 271
Delsarte, François (1811-1871)
  Sanctuary 140
Demosthenes (385?-322 B.C.)
  Fable 29
  Flags 43
  Sartoris 53
  Notes on a Horsethief 283
Dempsey, William "Jack" (1895-)
  Big Woods 21
  Go Down, Moses 62
  Pylon 116
  "Cheest" 218
  "Lion" 258
Desmoulins, Camille (1760-1794)
  Fable 29

De Soto, Hernando (1500?-1542)
  Sound and Fury 160
Devil (see Satan)
Dewey, George (1837-1917)
  "Once Aboard Lugger" 288
Diamond Dick
  Wild Palms 190
Diana
  "Out of Nazareth" 289
  "Elmer" 348
  "Love" 351
Dickens, Charles (1812-1870)
  Fable 29
  Mansion 100
  Notes on a Horsethief 283
Dickson, David (?-1836)
  Requiem 131
Dillinger, John (1902-1934)
  Requiem 131
  "Name for the City" 279
Don Giovanni
  "Don Giovanni" 228
Don Juan
  Absalom 10
  Mosquitoes 110
  Wild Palms 190
  "Knight's Gambit" 254
Don Quixote
  Pylon 116
  Wild Palms 190
Donne, John (1572-1631)
  Mansion 100
  Town 175
Dreiser, Theodore (1871-1945)
  Flags 43
  Sartoris 53
Du Guesclin, Bertrand (1320?-1380)
  Absalom 9
Dumas, Alexandre (1802-1870)
  Flags 43
  Sartoris 53
  Unvanquished 183
Duse, Eleonora (1859-1924)
  Requiem 131

Early, Jubal A. (1816-1894)
  "My Grandmother Millard" 277
Edward, Prince of Wales (1330-1376)
  "With Caution and Dispatch" 340
Edward VIII (1894-1972)
  "Devil Beats His Wife" 345
Eggleston, Beroth B. (?-1891)
  Requiem 131
Einstein, Albert (1879-1955)
  Town 175
  "Golden Land" 241
  "Smoke" 314
Eisenstein, Sergei (1898-1948)
  Wild Palms 188
Elijah
  "Black Music" 213
Ellis, Havelock (1859-1939)
  Mosquitoes 109
Emerson, Ralph Waldo (1803-1882)
  Mosquitoes 109
Ericsson, John (1803-1889)
  Fable 29
Erinys
  Requiem 134
Esculapius
  "Golden Land" 241
Euboeleus (Eubuleus)
  Sound and Fury 161
Eve
  Absalom 10
  Fable 32
  Mansion 102
  Sanctuary 140
  Sanctuary (original) 146
  Town 176
  Notes on a Horsethief 284
  "Portrait of Elmer" 295
  "Elmer" 348

Falstaff
  Wild Palms 190

Faulkner, William (1897-1962)
  "Al Jackson" 197
Fauntleroy, Little Lord
  Absalom 10
  "Brooch" 214
Faure, Elie (1873-1937)
  "Elmer" 348
Faustus
  Absalom 10
  Light in August 88
  Reivers 126
Fielding, Henry (1707-1754)
  Mansion 100
Fields, Lew (1867-1941)
  "Death-Drag" 224
Fink, Mike (1770?-1822?)
  Big Woods 21
  Requiem 131
Fitzgerald, F. Scott (1896-1940)
  Mansion 100
Fonck, René (1894-1953)
  Fable 29
Ford, Henry (1863-1947)
  Fable 30
  Mosquitoes 109
  Reivers 125
  Notes on a Horsethief 283
Forrest, Nathan Bedford (1821-1877)
  Absalom 9
  Big Woods 21
  Flags 43
  Sartoris 53
  Go Down, Moses 62
  Mansion 100
  Reivers 125
  Requiem 131
  Unvanquished 183
  "Big Shot" 211
  "Dull Tale" 230
  "Mississippi" 267
  "My Grandmother Millard" 277
  "A Return" 304

Master Character Index 413

"Shall Not Perish" 309
"Unvanquished" 333
"Vendée" 335
Fort, Paul (1872-1960)
  "Rose of Lebanon" 353
Francesca da Rimini (d. 1285?)
  Mansion 100
Francis, Saint (1182-1226)
  Sound and Fury 161
  Mayday 263
  Wish.ng Tree 339
Franco, Francisco (1892-1976)
  Mansion 100
Frankenstein
  Mosquitoes 110
Franz Josef (1830-1916)
  Wild Palms 188
Freud, Sigmund (1856-1939)
  Mosquitoes 109
Frost, Robert (1874-1963)
  "Out of Nazareth" 289

Gabriel
  Requiem 134
  "Music--Sweeter" 275
Galahad
  Soldiers' Pay 153
  Sound and Fury 161
  "Big Shot" 211
Galilean (see Jesus)
Gamelin, Maurice G. (1872-1958)
  Mansion 100
Garbo, Greta (1906-)
  Wild Palms 188
Garibaldi, Giuseppe (1807-1882)
  Sound and Fury 161
Garnett, Richard B. (1819-1863)
  Intruder 80
Gaudier-Brzeska, Henri (1891-1915)
  Fable 30
Gauguin, Paul (1848-1903)
  Fable 30
Genghis Khan (1162-1227)
  Fable 30

Town 175
Notes on a Horsethief 283
George II (1683-1760)
  "Appendix: Compson" 203
Gershwin, George (1898-1937)
  Mosquitoes 109
  Wild Palms 188
Gibbon, Edward (1737-1794)
  Soldiers' Pay 151
Gilbert, John (1897-1936)
  Sanctuary 140
  Sanctuary (original) 146
Gilbert, William (1836-1911)
  "All the Dead Pilots" 199
God (see Lord)
Goethe, Johann Wolfgang von (1749-1832)
  Town 175
  "Al Jackson" 197
  "Dull Tale" 230
Goldwater, Barry (1909-)
  Reivers 125
Goliath
  Fable 32
  Notes on a Horsethief 284
Gompers, Samuel (1850-1924)
  "Mirror of Chartres Street" 264
Grable, Betty (1916-1973)
  Town 175
Grant, Ulysses S. (1822-1885)
  Flags 43
  Sartoris 53
  Hamlet 72
  Light in August 87
  Requiem 132
  Sanctuary 140
  Sanctuary (original) 146
  Soldiers' Pay 151
  Town 175
  Unvanquished 183
  "Lizards" 260

Grant, Ulysses S. (cont.)
"My Grandmother Millard"
  277
"Shall Not Perish" 309
"Unvanquished" 333
"Rose of Lebanon" 353
Greeley, Horace (1811-1872)
  Mosquitoes 109
Grieg, Edvard (1843-1907)
  Mosquitoes 109
Guinevere
  Absalom 10
  Town 176
Guynemer, Georges Marie
  (1894-1917)
  Fable 30

Haig, Douglas (1861-1928)
  Fable 30
  "With Caution and Dispatch"
  340
Halleck, Henry W. (1815-1872)
  Flags 44
  Sartoris 53
Hals, Frans (1580?-1666)
  "Portrait of Elmer" 295
Ham
  Absalom 10
  Big Woods 21
  Go Down, Moses 63
  Requiem 134
Hamilton, Alexander (1757-
  1804)
  Mansion 100
Hamlet
  Absalom 10
Hampton, Wade (1818-1902)
  Reivers 125
Hancock, Winfield S. (1825-
  1886)
  Go Down, Moses 62
Handy, William C. (1873-
  1958)
  Town 175
Hannibal (247-183 B.C.)
  Fable 30
Hardy, Oliver (1892-1957)
  Pylon 116
Hardy, Thomas (1840-1928)
  "Knight's Gambit" 254

Hare, Joseph T. (?-1818)
  Big Woods 21
  Requiem 132
  "Mississippi" 267
Harlow, Jean (1911-1937)
  Pylon 116
  Town 175
Harpe, Micajah (1768-1799)
  Big Woods 21
  Requiem 132
  "Mississippi" 267
  "Name for the City" 279
Harpe, Wiley (1770-1804)
  Big Woods 21
  Requiem 132
  "Mississippi" 267
  "Name for the City" 279
Harriman, Edward H. (1848-
  1909)
  Mansion 100
Hebe
  "Leg" 256
Held, Anna (1873?-1918)
  Mosquitoes 109
Held, John (1889-1958)
  Mosquitoes 109
Helen
  Fable 33
  Hamlet 73
  Mansion 103
  Town 176
  Wild Palms 190
  Notes on a Horsethief
  284
Heliogabulus (204-222)
  Fable 30
Hemingway, Ernest (1899-
  1961)
  Mansion 100
  Pylon 116
  Requiem 132
Henry V
  Fable 33
Henry, Judith (1776?-1861?)
  Requiem 132
Hercules
  Wild Palms 190
  "Peter" 292

Herrick, Robert (1591-1674)
  Mansion 100
  Town 175
Hill, James J. (1838-1916)
  Mansion 100
Hinds, Thomas (1775-1840)
  Requiem 132
Hitler, Adolf (1889-1945)
  Go Down, Moses 62
  Mansion 100
  "Delta Autumn" 225
Holmes, Sherlock
  Mansion 103
  Notes on a Horsethief 284
Homer
  Fable 30
  Flags 44
  Sartoris 53
  Town 175
  "Name for the City" 279
  Notes on a Horsethief 283
Hooker, Joseph (1814-1879)
  Go Down, Moses 62
  Requiem 132
Hoover, Herbert (1874-1964)
  Mansion 100
  Wild Palms 188
Hoover, J. Edgar (1895-1972)
  Mansion 100
Hopkins, Harry (1890-1946)
  Mansion 100
Horace (65-8 B.C.)
  Hamlet 72
  Mansion 100
  Town 175
  "Appendix: Compson" 203
  "Knight's Gambit" 254
Houdini, Harry (1874-1926)
  "Once Aboard Lugger" 288
Housman, A.E. (1859-1936)
  "Out of Nazareth" 289
Hoyle, Edmund (1672?-1769)
  Soldiers' Pay 152
Hugo, Victor (1802-1885)
  Fable 30
  Notes on a Horsethief 283
Humphreys, Benjamin G. (1808-1882)
  Requiem 132

Ibsen, Henrick (1828-1906)
  Mosquitoes 109
Immelmann, Max (1897-1916)
  Fable 30
Ingersoll, Robert (1833-1897)
  "Beyond" 209
Isaac
  Fable 32
  Go Down, Moses 63
  Hamlet 72
  Notes on a Horsethief 284
Isaiah
  Wild Palms 189
Isolde
  Mansion 103
  Town 176
Israfel
  Mosquitoes 110

Jackson, Andrew (1767-1845)
  Mosquitoes 109
  Requiem 132
  Wild Palms 188
  "Al Jackson" 197
  "Appendix: Compson" 203
  "Courtship" 221
  "Mountain Victory" 273
  "Name for the City" 279
  "Out of Nazareth" 289
Jackson, Thomas J. "Stonewall" (1824-1863)
  Absalom 9
  Flags 44
  Sartoris 53
  Go Down, Moses 62
  Requiem 132
  Unvanquished 183
  "Monk" 270
  "Retreat" 302
  "Tall Men" 318
Jacob
  Mansion 102
James, Henry (1843-1916)
  Soldiers' Pay 152
  "Elmer" 348

James, Jesse (1847-1882)
  Requiem 132
  Wild Palms 189
  "Name for the City" 279
Jason
  Soldiers' Pay 153
Jekyll and Hyde
  Pylon 116
Jefferson, Thomas (1743-1826)
  Requiem 132
  "Name for the City" 279
Jesus (Christ)
  Absalom 10
  Fable 32
  Go Down, Moses 64
  Mansion 102
  Sanctuary (original) 146
  Sound and Fury 161
  Town 176
  Unvanquished 184
  "Beyond" 210
  "Carcassonne" 216
  "Cobbler" 218
  "Mirror of Chartres Street" 264
  Miss Zilphia Gant 265
  "New Orleans" 281
  Notes on a Horsethief 283
  "Raid" 299
  "Royal Street" 306
  "That Evening Sun" 320
  "Unvanquished" 333
Jezebel
  Hamlet 72
  Light in August 87
Joan of Arc (1412-1431)
  "Portrait of Elmer" 295
  "Elmer" 348
Job
  Hamlet 72
  "Portrait of Elmer" 296
John V, Count of Armagnac (1420?-1473?)
  Absalom 9
Johnson, Hugh S. (1882-1942)
  Mansion 101
Johnson, Jack (1878-1946)
  "With Caution and Dispatch" 340

Johnston, Albert S. (1803-1862)
  Requiem 132
  "A Return" 304
Johnston, Joseph E. (1807-1891)
  Absalom 9
  Flags 44
  Sartoris 53
  Reivers 125
  Requiem 132
  Unvanquished 183
  "Mississippi" 267
  "My Grandmother Millard" 277
  "Retreat" 302
Jonathan
  "Out of Nazareth" 289
Jonson, Ben (1573?-1637)
  Mansion 101
  Town 175
  "Leg" 256
Josephus, Flavius (37-100?)
  Unvanquished 183
Jove
  Soldiers' Pay 153
Judith
  Mansion 102
  "Knight's Gambit" 254
Juliet
  Fable 33
  Light in August 88
  Town 176
  "Adolescence" 195
  Notes on a Horsethief 284
Juno
  Hamlet 73
Jurgen
  Soldiers' Pay 153

Katzenjammer Kids
  Light in August 88
Keats, John (1795-1821)
  "Leg" 256
Kemper, James L. (1823-1895)
  Intruder 80

Master Character Index 417

Kilrain, Jake (1859-1937)
  Big Woods 21
  Go Down, Moses 62
  "Lion" 258
Kipling, Rudyard (1865-1936)
  Soldiers' Pay 152
  "Elmer" 348
Kitchener, Horatio Herbert
  (1850-1916)
  "All the Dead Pilots" 199
  "With Caution and Dispatch"
   340
Kosciusko, Thaddeus (1746-
  1817)
  "Mississippi" 267
Kreisler, Fritz (1875-
  1962)
  Mansion 101
Krupp
  Fable 30
Kubla Khan (1216-1294)
  Fable 30

Lafayette, Marquis de (1757-
  1834)
  Go Down, Moses 63
Lafitte, Jean (1780?-1826?)
  Pylon 116
Lamar, Lucius Q.C. (1825-
  1893)
  Requiem 132
Lao T'se (c.604-531 B.C.)
  Town 175
Lattimore, William (1774-
  1843)
  Requiem 132
Launcelot (Lancelot)
  Absalom 10
  Town 176
  "Big Shot" 211
Laurel, Stan (1890-1965)
  Pylon 116
Lazarus
  Pylon 116
Lear
  Mosquitoes 110
Leda
  Mosquitoes 110
  Sound and Fury 161
  "Elmer" 348

Lee, Robert E. (1807-1870)
  Absalom 9
  Flags 44
  Sartoris 53
  Go Down, Moses 63
  Intruder 80
  Mansion 101
  Requiem 132
  Town 175
  Unvanquished 183
  "My Grandmother Millard"
   277
  "Unvanquished" 333
  "Wash" 337
Le Fleur, Louis (?-?)
  Requiem 133
Leflore, Greenwood (1800-
  1865)
  Requiem 133
Legree, Simon
  Mansion 103
Lenin, Nikolai (1870-1924)
  Mansion 101
Lewis, John L. (1880-1969)
  Mansion 101
Lewis, Sinclair (1885-1951)
  Pylon 116
Lilith
  Absalom 10
  Fable 33
  Hamlet 73
  Mansion 103
  Requiem 134
  Town 176
  Wild Palms 190
  Notes on a Horsethief
   284
Lincoln, Abraham (1809-1865)
  Absalom 9
  Go Down, Moses 63
  Light in August 87
  Sound and Fury 161
  Unvanquished 183
  "Appendix: Compson" 203
  "Shall Not Perish" 309
  "Skirmish" 312
  "Unvanquished" 333
  "Wash" 337

Lind, Jenny (1820-1887)
  Requiem 133
Lindbergh, Charles (1907-1976)
  Pylon 116
Lindsay, Vachel (1879-1931)
  Soldiers' Pay 152
Littleton, Thomas (1589-1645)
  Absalom 9
  Fable 30
  Requiem 133
  Unvanquished 183
  Notes on a Horsethief 283
Livy (59 B.C.-17 A.D.)
  "Appendix: Compson" 203
Lochinvar
  Fable 33
  Mosquitoes 110
  Sound and Fury 161
  Notes on a Horsethief 284
Long, Huey P. (1893-1935)
  Mansion 101
  "By the People" 215
  "Knight's Gambit" 254
Longstreet, James (1821-1904)
  Absalom 9
  Go Down, Moses 63
  Intruder 80
  Requiem 133
  "Mountain Victory" 273
Lord (God)
  Absalom 10
  As I Lay Dying 16
  Big Woods 21
  Fable 32
  Flags 45
  Sartoris 54
  Go Down, Moses 63
  Hamlet 72
  Intruder 80
  Light in August 87
  Mansion 102
  Mosquitoes 110
  Reivers 125
  Requiem 134
  Sanctuary 140
  Sanctuary (original) 146

Soldiers' Pay 153
Sound and Fury 161
Town 176
Unvanquished 184
Wild Palms 189
"Ambuscade" 200
"Appendix: Compson" 203
"Artist at Home" 205
"Beyond" 210
"Black Music" 213
"By the People" 215
"Damon and Pythias" 222
"Death-Drag" 224
"Delta Autumn" 225
"Doctor Martino" 227
"Evangeline" 234
"Fool About a Horse" 235
"Fox Hunt" 237
"Frankie and Johnny" 237
"Golden Land" 241
"Home" 245
Idyll in the Desert 248
"Jealousy" 249
"Knight's Gambit" 254
"Leg" 256
"Lizards" 260
"Lo" 261
Mayday 263
"Mistral" 269
"Monk" 270
"Mr. Acarius" 274
"Music--Sweeter" 275
"New Orleans" 281
Notes on a Horsethief 284
"Once Aboard Lugger" 288
"Pantaloon" 291
"Pennsylvania Station" 291
"Peter" 292
"Priest" 296
"Raid" 299
"Retreat" 302
"A Return" 304
"Royal Street" 306
"Sepulture South" 308
"Shall Not Perish" 309
"Shingles" 311
"Skirmish" 312

"Smoke" 314
"That Evening Sun" 320
"That Will Be Fine" 322
"Uncle Willy" 331
"Unvanquished" 333
"Vendée" 335
"Victory" 336
"Wash" 338
"Love" 351
Lothair
"Knight's Gambit" 254
Lothario
Absalom 10
Wild Palms 190
Louis IX (1214-1270)
Requiem 133
Louis XV (1710-1774)
"Red Leaves" 300
Lowell, James Russell (1819-1891)
Mosquitoes 109
Lucifer (see Satan)
Lucullus, Lucius Licinius (c. 70 B.C.)
"A Return" 304
Ludendorff, Erich Friedrich Wilhelm (1865-1937)
"With Caution and Dispatch" 340
Lufbery, Raoul (1885-1918)
Soldiers' Pay 152

MacArthur, Douglas (1880-1964)
"Two Soldiers" 329
McClellan, George B. (1826-1885)
Requiem 133
McCudden, James T.B. (?-?)
Fable 30
McDowell, Irvin (1818-1885)
"Sepulture South" 308
McLaurin, Anselm J. (1848-1909)
Requiem 133
Machiavelli, Niccolò (1469-1527)
"Turn About" 327

Mackaill, Dorothy (1903-)
Mosquitoes 109
Maecenas, Gaius (70?-8 B.C.)
Mosquitoes 109
Magdalen
Hamlet 72
Maingault
Requiem 133
Sound and Fury 161
Malbrouck
"All the Dead Pilots" 199
"Barn Burning" 206
"Mistral" 269
Mallarmé, Stéphane (1842-1898)
"Rose of Lebanon" 353
Malraux, André (1901-1976)
Mansion 101
Maltby, Jasper A. (1826-1867)
"Dull Tale" 231
Manet, Edouard (1832-1883)
"Portrait of Elmer" 295
"Elmer" 348
Manigault
Requiem 133
Mannock, Edward (1888-1918)
Fable 30
Marguerite
"Knight's Gambit" 254
Maria (Mary)
Fable 32
Sound and Fury 161
Mayday 263
"Mirror of Chartres Street" 264
Miss Zilphia Gant 265
"New Orleans" 281
Notes on a Horsethief 284
"Priest" 296
"Royal Street" 306
Marion, Francis (1732?-1795)
Requiem 133
"My Grandmother Millard" 277

Mark
  Mayday 263
Marlborough, Duke of (John
    Churchill, 1650-1722)
  Fable 30
  Notes on a Horsethief 283
Marlowe, Christopher (1564-
    1593)
  Mansion 101
  "Leg" 256
Mary (see Maria)
Mason, Samuel (1750?-1804?)
  Big Woods 21
  Requiem 133
  "Mississippi" 267
  "Name for the City" 279
Massenet, Jules Émile Frédéric
    (1842-1912)
  Sanctuary 140
  Sanctuary (original) 146
Masters, Edgar Lee (1869-
    1950)
  Wild Palms 189
Matisse, Henri (1869-1954)
  "Portrait of Elmer" 295
  "Elmer" 348
Maximilian (1832-1867)
  Requiem 133
Mazarin, Jules (1602-1661)
  Fable 30
  Notes on a Horsethief
    283
Meade, George G. (1815-1872)
  Go Down, Moses 63
Medusa
  Wild Palms 190
Mendelssohn, Felix (1809-1847)
  "Mirror of Chartres Street"
    264
Menelaus
  Mayday 263
Mercury
  Soldiers' Pay 153
Messalina (?-48 A.D.)
  Mansion 101
  Town 175
Micawber
  Wild Palms 190

Michael
  Light in August 87
  "Shingles" 311
Michelangelo (1475-1564)
  Fable 30
Midas
  "Knight's Gambit" 254
Milton, John (1608-1674)
  Flags 44
  Sartoris 53
  Mansion 101
  Soldiers' Pay 152
  "Leg" 256
Mistinguette (1875-1956)
  Requiem 133
Mithridates (c.132-63 B.C.)
  Fable 30
Moloch
  Absalom 11
Momus
  Pylon 116
Monet, Claude (1840-1926)
  "Portrait of Elmer" 295
Monroe, Marilyn (1926-1962)
  Town 175
Montague
  Go Down, Moses 64
  "Point of Law" 294
Montesquieu, Charles Louis,
    Baron de (1689-1755)
  "Beyond" 209
Moore, George (1852-1933)
  "Elmer" 348
Morgan, John Hunt (1825-
    1864)
  Go Down, Moses 63
  Unvanquished 183
  "Shall Not Perish" 309
Morgan, J.P. (1837-1913)
  Mansion 101
  "Portrait of Elmer" 295
  "Elmer" 348
Mortemar
  Sound and Fury 161
Moses
  Fable 32
  Hamlet 72
  Light in August 87

Sound and Fury 161
Wild Palms 189
Notes on a Horsethief 284
Mozart, Wolfgang A. (1756-1791)
    Mansion 101
Murat, Joachim (1767?-1815)
    Fable 30
    Mansion 101
    Notes on a Horsethief 283
Murrell, John A. (1804?-1844)
    Big Woods 21
    Fable 30
    Requiem 133
    "Mississippi" 267
    "Name for the City" 279
    Notes on a Horsethief 283
Mussolini, Benito (1883-1945)
    Mansion 101
    Mosquitoes 109
    "Mistral" 269

Napier, John (1550-1617)
    "Leg" 256
Napoleon (1769-1821)
    Fable 31
    Mosquitoes 109
    Requiem 133
    Soldiers' Pay 152
    Unvanquished 183
    Wild Palms 189
    "Appendix: Compson" 203
    "Big Shot" 211
    "Don Giovanni" 228
    "Home" 245
    "Mississippi" 268
    "Mountain Victory" 273
    "Name for the City" 279
    "New Orleans" 281
    Notes on a Horsethief 283
    "Royal Street" 306
    "Elmer" 348
Narcissus
    Soldiers' Pay 153
Nero (37-68)
    Wild Palms 189

Nesbit, Evelyn (1884-1967)
    "Mistral" 269
Neville
    Go Down, Moses 63
Newton, Isaac (1642-1727)
    Fable 31
    Mansion 101
Nightingale, Florence (1820-1910)
    "Doctor Martino" 227
    "Love" 351
Nijinsky, Waslav (1890-1950)
    Wild Palms 189
Niobe
    Absalom 11
    Fable 33
    Soldiers' Pay 153
Noah
    Go Down, Moses 64
    Intruder 80
Nucingen
    "Dangerous Man" 223
Nungesser, Charles (1892-1927)
    Fable 31

O'Leary, Mrs.
    Wild Palms 189
Orleans
    Fable 31
Othello
    Soldiers' Pay 153
Ovid
    "Knight's Gambit" 254

Paine, Thomas (1737-1809)
    "Beyond" 209
Pan
    "Black Music" 213
Paris
    Fable 33
    Mansion 103
    Town 176
    Notes on a Horsethief 285
Patton, James (?-?)
    Requiem 133

Paul
　Fable　32
　Notes on a Horsethief　284
Peer Gynt
　Mosquitoes　110
Pemberton, John C. (1818-1881)
　Requiem　133
　Unvanquished　183
　"Ambuscade"　200
　"Mississippi"　268
Pershing, John J. (1860-1948)
　Mansion　101
　Soldiers' Pay　152
　"Al Jackson"　197
Peter
　Fable　32
　Idyll in the Desert　248
　Notes on a Horsethief　284
　"Victory"　336
Peter I (1672-1725)
　Fable　31
Peter the Hermit (1050?-1115?)
　"Elmer"　348
Petrarch (1304-1374)
　"Lo"　261
Petronius (1st century A.D.)
　Light in August　87
Phidias (5th century B.C.)
　Fable　31
Philip II (382-336 B.C.)
　Fable　31
Picasso, Pablo (1881-1973)
　"Mr. Acarius"　274
　"Portrait of Elmer"　295
　"Elmer"　348
Pickens, Francis W. (1805-1869)
　Flags　44
　Sartoris　53
Pickett, George E. (1825-1875)
　Absalom　9
　Intruder　80
Pico della Mirandola (1463-1494)
　Soldiers' Pay　152

Pilate, Pontius
　"Beyond"　209
Pistol
　Town　176
Pitt, William (1759-1806)
　Fable　31
　Notes on a Horsethief　283
Pocahontas (1595?-1617)
　Intruder　80
Pompadour, Marquise de (1721-1764)
　"Red Leaves"　300
Pope, Alexander (1688-1744)
　"Artist at Home"　204
Pope, John (1822-1892)
　Flags　44
　Sartoris　53
　Requiem　133
Porter, Fitz-John (1822-1901)
　Reivers　125
Prentiss, Seargent S. (1808-1850)
　Requiem　133
Prester John
　Fable　31
　Notes on a Horsethief　283
Priam
　Big Woods　21
　Go Down, Moses　64
　"Bear"　207
Priapus
　Absalom　11
Prince of Hell
　Hamlet　72
Ptolemy (2nd century A.D.)
　Mansion　101
Pushkin, Aleksander S. (1799-1837)
　Mansion　101
Pyramus
　Absalom　11
　Fable　33
　Notes on a Horsethief　285

Rachel
  Fable 32
Rameses II (c.1270 B.C.)
  "Mirror of Chartres Street" 264
Rand, Sally (1906-1979)
  Go Down, Moses 63
Rembrandt (1606-1669)
  Pylon 116
  "Portrait of Elmer" 295
Rhys-Davis, A.P.E. (?-?)
  Fable 31
Richard I (1157-1199)
  Absalom 9
  Flags 44
  Sartoris 54
  Town 175
  "Elmer" 348
Richthofen, Manfred von (1892-1918)
  Fable 31
  Flags 44
  Sartoris 54
Rickard, Tex (1871-1929)
  "Once Aboard Lugger" 288
Rickenbacker, Eddie (1890-1973)
  Mansion 101
Rima
  "Brooch" 214
Robespierre (1758-1794)
  Fable 31
Rockefeller, John D. (1839-1937)
  "Fox Hunt" 237
Rodin, Auguste (1840-1917)
  "Afternoon of a Cow" 196
Roland
  Absalom 11
  "Knight's Gambit" 254
Romeo
  Fable 33
  Light in August 88
  Town 177
  "Adolescence" 195
  "Notes on a Horsethief" 285

Roosevelt, Eleanor (1884-1962)
  Reivers 125
Roosevelt, Franklin D. (1882-1945)
  Go Down, Moses 63
  Mansion 102
  Wild Palms 189
  "Hog Pawn" 245
Rousseau, Jean Jacques (1712-1778)
  Soldiers' Pay 152
  "Golden Land" 241
Roxane
  Mosquitoes 110
  Wild Palms 190
Ruth, George Herman (1895-1948)
  Reivers 125
  Sound and Fury 161

Sabatini, Rafael (1875-1950)
  Flags 44
  Sartoris 54
Sabrina
  "Leg" 256
St. Elmo
  "Knight's Gambit" 255
Sampson, Batchelor
  "Knight's Gambit" 255
Samson
  Mansion 103
  Town 176
  Notes on a Horsethief 284
Samuel
  "Portrait of Elmer" 296
Samuel's father (Elkanah)
  Fable 32
  Notes on a Horsethief 284
Sandburg, Carl (1878-1967)
  Wild Palms 189
Santa Claus
  As I Lay Dying 16
  Flags 45
  Sartoris 54

Santa Claus (cont.)
  Sound and Fury   161
  Town   177
  Wild Palms   190
  "Mississippi"   268
  "That Will Be Fine"   321
Sassoon, Siegfried (1886-1967)
  Mosquitoes   109
Satan (Devil; Lucifer)
  As I Lay Dying   16
  Fable   32
  Light in August   87
  Mansion   103
  Reivers   125
  Town   176
  Unvanquished   184
  Wild Palms   189
  Notes on a Horsethief   284
Savonarola, Girolamo (1452-1498)
  Soldiers' Pay   152
  "Priest"   296
Schiller, Johann (1750-1805)
  Town   175
Schopenhauer, Arthur (1788-1860)
  Wild Palms   189
Scott, Walter (1771-1832)
  Absalom   9
  Unvanquished   183
  "Al Jackson"   197
Scriabin, Alexander (1872-1915)
  Sanctuary   140
  Sanctuary (original)   146
Semiramis
  Flags   45
  Mansion   103
  Sound and Fury   161
  Town   177
Sevier, John (1745-1815)
  Unvanquished   183
Shakespeare, William (1564-1616) (see also the Swan)
  Absalom   9
  Flags   44
  Sartoris   54

Mansion   102
Mosquitoes   109
Requiem   134
"Knight's Gambit"   254
"Leg"   256
Shelley, Percy Bysshe (1792-1822)
  Mosquitoes   109
  "Artist at Home"   204
Sheridan, Phillip H. (1831-1888)
  "Tall Men"   318
Sherman, William T. (1820-1891)
  Absalom   9
  Big Woods   21
  Flags   44
  Sartoris   54
  Reivers   125
  Requiem   134
  Soldiers' Pay   152
  Unvanquished   183
  "Ambuscade"   200
  "Bear Hunt"   208
  "Evangeline"   234
  "Mississippi"   268
  "Raid"   299
  "Wash"   337
Shields, James (1806?-1879)
  "A Return"   304
Shylock
  "Thrift"   324
Sibelius, Jean (1865-1957)
  Mosquitoes   109
Simeon, Saint (390?-459)
  Fable   31
Smith, Alfred E. (1873-1944)
  Soldiers' Pay   152
  Town   175
Smith, Andrew J. (1815-1897)
  Unvanquished   183
  "Appendix: Compson"   203
  "My Grandmother Millard"   277
  "Unvanquished"   333
Smith, John (1580-1631)
  "Mississippi"   268

Smith, Thorne (1892-1934)
  "Appendix: Compson" 203
Smollett, Tobias George
    (1721-1771)
  Mansion 102
Solomon
  Wild Palms 189
  "Courtship" 221
Spenser, Edmund (1552-1599)
  Mansion 102
  "Leg" 256
Stalin, Josef (1879-1953)
  Mansion 102
Stone, Philip A. (1893-1967)
  Town 175
Strauss, Johann (1825-1899)
  Sanctuary 140
  Sanctuary (original) 146
Stuart, Charles Edward (1720-
    1788)
  "Appendix: Compson" 203
Stuart, James Ewell Brown
    (1833-1864)
  Flags 44
  Sartoris 54
  Go Down, Moses 63
Suckling, John (1609-1642)
  Mansion 102
Sullivan, Arthur (1842-1900)
  "All the Dead Pilots" 199
Sullivan, John L. (1858-1918)
  Absalom 9
  Big Woods 21
  Go Down, Moses 63
  "Lion" 258
Sunday, Billy (1862-1935)
  Fable 31
  Notes on a Horsethief 283
Swan, The (William Shakespeare)
  Reivers 125
Swanson, Gloria (1898-   )
  "Once Aboard Lugger" 288
  "Portrait of Elmer" 295
  "Elmer" 348
Swedenborg, Emanuel (1688-
    1772)
  Mosquitoes 110

Swift, Jonathan (1667-1745)
  Soldiers' Pay 152
Swinburne, Algernon Charles
    (1837-1909)
  Mosquitoes 110
  Soldiers' Pay 152

Taft, William H. (1857-
    1930)
  Go Down, Moses 63
Talleyrand-Perigord, Charles
    Maurice de (1754-1838)
  Fable 31
  Notes on a Horsethief 283
Tamerlane (1336?-1405)
  Town 176
Tancred (1078?-1112)
  Town 176
  "Carcassonne" 215
Tanguay, Eva (1878-1947)
  Mosquitoes 110
Tarleton, Banastre (1754-
    1833)
  "Appendix: Compson" 203
Tartuffe
  Fable 33
Taylor, Jeremy (1613-1667)
  Unvanquished 183
Tchekov, Anton (1860-1904)
  Pylon 116
Teasdale, Sara (1884-1933)
  Wild Palms 189
Tennyson, Alfred (1809-
    1892)
  Light in August 87
Thackeray, William (1811-
    1863)
  Mansion 102
Thaw, Harry K. (1871-1947)
  "Mistral" 269
Thisbe
  Absalom 11
  Fable 33
  Notes on a Horsethief 285
Thomas, Norman M. (1884-1968)
  Mansion 102

Thucydides (471?-400? B.C.)
  Hamlet 72
  "Nympholepsy" 285
Tiberius Caesar (42 B.C.-37 A.D.)
  Fable 31
Titania
  Flags 45
  Sartoris 54
Tom O'Bedlam
  Mosquitoes 110
Tristan (Tristram)
  Mosquitoes 111
  Town 177
  Mayday 263
Truman, Harry S. (1884-1972)
  Mansion 102
Tschaikovsky, Petr Ilich (1840-1893)
  Sanctuary 140
  Sanctuary (original) 146
Tunney, James J. (1898-1978)
  Big Woods 21
  Go Down, Moses 63
  "Lion" 258
Turner, Joseph M.W. (1775-1851)
  Mosquitoes 110
Twain, Mark (1835-1910)
  Requiem 134

Uncle Remus
  Reivers 126
Uriah's wife (Bathsheba)
  Flags 45
Ur-Neill
  "Ad Astra" 194
Uther Pendragon
  Mayday 263

Vanderbilt, Cornelius (1794-1877)
  Wild Palms 189
  "Wild Palms" 354
Van Dorn, Earl (1820-1863)
  Flags 44
  Sartoris 54
  Light in August 87

Unvanquished 183
"Dull Tale" 231
"A Return" 304
"Shall Not Perish" 309
"Rose of Lebanon" 353
Vardaman, James K. (1861-1930)
  Flags 44
  Sartoris 54
  "Mississippi" 268
Venus
  Fable 33
  Hamlet 73
  Mansion 103
  Mosquitoes 111
  Soldiers' Pay 153
  Wild Palms 190
Verdi, Giuseppe (1813-1901)
  Mosquitoes 110
Verlaine, Paul (1844-1896)
  "Portrait of Elmer" 295
Victor Emmanuel III (1869-1947)
  "Elmer" 348
Victoria (1819-1901)
  Flags 44
  Sartoris 54
  Requiem 134
Virgil (70-19 B.C.)
  Town 176
Volstead, Andrew Joseph (1860-1946)
  "Big Shot" 211
Voltaire (1694-1778)
  Hamlet 72
  "Beyond" 210
Voss, Leutnant Werner (?-?)
  Fable 31
Vulcan
  Hamlet 73

Wagner, Richard (1813-1883)
  Mansion 102
  Town 176
  "Al Jackson" 197
Warwick
  Fable 31
  Notes on a Horsethief 283

Washington, Booker T. (1856–1915)
  Mansion 102
Washington, George (1732–1799)
  Go Down, Moses 63
  Soldiers' Pay 152
  Sound and Fury 161
  "Lo" 261
  "Devil Beats His Wife" 345
Watson, Tom (1856–1922)
  Soldiers' Pay 152
Weber, Joseph M. (1867–1942)
  "Death-Drag" 224
Webster, Daniel (1782–1852)
  Fable 31
  Notes on a Horsethief 283
Webster, Noah (1758–1843)
  Town 176
Western, Squire
  Mosquitoes 111
Wheeler, Joseph (1836–1906)
  "My Grandmother Millard" 277
White, Stanford (1853–1906)
  "Mistral" 269
Whitman, Walt (1819–1892)
  Wild Palms 189
Wilcox, Cadmus M. (1824–1890)
  Intruder 80
Wilcox, Ella (1850–1919)
  Soldiers' Pay 152
Wilde, Oscar (1854–1900)
  Absalom 9
Wilkinson, James (1757–1825)
  "Appendix: Compson" 203
  "Red Leaves" 300
Willkie, Wendell L. (1892–1944)
  Go Down, Moses 63
Wilson, Woodrow (1856–1924)
  Fable 31
  Flags 44
  Sartoris 54
  Mansion 102
  Soldiers' Pay 152
  "Al Jackson" 197

Wister, Owen (1860–1938)
  Wild Palms 189

Yseult
  Mosquitoes 111
  Mayday 263